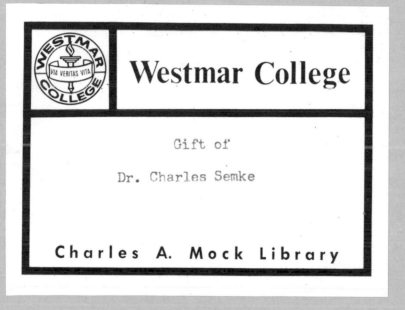

HUMAN BEHAVIOR IN THE WORK ENVIRONMENT

The Goodyear Series in Administration and Business Management

Lyman W. Porter,
Joseph W. McGuire,
Series Editors

ROBERT H. MILES, *Macro Organizational Behavior* (1980)

ROBERT H. MILES, *Resourcebook in Macro Organizational Behavior* (1980)

Y. N. CHANG, F. CAMPO-FLORES, *Business Policy and Strategy:
Text and Cases* (1980)
Business Policy and Strategy (soft-cover version—text only) (1980)

G. JAMES FRANCIS, GENE MILBOURN, JR., *Human Behavior in the
Work Environment* (1980)

MICHAEL BEER, *Organization Change and Development: A Systems View* (1980)

HUMAN BEHAVIOR

IN THE WORK ENVIRONMENT:
A Managerial Perspective

G. James Francis
Colorado State University

Gene Milbourn Jr.
University of Baltimore

Goodyear Publishing Company, Inc. Santa Monica, California

Library of Congress Cataloging in Publication Data

FRANCIS, GLENN JAMES, 1942-
    Human behavior in the work environment.

    (The Goodyear series in administration and business
management)
    Includes indexes.
    1. Organizational behavior.   2. Psychology, Indus-
trial.   3. Personnel management.   I. Milbourn, Gene.
II. Title.   III. Series: Goodyear series in administration and business management.
HD58.7.F7   658.3   79-22720
ISBN 0-87620-392-6

Copyright © 1980 by Goodyear Publishing Company, Inc.
Santa Monica, California

Current printing (last number):

10 9 8 7 6 5 4 3 2 1

ISBN: 0-87620-392-6

Y-3926-6

Designer: Linda M. Robertson
Production Editor: Hal Humphrey
Photographers: Christopher Johnson, p. xviii; courtesy of
Westinghouse Corporation, p. 20; Vince Romano, p. 90;
Peter Southwick, p. 140; Harry Riddle, p. 216;
Hugh Rogers, p. 300; and Marshall Licht, p. 372.

To Saundra and Sally.

Contents

Preface

Seeking to understand human behavior in the work environment is one of the most challenging and worthwhile objectives for anyone who has ever worked with another individual. This text is our effort to contribute to the knowledge and understanding of human behavior in the work environment. It is a blend of a theoretical foundation and practical application so that it is relevant to the tempo of our life today. The book is designed to be used in the teaching of management courses in human relations, organization behavior, or other introductory behavior courses.

The organization of the book is based upon a building block approach. After a brief historical account of the foundations of a behavioral approach to work (Part I), there is an examination of those factors involved with the job and the work environment that influence human behavior (Parts II and III). Parts IV and V investigate the ways in which managerial techniques impact upon behavior, and Part VI points out how special groups affect people's behavior at work. Part VII demonstrates the importance of managing change and the potential of organization development to influence positively human behavior in the work environment. Each of the seven parts is introduced by a brief synopsis of the material to be covered. Chapters begin with learning objectives and end with a summary, key terms, discussion questions, and a case study.

Historical information is kept to a minimum, with an emphasis placed upon the major contributions to the study of human behavior in the work environment. Results of current research are provided in order to demonstrate what the real impact of some of the more popular theories has actually been. Examples, analogies, and case studies are used to illustrate how theories are applied and, in some instances, how they fail.

There have been many people who have contributed to the development of this text. We would like to thank the following people for their reviews and suggestions: Dean Lyman Porter, University of California, Irvine; Joe McGuire, University of California, Irvine; W. Bruce Handley, Weber State College; Vance Mitchell, University of British Columbia; Stuart Murray, University of Tulsa; Jack L. Simonetti, University of Toledo; and Donald D. White, University of Arkansas.

We would also like to express our appreciation to Roger Holloway and Hal Humphrey of Goodyear Publishing for their guidance and assistance throughout this project and to Floye Johnson of Colorado State University for help in the preparation of the manuscript. And finally we are especially indebted to Saundra Francis for her continued support and the many hours she has devoted to this book.

HUMAN BEHAVIOR IN THE WORK ENVIRONMENT

PART ONE
INTRODUCTION

The behavioral approach to work assumes that people can contribute more to an organization than just the performance of a specific task. It also assumes that people will in turn receive more from the work experience than just the pay. While these assumptions may seem very logical to today's managers and students of management, the evolution of this type of thinking is fairly recent.

Chapter 1 will present a brief account of some of the major contributions in the development of the foundations of a behavioral approach to work. Why people work and the nature of the work role will be explored in order to provide insight into the reasoning behind the two assumptions stated at the beginning of this introduction. The discussion will then be directed toward how a behavioral approach actually influences organizational effectiveness.

Throughout this book the primary concern will be understanding human behavior in the work environment and the ways in which behavior can be positively affected. Therefore, the topics covered include an examination of those elements of the work environment that have an impact upon employees' behaviors, as well as the various behavioral management techniques that are designed to improve the rewards to individuals and to the organization. Since the human resources are generally considered to be the most important and most variable resources of any organization, it is essential that we strive to better understand and utilize them. In an effort to help accomplish these rather lofty objectives, this book will present a managerial perspective of human behavior in the work environment.

1

Foundations of a Behavioral Approach to Work

LEARNING OBJECTIVES

Upon completion of this chapter the student should be able to:

- Define the term "human relations."
- Trace the development of the human relations movement.
- Identify the more significant contributions to the behavioral approach to management.
- Discuss several reasons why people work.
- Recognize that the satisfaction of individual needs and organizational goals can be compatible.
- Demonstrate how a job satisfies several personal needs.
- Explain the importance of good human relations practices to organizational effectiveness.

The behavioral approach to work is not what most people think it is—and this is probably just as well. Too many people, including some practicing managers, believe the behavioral approach to work is one that stresses "glad handing" and "back slapping." Behavioral management is seen as the manipulation of people by bribes, a lot of smiling, and the uttering of syrupy compliments to subordinates and superiors alike.

This view of behavioral management is a misconception. It implies that there is no real control over employees other than that which being friendly provides. In short, such management would make for a pleasant work environment, but productivity would suffer and the costs of having behaviorally oriented managers would be prohibitive.

In the past this people-oriented practice of management has been commonly referred to as "human relations." While common usage suggests a very positive interpretation, the term "human relations" should be viewed as simply a descriptive one that applies to all interactions among human beings—good and bad. Thus, the behavior of people at work and how various elements of the work place affect the people are the keys to the study of human relations in organizations. Human behavior in the work environment includes the interchanges between superiors and subordinates, the interaction of peers, and the ways individuals interface with machinery, formal organizations, and informal groups.

It should be noted that the study of human behavior in the work environment covers more than just the activities involved with the actual work itself. There are certain elements in the work environment that influence both the formal and the informal interactions of people at work. These elements may vary from the particular leadership style of a supervisor to the racial mix of a work group. Since these elements or variables in the work environment have an impact upon human behavior in the work place, they will be identified and discussed throughout the book. In most cases the discussions will be equally applicable to the behavior of people in private, public, and not-for-profit organizations.

Within the framework of this book we are primarily concerned with achieving a better understanding of the behavior of people in the work environment. This chapter will provide a brief historical perspective of the behavioral movement in management, describe the reasons why people work and how jobs meet their needs, introduce the nature of the work role, and discuss some of the ways in which a behavioral approach to work can contribute to organizational effectiveness.

A BRIEF HISTORY OF THE BEHAVIORAL MOVEMENT IN MANAGEMENT

While it is difficult to pinpoint the exact beginning of the behavioral movement, the work of several people is particularly noteworthy. This brief overview of the evolution of this movement in management examines some of the contributions which advanced the value of human beings in the work place.

Most early thinkers and writers in the management field were engineers who were necessarily concerned with such factors as machines, plant layout, time studies, and administrative procedures. They believed that increased productivity could only be realized through better machines, better plant layouts, better utilization of the workers' time, and better administrative procedures. Several people emerged during this early management era as being different from the "efficiency experts." They approached the problem of increasing productivity as a human problem rather than as a mechanical one. Among the people who recognized the role and value of human beings in organizations were Robert Owen, Henri Fayol, Elton Mayo, and, more recently, Douglas McGregor. Each of these individuals contributed to the development of a behavioral approach to management.

Robert Owen

Robert Owen was a successful manager of a textile mill in Scotland from 1800 to 1828. He believed that the productivity of his work force was affected by many factors, including keeping the equipment in good repair and paying attention to the individual worker, whom he referred to as a "vital machine." In an 1813 publication, he reported that his attention to worker interests, attitudes, and "sentiments" resulted in a 50 percent return on investment. He advised other managers that the "movements in the minds of workers" are just as important as the movements of machine parts. To Owen, it was essential that managers treat each "vital machine" with kindness, "that its mental movements might not experience too much irritating friction."[1]

Before this time there was little concern for the individual worker other than in trying to keep him busy and "pushing him for more output." The very idea of devoting large segments of time to talking to employees about what they want and how they feel was not considered significant by managers.

Henri Fayol

Henri Fayol is regarded as the "father of management." He was a French engineer who successfully managed a large mining company. His success, he modestly reasoned, was due to the application of a set of general principles of management rather than to his personal leadership qualities. The set of fourteen general principles or guidelines of management was first published in French in 1916 in his book *General and Industrial Management* but was not published in English until 1949.[2] Although most of the principles were essentially administrative in nature, some emphasized human relations, such as:

Equity—refers to the employees' needs for "kindness," "justice," and fair treatment.

Esprit de corps—refers to a company's need to maintain a high level of morale.

Stability of Tenure—refers to workers' needs to feel secure in their jobs.

Order—refers generally to the idea of "a place for everything and everything in its place." Typically, this principle is thought to apply only to machines, raw materials, and other environmental objects. Today it is more broadly interpreted as meaning that people should have the opportunity to become competent in their work through having the necessary resources, material, equipment, and training to do their work without problems or interferences.

Elton Mayo

Elton Mayo conducted two well known experiments during the 1920s that showed that social and psychological factors were major influences on worker productivity.[3] Although Robert Owen, one hundred years earlier, was the first to be concerned with worker interests and attitudes, Mayo gained the most renown because his theories were better documented and disseminated.

Mayo's first experiment, called "The First Inquiry," was conducted in a troubled department of a Philadelphia textile mill. Morale was low, which reflected in a turnover rate of 250 percent. When the problem was first discovered, the mill had hired efficiency experts to remedy the situation through a financial incentive system—hoping money was what the workers wanted. It was not, as none of the workers were inspired enough to exceed the work standards and turnover continued to be high. Mayo suggested that the workers take four short rest breaks during the day to relieve the fatigue caused by standing all day. Not only did the rest breaks increase productivity in the troubled department, but also in work units which knew of the experiments. Later in the program the top manager allowed the workers the opportunity to schedule the rest breaks to suit their interests. After the changes, turnover dropped to a normal level and a bonus was given to the workers for exceeding the production standards. The experiment confirmed what Robert Owen had found much earlier. Opportunities for authentic expression of interests, more social interaction, and more participation in decision making have important influences on employee behavior.

The second experiment was conducted at the Hawthorne, Illinois, plant of the Western Electric Company in the late 1920s and early 1930s. Mayo first studied the effects of different levels of illumination on the output of women assemblers. He discovered that productivity increased not only in the group where the level of light was being altered (the experimental group) but also in the control group which experienced no changes at all. Productivity increased in the experimental group when the lights were quite dim as well as when the lights were very bright. Mayo concluded that the productivity increase was due to social and psychological factors rather than to environmental changes. Important to this increase was the realization by the workers that managers and supervisors were paying attention to them as human beings, rather than as objects of production.

Mayo conducted a similar study using various changes in the number and length of rest periods in another department at Western Electric and again confirmed the value of showing interest in workers. Production increased along with the increases in the length of the rest periods. Even when the rest periods were cut back in number and in length, production continued to increase. Again, it became apparent that people will put forth an extra effort when they are made to feel special. This phenomenon has since become known as the "Hawthorne Effect." While this explanation of the Hawthorne Effect is an oversimplification, it does illustrate the importance of giving more attention to the human element. If people can be made to feel that they are being given special attention, regardless of the reason, they will usually respond with higher levels of productivity and better morale.

Douglas McGregor

Douglas McGregor, a more recent scholar in the field of management, wrote *The Human Side of Enterprise* in 1960.[4] This widely read book intrigued both management practitioners and academicians. He thought that many managers were managing people as though the subordinates were lazy, stupid, dishonest, security-seeking, and work- and responsibility-avoiding. McGregor called these ideas "Theory X" assumptions about the nature of man. McGregor felt that managers who believed the Theory X assumptions to be true would be autocratic. In contrast to Theory X was a set of assumptions he proposed as "Theory Y." These assumptions were more consistent with his view of the inherent nature of man as an optimizer of capabilities. The Theory Y assumptions include:

1. Work is as natural as play or rest.
2. The average human being learns, under proper conditions, not only to accept responsibility but to seek responsibility.
3. The capacity to exercise imagination, ingenuity, and creativity in the solution of organizational problems is widely, not narrowly, distributed.
4. The intellectual potentialities of the average human being are only partially utilized in modern industrial life.
5. People can exercise self-control and self-direction in the pursuit of organizational goals.[5]

McGregor held that those managers who believed the Theory Y assumptions would generally practice some form of participative management style.

The Theory X-Y explanation of leadership behavior is one of the better known theories among management practitioners. It has influenced top level managers to increase the role of subordinate managers through such approaches as decentralization, delegation of authority, job enrichment, and management by objectives (MBO). Each of these approaches to management allows subordinates more responsibility for independent thinking and performance.

While there have been many others who have contributed to the development of a behavioral approach to management, the people mentioned above have been among the most significant. Throughout this book other contributions to the behavioral movement will be discussed. The recognition of the importance of the individual in the work environment is the one thing almost all of these contributions have in common.

The remainder of this chapter will provide an introduction to many of the concerns that have guided management academicians and practitioners in the development of behavioral theories and practices. This introduction includes: determining why people work; people's needs and how they can be satisfied in the work environment; the importance of the work role; how goal-oriented behavior can be encouraged; and how a behavioral approach to work has an impact upon organizational effectiveness. The brief discussion of these topics is meant to give an overview which will provide a better foundation for more detailed coverage later in the book.

SATISFYING INDIVIDUAL NEEDS IN THE WORK ENVIRONMENT

Why Do People Work?

If you believe the response to this question is quite obvious and that the only reason people work is for the pay, this may tell you something about how you view people. Actually, if this question were to be asked of a randomly selected sample of the work force, the answers would undoubtedly vary a great deal. Many people would respond in terms of money or what the money earned allows them to do. Others would be more interested in the challenge their jobs offer and the potential to achieve. People with high levels of social needs may see their employment as being the primary way of satisfying those needs. There will also always be a certain percentage of wealthy, bored, or retired people who work "for something to do." The liberated woman may likewise work "for something meaningful to do." There are, of course, countless reasons why people work and why their jobs are important. Individuals will have reasons that match their values, personalities, and lifestyles.

Regardless of why each of us works, the jobs we hold help us in establishing a self-definition and a perception of ourselves. All of us would like to perceive ourselves as competent individuals performing worthwhile jobs. Unfortunately, some individuals see their jobs, their organizations, and themselves in a more negative way. If a negative attitude toward a job exists, it is a fairly safe assumption that the individual stays on the job only for the money and/or security it provides. A person's job should be a more meaningful experience than that. Most people spend at least half of their waking hours on the job five days of the week—a substantial period of time. It seems that during the approximately forty hours of work each week everyone should expect to be able to satisfy more than just the basic needs. Generally, the more needs a job satisfies, and the more completely the job satisfies those needs, the more important the job itself is to the individual.

The Hierarchy of Needs

Even though the late Abraham Maslow, a noted American psychologist, did not design his well known hierarchy of needs for use in the motivation of people at work, it has been widely accepted as an important contribution to modern motivational theory. The needs recognized by Maslow are certainly applicable to all human beings. Whether it is a hierarchy or not seems to be debatable. (This issue will be discussed in more depth in Chapter 7, but for now it is important to recognize that individuals expect to satisfy many of their individual needs within the organizational framework.) The need hierarchy recognizes five different levels of needs, progressing from the most basic physiological needs to the more refined psychological needs of self-actualization. Basic to the application of the need hierarchy is the assumption that the lower level needs must be met before the higher levels of needs can be satisfied. This implies that once most of the physiological needs are taken care of, the individual will be concerned with safety and security needs, then the social needs, and so on up the hierarchy. The five levels of the hierarchy are shown below:

- Level 1 Physiological needs
- Level 2 Safety and security needs
- Level 3 Belonging and social needs
- Level 4 Esteem (ego) and status needs
- Level 5 Self-realization or -actualization needs[6]

Managers must recognize the existence of these needs within employees and be aware that the needs will vary in intensity from one individual to the next. With an understanding of human needs, managers will be more capable of utilizing managerial practices that will contribute to the creation of a work environment in which employees can satisfy their needs. Table 1.1 shows a representative sample of how employee needs may be satisfied from various sources within the work environment.

All organizations have great unused potentials for satisfying social, ego, and self-actualization needs. Since people spend so much of their time working in organizations, an important management concern should be that of designing a need-fulfilling work environment. It is known, for example, that ego needs are basically fulfilled through the praise and recognition that come from other people. This can be applied to organizational life by saying that the ego of a worker is best strengthened and satisfied through praise and recognition from co-workers, supervisors, and managers. As is shown in Table 1.1, there are ample opportunities for

TABLE 1.1   Sources of Satisfaction of Employee Needs in the Work Environment

Physiological Needs
1. Wage and/or salary which pays for food, clothing and shelter
2. Exercise
3. Rest

Safety Needs
1. Job security
2. Safe working conditions
3. Assurance of economic well-being provided by insurance, pensions, and other fringe benefits

Social Needs
1. Co-worker friendship
2. Membership in close knit department
3. Participation in departmental activities
4. Participation in organizational activities

Ego Needs
1. Praise and recognition from co-workers, supervisors and top managers
2. Job competence
3. Setting own goals
4. Making own decisions

Self-Actualization Needs
1. Performing work for sense of accomplishment
2. Performing work for sense of challenge
3. Doing excellent work to feel good about oneself
4. Fulfilling one's potential

individuals to have many of their needs satisfied while performing a job. In fact, the way the job is designed will be a determinant of the person's work role and how well that role helps to satisfy personal needs.

Nature of the Work Role

A job is a collection of individual tasks that a worker performs. It is the formal link with the organization and an important part in the formation of the individual's work role. A person's work role also includes the supervisor, pay, promotional opportunities, co-worker relationships, working conditions, and hours of work. The work role can thus be said to:

1. Provide wages to the worker in return for services
2. Require the expenditure of mental and physical energy
3. Permit the employee to contribute to the production of goods or services
4. Permit or require social interaction from the worker
5. Define, at least in part, the social status of the employee[7]

Each of these functions of the work role is rewarding and pleasurable for most employees. Earning wages, feeling worthwhile by contributing to the production of goods and services, interacting with co-workers, and having an identifiable social status are rewarding experiences. The expenditure of mental and physical energy can also be rewarding as it is required to maintain a comfortable level of stimulation and alertness. In combination, all of these factors influence how people behave on the job and how they feel about the organization.

A good manager attempts to design a work role that is compatible with the worker and his needs. By doing this, the manager can aid the worker to maintain a healthy attitude toward organizational life. Generally, a challenging and meaningful job with trusting, supportive supervision will produce better work attitudes than will a simple and boring job with autocratic supervision.

Matching people with the right work-role factors should always be one of the main tasks of good managers and supervisors. It is not as easy as it sounds since individuals have different needs, values, and personalities that influence the formation of work preferences. These work preferences are seen by employees as the best way to satisfy their needs and to obtain work experiences compatible with their personalities and their personal values. When employees see the satisfaction of their needs as possible, it will cause them to direct their behavior toward attainment. Thus, this relationship between needs and the potential satisfaction of these needs in the work environment leads to goal-oriented behavior.

THE INFLUENCE OF A BEHAVIORAL APPROACH UPON ORGANIZATIONAL EFFECTIVENESS

Goal-Oriented Behavior

During our lives we may try to accomplish certain personal goals, such as being a competent musician, artist, athlete, student, craftsman, executive, or parent. Usually we have multiple goals rather than just one goal. For most people a single goal simply does not require a sufficient range of activities in which to be engaged unless it is stated in very general terms, such as "to be a better person." We continually evaluate ourselves on how well we are meeting our many goals or working toward their accomplishment. If the goals are inappropriate or unrealistic (playing major league baseball or becoming a movie star), they are adjusted to better reflect reality or they are dropped. When goals are dropped we usually replace them with others. Some will be short-term in nature and provide us with the opportunity for immediate feedback. Some will be of an intermediate time span and some will be long-term and will be tied into our long-range plans. The presence of goals creates within us what is known as goal-oriented behavior. We are involved with activities with some result or goal in mind. The goals direct our behavior. Behavior that contributes to goal achievement is productive and that behavior which does not contribute to goal achievement is nonproductive.

The entire process of setting goals, adjusting them, replacing them, evaluating efforts toward goal achievement, and finally establishing new goals when the old ones are met is precisely what organizations do. Although the goals themselves and the process of attaining them are more sophisticated and complex, the organizational attempts at goal-oriented behavior are similar to those of individuals.

Allowing individuals to set work related goals and making sure those goals are compatible with the organization's goals is a critical managerial task. When this task is accomplished in a way that makes the individual feel like an important part of the organization, there is generally a noticeable positive impact upon the employee's work behavior. Thus, a behavioral orientation by a manager will not only help to satisfy employee needs but will also lead to greater organizational effectiveness.

Human Dimensions that Influence Organizational Success

According to Rensis Likert, a well-known authority on management, there are five key human dimensions that strongly influence a firm's success:

- Managerial leadership
- Organizational climate

- Group processes
- Peer leadership
- Subordinates' satisfaction[8]

Managerial and peer leadership place importance on supporting, encouraging, and helping an individual do the best possible job. Effective group processes refer to procedures that instill mutual trust, confidence, and teamwork among members of a work group. Organizational climate (organizational personality) can contribute to organizational effectiveness when it creates within employees the feeling that the company is concerned with their ideas, involvement, and participation. As we know, some of our friends have more trusting and supportive personalities than others do. We are more open, more honest, and more communicative when dealing with trusting personalities than we are with defensive and dull personalities. The personalities of companies vary in the same way.

Likert found that people working in healthy organizations all tended to describe the human dimensions in about the same way.[9] The people working in less successful companies described the key human dimensions in an opposite manner. For example, in healthy firms leadership was described as supportive and participative, while in the unhealthy firms leadership was described as exploitative and autocratic. The organizational climate was viewed as friendly in successful firms and cold and unfriendly in less successful companies.

Departments in successful companies operated in the following manner:

1. Each department made all the decisions that affected it.
2. All members of the work group participated in making the decisions.
3. All decisions were made by group consensus.[10]

Most employees feel more a part of their organization when their ideas are put into action. Indeed, the feeling of belonging to an organization is often closely linked to a feeling of commitment or ownership. For instance, when people say "Our company is doing more than any other to fight air pollution," or "Our agency services more people than any other state agency," it is a good indication that there is a feeling of ownership and belonging. The more "ownership" and feelings of belonging there are, the better for the organization. People take care of what they own. Although no organization operates exclusively on the three principles stated above all the time, the more successful organizations make an attempt to implement them when possible.[11]

Table 1.2 provides descriptions of a behavioral orientation for each of the dimensions identified by Likert as influencing productive effi-

TABLE 1.2   Descriptions of a Behavioral Orientation in the Implementation of Key Human Dimensions.

MANAGERIAL LEADERSHIP—Extent to which managers display the following:
  Support—pays attention to what you are saying
  Goal emphasis—encourages best effort
  Help with work—shows ways to do a better job
  Team building—encourages subordinates to work as a team
GROUP PROCESS—Extent of:
  Planning together, coordinating efforts
  Having confidence and trust in other members
PEER LEADERSHIP—Extent peers display the following:
  Support—friendly
  Goal emphasis—maintains high standards
  Help with work—group shares with each other new ideas, solutions
SATISFACTION with:
  Co-workers, superior, job, pay, and promotional opportunities
ORGANIZATIONAL CLIMATE
  Communication flow—employees know what is going on
  Decision making practices—employees are involved in setting goals
  Concern for persons—the organization is interested in the individual's welfare and tries to improve working conditions
  Technological adequacy—improved methods are quickly adopted

Source: Adapted from Rensis Likert and David Bowers, "Improving the Accuracy of P/L Reports by Estimating the Change in Dollar Value of the Human Organization," Michigan Business Review 23 *(March 1973): 17–18.*

ciency. People in successful organizations create a work environment that is characterized by the factors described in this table. In well-run companies, managers pay attention to what people are saying, encourage best efforts from everyone, show people ways to do a better job, and encourage group members to work as a team. Successful group or department work is characterized by group members planning together, coordinating their efforts, and having confidence and trust in each other. Peer leadership in healthy companies is demonstrated by group members offering support, helping with work, and encouraging teamwork.

An Example of Improving Organizational Effectiveness with a Behavioral Approach to Work

In the Atlanta, Georgia, area General Motors has two automobile assembly plants, Lakewood and Doraville. Compared to the outstanding Doraville operation, at one time the Lakewood plant was a disaster area. Organizational effectiveness was low as measured in terms of product quality, tool breakage, scrap loss, and grievances. Doraville, on the other hand, was rated very high in all areas of organizational health and success. The Doraville human dimensions (see Table 1.2) were very positive, whereas the descriptions of the human relations factors at Lakewood were very negative.

Employees at the Doraville plant were provided important decision-making activities at the departmental level. Most decisions approximated a group consensus with all group members taking an active role. The idea that "an informed employee is an involved employee" was a reality at Doraville. The Lakewood plant was a sort of dictatorship where the rank-and-file workers were not allowed a voice in important decision-making activities.

A three-year program (1969–1972) was started to change the Lakewood plant into an operation resembling the Doraville plant.[12] At the outset, the Lakewood supervisors and managers were trained to upgrade their leadership and communication skills, goal-setting practices, and team-building activities. The sessions emphasized the roles of mutual understanding, trust, and support between workers and leaders. Each supervisor was given a "utility trainer" to help with some functions such as training new employees, trouble shooting, rearranging operations, controlling salvage, checking fixtures, and so on. The utility trainers enabled the supervisors to spend more time attending to the needs, interests, and expectations of their subordinates.

The Lakewood workers were given a total of 20,000 hours of classroom training on human relations skills and on plant operations. They received and exchanged information in these classroom sessions on future products, organizational changes, selected cost data, labor cost figures, product quality, and labor efficiency. Most importantly, these classroom sessions provided the workers an arena where they could participate in designing the environment where they worked. Feelings of commitment to the organization increased.

In 1972, only three years after the workers were given the training and provided upgraded decision-making opportunities, many important positive improvements were realized by Lakewood:

- Grievances decreased 60%
- Product quality increased 10%
- Scrap loss decreased 75%
- Indirect labor efficiency improved 20%
- Direct labor efficiency improved 10%[13]

These improvements were attributed to the upgrading of the five human dimensions shown in Table 1.2. In the beginning of the project, Lakewood's scores on managerial and peer leadership, organizational climate, satisfaction, and group processes were very low compared to Doraville's. After the training and classroom activities Lakewood's scores significantly improved, almost to the level attained by Doraville.

MEETING THE CHALLENGES OF
A BEHAVIORAL APPROACH TO WORK

It is often said that managers manage people or things. They are not mutually exclusive. Even in high technology situations and in capital intensive organizations, people remain the most important resource. Managing "things" such as inventory, for example, also requires the supervision of people. To become people-oriented is especially hard for individuals with a technical background, but it is becoming increasingly clear that a behavioral approach translates into better productivity and cost records.

An important role of managers and supervisors is to create a work environment where people can contribute to the organization, become competent, and be satisfied. At work, individuals experience the feelings of competence and satisfaction when they do well in a meaningful job. This opportunity is made possible when important factors in the person's work environment fulfill each individual's needs and expectations.

The effective management of people is a challenge. Managing things is relatively easy when compared to managing people. Seldom does inventory talk back, complain, or ask for more pay. Therefore, the coverage of topics in this book will give primary attention to understanding human behavior in the work environment and how the many different variables or elements of the work environment can influence behavior. A managerial perspective will be emphasized throughout the book in order to assist managers and prospective managers in understanding human behavior and in successfully implementing a behavioral approach to management.

A brief synopsis of the topics to be covered in the remaining parts of the book is presented below:

- Part II—Human Behavior and the Work Itself (Chapters 2–4) examines how an individual fits into the work environment and the importance of job design and job satisfaction.
- Part III—Human Behavior and the Climate of the Work Environment (Chapters 5 and 6) explains how an organizational climate is created, how to develop a positive organizational climate, and how to recognize those things in the work environment that may negatively influence behavior causing stress among the employees.
- Part IV—Understanding Motivated Behavior (Chapters 7–9) explores motivational theories and the role of money, and demonstrates how to positively reinforce employee behavior.
- Part V—Leadership and Human Behavior in the Work Environment (Chapters 10–13) deals with how the communication flows and the leadership within an organization influence human behavior.

- Part VI—Special Groups and Their Influence on Behavior in the Work Environment (Chapters 14–16) discusses how special groups—such as knowledge resources, women and minorities, and labor unions—affect the behavior of the members of such groups and the people who must manage them.
- Part VII—Human Behavior and Organization Development (Chapters 17 and 18) provides an introduction to organization development and gives an overview of a behavioral approach to management.

SUMMARY

The foundations of a behavioral approach to work can be discovered in the contributions of several people. Many of the early contributors to the behavioral approach were engineers who were concerned with efficiency of operations. They discovered that by being more concerned with the role and the value of human beings in the organization, productivity could be increased. However, not until Elton Mayo's experiments in the late 1920s and early 1930s did the human relations movement receive much attention. Since then, significant contributions have been made to the study of human behavior in organizations.

When studying human behavior in organizations it is necessary to examine the overall impact of the work environment on the quality of work life offered to members of the organization. When there is evidence of a behavioral approach to work, there is also a high quality of work life within the work environment. Where there is a low quality of work life, there is not only poor human relations but also a host of costly human problems such as poor product quality, tardiness, turnover, complaints, and low will to work.

One of the most important roles of managers and supervisors is to create a work environment where people can make a contribution, become competent, and be satisfied. When people feel competent, they feel important and worthwhile. At work, an individual experiences the feelings of competence and satisfaction when he or she does well in a meaningful job. The employee must, therefore, have the opportunity to do meaningful work that will allow the fulfillment of some personal needs and expectations.

The nature of the work role will be very important to the individual's satisfaction of needs. A work role includes the supervisor, pay, promotional opportunities, co-worker relationships, working conditions, hours of work, and, of course, the job itself. When a manager helps employees satisfy their personal needs, while at the same time meeting organizational goals, the result is goal-oriented behavior. Goal-oriented behavior by the employees of an organization is usually an important outcome of a behavioral approach to work.

Rensis Likert has identified five important human dimensions which strongly influence a firm's success: managerial leadership, organizational climate, group processes, peer leadership, and subordinates' satisfaction. When looking at the costs associated with the failure to recognize these human dimensions, it can be shown that these dimensions contribute much more to the financial well-being of a firm than some managers realize. With new, more sophisticated, methods of measuring the costs associated with human resources, it is becoming more obvious than in the past that there is a definite relationship between a behavioral approach to management and organizational effectiveness.

The improvements made in the General Motors Lakewood, Georgia, plant demonstrate the cost savings a behavioral approach can generate. After three years of training and upgraded decision-making practices, there was a decrease in grievances, an increase in product quality, a large decrease in scrap loss, and an increase in labor efficiency. Improving upon the human dimensions had a very definite impact upon organizational effectiveness.

NOTES

1. ROBERT OWEN, *A New View of Society* (New York: E. Bliss & F. White, 1825), pp. 57–62. This is the first American edition from the third London edition.

2. HENRI FAYOL, *General and Industrial Management* (London: Sir Isaac Pitman and Sons, 1949). Fayol's "General Principles of Management" first appeared in 1916 in an industrial bulletin published in France.

3. ELTON MAYO, *The Human Problems of an Industrial Civilization*, 2nd ed. (Boston: Harvard Business School, Division of Research, and New York: Macmillan Co., 1946); and F. J. ROETHLISBURGER and W. S. DICKSON, *Management and the Worker* (Cambridge, Mass.: Harvard University Press, 1939, 1950).

4. DOUGLAS MCGREGOR, *The Human Side of Enterprise* (New York: McGraw-Hill Book Co., 1960).

5. Ibid., pp. 47–8.

6. ABRAHAM MASLOW, "A Theory of Human Motivation," *Psychological Review* 50 (1943): 370–96.

7. VICTOR VROOM, *Work and Motivation* (New York: John Wiley and Sons, 1964), p. 30.

8. RENSIS LIKERT, *New Patterns of Management* (New York: McGraw-Hill Book Co., 1961).

9. RENSIS LIKERT and DAVID BOWERS, "Improving the Accuracy of P/L Reports by Estimating the Change in Dollar Value of the Human Organization," *Michigan Business Review* 23 (March 1973): 19.

10. Ibid.

11. Ibid.

12. See William F. Dowley, "System 4 Builds Performance and Profits," *Organizational Dynamics* 3 (Winter 1975): 32.

13. Ibid.

QUESTIONS FOR THOUGHT AND DISCUSSION

1. In your opinion why has the behavioral approach been associated with manipulation and bribing of employees to get work done? Are these criticisms justified?

2. How can a behavioral approach to work help minimize some of the more common manpower problems, i.e., absenteeism, tardiness, and turnover?

3. Can a behavioral approach to work contribute anything to the organization in terms of dollars and cents?

4. What is the relationship between a behavioral approach to work and goal-oriented behavior?

5. How can a behavioral orientation in the implementation of key human dimensions help satisfy the needs described by Maslow?

KEY TERMS

The student should be able to discuss the significance of these terms to the study of human behavior in the work environment.

Human relations	Theory X
Vital machine	Theory Y
Father of management	Hierarchy of needs
The First Inquiry	Work role
Hawthorne studies	Goal-oriented behavior
Hawthorne Effect	Key human dimensions

AN EXPERIENTIAL CASE

Informally interview three to five people who hold full-time jobs. Record the reasons why these people work and the priority of the reasons. Have the people rank their organization according to the five human dimensions identified by Likert. Compare the lists of why people work and the lists of human dimensions. Can the differences in priorities be explained? How?

PART TWO

HUMAN BEHAVIOR AND THE WORK ITSELF

Perhaps one of the most important factors outside the individual in influencing work behavior is the actual job a person performs. Because of the amount of time an employee spends on a job, behavior will necessarily be affected by the nature of the job duties. Job design and employee selection are critical in bringing about a match between an employee's self-image and the job. The job will also determine the number and nature of interpersonal relationships. Standard of living, career paths, and degree of job satisfaction are all influenced very strongly by the nature of the task to be performed. Even the length of time an individual has held a job affects that person's behavior in the work environment. People will usually behave somewhat differently after becoming accustomed to their jobs and to their work environments. The success they have in making the necessary adjustments may be dependent upon their socialization process as well as the training and orientation they receive.

Chapters 2, 3, and 4 show how the work environment, the structure of the task itself, and the satisfaction received from the job are important to the on-the-job behavior of the individual. As pointed out in Chapter 1, the first changes in the work environment resulting from a more behavioral approach to management are usually directed toward improving the actual work conditions and updating the design of jobs. Even though working conditions have improved substantially from the days of Robert Owen, the design of the job itself is still one of the most important determinants of job satisfaction and human behavior in the work environment.

2

The Individual and the Work Environment

LEARNING OBJECTIVES

Upon completion of this chapter the student should be able to:

- Define what constitutes a work environment.
- Explain the formal and informal socialization process.
- Identify the variables in the development of a role in the work environment.
- Differentiate between role conflict and role ambiguity.
- Recognize the existence of incongruencies between organizations and individuals.
- Explain the relevance of transactional analysis to organizational relationships.
- Describe some of the ways to bring individuals and organizations into congruence.

When undergraduates are asked what their majors are, they are quick to reply with a specific answer such as "management." In fact they may even give their rationale for selecting a particular major, citing any number of reasons including an abundance of jobs in the field, good starting salaries, or the challenging nature of the work. But when they are asked, "What will you do when you graduate?" the reply usually becomes somewhat vague and is generally something like: "I guess I'll get a job someplace as a management trainee." When they are queried further about what it is that management trainees do, the reply remains imprecise: "You know, manage people, learn about the business, and help the company reach its objectives."

This is not to imply that management majors are any less prepared for what to expect than any other majors are. Marketing majors, accounting majors, psychology majors, and majors in just about any undergraduate field will typically be vague about what to expect regarding the nature of the jobs available to them.

Expectancies of people entering the work force for the first time on a permanent basis, especially for those entering at a management level, are understandably very general and sometimes not too realistic. But the more realistic the expectancies are, the greater the chance for those expectancies to be met. Accordingly, when there is a greater chance for expectancies to be met, there is a stronger probability of the individual having job satisfaction. The chances of having realistic expectancies and of having these expectancies met appear to be improved when the organization provides the individual with specific kinds of information before hiring and when the organization helps the individual in the organizational socialization process. This chapter will examine individual socialization into the work environment, the development of a role, and those things that are important to the individual and the organization in managing a work environment in such a way as to allow individual contribution and satisfaction.

SOCIALIZATION INTO THE WORK ENVIRONMENT

What exactly is a work environment? The answer to this question appears to be rather simple—it is where an individual performs job related tasks. But it is more than just the *where*. The work environment includes a number of factors, any one of which may be considered the most important element by different people. Location of the organization; size of the organization; work conditions; nature of the job; fellow employees; the reward systems; internal rules and policies; the industry; the local, state and federal regulations that apply to the industry; the relationship with competitors; the relationship with the public; the managerial philosophy; the leadership styles; and the organizational structure all contribute to what is broadly defined as the work environment.

Given all these elements it becomes clear that the assimilation of the individual into the work environment is much more than just being able to do the job. There are adjustments to be made regarding rules and regulations, formal job requirements, expectations of informal groups, individual relationships, and on and on. This process of adjusting to, and fitting into, an environment is known as socialization.

The organizational socialization of an individual is a process whereby individual values, attitudes, and behavior become compatible with the expectancies of the formal organization.[1] Most organizations will expect individuals to have or to develop a set of values that are consistent with those of the firm. While values and attitudes will not always be known explicitly to others, the behavior of an individual will be perceived as a display of his or her values and attitudes. It is unlikely that employees will have an exact match of values, attitudes, and behavior with their organization, but the socialization process is an ongoing activity in which the employee is moving closer toward such a match with the organization. Some people may never accept certain values of an organization, but as long as they are not in direct opposition or moving further away from those formal values, there can still be a socialization process taking place.

One of the important aspects of socialization is the feeling an individual gets when he or she has a sense of belonging. Feeling a part of the work environment and being comfortable with the work environment would indicate that socialization is taking place. This comfortableness or "fit" with the work environment is dependent not only upon the formal aspects of the job but the informal as well.

Being accepted as part of an informal work group in the work environment may contribute significantly to the organizational socialization process. Informal groups may help the individual to develop some of the values and attitudes that are upheld by the formal organization. But it is a fact of organizational life that some informal groups may possess values that are not always consistent with those of the organization.[2] In such cases it may mean the individual must be involved in two somewhat separate socialization processes—one with the formal organization and one with the informal group. However, even where there may be some differences of values between the formal and informal groups, it has been found that the informal group may provide a socialization influence that is, for the most part, compatible with the values of the formal organization.[3] This positive influence of informal groups apparently stems from the fact that the groups recognize that they owe their existence to the formal organization.[4]

The rate at which the individual becomes a real part of the work environment and the degree to which the individual is socialized will have a great influence on that person's perceived role within the organization. Conversely, the development of a role in the work environment will greatly assist the socialization process. The relationship could, therefore, be said to be circular and indeterminable with regard to primacy.

ASSUMING A ROLE
IN THE WORK ENVIRONMENT

When an individual accepts a position with an organization, he or she has accepted a certain role that is expected to be carried out. That role is defined in formal terms by the job description, which outlines the tasks and duties to be performed; by the job specification, which prescribes the expected background and abilities an individual will bring to the job; and by the organizational structure, which provides the framework for the formal vertical and horizontal relationships. The individual's pattern of actions or role has been set forth by the organization. Whether or not the individual successfully assumes the role will be dependent upon several variables.

These variables are really types of expectations that can be divided into two categories:

1. The expectations of the individual
2. The expectations of the organization

Table 2.1 shows the two lists of expectancies. When examining the two lists of expectations, remember they are presented as examples. Every individual and organization will have a unique list of expectancies. The ones appearing in the table are of a fairly general nature and are representative of the kinds of expectations that will exist. It should also be noted that the two lists actually amount to four sets of expectancies. An individual will have expectancies of (1) what will be given to the organization, and (2) what the organization should provide. Likewise the organization will have certain expectancies of (3) what employees should provide, and (4) what the employees should receive from the organization for their particular services.

The key to a successful assumption of a particular role in a formal organization is the extent to which the individual expectancies and the organizational expectancies given in Table 2.1 match. It is not necessarily simply a matter of equating a higher number of matches to a high level of

TABLE 2.1   Types of Expectations*

(a)

The following listed thirteen items are examples of areas in which an individual has expectations of receiving and an organization has expectations of giving. That is, for each item in this list, the individual will have an expectation about what the organization will offer him or give him in that area. Likewise, the organization has an expectation about what it will offer or give the individual in that area.

1. A sense of meaning or purpose in the job
2. Personal development opportunities
3. The amount of interesting work (stimulates curiosity and induces excitement)
4. The challenge in the work
5. The power and responsibility in the job
6. Recognition and approval for good work
7. The status and prestige in the job
8. The friendliness of the people, the congeniality of the work group
9. Salary
10. The amount of structure in the environment (general practices, discipline, regimentation)
11. The amount of security in the job
12. Advancement opportunities
13. The amount and frequency of feedback and evaluation

(b)

The following listed seventeen items are examples of areas in which an individual has expectations of giving and the organization has expectations of receiving. That is, for each item in this list, the individual will have an expectation about what he is willing or able to give or offer the organization in that area. Likewise, the organization has an expectation about what it will receive from the individual in that area.

1. The ability to perform nonsocial job-related tasks requiring some degree of technical knowledge and skill
2. The ability to learn the various aspects of a position while on the job
3. The ability to discover new methods of performing tasks; the ability to solve novel problems
4. The ability to present a point of view effectively and convincingly
5. The ability to work productively with groups of people
6. The ability to make well-organized, clear presentations both orally and written
7. The ability to supervise and direct the work of others
8. The ability to make responsible decisions well without assistance from others
9. The ability to plan and organize work efforts for oneself or others
10. The ability to utilize time and energy for the benefit of the company
11. The ability to accept company demands which conflict with personal prerogatives

TABLE 2.1   (continued)

12. Social relationships with other members of the company off the job
13. Conforming to the folkways of the organization or work group on the job in areas not directly related to job performance
14. Further education pursued off company time
15. Maintaining a good public image of the company
16. Taking on company values and goals as one's own
17. The ability to see what should or must be done, and to initiate appropriate activity

*These thirty types of expectations were adapted from earlier research by David E. Berlew and Douglas T. Hall, "The Socialization of Managers: Effects of Expectations on Performance," *Administrative Science Quarterly* (September 1966): 207–23.

Source: John Paul Kotter, "The Psychological Contract: Managing the Joining-Up Process," in People and Productivity, *ed. Robert A. Sutermeister (New York: McGraw-Hill, Inc., 1976), p. 285.*

job satisfaction or successful role assumption. Each individual and each organization will have priorities that will make some expectancies much more important than the rest. Those expectations that are viewed as being very important to either party are, of course, the most critical in determining the successful assumption of a role. A mismatch of one or more of this type of expectancy could mean dissatisfaction on the part of either (or both) the individual and the organization. By the same token, the less critical an expectancy to either party, the less likely it is that a mismatch will contribute to dissatisfaction.

The successful assumption of a role within a formal organizational structure is most difficult to predict. There will always be some information regarding expectations that is incomplete or left out completely. It is necessary, of course, for both job performance and job satisfaction that employees understand precisely what their job is. The extent to which the employee understands job related tasks and objectives is known as role clarity. But role clarity by itself does not always mean improved performance. There must be an acceptance by the individual of the work role. When there is both role clarity and role acceptance, there is a great likelihood of goal commitment, job involvement, and job satisfaction.[5]

While it might be natural to assume that informational gaps will be filled over a period of time, the problem does not disappear entirely as the expectations of both the employees and the organization undoubtedly will continue to change. In some instances a change in an expectation may be communicated, especially if it is a change on the part of the organization, but unfortunately this is not always the case when individual expectations change. There may be attempts to communicate major changes in expectancies, but minor changes may be more evident by changes in behavior and work performance. On occasion these evident changes of behavior may be due to a feeling of uncertainty as to what the formal requirements of the job really are.

ROLE AMBIGUITY

Poor role definition or lack of clarity concerning one's role is indicative of role ambiguity. Unlike role conflict (where there is a choice to be made between two or more differing expectations that have been stated or implied), the state of role ambiguity is one of uncertainty. The existence of ambiguity in the work environment can usually be blamed upon poor communications. Incomplete and/or vague instructions and explanations will leave the individual in a position of not knowing exactly what is expected of him.

An employee who is left to his or her interpretation of the situation may take some action that is considered inappropriate by the organization. Without guidelines to channel the employee's actions, the behavioral alternatives available are almost unlimited. Consistency of action is quite improbable, and meeting the expectations of superiors and others within the organization becomes a trial-and-error experience.

When an individual accepts a certain role as defined by the formal organization, the level of satisfaction and performance can be affected by the lack of role clarity and role acceptance. If both parties believe there is a successful matching of expectancies and the role is clearly understood and accepted, it can be assumed the individual will fulfill the formal role assigned. However, when there are mismatches of expectancies that are not immediately resolved, there is the possibility that the individual will suffer from role conflict.

ROLE CONFLICT

On occasion there will be forces in the work environment which cause an individual to feel that there are opposing demands being placed upon him or her. When these demands are in conflict with one another, the individual is placed in an "either-or" situation. There would be no way to satisfy both, so there must be a choice as to which demand to meet. Being caught between such opposing forces puts a person in role conflict.

A mismatch in the expectations of an organization and an individual can cause such a role conflict. Similarly, the expectations of colleagues can put a person in a role conflict situation. For example, a new employee might be torn between abiding by company policy, which calls for a strict adherence to the job description, and giving in to the requests of another department for assistance that would mean going beyond the job descrip-tion. This problem frequently occurs because the former holder of the job did many things not included in the job description, which came to be expected by colleagues as services that should be rendered by anyone holding that job. New employees who are somewhat unsure of their roles seem to be more susceptible to this kind of role conflict.

Differences in the values of the formal and informal groups can also create role conflict. The choice between obeying rules or orders from the formal organization or yielding to the peer pressure of an informal group in an attempt to resist the rules or orders can be a traumatic decision-making process.

In addition there is the possibility of a conflict between personal and organizational goals. Recent college graduates who are ecology minded and find themselves working for a company that is a major polluter of the rivers and streams near the plant site would be examples of employees whose role conflicts are the result of personal beliefs and values being in conflict with those of the organization.

Role conflict is fairly common in most work environments and can be caused in a number of ways. Usually the existence of role conflict is due to a particular incident and is of relatively short duration. If a role conflict is considered to be major and is of an enduring nature, most individuals would find the pressure intolerable and would quit the job. Chris Argyris (a noted professor and management consultant), however, believes that role conflict is inevitable in formal organizations because of the differences in the needs of a healthy personality and those of the organization. He refers to these differences as a "basic incongruency."

INCONGRUENCY THEORY AND ROLE CONFLICT

Incongruencies between the needs of people and the requirements of the organization will exist, according to Argyris, in those organizations which implement formal principles of organization.[6] He contends that the incongruencies will be worsened by the growth of a healthy personality toward maturity and the necessity of the organization to make people dependent upon the organization. Although there are probably very few organizations that still cling exclusively to the ideal principles of formal organization, Argyris chose to use the extremes in order to help analyze the degree to which individuals and organizations tend toward the ex-tremes. Thus, the greater an individual's desire to constantly move toward maturity and the greater the desire of the organization to make people passive and dependent, the greater the incongruency.

There are many organizational practices which Argyris believes keep people psychologically immature—at the child level of personality development.[7] The following are examples of how some organizational practices keep employees psychologically immature.

1. *Specialization:* The breaking up of a whole job into small, simple, and routine tasks. Each task becomes a job for one person.
2. *Short Span of Control:* A small number of workers are closely supervised by one person. This practice tends to make the workers feel policed in their organizational life.
3. *Unity of Direction:* The creation of one plan by the head of a department without asking for any input or suggestions from others. This makes employees feel detached from important decision-making activities.
4. *Chain of Command:* The line of authority from the top of the organization down to the first-line supervisor. The worker feels that all the important power and authority rests with a few people at the top.

Table 2.2 shows the child and adult personality characteristics as identified by Argyris.[8]

Argyris contends that people want to work hard and to control important factors in their organizations. Usually they are blocked by one or more of the four organizational practices that are closely followed by managers at all levels. When formal organizational principles are applied in such a manner, people will find themselves in a work environment which:

1. Allows them minimal control over their jobs
2. Expects them to be passive and dependent
3. Expects them to have a short-time perspective
4. Encourages them to use shallow abilities
5. Expects them to produce under conditions which may lead to psychological failure[9]

For example, unity of direction implies that only one individual has the authority and responsibility for thinking ahead and creating the plan for others to follow. Implicitly the individual worker is asked to be passive and dependent, to have only a short-term perspective, and to be subordinate to the superior. In a similar fashion, specialization influences an individual to have shallow job and organizational interests and to be able to behave in only a few ways.

Besides being repetitive and boring, specialized jobs offer little in the way of feedback. A person working on an assembly line performing a highly specialized job is not always aware of the importance of the job,

TABLE 2.2 Trends in Personality Development

CHILD	ADULT
passive	active
dependent	independent
behave in few ways	behave in many ways
shallow interests	deep, intellectual interests
short-time perspective	long-time perspective
subordinate feelings	equal or superordinate feelings
lack of awareness	awareness and self-control

nor is there a feeling of accomplishment associated with the job. Such jobs are not limited to blue-collar tasks requiring few skills. One individual who described himself as a victim of specialization was a computer programmer at a large midwestern university. After approximately three years of programming the same kinds of statements and working with the same kinds of problems, he became a dropout from the white-collar world of work. He started his own custom home construction business in which he did a large share of the work. He claimed the increased job satisfaction was largely due to the feeling of accomplishment that came with the feedback of actually seeing his finished product. He could say to someone else, "See that house? I built it." For people with this need for feedback, job specialization does not offer much job satisfaction.

Furthermore, Argyris believes that the problems stemming from the basic incongruencies will be exaggerated by the following:

- The lower an individual is in the organization
- The more mature an employee is
- The more formalized the organization
- The more mechanized the jobs[10]

It would appear that if the incongruency theory is correct we can expect more behavioral problems in organizations that are extremely formalized bureaucracies where specialization is emphasized and the leadership style is one which stresses employee dependence. In such a work environment it would not be surprising to see an abundance of job dissatisfaction and role conflict. Identifying the cause of the human oriented problems would not be difficult in a situation so extreme. However, in the real work environment, where there are generally not these extremes, the identification and solution of human problems becomes more difficult.

Argyris' model provides insight as to some of the probable causes and possible solutions to situations where incongruencies between the organization and individual occur.

ROLE AND STATUS

Formal Status

With the assumption of a role in an organization comes not only authority and responsibility, but also a certain status or social ranking. Status that is derived from the formal organization is based upon position in the hierarchy. The status that normally accompanies a certain position can be expanded upon by the behavior of the individual or, of course, it can also be diminished.

A new employee will learn of the formal status system and the various status symbols over a period of time. Ironically, new employees learn more about the formal status system by informal means than they are told formally. It is rare indeed for any corporation or public agency to officially announce that when one is promoted to manager, an oil painting will be provided for the office wall, a wooden desk will replace the grey steel one, and the office space provided will be twenty square feet larger. While these status symbols are not formally announced, there seems to be little need to do so. It becomes understood by all employees which status symbols go with which jobs.

Although level in the hierarchy serves as a guide, there are other factors that may contribute to a particular status. In some organizations there may be marked distinctions between the status of a line manager and a staff manager who appear to be on the same level in the hierarchy. The nature of the job may also determine how much status a person has. For instance, in one corporation that has a sizable international marketing department the people within that department seem to enjoy a higher status than those of equal rank who are involved with the marketing effort in the United States. Other factors such as pay, seniority, level of education, and work conditions may also be determinants of formal status.

Informal Status

Informal status is granted by the people with whom an individual associates. This type of social ranking is determined by how people feel toward the individual. Status may come in an informal group as a result of some type of behavior that is especially valued by the group. It may be accorded to those who have recognized expertise, skills, seniority, strength, or even the ability to tell stories better than anyone else. Informal status is an earned ranking that comes from the people who know the individual the best. In this sense it could be argued that it may be equally important to the satisfaction of ego needs as the status granted by the formal organization.

TRANSACTIONAL ANALYSIS AND ROLE

Many trainers and seminar leaders today are using transactional analysis to help managers and management trainees better understand behavior and perceived roles. An important contribution of transactional analysis (TA) has been the attempt to explain behavior in terms of a number of separate but related transactions. A transaction is essentially an interaction between people. All social, psychological, material, and spiritual contacts between individuals can be defined as transactions.[11]

The TA approach holds that in order to analyze behavior one must first understand that the basic component of behavior is an ego state.[12] An ego state is defined as a "consistent combination of thought-feelings and related behavior."[13] There is, in other words, a consistency in the manner in which people combine logic, emotions, and behavior in situations which call for a response.

There are three ego states within every individual:

- The parent ego state
- The adult ego state
- The child ego state

Sources of ego states can usually be attributed to:

- The behavior of parental figures (parent)
- Behavior based upon objective reality (adult)
- Behavior that duplicates that of childhood (child)

Table 2.3 provides an overview of the ego states.

The selection of an ego state for a particular situation is dependent upon the person's perceived role and the consequences desired. Simply put, role perception is how the individual believes he or she should act given the set of circumstances and personalities involved. If a manager is dealing with a group of subordinates, the perceived role will be one that is influenced by the job description. Thus, the perceived role will be one of authority, power, and responsibility. Since the role is perceived as one of authority that is autocratic or paternalistic in nature, the ego state selected will probably be that of the parent.

TABLE 2.3   Structure of the Personality

PERSONALITY STRUCTURE	PARENT EGO STATE	ADULT EGO STATE	CHILD EGO STATE
Concept of Life	Taught concept of life: "How to" lists, rights and wrongs. Source of quick evaluative judgments.	Thought concept of life: Center of (1) data processing; (2) probability estimating; (3) decision making.	Felt concept of life: Source and seat of emotions.
Basic Concern	To be right, to be "on target."	To be respected as competent, recognized as good decision maker.	To be liked.
Special Attributes	Storehouse of standards of social controls and emotional norms, lists of "shoulds" and "should nots"—conscience	Only data processor in here-and-now, awareness of no certainty for success, only some degree of probability for success or failure.	Wants immediate results, guarantees and certainties, instant gratification—vastly more willing to receive than to give.

Source: Reprinted, by permission of the publisher, from Transactional Analysis and the Manager, *Dudley Bennett,* © *1976 by AMACOM, a division of American Management Association, p. 3.*

Of course, the hoped for result of the transaction is also important to the selection of an ego state. Generally the role perception and the wanted outcome will be compatible. When they are not, it is most likely that the outcome desired will have the greater influence on the selection of an ego state.

Everyone will, on occasion, assume each one of the three ego states. Just because a person is a fully grown, fairly mature individual does not mean he or she will never again be in a child ego state. The relationships adults have with their parents may serve as an example. A person may be thirty years old, married, have children, have an advanced degree, and hold a very responsible, well-paid position within an organization and still be treated as a child by his or her parents. That is not surprising. But most people will also still respond to their parents in a child ego state, at least in certain situations. In addition, in cases where employees feel subordinate in the formal organization, they may slip into the child ego state. This may be done because the employees feel it is necessary in order to survive organizationally. The resultant feelings and behavior will cause the employees to experience role conflict, and thus, this situation lends credibility to the incongruency theory.

PUTTING THE WORK ENVIRONMENT IN CONGRUENCE WITH THE INDIVIDUAL

This chapter has pointed out some of the factors that seem to cause incongruencies between organizations and the employees. However, it is important to note that many companies have taken steps to minimize the conflicts. Successful corporations such as Hewlett-Packard and Texas Instruments have created a more informal work environment and have diminished some of the more damaging side effects of a formalized bureaucracy. By allowing people to come to work without wearing ties, by doing away with many of the status symbols usually associated with management positions, and by encouraging creative thinking these two technically oriented companies have developed a climate that makes the socialization process easier. Even though some of the things that can be done to make a work environment more "livable" sound rather trite, this should not detract from their importance.

Once some of the more superficial requirements of a formalized organization have been dropped, the organization usually reaps the benefits stemming from improved employee morale and loyalty. When people learn that it is the result and not the procedure that is valued, the work environment has taken a step toward improvement. When a new employee learns that innovation and unique thinking are valued commodities, some assumed incongruencies may disappear. And when contribution and ability appear more important to advancement than a three-piece suit and a pair of wingtips, some of the causes for value conflict have been minimized.

Besides just changing managerial philosophies and attitudes, there are several actions that can be taken to provide more congruence between the people and the company. Improving upon existing orientation sessions and initiating reorientation sessions for everyone would be an example, as would training middle- and top-level managers and first-line supervisors in how to deal with employee role conflict and role ambiguity. Perhaps through the use of some participative approach which encourages open communications between superior and subordinate, management can demonstrate and emphasize the goal compatibility of the employee and the company.

Throughout the remainder of this book there will be discussions of various behavioral problems in the work environment and possible solutions. The perceived roles of the employees, whether real or not, will in many cases be a contributor to these problems. Likewise role conflict and role ambiguity can be seen as contributors to many of the difficulties in the work environment. Managers must become more behaviorally oriented so that they will be better prepared to properly diagnose and deal with problems that are caused by incongruencies between employees and the organization.

SUMMARY

When employees have realistic job expectancies, there is a greater chance that their expectancies will be met. With more fulfillment of expectancies comes a higher level of job satisfaction. It is, therefore, important that organizations inform employees early in their employment, or even before they are hired, about what the organization expects to receive and what it in turn expects to provide.

Having this kind of information can help the individual in the socialization process and help reduce the potential for role conflict and role ambiguity. While going through this process of "fitting in," the more information the employee has concerning the work environment, fellow employees, job requirements, and expectancies of the formal and informal groups, the more readily the individual will be able to assume his or her role. Since on-the-job behavior is a reflection of a perceived role, the quantity and quality of communications to the new employee greatly influences the likelihood of the perceived role matching the expectations of the organization.

Incongruencies between individuals and formal organizations appear to be greater the more formalized the organization is and the more mature the individual. Many corporations and public agencies have attempted to do away with these incongruencies by training supervisors and managers in leadership styles, communications, and transactional analysis. By creating a more informal work environment, by having better prepared managers, and by making adjustments of managerial philosophies, policies, and regulations, it is possible to get greater goal compatibility between employees and the organization. When the individual can be in harmony with the work environment, there will be better performance in the long run and more satisfaction for both the superior and the subordinate.

NOTES

1. PATRICK E. CONNOR, "A Critical Inquiry into Some Assumptions and Values Characterizing OD," *Academy of Management Review* 2 (October 1977): 642.

2. Ibid.

3. See ROBERT PRESTHUS, *The Organizational Society* (New York: Random House-Vantage Books, 1962), pp. 156–63.

4. Ibid.

5. See RICHARD M. STEERS, *Organizational Effectiveness, a Behavioral Review* (Santa Monica: Goodyear Publishing Company, Inc., 1977), p. 126.

6. CHRIS ARGYRIS, "A Basic Incongruency between the Needs of a Mature Personality and the Requirements of Formal Organization," in *People and Productivity*, ed. Robert A. Sutermeister (New York: McGraw-Hill, Inc., 1976), p. 207.

7. See CHRIS ARGYRIS, *Personality and Organization* (New York: Harper and Row, Inc., 1957).

8. Ibid.

9. ARGYRIS, "A Basic Incongruency," p. 207.

10. DUDLEY BENNETT, *Transactional Analysis and the Manager*, AMACOM (New York: 1976), p. 28.

12. Ibid., p. 1.

13. Ibid.

QUESTIONS FOR THOUGHT AND DISCUSSION

1. What has been involved in your socialization to the college campus? In what ways is the socialization process on-going?

2. Compare role ambiguity and role conflict. What do you believe to be the best methods of assuring role clarity for new employees?

3. In your opinion do organizations desire to make their employees passive and dependent? What specific organizational practices (of any private or public organization) are you aware of that encourage employees to be psychologically immature?

4. What is the importance of transactional analysis to managers?

5. What do you believe to be the best way to put the work environment in congruence with the individual? Support your answer.

KEY TERMS

The student should be able to discuss the significance of these terms to the study of human behavior in the work environment.

Socialization process	Span of control
Work environment	Unity of direction
Role	Chain of command
Individual expectancies	Role ambiguity
Organizational expectancies	Formal status
Role clarity	Informal status
Role acceptance	Transactional analysis
Role conflict	Role perception
Incongruency theory	Ego state
Specialization	

CASE INCIDENT

As a staff manager of Technical Training in the Human Resource Development Group, Fred West was recognized as one of the brightest and hardest working people in the entire Employee Relations Department of Consolidated Systems Unlimited. Fred was a brilliant statistician and computer programmer who was responsible for designing and teaching training programs for programmers and systems analysts as well as many other technically oriented sessions for engineers. He had published a number of articles in professional journals and was gaining somewhat of a reputation throughout the nation. Consequently he was asked to give talks and conduct workshops and seminars in his free time. However, Fred's ambition was causing problems with one of his superiors.

Fred's immediate superior, Rob, was quite supportive and encouraged Fred in whatever he did. Rob's boss, Ron, was not particularly pleased with Fred's activities outside the company and wanted him to slow down a bit and become more concerned with his job within the department.

When confronted by Ron and told he would not be allowed to continue his consulting outside the company, Fred reminded Ron that his contract allowed him two days off a month for consulting or personal development and that the seminars he conducted on weekends, vacations, or after work hours should be of no concern to the company. Ron expressed the belief that Fred could actually be training people who could end up competing with Consolidated Systems and that other people within the company would be jealous of his outside involvement. Besides that, Ron was concerned that Fred was not devoting his full attention to his job when he was involved with outside activities. Fred reminded Ron that fellow employees Fletcher and Glenn had the same kind of employment contracts and that they too were in demand by other groups because of their expertise. Ron's reply was a rather terse acknowledgement of the situation, adding that they too would have to give up all outside activities.

Fred did not want to lose his job but neither did he want to quit consulting and giving talks and seminars. He approached Rob, his immediate superior, with the problem. Upon hearing Ron's request Rob became irate.

Rob: Do you know how much time our omnipotent leader takes off from his job to do the exact same thing you are doing?

Fred: No, not really.

Rob: Well, if you had to try to find him sometime to get some requisition signed or approval to make a move, you would know that he is hardly here. And he, of course, is giving these talks and seminars in the interest of public relations.

Fred: I'll bet.

Rob: If we had the income he gets in one year from those "P.R." talks it would double our salary.

Fred: That's not saying much. I learned at the last American Institute for Decision Sciences meeting that I'm about $3,000 below average. I have to do something on the outside just so I can continue living here. Does Ron really want us so dependent on the company that he is afraid to let us do anything on our own?

Rob: I don't understand his reasoning. It's a "do as I say not as I do" kind of policy.

Fred: Well, he has told me that I have a conflict of interest and it's not fair to the other employees because I have this opportunity and they don't.

Rob: Boy, that's something else. I can't believe he is doing this. I'll talk to him. He is out of line bypassing me anyway.

Questions for Discussion

1. Is there a role conflict? Explain.

2. Does Fred have a conflict of interest?

3. What alternatives are available to Rob? Which one do you feel is the best alternative?

4. Does Ron have the right to prohibit Fred from doing any more outside work?

5. Relate this situation to Argyris' incongruency theory.

3

The Importance of Job Design

LEARNING OBJECTIVES

Upon completion of this chapter the student should be able to:

- Define job design and recount the history of its development.
- Discuss why apathy, boredom, restlessness, and dissatisfaction are consequences of poor job design.
- Outline the characteristics of good jobs and their impact upon people.
- Explain how jobs once stimulating become routine and, perhaps, boring to some people.
- Recognize why the intrinsic job factors such as achievement and responsibility have more influence on workers' behavior than extrinsic factors such as company policies and procedures.
- Identify those job factors important to enriching a job.
- Contrast the reasons some people want enriched jobs while others do not want their jobs enriched.
- Suggest guidelines to follow when implementing job redesign programs.
- Differentiate between job enrichment and job enlargement.

Work attitudes and behavior are influenced by an individual's parents, church or synagogue, and teachers, and by various laws and societal norms. As has been said many times, each of us is, in a large part, the product of an environment. The organization in which one works is part of such an environment and naturally has a major influence. An important part of the work environment is the actual job performed. The design of that job, or the nature of the tasks and how they must be carried out, will greatly affect on-the-job behavior. A poorly designed job can cause boredom, stress, and low motivation. There are many observable behaviors that are symptoms of the problems that can be attributed to poor job design.

Think about the last time you were in a large business office for over five minutes. How often did you see people running off to get coffee or a soft drink, stretching, engaging in social conversations, horsing around, daydreaming, changing positions while seated at their desk, or comparing pictures of their families? While it is not always the case, many times it is job boredom that causes such behavior. The workers are not being stimulated by their jobs so they seek activities that are more interesting or those that simply provide a break from a tedious and boring task.

In any of your classes try to notice the frequency of students shifting around in their chairs, conversations not related to the course, doodling, passing notes, or even sleeping. Boredom with the class is probably the cause of these behaviors. The students engaging in such activities are not stimulated by the class.

Also take note of the number of times your professor starts discussing something not important to the course. Does the professor talk about tennis, golf, art, taxes, parking, cars, or dissertations? Boredom with the topic of discussion for the class may be the cause for the introduction of other topics. Perhaps the professor is not stimulated or perhaps the professor senses that the students are not stimulated. The introduction of subjects which appear to be irrelevant may be a method used to regain or keep the attention of students and allow a brief respite from academic pursuits for students whom the professor perceives as getting bored.

Think about the last time you put off studying for final exams. All of a sudden you had to prepare for three or four tests at the same time. Did you find yourself extremely nervous or anxious? Could you concentrate? Did you feel overwhelmed by the amount of information you had to learn? If you were nervous, unable to concentrate, and felt overwhelmed, you experienced the opposite of boredom. You were overstretched or overstimulated by the amount of work you had to do.

Think about the last time you played in some athletic event against a superstar. If you have not had this kind of experience, think about the last time you met someone really important, popular, or powerful. Did you feel awkward? Did you fail to do well or as well as you had hoped? If you felt you made a fool of yourself, you were probably overstimulated and/or overwhelmed by the situation.

In this chapter, we will explain how a job can be designed so that workers are stimulated by the work but not to the point where they are overwhelmed by the demands of a job. The process is called job design, or more appropriately, job redesign, since jobs occupied by people have already been designed at least once. This chapter presents the groundwork for designing jobs to better meet the needs of employees.

THE EVOLUTION OF JOB DESIGN

Before the advent of large manufacturing plants the majority of Americans lived on farms. That agrarian society was made up of a very self-reliant people. It was necessary for the farmers to possess a number of skills for the many jobs they had to perform. Today's more industrial society has caused people to grow away from the self-reliance of the past. It seems we have gone to the other extreme where the possession of a specialized skill is more highly valued than having several skills that have not been fully developed.

The emphasis on job specialization was the result of the scientific management movement of the late 1800s and early 1900s. Before this movement people were craftsmen doing "complete" jobs. They planned the job, did the job, evaluated their job performance and took corrective action to improve their performance. As a result of the scientific management approach the worker was left with just doing the job. The planning and evaluation dimensions were removed from the individual's responsibility.

This meant that most workers were doing simple, fragmented tasks requiring little thinking. Specialization does, of course, offer several advantages to management:

1. It reduces training time since a worker needs to learn only a few skills rather than many.
2. High precision can be attained by a worker performing one task and repeating it many times.
3. Machines and other equipment can be designed to fit each specialized job.

Since all of these advantages help to reduce operating costs while increasing productivity, specialization is well grounded economically. In this regard the idea of specialization appeared to be a welcome solution to the problems faced by the management of organizations at the turn of the century.

But specialization brought with it a host of human problems. Workers entering large organizations were generally farmers and other rural workers who were accustomed to doing an entire piece of work. Their work on a farm had nearly always provided what is referred to as job closure, the experience of seeing the results of one's efforts. Shining a pair of shoes, washing a car, or preparing and consuming a dinner are examples of closure.

As pointed out in Chapter 1, concern for the plight of the workers did not occur in any organized form until the human relations movement of the 1920s and 1930s. During this period, methods of questioning, interviewing, and testing workers were developed. This allowed human problems in organizations to be seriously investigated. It was during this period that topics relating to worker discontent, alienation, attitudes, motivation, and satisfaction began to be scientifically studied.

Starting in the late 1960s and throughout the 1970s the focus shifted to the subject of job design. Indeed, there have been so many articles published that it would appear that the subject of job design has received enough attention to qualify it as one of the more popular management fads. However, most management scholars believe that the current focus on job design is not merely a fad but rather an attempt to significantly improve the quality of work life.

There are several reasons why the work itself rather than some other factor is getting more interest and research effort. When workers are unhappy with the jobs they were hired to do, managers may feel they have to counter this dissatisfaction by introducing something pleasant into an employee's work life. For instance, job dissatisfaction may be temporarily neutralized when a worker receives a pay raise or an increase in benefits. In this situation, the worker might be thinking, "Well, although I can't stand my job, the pay is good, so I'll stick with it a little longer." There are other things that could be done to make employees temporarily forget their dissatisfaction. Such methods, however, end up costing more in the long run. The best answer is to design the job so that it can provide some satisfaction and insure that it is compatible with the worker's needs. As one manager has observed, "If people liked their jobs, you would not need supervisors, fancy pay plans, company picnics, or any of those other human relations tricks." This observation reflects an extreme point of view that fails to recognize that one of the "human relations tricks" is to design jobs in a manner that allows people to like their jobs.

THE NEED FOR BETTER JOB DESIGN

The work people perform is one of the most important factors in influencing the quality of work life. The work or job factor strongly affects job attitudes, performance and the will to work. Imagine how terrible some people who need challenges must feel after having worked eight hours on a simple and meaningless job. Some common complaints heard from workers doing this kind of work include dissatisfaction, fatigue (a result of being bored), a feeling of uselessness, apathy, and low motivation and creativity. Many people have lived with these types of complaints a large portion of their working lives. On the other hand, some companies with innovative managers have thought about better ways of combining the different tasks which comprise a job. These managers have created jobs that match a worker's needs and expectations. When there is a match between what a worker wants from a job and what is offered from a job, high levels of satisfaction and motivation will be felt by the worker. Good jobs give workers the opportunity to demonstrate competence on worthwhile and challenging activities. These jobs also perform the following functions:

1. Allow a worker to feel personally responsible for a meaningful portion of work rather than a fragmented part of a job
2. Provide rewards which are intrinsically meaningful or otherwise experienced as important by the worker
3. Provide feedback to the worker about how well he or she is working

In recent years popular magazine and newspaper accounts have painted a bleak picture of the calibre of jobs offered to the American worker. It seems that many workers find it difficult to commit themselves to work which is void of personal meaning and significance. Not only are simple jobs generally disliked by many people, but they are also incompatible with the healthy adult personality (as was discussed in Chapter 2). That chapter mentioned that routine work provides workers little control over their work environment and forces them to perfect and value the frequent use of a few skin-surface, shallow abilities. All of us feel significant when we use our important abilities and skills in doing something well, but we don't feel significant using only our shallow abilities. Most individuals need challenging and responsible work in order to feel competent in organizational life.

The job stimulation issue presents a complicated problem. An individual's perception of the same job will change over time. When workers are first hired they find most jobs rather confusing because they do not know how the jobs should be done. However, once-challenging jobs become routine and nonchallenging after the workers have been trained and have practiced doing the jobs many times. Successful managers can sometimes tell when boredom sets in by observing the day-to-day behavior of workers. When workers are bored (and the same goes for students) they start doing things which increase stimulation. Bored workers walk around too much, take too many breaks, become tired too soon, and generally engage in too many nonjob activities.

THE JOB/PERSON MATCH

Job design is defined as any activity that involves changing a job "with the intent of increasing both the quality of the employees' work experience and on-the-job productivity." Since people differ in their psychological make-up, a perfect job for one person could be poorly suited for another.

Importance of Matching the Job with the Person

People want jobs that match their needs, values, and personalities. High levels of motivation and satisfaction and low levels of absenteeism and turnover result from a good job/person match. A mismatch leads to frustration, boredom, dissatisfaction, and the lack of the will to work.

Studies have shown that a worker who occupies a job that requires the use of his skills derives a "sense of competence" from mastering his work. R. W. White, a well-known psychologist, sees a strong relationship between competence and self-esteem.[1] People are happy when they believe themselves to be competent in performing meaningful work. Since most people strive to master important activities in their lives, it is not surprising that the mastery of skills performed on the job involves a certain amount of pride. After all, work for most people is the most important activity influencing their self-esteem.

The famous ego psychologist Eric Erikson coined the phrase "sense of industry" to refer to a person's attempts to feel useful, competent, and productive.[2] He believes that often people are distressed with their personal development because of problems in identifying with an occupation. However, once a career choice takes place and the process of job mastery begins, psychological health improves.

Competency and psychological health are also important to Abraham Maslow's hierarchy of needs.* As explained in Chapter 1, the highest level of need identified by Maslow is self-actualization.[3] Self-actualization refers to a very high level of human development and personal adjustment. It is often defined in general terms as "becoming all that one is capable of becoming." Doing the best that we can on each job that we do—however tedious or boring—contributes to feelings of competence, high self-esteem, and self-actualization. Admittedly, people sometimes have to "talk themselves into" demonstrating competence on lower organizational jobs that are generally not as exciting or important as top

---

*Maslow's hierarchy of needs is discussed in detail in Chapter 7.

managerial jobs. Nevertheless, competence shown on lower organizational jobs leads to the opportunity to experience competence and self-
actualization in upper organizational positions.

Determining the Job/Person Match

The work people perform may range from the very simple and routine
(short-cycle jobs) to the very complex and unpredictable (long-cycle jobs).
A short-cycle job refers to one where the worker is essentially performing
only a few activities many times during the work day. Pumping gasoline is
a short-cycle job. A week's experience pumping gasoline is like one
hour's experience forty times over. Long-cycle jobs are complex, challenging, and unpredictable. For example, a job such as developing a marketing strategy for a corporation, which would require implementing
changes over a period of time to meet the varying customer desires and
market competition, would be a long-cycle job. The contrast between
short-cycle and long-cycle jobs can be seen more closely by looking at the
characteristics of each type of job. A worker is performing a short-cycle
job when the worker:

1. Uses only a few relatively important skills and talents
2. Performs only a fragment of a job rather than a whole, complete job
   where the person can see the results of his or her efforts
3. Does not believe the job to be essential to company success
4. Does not have control over work methods and work pace

An employee is performing a long-cycle job when the person:

1. Uses many different, important skills and abilities
2. Does a whole job where the person can see the beginning and end of
   the completed job
3. Knows that the job is important to company success
4. Has control over work methods and work pace

As illustrated in Figure 3.1 the long-cycle jobs tend to be in the
upper part of the organization, whereas the short-cycle jobs tend to be in
the lower part of the hierarchy. Ordinarily, the work performed at the
upper levels of an organization is more ambiguous and nonroutine than
jobs performed at lower organizational levels.

Some people want highly stimulating and unpredictable activities in
their lives all the time. If properly trained, these people would feel right at
home in a job that was constantly changing. Conversely, some individuals

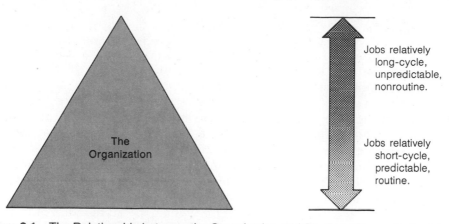

Figure 3.1   The Relationship between the Organization and Short- and Long-Cycle Jobs. Ordinarily, upper organizational jobs are more nonroutine than lower organizational jobs.

actually prefer the predictable and routine jobs. They prefer to design their lives around clear and predictable activities. (This notion is referred to as Activation Theory and it will be fully discussed in Chapter 7.)

Some studies which have been conducted within the last four years have come up with interesting results concerning the length of job cycles.[4] The long-cycle, complex jobs are preferred by people seeking fulfillment of strong achievement and self-actualization needs. The research has also found that long-cycle jobs are liked by people who believe strongly in the Protestant work ethic. A person subscribing to the work ethic believes that hard work in organizations will "pay off." For this person, high self-esteem is realized when the person does well in work activities rather than in nonwork activities.

The short-cycle jobs are preferred by people seeking fulfillment of security, social, and monetary needs in organizations. People who react favorably to short-cycle jobs probably do not believe in the work ethic as much as others. This is not to say that they do not want to work hard. It only suggests that work to these people is not the dominant reason for living. Many people derive feelings of achievement and personal development from activities outside of work. Activities such as hobbies, athletics, and family concerns are their primary means through which feelings of personal development and achievement may be realized.

People vary a great deal with regard to what they want from a job. In much the same way as people have different preferences for cars, food, clothing, and the like, they have job preferences that are just as varied. When these job preferences can be met fairly closely, people will work longer, harder, and more effectively than when their preferences are not met.

INTRINSIC AND EXTRINSIC JOB FACTORS

Frederick Taylor is given credit for being the first serious "modern" management thinker to redesign jobs. While studying jobs during the early 1900s, he discovered that output would increase if the planning and controlling aspects of a person's job were removed—leaving the person just doing the job. To many current observers, this was the beginning of job specialization. Much later, in the mid-1950s, Frederick Herzberg and associates stimulated a great deal of discussion and controversy about job design, although their immediate concern was examining the causes of job satisfaction.[5] Their theory (to be discussed in more detail in Chapter 7) proposes that the causes of employee satisfaction and motivation are, for the most part, within the work that is being done, in the form of intrinsic rewards. These rewards include recognition, achievement, responsibility, personal growth and development, and advancement. A person experiences these rewards by performing well on a challenging job. These factors are called "satisfiers" or "motivators" because they are believed to be effective in motivating workers toward superior job performance.

On the other hand, the "hygiene" factors such as pay, working conditions, job security, co-workers, supervisory style, and company policies are mostly extrinsic or outside of the task being done.[6] These hygiene factors, according to Herzberg, are not powerful in inspiring workers toward higher performance goals, but they can cause dissatisfaction. In short, the satisfiers or motivators are generally intrinsic and the dissatisfiers or hygiene factors are mostly extrinsic.

INTRINSIC JOB FACTORS AND JOB TENURE

Why do some workers stay on a job longer than others? Many authorities believe that meaningful jobs—those offering the worker ego involvement—strongly influence the longevity of the employment relationship. Such work is believed to be pleasurable to the worker. The logic is simple: when the work a person performs is felt to be worthwhile, ego involving, challenging, and rewarding, the work is experienced as pleasurable. People seek and return to pleasurable situations while they avoid or do not return to unpleasurable and painful situations.

The length of time an individual stays on a job tends to be influenced more by factors within the work itself (intrinsic factors) than by factors outside of the work itself (extrinsic factors). One researcher put this idea to an empirical test with dentists, nurses, policewomen, social workers, and youth counselors. (Most of the people in the sample were females.) He discovered that the intrinsic factors strongly influenced a person's longevity on the job. Workers reporting concern for intrinsic factors stayed on the job longer than those not so concerned with these factors. On the other hand, workers reporting strong interests for the extrinsic factors did not have strong staying power.[7]

A second test of the power of intrinsic factors was performed with a different set of workers. The 1,027 workers in this study were teachers, special education teachers, laboratory workers, and building workers. The results were the same as in the first study. Workers who were mainly concerned with intrinsic factors stayed on the job longer than those who were concerned with the extrinsic factors.[8]

JOB ENRICHMENT

Recent attempts to increase employees' job satisfaction have been concerned with redesigning jobs so that they are intrinsically more rewarding. These efforts are examples of job enrichment. Job enrichment is defined as being:

> . . . concerned with designing jobs that include a greater variety of work content; require a higher level of knowledge and skill; give the worker more autonomy (independence) and responsibility for planning, directing, and controlling his own performance; and provide the opportunity for personal growth and meaningful work experience.[9]

In short, job enrichment will allow a worker to be involved in planning, directing, and controlling how a job is to be done.

In some instances job enlargement is confused with job enrichment. Job enlargement expands the duties of the job without necessarily allowing the individual any more control over the job. The process of simply adding duties to a job should not be viewed as an attempt to enrich the job. Enlargement is known as the "horizontal loading" of a job. Duties are added horizontally which means the job holder simply has more duties of the same nature to perform. Enrichment, on the other hand, is the "vertical loading" of the job. While this will also entail more duties, they are managerial kinds of tasks such as planning and controlling. A simple way to remember the difference is to equate enlargement with quantitative changes in the job and enrichment with qualitative changes.

Table 3.1 shows the types of job changes Herzberg believes lead to high motivation. Each of the seven principles of job design shown affects one of the intrinsic factors. For example, principle "F"—"introducing new and more difficult tasks" to a person's present job—is believed to increase a worker's feelings of personal growth and development. Principle "B"—"increasing the accountability of individuals"—is believed to increase job responsibility and recognition.

One serious shortcoming of this theory is that it does not provide for individual differences between people in their preferences for job en-

TABLE 3.1 The Herzberg Job Enrichment Ideas

PRINCIPLE	MOTIVATORS INVOLVED
A. Removing some controls while retaining accountability	Responsibility and personal achievement
B. Increasing the accountability of individuals for own work	Responsibility and recognition
C. Giving a person a complete natural unit of work (module, division, area, and so on)	Responsibility, achievement, and recognition
D. Granting additional authority to an employee in his activity; job freedom	Responsibility, achievement, and recognition
E. Making periodic reports directly available to the worker himself rather than to the supervisor	Internal recognition
F. Introducing new and more difficult tasks not previously handled	Growth and learning
G. Assigning individuals specific or specialized tasks, enabling them to become experts	Responsibility, growth, and advancement

Source: Frederick Herzberg, "One More Time: How Do You Motivate Employees?" Harvard Business Review 46 (January–February 1968), 59. Copyright © 1967 by the President and Fellows of Harvard College. All rights reserved.

richment. Many people do not like complex and challenging jobs. Enriching a job for such people would cause dissatisfaction and would probably prove to be a waste of time and money.

Another shortcoming is the absence of a method of measuring the existence of the intrinsic factors. While one individual may consider a job quite challenging and stimulating, another may find the same job to be totally lacking in intrinsic rewards. Matching a job with a person is, therefore, nearly impossible without some kind of method of first comparing the intrinsic rewards of the job with the needs of the individual.

THE INTRINSIC WORK MOTIVATIONAL MODEL

The major task in job design projects is to match a person's need for growth and accomplishment with certain job factors. The important job factors that managers can change are shown in Figure 3.2.

Figure 3.2 The Five Job Factors Changeable in Job Design

Each of these job factors is defined in the following manner:

Skill variety—The degree to which a job requires a variety of different activities in carrying out the work, which involve the use of a number of different skills and talents of the employee.

Task Identity—The degree to which the job requires completion of a "whole" and identifiable piece of work.

Task significance—The degree to which the job has a substantial impact on the lives or work of other people.

Autonomy—The degree to which the job provides substantial freedom, independence, and discretion to the employee in scheduling the work and in determining the procedures to be used in carrying it out.

Feedback—The degree to which carrying out the work activities required by the job results in the employee obtaining direct and clear information about the effectiveness of his or her performance.[10]

A job can be high or low on any of the job factors. Generally, the higher the job rates on these factors, the better it is for those people needing accomplishment and growth. The job of college professor is high on the autonomy (independence) factor as well as on the feedback factor. The job of being a college student is high on the skill variety factor while moderately low on the feedback dimension. Seldom does a student receive "direct and clear information" on the effectiveness of all of his or her inputs. Time lags in the feedback of information and incomplete feedback on performance cause the ratings to be moderately low in feedback. If professors could discover better ways of keeping students informed of their course progress, the feedback factor could be rated higher. The job of quarterback for the Dallas Cowboys is extremely high on task significance and feedback, moderately high on task identity and skill variety, and average on autonomy.

Figure 3.3 shows that workers can be divided into two groups for job design purposes: those concerned with fulfilling high growth needs (Group I) and those concerned with satisfying low growth needs (Group II). Job enrichment benefits the workers desiring growth and accomplishment while it does not benefit, and perhaps alienates, workers not seeking additional growth through their work.

The five job factors are real and measurable qualities of a job. A pencil-and-paper survey questionnaire could be administered to employees to find out how much of each factor a job contains. It is of equal importance to understand how these qualities or factors are perceived by workers. As shown in Figure 3.3, upgrading the job factors for workers who are concerned with personal growth will lead to consequences which are vastly different than for individuals not concerned with personal growth through work. The "psychological states" shown in Figure 3.3 play a key role in determining if job enrichment projects are successful. The three psychological states are defined as follows:

Experienced meaningfulness of the work—The degree to which the employee experiences the job as one which is generally meaningful, valuable, and worthwhile.

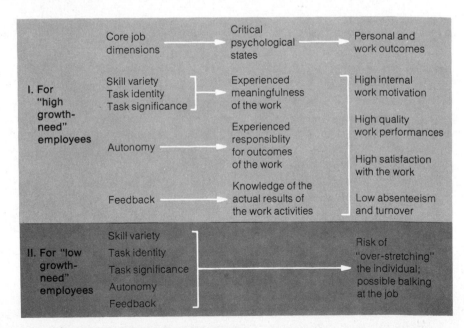

Figure 3.3   The Intrinsic Work Model of Motivation

(Source: J. R. Hackman, G. R. Oldham, R. Janson, and K. Purdy, A New Strategy for Job Enrichment. *New Haven, Conn.: Yale University Technical Report No. 3, 1974, p. 14.)*

Experienced responsibility for work outcome—The degree to which the employee feels personally accountable and responsible for the results of the work he or she does.

Knowledge of results—The degree to which the employee knows and understands, on a continuous basis, how effectively he or she is performing the job.[11]

These psychological states are not activated for low growth-need individuals by changes in the job factors. This is understandable since such people do not perceive the five job factors in the same favorable light as do the workers desiring growth. If these people with low growth needs were placed in enriched jobs, they would be overwhelmed by the increased job challenges and responsibilities and would probably rebel in one way or another.

Workers needing personal growth through work will realize that the job factors of skill variety, task identity, and task significance influence job "meaningfulness." Autonomy will provide "responsibility" and feedback, "knowledge of results." When enriched jobs are felt to be meaningful and responsible, they will lead to high work motivation, high quality performance, and high satisfaction. Internal work motivation is defined as the degree "to which the employee is self-motivated to perform effectively on the job—that is, the employee experiences positive internal feelings when working effectively on the job, and negative internal feelings when doing poorly."[12]

Does the Intrinsic Work Motivational Model Work?

Recently, the model was put to a scientific test to examine the validity of the theory. The model was tested with 658 employees who worked on sixty-two different jobs in seven organizations. The workers occupied blue-collar, white-collar, and professional jobs in both service and industrial organizations.[13] The researchers wanted to know if people who are very concerned with personal growth would react more positively to job enrichment than those who were not so concerned.

The results showed that job enrichment has much greater positive effects for people who are very concerned with personal growth than for the others. The model is correct. Individual perceptions of the job factors vary greatly and these differences are rooted in a person's need for greater work accomplishment.

Hygiene Factors and the Intrinsic Model

After successfully confirming the Intrinsic Work Motivational Model for a second time with 210 employees engaged in twenty-five different jobs in a bank, the investigators outlined the relationships between the Herzberg work context or hygiene factors (such as pay, supervision, company policies, promotional opportunities) and the job enrichment model. Their findings are presented below:

1. When employees are well-satisfied with the work context factors and have strong needs for personal growth through the job, job enrichment has very favorable effects on work satisfaction, performance, and motivation.

2. When employees are well-satisfied with the work context factors but have weak needs for personal growth through work, job enrichment has only moderately weak effects on satisfaction, performance, and motivation.

3. When employees are dissatisfied with the work context factors and have weak needs for personal growth through work, job enrichment has no effect on satisfaction, performance, and motivation.

4. When employees are dissatisfied with work context factors and have strong needs for personal growth through work, job enrichment has a favorable effect on work satisfaction, performance and motivation.[14]

These researchers are saying that the success of job enrichment is dependent upon the level of satisfaction with the work context and the level of personal growth needs of the individual. For people with low growth needs, job enrichment seems to have little favorable impact even when there is satisfaction with job context. However, the rewards appear to be much greater when high growth-need individuals are involved. The potential for increasing performance and motivation even for these kinds of people is higher for those who are satisfied with job context.

JOB ENRICHMENT FOR MANUAL JOBS

While most of the efforts at enriching jobs have involved higher level jobs, there is no reason why the jobs held by the rank-and-file cannot be enriched. Indeed, this is usually where enrichment is needed most. Table 3.2 shows several techniques that have been applied to manual or machine shop work.

Most of the job changes allow the worker to do more job planning and job evaluating on top of just doing the job. This allows the workers to feel more of an ownership and more control over their work lives when they can perform more of a whole job. For example, when the workers are given the responsibility for machine maintenance and replacement of parts, they will sense increased control over something important in their work environment—their own machines. When work teams plan the

TABLE 3.2   Job Enrichment for Manual Jobs

OLD SITUATION	SITUATION AFTER JOB ENRICHMENT
Each employee rotated among all machines.	Each employee assigned to only two machines.
When machine failure occurred, operator called on maintenance group.	Each operator given training in maintenance; each conducts preventive and corrective maintenance on the two machines for which he is responsible.
Operator changes the slicing blade (the most important component of the machine) following a rigid rule contained in a manual.	Operator given authority to decide when to replace blade, based on his judgment.
Supervisor monitors operator and corrects unsatisfactory performance.	Performance feedback system developed that provides daily information on their work quality directly to operators.
Individual performs specialized task on units passing by him.	Three- to five-man teams build entire unit.
Supervisor decides who should do what.	Team decides who should do what.
Inspectors and supervisor test output and correct performance.	Team conducts own quality audits.

Source: Ross A. Weber, Management *(Homewood, Ill.: Richard D. Irwin, Inc., 1975), pp. 124–5.*

product, build the product, and evaluate the final product, each worker will feel that he or she was significant to the production process.

Having learned of several bad side-effects of specialization and short span of control, a president of a large manufacturing company asked Chris Argyris what he would recommend to upgrade the work situation for assemblers. Argyris observed that twelve women were involved in performing very simple, fragmented, and routine tasks in assembling a radiolike product. The twelve women were not only performing repetitious short-cycle work but were also being very closely supervised by a foreman, an inspector, and a packer.

Argyris suggested that each of the women be completely responsible for properly assembling the entire product, packing it, and handling consumer complaints. They even had to put their names on the product before it left the factory. At first the results were disastrous. Production had dropped over 70 percent after six weeks. However, after fifteen weeks production had increased higher than ever before. Also, dollar costs due to mistakes and waste dropped 94 percent. Letters of complaints dropped 96 percent.[15]

A major change involving how work is done is bound to decrease productivity for awhile. Learning the new procedures and methods combined with temporary nervousness, anxiety, and lack of confidence prohibits immediate increases in output. Even when the workers are looking forward to a change, such as a move into a new plant, the change frequently brings about a drop in the productivity level. Often the temporary decreases in productivity and worker "comfort" cause many managers to return to their earlier method of managing before good results are allowed to occur. Although this is understandable, it is unfortunate. Some managers are realizing outstanding benefits from enriching jobs on even the lowest levels of the organization.

WHO WANTS JOB ENRICHMENT?

There are three approaches to finding out who wants "job enrichment":

- The urban versus rural method
- The strong versus weak belief in the Protestant work ethic
- High versus low strength for higher order growth needs[16]

In general, but not always, worker satisfaction after job enrichment is high when workers have grown up in rural areas, have a strong belief in the Protestant work ethic, or have strong concern for personal growth through work.

The prediction that urban blue-collar workers do not like enriched jobs stems from the belief that they are alienated from middle-class norms and values. Some examples of middle-class values include:

- "Work is the path to salvation"
- "Hard work leads to a better life"
- "Hard work is always worthwhile"

This method of grouping workers by where they were reared is obviously convenient but will include some people who psychologically do not belong. That is, there are some urban blue-collar workers who believe in hard work and some white-collar workers who do not. However, this scheme must be credited for providing the first insight on the influence of individual differences on job enrichment effectiveness.

Please indicate your agreement or disagreement with each of the statements below. There are no right or wrong answers. The important thing is to state how you feel about each item. Please use the 6-point scale to rate your agreement or disagreement.

1	2	3	4	5	6
Strongly Agree	Agree	Mildly Agree	Mildly Disagree	Disagree	Strongly Disagree

_____ 1. Hard work makes you a better person.
_____ 2. Wasting time is as bad as wasting money.
_____ 3. A good indication of a person's worth is how well he or she does the job.
_____ 4. If all other things are equal, it is better to have a job with a lot of responsibility than one with little responsibility.

Figure 3.4 The Work Value Method

(Source: John Wanous, "Who Wants Job Enrichment," SAM Advanced Management Journal 41, Summer 1976: 18.)

The work value method of predicting worker reaction to enriched jobs is believed to be a more exacting and direct way to determine if people would react positively to job enrichment. A sample questionnaire is found in Figure 3.4. Low scores on this questionnaire indicate that a worker would benefit from enriched work because low scores reflect a need for personal growth and accomplishment through work.

One serious shortcoming of using this questionnaire is that the answers can easily be faked. To help insure honest questionnaire responses, management must attempt to guarantee the worker's anonymity. One way of doing this is to hire a management consultant to administer and score the questionnaires.

The third method of examining worker dispositions toward enrichment is through the need-strength approach. An example of a questionnaire is shown in Figure 3.5. High scores on this test are indicative of an attitude favoring enriched jobs.

The need-strength method appears to be the best way to find out who wants enrichment. According to one expert on the topic:

The results showed that the need-strength method produced the most pronounced differences of the three methods. Those designated as having strong needs for job enrichment showed a strong relationship between job enriching characteristics and increased job satisfaction. And those identified as having weaker needs for such jobs reported they felt job enriching characteristics were unnecessary for their job satisfaction.[17]

Although the need-strength approach is plainly preferred, all three techniques have been used successfully by other management experts.

Listed below are a number of characteristics that could be present on any job. People differ about how much they would like to have each one present in their own jobs. We are interested in learning how much you personally would like to have each one present in your job. Using the scale below, please indicate the *degree* to which you *would like* to have each characteristic present in your job.

1	2	3	4	5	6	7

would like having
this *moderately*
(or less)

would like
having this
very much

would like
having this
extremely

_____ 1. Stimulating and challenging work.
_____ 2. Chances to exercise independent thought and action in my job.
_____ 3. Opportunities to learn new things from my work.
_____ 4. Opportunities to be creative and imaginative in my work.
_____ 5. Opportunities for personal growth and development in my work.
_____ 6. A sense of worthwhile accomplishment in my work.

Figure 3.5   The Need-Strength Approach
(Source: John Wanous, "Who Wants Job Enrichment," SAM Advanced Management Journal 41, Summer 1976: 19.)

BENEFITS OF JOB ENRICHMENT

When there is a match between job enrichment efforts and people who are desirous of holding more challenging jobs, job enrichment can offer several benefits. These benefits accrue to both the job holders and the organization. The individual gains a good deal more personal satisfaction from the job and the organization can realize savings and economies that can be expressed in dollars and cents.

Benefits for the individual include:

- More job satisfaction
- Greater responsibility and authority
- The opportunity to experience more growth and development
- A greater sense of achievement
- More job autonomy
- A greater diversity of job experiences
- More practice at making decisions

Benefits for the organization include:

- Higher levels of job performance

- Improvement in quality of decisions
- More employee loyalty to the organization
- Fewer absences
- Lower turnover rate

GUIDELINES FOR THE JOB ENRICHMENT PRACTITIONER

One recent survey found that only 5 of 125 firms studied made any formal, systematic attempt to enrich jobs.[18] These firms were randomly selected from 300 of the top 1,000 *Fortune* industrial organizations. This very low rate of use signals the apparent lack of understanding of job design by management practitioners.

However, job enrichment has not been around all that long. Only since about 1970 have management scholars and practitioners made healthy strides toward really understanding the nature of the relationship between job factors and worker characteristics such as personal need for growth through work. A checklist for those thinking about beginning a job enrichment program has been developed. Several items from the checklist are presented below.[19] The more "yes" answers to the six questions, the stronger is the argument for job enrichment.

1. *Is there widespread discontentment among the employees?* Discontentment may be reflected in such things as: high turnover, absenteeism, sabotage, poor work quality, excessive grievances, indifferent or apathetic attitudes, and/or a large number of personal conflicts. If the operation runs smoothly, there is little reason to jeopardize the current efficiency by changing the environment.

2. *Can the job be economically changed at this time?* The easiest way to implement job enrichment is to have the employee assume the responsibilities for checking the quality of the product. This may be a desirable approach, but does the checking function require a deceptively high amount of skill which would necessitate extensive retraining and the procurement of additional testing equipment?

3. *Can the employee be given control over his task?* Studies indicate that monotony, boredom, and decreased job satisfaction are likely to stem from highly fragmented jobs. The cost of production due to employee absenteeism and turnover is reduced when the employee achieves additional satisfaction from his task.

4. *Does the employee perceive the task as meaningful to society?* In our rapidly changing, "throw-away" society, the production of a poorly designed and poorly produced product does not lend itself to em-

ployee involvement. There is no degree of craftsmanship involved in such a product, so it is unlikely the employee will wish to identify with the product by assuming more responsibility.

5. *Is there a reward to the employee for assuming increased responsibility?* Effective job enrichment occurs when an employee feels a sense of accomplishment upon completion of a task. The job should be designed to fill the employee's need for recognition and self-actualization. Since many jobs would become more difficult after enrichment, there may be a need to increase an employee's base pay.

6. *Can a system be designed to furnish feedback to the employee?* If detailed information is not available to the employee on current production and quality output for his department, it will be difficult for the employee to effectively control his task once it becomes enriched. The most meaningful kinds of responsibilities to be turned over to the employee are those which involve him in the determination of undesirable variations to encourage him to initiate self-corrective action.

SUMMARY

Job design is the process of matching job factors with worker needs for growth and accomplishment through work. Most attempts at job design or job redesign normally include job enrichment since most jobs suffer from being too simple, fragmented, and routine rather than worthwhile and challenging. Job enrichment is any activity that involves the alteration of specific jobs with the intent of increasing both the quality of employees' work experiences and their on-the-job productivity.

Job design is concerned with making sure workers are properly stimulated through their work. When workers are not stimulated, they become bored. This feeling of boredom may lead to many types of nonjob activities such as horseplay and taking prolonged and unauthorized coffee breaks.

The job stimulation issue presents a complex problem. An individual's perception of the same job will change over time. Most jobs are rather confusing to new employees because they do not know how the jobs should be done, but once-challenging jobs become routine and non-challenging after workers have been trained and have practiced doing the jobs many times.

One of the theories supporting job design is called the intrinsic work motivational model. The model deals with the intrinsic job variables since workers are motivated by the feelings of growth, achievement, and worthwhile accomplishment that come from doing well on a meaningful job.

To enrich a job a manager changes the factors composing the work people perform. There are five factors: skill variety, task identity, task significance, autonomy, and feedback. Generally, job enrichment programs are very successful when workers have a strong need for personal accomplishment. When workers do not possess such a need, job enrichment programs may not be very beneficial.

Enriched jobs in many ways require more effort from the worker; therefore, enriched jobs tend to be more difficult and more challenging than simple and repetitive jobs. Three methods of grouping workers, by rural versus urban upbringing, by work values, and by need/strength, were shown to be helpful in determining the type of worker who would benefit from job enrichment and enjoy having the additional challenges associated with the vertical loading of a job.

NOTES

1. See R. W. WHITE, "Motivation Reconsidered: The Concept of Competence," *Psychological Review* 66 (September 1959): 297–333.

2. ERIC ERIKSON, "Identity and the Life Cycle," *Psychological Issues*, International University Press, Monograph 1 (New York: 1959).

3. ABRAHAM MASLOW, *Motivation and Personality* (New York: Harper and Brothers, Inc., 1954).

4. See, for example, MATTHEW R. MERRENS and JAMES GANETT, "The Protestant Ethic Scale as a Predictor of Repetitive Work Performance," *Journal of Applied Psychology* 60, No. 1 (1975): 125–127; GREG OLDHAM, J. R. HACKMAN and J. F. PEARCE, "Conditions under Which Employees Respond Positively to Enriched Work," *Journal of Applied Psychology* 61, No. 4 (1976): 395–403; J. R. HACKMAN and GREG OLDHAM, "Development of the Job Diagnostic Survey," *Journal of Applied Psychology* 60, No. 2 (1975): 159–70; and JOHN WANOUS, "Individual Differences and Reactions to Job Characteristics," *Journal of Applied Psychology* 59, No. 5 (1974): 616–22.

5. FREDERICK HERZBERG, BERNARD MAUSNER, and BARBARA SNYDERMAN, *The Motivation to Work*, (New York: John Wiley and Sons, 1959).

6. Ibid.

7. M. I. MEIR, "The Relationship Between Intrinsic Needs and Women's Persistence at Work," *Journal of Applied Psychology* 56, No. 4 (1972): 293–6.

8. M. I. MEIR and AZY BURAK, "Pervasiveness of the Relationship Between Intrinsic and Extrinsic Needs and Persistence at Work," *Journal of Applied Psychology* 59, No. 1 (1974): 103–4.

9. FRED LUTHANS and W. E. REIF, "Job Enrichment: Long on Theory, Short on Practice," *Organizational Dynamics* 2, No. 3 (1974): 31.

10. HACKMAN and OLDHAM, "Development of the Job Diagnostic Survey," p. 162.

11. Ibid.

12. Ibid.

13. J. Richard Hackman and G. R. Oldham, "Motivation Through the Design of Work: A Test of a Theory," *Organizational Behavior Human Performance* 16, No. 2 (1976): 250–79.

14. Oldham, Hackman, and Pearce, "Conditions under Which Employees Respond," pp. 395–403.

15. In N. Breman, *The Making of a Moron* (New York: Sheed and Ward, 1953). Argyris also describes a second incident where mentally retarded women in a knitting mill functioned as well as or better than others about the same age.

16. John Wanous, "Who Wants Job Enrichment," *SAM Advanced Management Journal* 41 (Summer 1976): 15–22.

17. Ibid., 19.

18. Luthans and Reif, "Job Enrichment," pp. 30–49.

19. Peter Mears, "Guidelines for the Job Enrichment Practitioner," *Personnel Journal* (May 1976): 210–12. Abridged with permission. *Personnel Journal* copyright May 1976.

QUESTIONS FOR THOUGHT AND DISCUSSION

1. Comment on this quotation: "If people liked their jobs, you would not need supervisors, fancy pay plans, company picnics, or any of those other human relations tricks."

2. Think of the last time you were working and observed some workers who were seemingly bored. List the actions these workers engaged in to increase their job stimulation. What things could be done to increase the "bored" workers' job stimulation?

3. Using the table entitled "The Herzberg job enrichment ideas" design either an auto mechanic's or a secretary's job with as many motivators as you can.

4. On a 1 to 10 scale (1 being low, 10 high) rank your present or last job on skill variety, task identity, task significance, autonomy, and feedback. Which ones were the most important to you? Explain how three of the five job dimensions could be altered to increase your positive feelings toward the job.

5. Of what importance is the idea of low and high strength for growth needs in job enrichment programs? How do managers determine if their subordinates are high in such need-strength?

KEY TERMS

The student should be able to discuss the significance of these terms to the study of human behavior in the work environment.

Specialization

Scientific management movement

Job design

Job stimulation

Sense of competence or sense of identity

Self-actualization

Short-cycle jobs

Long-cycle jobs

Intrinsic job factors

Hygiene job factors

Job enrichment

Skill variety

Task identity

Task significance

Autonomy

Job feedback

The intrinsic work motivational model

Critical psychological states

The urban vs. rural issue

The work-value and the need-strength approaches

CASE INCIDENT

Jack Femmerman is the president of a medium-sized, full-line insurance company employing 4,800 people. The company has several offices throughout the United States and is headquartered in a fairly large city in the mid-Atlantic region. Most of the employees have urban backgrounds and at least a high school diploma. Many have completed two years of college at one of several junior colleges in the vicinity.

Mr. Femmerman, an avid reader of various management publications, has noticed a trend toward offering workers greater job responsibilities and authority, more opportunities for growth and development, increased job autonomy, more performance feedback, greater diversity of job experiences, and more closure (doing a complete job). He has also noticed a trend toward differentiating workers in terms of their "will to work." That is, a manger generally should not lead people who believe in the Protestant work ethic in the same way that he leads people who do not believe in the work ethic.

Being an insurance company, the firm has several hundred secretaries and clerks. While tardiness, absenteeism, and turnover are not uncommonly high for this company, these three consequences of job dissatisfaction could be lowered. Mr. Femmerman is mostly concerned with the general lack of enthusiasm and morale among the clerks and secretaries. They simply do not appear stimulated by their jobs. This is particularly evident among the older, more experienced workers who perform routine and predictable jobs in a dependable but unmotivated manner. The general managers, along with Jack, believe that much too much time is being frivolously wasted by the secretaries in nonjob-related conversations, social horseplay, doodling, meandering about the office, and going for coffee and soft drinks.

The president hired an outside consultant to measure the secretarial job characteristics. The consultant used a questionnaire to measure the amount of job variety, job closure, autonomy, feedback, and opportunities for friendship. The data collected from the questionnaires show that the secretaries have a good deal of time on their hands to create and nurture friendships at work. The data also show that their jobs are *unsatisfactory* in terms of variety, autonomy, feedback and closure.

The consultant and Jack Femmerman are in agreement that the secretarial jobs do need to be redesigned in some way to offset the unfavorable consequences of routine work. They obtained the following copy of a typical secretarial job description and are reviewing it for job redesign purposes.

Description of Work:

General Statement of Duties: Performs a variety of secretarial and clerical work requiring some exercise of independent judgment.
Supervision Received: Works under general supervision of a technical or administrative superior.
Supervision Exercised: Exercises supervision over clerical personnel as assigned.

Example of Duties:

Types correspondence, reports, forms and other items requiring some independence of judgment as to content, accuracy and completeness.

Takes dictation as required. Transcribes to draft or final copy, as appropriate.

Receives telephone calls and personal visitors, handling any questions or matters of a less technical or routine nature and directing others to the appropriate staff members. Assists job applicants in filling out forms and applications.

Screens incoming correspondence and refers to appropriate staff members with relevant attachments or notes for their instruction or disposition.

Establishes and/or maintains filing systems, control records, and indexes, using some independence of judgment.

Schedules appointments, makes reservations, arranges conferences and meetings.

Composes routine correspondence and refers to appropriate staff members with relevant attachments or notes for their instruction or disposition.

Operates a variety of office equipment.

Questions for Discussion

What steps or procedure should be taken to redesign the secretarial jobs? How could the job description be rewritten so that it reflects greater variety, feedback, and autonomy?

4

Job Satisfaction

LEARNING OBJECTIVES

Upon completion of this chapter the student should be able to:

- Correct the old adage "a happy worker is a productive worker."
- Define job satisfaction in general terms.
- Contrast global and facet satisfaction.
- Explain the role of expectancies in the determination of job satisfaction.
- Outline how a person determines his or her level of satisfaction.
- Recognize the relationship of job satisfaction and organizational effectiveness.
- Describe how job satisfaction influences life satisfaction.
- Explain why some employees protect their mental health by giving up thoughts of an improved work situation.

Interviewer: Tell me Harold, how do you like your job?

Harold: I love my job.

Interviewer: What is it that you like about your job?

Harold: I like the pay and the benefits, and the people I work with are OK, too.

Interviewer: How about the job content?

Harold: You mean the work I actually do? It's boring as hell.

Interviewer: Doesn't the work you do provide you with any satisfaction?

Harold: You've got to be kidding! My job takes no special skill or education. I do the same thing over and over again, five days a week.

Interviewer: Is there any challenge involved with it?

Harold: Oh for sure. Ron, the guy next to me, and I see who can hold our breath the longest. And we also play trivia. That's kind of challenging.

Interviewer: What is the most stimulating thing about your job?

Harold: Trying to estimate exactly my production for the day.

Interviewer: Can you?

Harold: You bet, right on the nose. It's the same every day.

Interviewer: Could you do more?

Harold: Probably between two and three times more.

Interviewer: Why don't you?

Harold: Why should I?

Interviewer: But you are satisfied with your job?

Harold: Sure! I love it, I told you.

Does Harold really have job satisfaction? He claims to love his job but does not seem that enthusiastic about the actual tasks he must perform. The old adage that "the happy worker is a productive worker" was believed to be true for many years. Now, however, the reverse of that is accepted as the truth: it is a productive worker who is a happy worker. But as Harold's case shows, job satisfaction is not easily defined. It seems to be interpreted differently by different people.

In 1970, it was estimated that there had been over five thousand articles published on job satisfaction.[1] Even given this amount of research, the cumulative results on job satisfaction have been inconsistent. There have been no definitive studies that demonstrate clearly how satisfaction and/or dissatisfaction affect employee job behavior and organizational effectiveness. It is certain only that academicians are discussing this relationship, researchers are trying to identify, define, and measure it, industrialists are seeking it, and the government is supporting it. This chapter is an attempt to provide a better understanding of what is meant by job satisfaction, the factors and processes influencing satisfaction, and the behavioral consequences of different levels of satisfaction.

DEFINITION OF JOB SATISFACTION

If a person "feels good" about his or her job, is that an indication of job satisfaction? How about an individual who is very happy with the way the job pays—is that the same as job satisfaction? Or can someone be satisfied with a job that is not too challenging but is a stepping stone to a more interesting position?

A pair of researchers in 1972 examined nine definitions of job satisfaction advanced during the previous several years and found that people attached different meanings to "what it is to be satisfied."[2] In another study, job satisfaction was defined as the "pleasurable emotional state resulting from the appraisal of one's job as achieving or facilitating the achievement of one's job values."[3] In contrast, job dissatisfaction was defined as "the unpleasurable emotional state resulting from the appraisal of one's job as frustrating or blocking the attainment of one's job values or as entailing disvalues."[4] Both satisfaction and dissatisfaction were seen as "a function of the perceived relationship between what one wants from one's job and what one perceives it as offering or entailing."[5] Other scholars have confined their definition of job satisfaction to "persistent feelings toward discriminable aspects of the job situation."[6] (Discriminable aspects refer to such factors as the work itself, pay, promotional opportunities, the supervisor, co-workers, and the hours of work.) Some definitions see morale and satisfaction as being synonymous. For example, one important psychologist believes that morale is "the extent to which an individual's needs are satisfied and the extent to which the individual perceives that satisfaction as stemming from his total job situation."[7]

Generally, job satisfaction is the result of the individual's perception of what is expected and what is received from different facets of the work situation. The closer the expectation is to what is actually received, the greater the job satisfaction. Job satisfaction sometimes refers to an overall feeling of satisfaction or satisfaction with the situation-as-a-whole (global satisfaction). At other times, job satisfaction refers to a person's feelings toward specific dimensions of the work environment (facet satisfactions). These dimensions or facets of the work environment refer to such things as pay, benefits, promotional opportunities, work conditions, supervision, the work itself, co-workers and the organizational structure. As everyone knows who has ever held a job, it is quite possible to be satisfied with some dimensions and dissatisfied with others. Global satisfaction, then, really amounts to a feeling toward all of these various facets of the work environment. If a person feels good about his or her job in a global sense, that individual probably does have job satisfaction. But when only a cumulative attitude such as this is known, it is difficult for people to influence and improve it. For practicing managers concerned with improving the work environment it is more helpful to obtain worker feelings about facet satisfactions than about global satisfaction. Managers can take more direct action in eliminating pockets of dissatisfaction when they know what facets are causing or contributing to low global dissatisfaction.

IMPORTANCE OF JOB SATISFACTION
TO THE ORGANIZATION

The importance of satisfaction to the firm is best studied through long-term research efforts. The study discussed below represents one of the very few major statistical efforts directed toward untangling the degree and direction of influence of the many factors influencing organizational efficiency.

Rensis Likert and his associates have been studying the importance of human behavior concerns such as satisfaction to organizational effectiveness since 1946.[8] Armed with information collected from more than 20,000 managers and 200,000 workers, they have mapped the relationships shown in Figure 4.1.

The researchers have grouped the six human organizational dimensions into causal, intervening, and end-result variables. Managerial leadership and climate are the causal variables which "determine the course of developments within an organization and the results achieved by the organization."[9] Peer leadership, group processes, and subordinates' satisfaction are the intervening variables. These variables "reflect the internal state and health of the organization, e.g., the loyalties, attitudes, motivations, performance goals, and perceptions of all members and their collective capacity for effective interaction, communication, and decision making."[10] Productive efficiency, the end-result variable, "reflects the achievements of the organization, such as its productivity, costs, scrap loss, and earnings."[11]

The width of each arrow reflects the degree of influence. The numerical figure next to each arrow is the coefficient of determination which indicates the relative strength of the relationship. For example, satisfaction is seen to be influenced by managerial leadership, organizational climate, peer leadership, and group processes. Similarly organizational climate influences peer leadership and group processes. The coefficient of determination of .49 between managerial leadership and satisfaction means that 49 percent of the variation in worker satisfaction is attributed

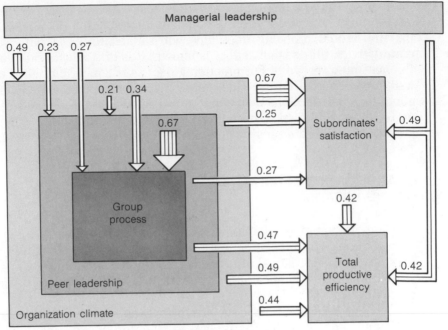

Width of arrow shows magnitude of relationship

Figure 4.1 Relationship among Human Organizational Dimensions. Shows the importance of job satisfaction to organizational efficiency. Over the long run, satisfaction is seen as an important determinant of organizational effectiveness.

(Source: R. Likert and D. Bowers, "Improving the Accuracy of P/L Reports by Estimating the Change in Dollar Value of the Human Organization," Michigan Business Review, March 1973: p. 19.)

to or explained by managerial leadership. Conversely, 51 percent of work satisfaction can be attributed to factors other than managerial leadership. The coefficient of determination of .42 between satisfaction and productive efficiency means that 42 percent of the variation of productive efficiency is accounted for, stems from or is explained by worker satisfaction.

Since satisfaction has been seen as a significant influence on organization efficiency, it is important to the firm to know when and why there is little or no job satisfaction. A very serious consequence of job dissatisfaction is turnover. While a lack of satisfaction appears to have an impact upon employee attitude and on-the-job efficiency, the ultimate expression of employee dissatisfaction is to leave the organization. One approach management may utilize to minimize turnover is to determine those facets of the work environment that are perceived by employees as having a negative impact upon their level of satisfaction.

However, the level of job satisfaction is not the only or necessarily the most effective predictor of turnover. Organizational commitment, which is defined as "the strength of an individual's identification with and involvement in a particular organization,"[12] may give a better indication of which employees are likely to leave. It has been found that commitment to the organization is derived over a longer period of time than is the determination of the level of job satisfaction.[13] Since commitment to an organization involves the feelings of the employee toward the organization's goals and the willingness to continue working toward the accomplishment of those goals, it is more global (situation-as-a-whole) than facet satisfaction. Facet satisfaction is more closely related to tangible aspects of the work environment and is more likely to change with any change in one of those aspects. While it is important to know employees' feelings toward various facets of the work environment in order to bring about more job satisfaction, it also may be necessary to become more concerned with the level of commitment to the organization in order to deal more effectively with turnover.

HOW SATISFACTION DEVELOPS

Two people doing exactly the same job in the same work environment may have drastically different feelings about their level of job satisfaction. But the various facets of job satisfaction could be the same for each person. For instance, let's compare two new physical education instructors at a university who bring to the job similar backgrounds in terms of experience and education. They both have the same work load, the same supervisor, equal promotional opportunities, identical pay and benefits, and work conditions that are as similar as possible. Yet one of the instructors claims to have no job satisfaction while the other believes himself to be highly satisfied. While they would have slightly different perceptions of their co-workers and management, would that be enough to cause the differences in satisfaction? It is difficult to say, but at least one other variable should be considered in such a situation—expectancies. Even though their training was much alike, one of the instructors had planned on being a coach. When no coaching jobs were available, the physical education job was taken with the attitude that it would be temporary until a coaching job came along. The job itself, therefore, did not match expectancies. The other instructor had always wanted to be a physical education teacher. Thus expectancies could be related to all facets of the job. There are expectancies that can be considered global and some that are related to the specific dimensions of job satisfaction such as pay and promotional opportunities. When there is a mismatch of either type of expectancy and reality, there is bound to be some dissatisfaction. This is especially true when the realities do not come up to the preconceived standards that constitute the expectancies. If reality is better than what

was expected, then of course job dissatisfaction is not as likely to occur because of the mismatch, but there will be some effects from it
nevertheless.

In short, when there is agreement between what is expected and
what is received, satisfaction is present within the individual. When that
which is expected exceeds what is received, dissatisfaction results. When
what is expected is less than what is received (overpayment), a state of
tension is felt.

Although equity theory will be discussed further in Chapter 9, it
does have relevance to job satisfaction. As has been pointed out, an individual's expectancies are very important in determining job satisfaction.
Equity theory is concerned, in part, with the origination of these expectancies. Some expectancies are formulated as a result of one's beliefs
about the rewards of others who have similar backgrounds, abilities, and
positions. These individuals with whom one identifies for comparison
purposes are known as referent others.

Thus, the rewards that an employee expects to receive from the job
are influenced by several factors: one's own perceived job inputs, the
perceived inputs and outcomes (rewards) of referent others, and by the
characteristics of the job itself. The greater the expectations concerning
these factors, the greater must be the rewards in order for the worker to be
satisfied. Dissatisfaction is more likely to occur when the individual and
the comparison person (referent other) occupy a high organizational level
or skill classification. In fact this comparison with a referent other seems
to cause more dissatisfaction among professionals and those with higher
levels of education than among rank-and-file workers with limited educations.

Some of the situations that effect dissatisfaction have been outlined
by Edward Lawler:

1. People with high perceived inputs will be more dissatisfied with a
   given facet than people with low perceived inputs.

2. People who perceived their job to be demanding will be more dissatisfied with a given facet than people who perceive their jobs as
   undemanding.

3. People who perceive similar others as having a more favorable
   input-outcome balance will be more dissatisfied with a given facet
   than people who perceive their own balance as similar to or better
   than that of others.

4. People who receive a low outcome level will be more dissatisfied
   than those who receive a high outcome level.

5. The more outcomes a person perceives his comparison other to receive, the more dissatisfied he will be with his own outcomes. This

should be particularly true when the comparison other is seen to hold a job that demands the same or fewer inputs.[14]

FACETS OF JOB SATISFACTION

As mentioned earlier, global job satisfaction refers to an emotion or feeling that an employee has toward the entire work situation. Although this type of information may be useful to operating managers, it is not as helpful in attacking the causes of dissatisfaction as knowledge about worker feelings toward the specific or discriminable facets of job satisfaction. Managers can alter the important objects, conditions, or situations affecting global satisfaction only after collecting job facet satisfaction data.

In order to determine the factors in the work environment that are important enough to elicit worker feelings or satisfactions, one researcher has reviewed the empirical literature and determined job satisfaction has, at a minimum, seven important facets. The seven important dimensions were found to be:

1. The work itself
2. Supervision
3. The organization and its management
4. Promotional opportunities
5. Pay and other financial benefits
6. Co-workers
7. Working conditions[15]

In another study a group of researchers found that workers have feelings toward five job facets:

1. The work itself
2. Pay
3. Promotional opportunities
4. Supervision
5. Co-worker interaction[16]

Figure 4.2 shows sample questions from their research instrument, the Job Descriptive Index (JDI), which is perhaps the most well-known instrument for securing job facet satisfaction measurements. A worker is instructed to put a "Y" next to an item describing his or her work, an "N" when an item does not describe the job, and a "?" when not certain. The

Think of your present work. What is it like most of the time? In the blank beside each word given below, write

__Y__ for "Yes" if it describes your work

__N__ for "No" if it does NOT describe it

__?__ if you cannot decide

Work on Present Job

_____ Routine

_____ Satisfying

_____ Good

_____ On your feet

Think of the opportunities for promotion that you have now. How well does each of the following words describe these? In the blank beside each word put

__Y__ for "Yes" if it describes your opportunities for promotion

__N__ for "No" if it does NOT describe them

__?__ if you cannot decide

Opportunities for Promotion

_____ promotion on ability

_____ dead-end job

_____ unfair promotion policy

_____ regular promotions

Think of the majority of the people that you work with now or the people you meet in connection with your work. How well does each of the following words describe these people? In the blank beside each word below, put

__Y__ if it describes the people you work with

__N__ if it does NOT describe them

__?__ if you cannot decide

Think of the pay you get now. How well does each of the following words describe your present pay? In the blank beside each word, put

__Y__ if it describes your pay

__N__ if it does NOT describe it

__?__ if you cannot decide

Present Pay

_____ income adequate for normal expenses

_____ insecure

_____ less than I deserve

_____ highly paid

Think of the kind of supervision that you get on your job. How well does each of the following words describe this supervision? In the blank beside each word below, put

__Y__ if it describes the supervision you get on your job

__N__ if it does NOT describe it

__?__ if you cannot decide

Supervision on Present Job

_____ impolite

_____ praises good work

_____ influential

_____ doesn't supervise enough

People on Your Present Job

_____ boring

_____ responsible

_____ intelligent

_____ talk too much

Figure 4.2   Sample Items from *The Job Descriptive Index.*

(The Job Descriptive Index *is copyrighted by Bowling Green State University. Source: Patricia Cain Smith, Lorne M. Kendall, and Charles L. Hulin,* The Management of Satisfaction in Work and Retirement, A Strategy for the Study of Activities. *Chicago: Rand McNally & Company, 1969.)*

JDI can be used for all job types, is completed quickly by respondents, and is easily scored. There is extensive normative data available for the JDI. This makes it possible for managers to compare a satisfaction profile of their own workers with profiles of employees from other companies.

The number of facets generally varies slightly from study to study due to the occupational group considered, the number and types of questions asked, and the method by which the responses are analyzed. However, most questionnaires are designed to measure at least five satisfaction facets.

Are there differences in the importance of certain facets to managerial, salaried, and hourly employees? This question is important because each work situation and job should be designed to provide for valued and important rewards. The rank order of importance of sixty-eight job characteristics has been examined using inputs from 1,311 managerial and supervisory employees, 3,653 salaried workers, and 6,192 hourly employees.[17] As reflected in Table 4.1, considerable agreement was found on the priorities of job characteristics.

The higher the number beside each characteristic, the more important is that characteristic to the group studied. Table 4.1 shows the rankings of the ten highest job characteristics for each of the three occupational groups. (There are more than ten for the managerial group because two characteristics were ranked as equally important.)

It is noteworthy that the two most important characteristics for all three groups are related to job design (type of work) and feelings of competence from doing a good job. The motivational importance of some of these factors will be examined in Chapter 7. "Pay" was not found to be in the top ten for the managers and was rated eighth in importance by salaried workers. However, "pay" was found to be tied with "satisfaction from good work" as most important to the hourly workers. "Job security" was not found to be important to salaried workers but was rated very important to both managers and hourly workers.

PERSONALITY AND JOB SATISFACTION

One of the most serious omissions in job satisfaction research has been the consideration of personality as an important influence. A well-known organizational psychologist has commented as follows on managerial satisfaction:

If we are to make real progress in understanding managerial satisfaction, we must reject the assumption that these differences are attributable solely to job content or work environment, and start looking at individual differences among managers in motives and abilities. . . . It seeks likely that we will find the effects of dimensions of the managerial role on satisfaction will vary markedly with differences in the personality of its occupant.[18]

TABLE 4.1 Rankings of Highest in Importance of Ten Job Characteristics from Sixty-eight Possible Characteristics

JOB CHARACTERISTIC	MANAGERIAL	SALARIED	HOURLY
Satisfaction from good work	13.6	11.2	9.4
Satisfaction from the type of work you do	9.4	8.1	7.3
Your contribution to company product	9.4	6.3	6.4[b]
Cooperation among your fellow workers	9.4	6.3	6.5[b]
Performance of subordinates	9.4	—[a]	—[a]
Company planning for the future	8.2	7.0	6.6
Company reputation	8.1	5.1[b]	5.8[b]
Higher management's support of your supervisor	8.0	5.5[b]	4.0[b]
Cooperation between departments	8.0	5.5[b]	4.3[b]
Freedom to make decisions in your work	8.0	7.0	5.6[b]
Morale of your co-workers	8.0	5.5[b]	5.7[b]
Management support of your decisions	8.0	—[a]	—[a]
Group insurance plan	7.1[b]	7.1	7.3
Fairness of promotion procedures	6.3[b]	6.3	6.5[b]
Opportunity to use your special skills and abilities	6.2[b]	6.2	5.7[b]
Pay for the work which you do	6.1[b]	6.2	9.4
Your pay compared to other (industry) companies	5.5[b]	5.0[b]	7.2
Vacation policy	6.2[b]	5.5[b]	7.2
Your work place	4.9[b]	4.9[b]	7.2
Opportunity to obtain good equipment, supplies, and materials	5.5[b]	4.7[b]	7.2
Your job security	6.5[b]	5.2[b]	6.6

[a] Not rated by this group.
[b] Not in top ten.

Source: W. W. Ronan, "Relative Importance of Job Characteristics," Journal of Applied Psychology, Vol. 54, No. 2, (1970), 199. Copyright © 1970 by the American Psychological Association. Reprinted by permission.

The study of personality and the study of job satisfaction are each very complex when investigated singularly and even more complex in combination. While research has been done concerning the relationship of personality and job satisfaction, the results have been too mixed to draw many useful conclusions.

It is known that personality is very important in job preference and job choice. In some instances occupational choice and occupational satisfaction are seen as being closely related, as noted below:

. . . the problems of occupational choice and occupational satisfaction seem inseparable. In attempting to predict occupational choice (or experiencing the process of vocational choice), one is, in effect, trying to identify a priori the occupation in which a person will obtain *satisfaction*. (original author's italics)[19]

Some experts believe that the impact of an individual's personality is dissipated during the vocational choice process. In other words, personality will have more of an impact upon the vocational choice than upon the job satisfaction experienced after the choice has been made.

One possible influence of personality on satisfaction can be partially explained by the role of one's self-concept. The self-concept is a dimension of personality which has received some attention in the explanation of job choice. People have a certain image of themselves and attempt to find a job which is compatible with this image. If the match between image and job is successful, an individual will be satisfied with the vocation. If the self-image and the job are not compatible, the person will be dissatisfied. One expert elaborates:

Individuals will tend to find more satisfying those jobs and task roles which are consistent with their self-cognitions. Thus, to the extent that an individual has a self-cognition of himself as a competent, need-satisfying individual, then, to that extent, he will find more satisfying those situations which are in balance with these self-perceptions.[20]

This implies that a person will be dissatisfied with a job which is not compatible with his or her self-image. Since dissatisfaction leads to absenteeism and turnover, at least one aspect of personality has shown some influence on employee behavior. Much more research is needed on this topic before managers are able to work with the complex topic of personality.

EXTENT OF JOB SATISFACTION/ DISSATISFACTION IN THE UNITED STATES

During the 1970s popular accounts of the human element in work organizations have tended to report on a "lack of a will to work," "general alienation from work," "creeping dissatisfaction," "blue-collar blues" and the like. A national study conducted by the Department of Labor in 1974, however, found that, in general, American workers are much more satisfied than dissatisfied and that the level of satisfaction had remained about the same over the previous decade.[21] Figure 4.3 and Table 4.2 report the national satisfaction profiles from seven surveys between 1958 and 1973.

Figure 4.3 shows that job satisfaction has not been decreasing as has been dramatically reported. But on the other hand, one may take the position that satisfaction had not increased significantly during the time

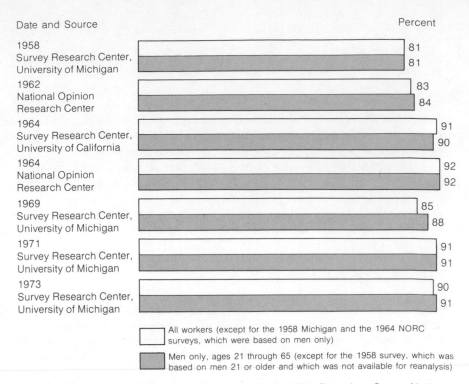

Date and Source	Percent

1958
Survey Research Center,
University of Michigan — 81 / 81

1962
National Opinion
Research Center — 83 / 84

1964
Survey Research Center,
University of California — 91 / 90

1964
National Opinion
Research Center — 92 / 92

1969
Survey Research Center,
University of Michigan — 85 / 88

1971
Survey Research Center,
University of Michigan — 91 / 91

1973
Survey Research Center,
University of Michigan — 90 / 91

☐ All workers (except for the 1958 Michigan and the 1964 NORC surveys, which were based on men only)

▨ Men only, ages 21 through 65 (except for the 1958 survey, which was based on men 21 or older and which was not available for reanalysis)

Figure 4.3 Percentage of "Satisfied" Workers, 1958–1973, Based on Seven National Surveys

(Source: R. P. Quinn, G. L. Staines, and M. R. McCullough, Job Satisfaction: Is There a Trend?, U.S. Dept. of Labor, Manpower Monograph no. 30. Washington, D.C., 1974, p. 4.)

period studied. None of the research centers measured satisfaction with the same technique. For this reason it is difficult to compare the findings of the different centers. Perhaps the best indication of change is to compare the differences found in satisfaction as recorded by one center. The University of Michigan studies, which used the same instrument, reported the percentage of satisfied workers increased from 81 percent to 91 percent between 1958 and 1971, followed by a 1 percent decrease in 1973.

Table 4.2 provides all of the results accumulated in the Department of Labor study. The conclusions point out the difference in job satisfaction experienced by groups broken down by race, age, sex, occupational categories, and level of education. For example, the job satisfaction of blacks tends to be lower than that of whites, young workers are not as satisfied with their work situation as are older workers, and male workers are usually found to be more satisfied than female employees. Also, as the reader would expect, it was found that the highly educated professional and managerial workers are more satisfied than workers in the lower levels of a company's hierarchy.

TABLE 4.2   Satisfaction Trends 1958–1973: The Quinn, Staines, and McCullough Study

1. In spite of public speculation to the contrary, there is no conclusive evidence of a widespread, dramatic decline in job satisfaction.

2. Job satisfaction among blacks and other minority groups has been consistently lower than that of whites.

3. Younger workers are less satisfied with their jobs than older workers.

4. Among occupational categories, professional-technical workers, managers, officials, and proprietors register the highest levels of job satisfaction, while operatives and nonfarm laborers register the lowest.

5. Women workers, by and large, are about as contented with their jobs as are men.

6. Among workers without a college degree, there is little relationship between educational level and job satisfaction.

7. When asked to identify the individual facets of the job which were of greatest importance to them, most workers in a national sample gave high ratings to the availability of the resources needed to perform well and to the challenge of their jobs and lower ratings to financial rewards and "comfort" factors.

8. A long list of job-related stresses have been implicated in various types of physical and mental illnesses, indicating that expressions of job dissatisfaction may be viewed as an important early warning system to both employees and employers.

9. There is no convincing evidence of the existence of a direct cause-effect relationship between job satisfaction and productivity.

10. Most recent experiments concerning such currently disputed matters as the impact on workers' attitudes of changing work schedules and job redesign have been conducted and evaluated too unscientifically to permit any reliable estimation of their success.

Source: R. P. Quinn, G. L. Staines, and M. R. McCullough, Job Satisfaction: Is There a Trend?, *U.S. Dept. of Labor, Manpower Monograph no. 30 (Washington, D.C., 1974), p. 4.*

JOB SATISFACTION AND JOB BEHAVIOR

It seems intuitively reasonable that since workers derive different levels of satisfaction from their work roles, these satisfactions are somehow systematically related to their behavior in the work place. However, the research findings suggest that job dissatisfaction only consistently influences absenteeism, turnover, and other "costs" of the corporation. People tend to approach or return to satisfying situations and avoid unrewarding or punishing situations. Unfortunately, the relationship between satisfaction and task performance is not always as clear cut as the one between satisfaction and "costs."

The levels of satisfaction and performance are affected by different factors. Performance is influenced by effort, abilities and skills, and problem-solving approaches. Satisfaction is influenced by perceived equity of rewards. Performance and satisfaction may be related if the organization clearly ties rewards to task performance and makes this visible to employees. Salespeople compensated entirely on a commission basis and other workers paid on an incentive pay plan or on a piece-rate system are good examples of linking performance and rewards.

A different line of reasoning is advanced by a pair of social psychologists.[22] They believe that workers belong to four social structures:

1. A system outside of the plant and within the plant
2. A system of relationships with other workers
3. A system of formal union structure
4. An organizational system of the company itself

High performance is commonly believed to be a means of acquiring social status, recognition, and prestige in the social system outside of the plant. However, the evidence that has been accumulated indicates that factory workers are not motivated toward prestige or social status outside of the plant but are motivated toward status in the peer group within the plant.[23] High levels of task performance may be incompatible with peer group membership and associated benefits stemming from this membership. There is no obvious reason to believe the industrial factory workers seeking peer group membership and satisfaction will be concerned with high work output when high levels of output are perceived to be in conflict with peer group norms. Satisfaction and job performance are, therefore, seen as being influenced by different factors.

A similar situation has been witnessed by nearly all students. At certain points during a student's schooling it seems that scholarly pursuits are held in very low regard by some groups of children. This appears to occur with greatest frequency during the junior high (or middle school) years. It also seems more prevalent among boys than girls. A young man who puts his hand up in response to a teacher's question or who admittedly has studied a number of hours for an exam is likely to be treated with disdain for being a "curve breaker." In such cases high performance is probably incompatible with peer group membership. Generally this is but one phase in the evolution of most students. Later, in high school and college, high performance receives more respect and is usually seen as adding to the level of satisfaction of most students.

One study examined the typical employee responses toward work factors evaluated as satisfying and dissatisfying. Table 4.3 shows worker responses toward ten situations or job conditions. The findings suggest that the consequences of dissatisfaction with any one factor may not necessarily be similar to the consequences of dissatisfaction with another factor. For example, dissatisfaction with the supervisor leads to certain behavior which is not the same as the behavior resulting from dissatisfaction with the work itself. When a worker is dissatisfied with the supervisor, typical reactions may include:

1. Avoiding the supervisor
2. Complaining and arguing
3. Rejecting demands and advice

Work dissatisfaction may lead to the following reactions:

1. Seeking a transfer
2. Being absent or late
3. Taking rest breaks
4. Quitting

The author of the results of this study notes that Table 4.3 does not include all employee reactions to satisfying and dissatisfying job facets. However, managers and supervisors would benefit from studying the reactions to dissatisfying job facets in order to identify and change the job facets that tend to be linked with dysfunctional employee behaviors.

THE INFLUENCE OF JOB SATISFACTION ON LIFE SATISFACTION

Is there a relationship between job satisfaction and life satisfaction? It seems reasonable to assume that individuals who are happy with their jobs would tend to be happy with life in general. (Or are individuals who are happy with life in general happy with their job situation?) Alternatively, do people who dislike their jobs also tend to dislike important things in their life, for example, family and leisure activities?

One study did find that unhappy workers were also unhappy with life in general.[24] More importantly, the study concluded that job satisfaction influences life satisfaction more than life satisfaction influences job satisfaction. This relationship is especially significant when unhappy workers attach high importance to their jobs. When a worker attaches high importance to the job while, at the same time, being dissatisfied with it, general life discontent could very well develop. In the 1960s, it was thought that a dissatisfied worker would compensate for job discontent through rewarding activities outside of the organization, such as becoming more family oriented and getting more involved with fraternal and voluntary organizations or community projects. The above mentioned study argues against that idea. Dissatisfied workers on the job were dis-

TABLE 4.3   Types of Actions Typically Taken Following Positive and Negative Appraisals of the Job Situation and/or Its Aspects

OBJECT OF APPRAISAL	ACTIONS FOLLOWING POSITIVE APPRAISALS	ACTIONS FOLLOWING NEGATIVE APPRAISALS
Job as a whole	Stay on job	Be absent or late; quit
Work itself	Come early; work late; seek transfer (if satiated); stay on job	Seek transfer; be absent or late; take rest breaks; quit
Own past performance	Maintain performance; set new (higher) goal; stay on job	Increase effort; lower goal (and decrease effort); quit
Assigned work goals (quotas; bogeys)	Accept goal; stay on job	Reject goal (restrict output); complain; file grievance; strike; quit
Supervisor	Approach (seek company of); accept demands and advice; stay on job	Avoid; complain and argue; use defense mechanisms; reject demands and advice; conform to demands; file grievance; strike; physical attack; quit
Coworkers	Approach (interact with); conform to norms (out of liking); stay on job	Avoid; argue with; conform to norms (out of fear); be absent; quit
Subordinates	Praise and recognize; interact with; retain; promote; stay on job	Correct; teach; criticize; harass; fire; quit
Promotion	Raise aspirations; stay on job	Complain; increase or decrease effort; lower aspirations; use defense mechanisms; quit
Pay	Stay on job; modify effort (depending on judged connection to performance)	Complain; strike; solicit competing offer; modify effort (depending on judged connection to performance); quit
Working conditions	Stay on job	Tolerate; be absent or late; complain; quit

Source: E. Locke, "Job Satisfaction and Job Performance: A Theoretical Analysis," Organizational Behavior and Human Performance *5 (1970), p. 5.*

satisfied in life as well. Satisfied workers on the job were also satisfied with life.

Specifically, the study placed foremen into two groups. The unhappy, dissatisfied foremen were in Group A, while the happy, satisfied foremen were in Group B. Each individual completed a job satisfaction

and life satisfaction questionnaire, plus a questionnaire about job importance. Group A foremen who did not place high importance on the job
were happier off the job than the Group A members who did place high
importance on the job. These foremen simply protected their mental
health through giving up thoughts of an improved work situation. They
resigned themselves to their situation. The researchers explain:

Those men who were in a work environment that provided little job satisfaction
(foremen Group A) were more likely to be dissatisfied with other aspects of their life if
they felt aspects of the job such as promotions, supervision, and work to be
important for their job satisfaction. It would appear that when men are in a job
situation that provides little satisfaction, disavowing the importance of the job may be
a healthy response.[25]

In other words, for workers who find little satisfaction or the possibility of
satisfaction in the work situation, it may be best to attach less importance
to the job. In fact, it could very well help the stability of a work environment where the jobs are typically repetitive and boring. This phenomenon of disavowing the importance of work has been found to help the
outlook of many of Detroit's automobile assembly line workers. Workers
not wanting promotions and advancement were happier and more content than others who placed high importance on challenging jobs, promotions, achievement, and the like.[26]

It is, of course, possible to have life satisfaction without having
much job satisfaction, but those who have more job satisfaction seem also
to have more life satisfaction. Once again, the determination of job satisfaction and, therefore, life satisfaction, to some extent seems to be dependent upon the expectancies of the individual and how those expectancies
match up with reality.

SUMMARY

Job satisfaction is seen as a consequence of performance rather than a
cause of it and represents the difference between what is expected and
what is received from different job facets. Satisfaction is a feeling a worker
has toward particular objects or conditions in his work environment. The
number of facets was seen to vary from study to study, but normally
ranged from five to seven dimensions. Satisfaction facets may include the
work itself, pay and benefits, promotional opportunities, supervision,
co-workers, the organization and its management, and working conditions.

Over the long run, satisfaction of workers strongly influences the
productive efficiency of a firm. This productive efficiency is generally
reflected on the "costs" side of the company's ledger. Absenteeism, turn-

over, alcohol and drug abuse, sabotage, and theft were reported as being linked to job dissatisfaction. The consequences of dissatisfaction must be evaluated with regard to the object of dissatisfaction. For example, pay dissatisfaction was seen to result in behavioral consequences that are different from the consequences associated with supervisory dissatisfaction.

Satisfaction of American workers with their work roles has not changed significantly in the recent past. National surveys depict the more satisfied person as being white, middle-aged, occupying a professional, technical or managerial work role, and college educated. Some people who are not satisfied with their jobs try to protect themselves from most of the behavioral consequences of job dissatisfaction by disavowing the importance of the job. However, it has been found that job satisfaction affects life satisfaction more than life satisfaction affects job satisfaction. Individuals who are happy and content on the job are generally happy and content off the job as well.

NOTES

1. E. E. Lawler, "Job Attitudes and Employee Motivation: Theory, Research, and Practice," *Personnel Psychology* 23 (Summer 1970): 223–37.

2. J. P. Wanous and E. E. Lawler, "Measurement and Meaning of Job Satisfaction," *Journal of Applied Psychology* 56, No. 2 (1972): 95–105.

3. E. A. Locke, "What Is Job Satisfaction?" *Organizational Behavior and Human Performance* 4, No. 4 (1969): 316.

4. Ibid.

5. Ibid.

6. P. C. Smith, L. M. Kendall, and C. L. Hulin, *The Measurement of Satisfaction in Work and Retirement; A Strategy for the Study of Attitudes* (Chicago: Rand McNally, 1969), p. 37.

7. R. M. Guion, "Industrial Morale (a symposium) 1. The Problem of Terminology," *Personnel Psychology* 11 (Spring 1958): 62.

8. R. Likert and D. Bowers, "Improving the Accuracy of P/L Reports by Estimating the Change in Dollar Value of the Human Organization," *University of Michigan Business Review* 25 (March 1973): 15–24.

9. Ibid., p. 27.

10. Ibid.

11. Ibid.

12. Lyman W. Porter, Richard M. Steers, Richard Mowday, and Paul Boulian, "Organizational Commitment, Job Satisfaction, and Turnover among Psy-

chiatric Technicians," *Journal of Applied Psychology* 59, No. 5 (1974): 604.

13. Ibid., p. 608.

14. E. E. LAWLER, *Motivation in Work Organizations* (Monterey, Ca.: Brooks/Cole, 1973), p. 77.

15. W. W. RONAN, "Individual and Situational Variables Relating to Job Satisfaction," *Journal of Applied Psychology Monograph* 54, No. 2 (1970): 3.

16. SMITH, KENDALL, and HULIN, *Measurement of Satisfaction*, Chapters 1–3.

17. RONAN, "Individual and Situational Variables," p. 3.

18. VICTOR VROOM, *Work and Motivation* (New York: John Wiley, 1964), p. 57.

19. B. W. TUCKMAN, "Personality and Satisfaction with Occupational Choice; Role of Environment as a Mediator," *Psychological Reports* 23, No. 6 (1968): 542.

20. A. K. KORMAN, "Task Success, Task Popularity, and Self-Esteem as Influences on Task Liking," *Journal of Applied Psychology* 52, No. 6 (1968): 485.

21. R. P. QUINN, G. L. STAINES, and M. R. McCULLOUGH, *Job Satisfaction: Is There a Trend*, U.S. Dept. of Labor, Manpower Research Monograph No. 30 (Washington, D.C., 1974).

22. D. KATZ and R. L. KAHN, "Some Recent Findings in Human Relations Research in Industry," in *Readings in Social Psychology*, ed. G. E. Swanson, T. M. Newcomb, and E. L. Hartley (New York: Henry Holt and Co., 1952), pp. 650–65.

23. W. L. WARNER and D. S. LUNT, *The Social Life of a Modern Community* (New Haven, Conn.: Yale University Press, 1941). Also see A. ZALEZNIK, C. R. CHRISTENSEN, and F. ROETHLISBERGER, *The Motivation, Productivity, and Satisfaction of Workers: A Prediction Study* (Boston: Harvard Business School, 1958); W. F. WHYTE, *Money and Motivation* (New York: Harper and Row, 1955).

24. BENJAMIN IRIS and GERALD BARRETT, "Some Relationships Between Job and Life Satisfaction," *Journal of Applied Psychology* 56, No. 4 (1972): 301–4.

25. Ibid., p. 303.

26. A. W. KORNHAUSER, *Mental Health of the Industrial Worker* (New York: John Wiley, 1965).

QUESTIONS FOR THOUGHT AND DISCUSSION

1. Select two ways of defining job satisfaction and discuss the arguments for and against each being used by managers in ongoing organizations.

2. Of what importance is job satisfaction to such "bottom-line" topics as labor costs and a firm's productive efficiency?

3. Drawing from Rensis Likert's work at the University of Michigan outline the factors that have an impact on job satisfaction. Why is the model of the "human organizational dimensions" important?

4. Using the determinants of satisfaction discussed in this chapter, explain the

manner you decide on how satisfied you are with your job. Be sure to identify a referent other.

5. Drawing from your last two work experiences, compare and contrast your estimates of your job satisfaction with the work itself, pay, promotional opportunities, supervision, and co-worker interaction. Although these are the five agents typically measured in job satisfaction research, are there others you think should be included?

KEY TERMS

The student should be able to discuss the significance of these terms to the study of human behavior in the work environment.

Job satisfaction
Job dissatisfaction
Global satisfaction
Facet satisfaction
Causal variables
Intervening variables
End-Result variables
Expectancies

Organizational commitment
Job descriptive index
Equity theory
Life satisfaction
Self-concept
Morale
Referent others

CASE INCIDENT

"What Price Job Satisfaction?"

When leaving a local night club Joe and his wife Jan spot an old buddy who Joe used to work with.

Joe: Hi, Ed! How're you doing?

Ed: Hi, Joe! I'm doing fine. How's that new job working out for you?

Joe: Great! I really like it so far. It is interesting to say the least.

Ed: I would imagine. How you can work with those bunch of dingbats in personnel is beyond me. Anyway, congratulations, moves like that just don't happen every day.

Joe: Thanks, Ed. You're right they don't happen every day, so I plan to take advantage of it.

Ed: Well, that's good as long as you enjoy it.

Joe: Oh, I do. It couldn't be better.

Ed: You should be in a good spot, that dummy boss of yours can't possibly last. See you later Joe. Good luck down there in personnel.

Joe: Thanks again, Ed. Take care.

After Joe and his wife leave, she questions his discussion with Ed.

Jan: Joe, I can't believe you! Every night you come home at six o'clock dead tired with no appetite except for martinis, and then you tell Ed how great your job is.

Joe: It's not so bad, honey. It's just that I have to spend a little more time on it until I get some things straightened out.

Jan: Only thing you are going to straighten out is yourself—on a slab if you don't quit this eleven and twelve hour workday. It seems that's all you think about anymore. I don't think you should have accepted the job.

Joe: It's quite a bit more money. We can use it. Besides I can't go back to my old job now, how would that look?

Jan: Who cares?

Joe: I care! I do have some pride you know. Anyway, I sort of like the stuff I do. You know I've always wanted to get into wage and salary. It sure as hell has more status than my old job.

Jan: Sure you enjoy it! I thought you said you missed all the personal contacts you had?

Joe: I do.

Jan: I also thought you said the job was about as exciting as watching grass grow.

Joe: Well, I did but . . .

Jan: You heard Ed call your boss a dummy. Everybody knows he's just riding his boss's coattails. The man isn't too bright, you know.

Joe: Well, I suppose there are smarter people in the world.

Jan: And how about that statement last night when you were complaining about being a glorified clerk?

Joe: I was just tired, I guess.

Jan: I am too, Joe, tired of that whole mess down there at the plant.

Questions for Discussion

1. How much job satisfaction does Joe have?
2. How would you rate Joe's global satisfaction and facet satisfaction?
3. What facets does Joe appear to be satisfied with?
4. What facets are causing dissatisfaction?
5. What should Joe do?

PART THREE

HUMAN BEHAVIOR AND THE CLIMATE OF THE WORK ENVIRONMENT

Just as every individual has a personality that makes each person unique, each organization has an organizational climate that clearly distinguishes its "personality" from other organizations. Chapter 5 explains how a climate is created and maintained and how it impacts upon the behavior of the people within the organization. It also discusses the ways in which employees bring about changes in an existing climate and the kinds of behaviors that are designed to offset certain actions taken by management.

Unfortunately, every organization's climate is made up in part by the amount of stress that the people perceive to be present in the work environment. Of course, the way in which an individual responds to stress will probably determine the amount of stress that person perceives to exist.

The ability to cope wtih stress has been related to personality types. Those who are least able to cope with the stress in their work environment are those who seem to suffer from a greater incidence of heart disease. It is also noted that many people attempt to deal with stress by turning to alcohol and/or drugs. Chapter 6 discusses some of these negative aspects of human behavior in the work environment; these behaviors and those things in the organization that may contribute to them must be understood so that corrective actions can be taken.

5

Organizational Climate

LEARNING OBJECTIVES

Upon completion of this chapter the student should be able to:

- Define organizational climate.
- Identify the components of organizational climate.
- Discuss how organizational components contribute to climate.
- Explain the reciprocal effect in the determination of organizational climate.
- Compare how managers and their subordinates contribute to the existing climate.
- Recognize the possible postures or behaviors employees may adopt as a reaction to management.
- Distinguish between cooperation and accommodation.
- Describe the difference between substantive issues and emotional issues as causes of conflict.

"The climate here stinks! Morale is low, no one seems to want to produce, my work is not challenging, and my colleagues don't stimulate me."

The employee making these comments was definitely not referring to the weather by using the word climate. Organizational climate is a concept that managers are recognizing as being closely related to job performance and job satisfaction. To get more satisfaction and better performance usually means an improvement in organizational climate is necessary. But before any manager can bring about these desired changes there must be an understanding of what the climate is at the time and what has contributed to its existence.

Every organization has its own unique "personality."[1] Just as in the development of a personality within an individual, there are a number of factors that seem to mold the existing personality or climate of an organization. Organizational history, financial status, reputation, standing in its industry, innovation and, of course, the people are but a few of the factors that contribute to the formation of an organizational personality. Personality is a fairly descriptive term, especially if an accepted definition of personality for individuals can be modified to fit organizations. For example, R. W. White's definition of personality as the organization of an individual's personal pattern of tendencies[2] could probably be applied with appropriate adjustments in wording to cover the unique patterns of tendencies of a formal group of people. However, the term organizational climate is more appropriate as its usage implies a somewhat broader concept than personality. Because of the interactions of the formal and informal groups and the impact of the physical work conditions, terms such as "environment" and "atmosphere" are also frequently used as synonymous with "climate." The following definitions of organizational climate will further illustrate how the term will be used throughout this chapter.

DEFINITION OF ORGANIZATIONAL CLIMATE

Organizational climate, although intangible, is a very real phenomenon. In the pertinent literature several different definitions of organizational climate have been proposed which are all quite similar. While there are some differences, there seems to be a greater degree of commonality. Forehand and Gilmer's definition is one which has been well accepted and is representative of other similar attempts to explain the construct of climate. They define organizational climate as a "set of characteristics that describe an organization and that (a) distinguish one organization from another, (b) are relatively enduring over a period of time, and (c) influence the behavior of people in the organization."[3] Another definition explains organizational climate as "a summary perception which people have of (or about) an organization. It is, then, a global impression of what the organization is."[4] Since the summary perception people have about an organization will tend to influence behavior, it can be said that organizational climate is a manifestation of the attitudes of organizational members (all employees) toward the organization itself.

These attitudes are, of course, based upon such things as management policies, supervisory techniques, the "fairness" of management, labor's reactions to management, and literally anything that affects the work environment. Lawrence James and Allan Jones have broken these factors that influence organizational climate into five major components:

1. Organizational context—goals and objectives, function, etc.
2. Organizational structure—size, degree of centralization and operating procedures
3. Process—leadership styles, communication, decision making and related processes
4. Physical environment—employee safety, environmental stresses and physical space characteristics
5. Systems values and norms—conformity, loyalty, impersonality and reciprocity[5]

Although it is recognized that any one individual may influence the organizational climate to some degree, the tracing of the effects of individual behavior on the climate would be quite burdensome and complex and beyond the scope of this chapter. The idea that it may be possible to have "as many climates as there are people in the organization"[6] is not rejected by the authors. But when viewed in concert, the actions of the individuals become more meaningful for viewing the total impact upon the climate and determining the stability of the work environment. It should also be noted that the climate will be viewed from a total system (organization) perception. While there may be differences in climates within subsystems (departments), these will be integrated to a certain extent just as the attitudes of individuals are integrated to form the existing organizational climate.

The fact that there are often differences in climate between work units suggests that the criteria for successful operations may be somewhat different from one department to the next. As has been noted, "an effective climate in a simple and static environment may prove to be dysfunctional in a dynamic and complex environment."[7] However, since the climates in organizational subsystems are seldom radically different, a view of the total organizational climate and its determination will be more meaningful to the student of human behavior in the work environment than a fragmented view of the subsystems.

HOW ORGANIZATIONAL COMPONENTS
CONTRIBUTE TO CLIMATE

There are certain elements of every organization that influence the existing climate more than others. In some it may be the structure, in others the physical environment or the high level of technology. The five organizational components identified by James and Jones are common to all organizations, profit and nonprofit, private and public. These will be discussed briefly to demonstrate in general terms how each may contribute to an organizational climate.

Organizational Context

Generally the prevailing management philosophy will be among the easiest factors to observe. It will be evident in the goals and objectives of the organization and the manner in which management pursues their attainment. For example, the reputation of a particular company regarding the treatment of employees would provide some indication of the managerial philosophy regarding the utilization of the human resources. This manpower philosophy of management is expressed by policies, rules, regulations and, of course, by the actions of members of management. The reaction of the employees and the degree to which they agree with management's philosophy is critical to the development of a favorable climate. If management has done an adequate job of employee selection (matching employees' goals to organizational goals), there is no reason why the expression of management philosophy in the form of managerial action should be a negative influence on climate. Although manpower utilization is but one example of the expression of management philosophy, the attitude toward treatment of employees is indeed a major contribution to the overall organizational climate.

Organizational Structure

The hierarchy or structure of an organization is usually regarded as an expression of management philosophy. An organizational structure is a framework which establishes formal relationships and delineates authority and functional responsibility. For example, the size of an organization will have some impact upon its climate. One would expect a firm of 175 people to have a more intimate kind of interpersonal environment than a business of 30,000 employees.

The actual arrangement of the structure or hierarchy is also critical to the climate. A management that believes in a high degree of employee input will probably have a decentralized structure. By having fewer levels in the hierarchy and more people on each level, such a structure will contribute to an attitude of participative decision making. In contrast, a top management team that would like to maintain a greater degree of consistency in decision making would want a more centralized structure. This would enable greater control over decisions and would probably encourage more centralized communications and information centers.

Process

Leadership styles and communication styles are representative of processes or means by which management carries out goals and objectives. As the supervisory or leadership style is very visible to the employees, they will undoubtedly consider it to be very high on the list of contributing factors to organizational climate. For each employee, his or her supervisor *is the company*, so the company is judged to a great extent by the immediate superior. It is the immediate superior who allows (or disallows) input in the decision-making process, gives assignments, does performance appraisals, conducts performance reviews, interprets policies, determines pay increments, and decides who has the potential to be promoted.

This relationship between superior and subordinate is not only of an interpersonal nature, but it also represents the primary interface between the organization and the employee. All managers must therefore be aware of the possible influence on climate when deciding the most appropriate supervisory technique for a particular situation. Failure to give consideration to the effect on climate would be a monumental error that could be reflected in the performance of the employees and abort any hope of attaining company objectives. Such a failure could cause the psychological costs of an unfavorable climate to rise appreciably. Decisions about leadership style become even more important when it is recognized that it is a major factor in the determination of the reciprocal action to be taken by the employees.

Physical Environment

An employee working in a relatively quiet, clean, and safe environment will probably have a more favorable perception of the organizational climate than one who works in a noisy, dirty, and dangerous environment. In fact studies today go beyond just the immediate conditions of the work itself. Research is being conducted that evaluates the importance of the external environment (physical terrain—mountains, deserts, etc.), the size and location of the building in which one works, the size of the city, and even the impact of the weather. All of these things affect the climate of an organization and consequently affect the level of job and life satisfaction. For instance, morale, job performance, and the ability to recruit qualified people were all purported to improve for a company which moved from a city in Kansas to Boulder, Colorado.

Even such things as office decor, office size, and the physical space a person has available to work in have been found important to the development of a favorable attitude toward the job. While the lack of space in a somewhat confining office does not seem to affect perform-ance to a great degree, it will make some people feel more competitive and aggressive. This is especially true of men. Women usually are not as bothered by cramped quarters as men in terms of affecting a behavioral change.

Noise has also been considered instrumental in influencing organi-zational climate. High levels of noise do tend to lead to some feelings of nervousness, frustration, and aggression. The downtown traffic and activ-ity of a large city would probably not be nearly so awesome without the noise. But even that level of noise is much more evident to someone from a small town than to someone who has been exposed to it for a long period. In fact, some degree of immunity to noise appears possible when it is a steady or constant part of the environment. However, loud, intermit-tent noises definitely have a negative effect upon organizational climate. We have only to think of the emotions caused by music and sound effects (which also heightened the visual experience) for such movies as *The Exorcist* and *Jaws* to recognize the potential impact of noise of all kinds in the work environment.

Systems Values and Norms

The formal value system of an organization is usually fairly evident. Cer-tain kinds of behavior are encouraged and rewarded and certain kinds of behavior will subject an individual to formal sanctions. These types of values are communicated through policies, rules, and regulations. Some-times they are interpreted differently by supervisors who have slightly different management philosophies. On the other hand, the informal value system is more difficult to ascertain. This may apply to actions and behavior within the peer group and within the formal constructs of the job. An activity that would have been rewarded at one organization may be cause for a reprimand at another.

The values of both formal and informal groups are very powerful in determining the climate of an organization. Why is one organization known for its conservative attitude while another is viewed as being very innovative and progressive? The encouragement of creativity in the work environment is obviously going to cause a different climate than the en-forcement of a dress and grooming code would cause. Similarly, the or-ganization that treats employees with respect and understanding will have a different climate than one which is very cold and impersonal. Whatever actions or position management takes, there will be a reaction by the employees of the organization. This reaction can be referred to as a reciprocal response.

THE RECIPROCAL EFFECT

The response of employees to their work environment and the actions taken by them in an effort to control and adapt to their environment constitute the reciprocal effect of the determination of organizational climate. All employees of an organization, whether labor or management, are engaged in behavior that is a reaction to their work environment. The reciprocal effect for many employees is visible only in their department or in their relationship with their superior. Some employees, on the other hand, have the ability, due to their cohesiveness and ability to organize, to take reciprocal actions that have an impact upon the entire organization. For illustrative purposes this discussion will be concerned with the relationships of employees and management and how their actions and reactions affect organizational climate.

Because of the contact between most employees and management on a daily basis, and the necessary give-and-take in their relationship, the reciprocal behavior from both parties is a never ending cycle. All aspects of their relationship influence the organizational climate. Therefore, in some cases, the causes and effects of adjustments in the climate of the organization would appear to be indeterminate.

There are many different ways people may influence climate, intentionally or unintentionally. It may be done in some instances quite effectively without any formal organization, or it may require the existence of a union in order to wield the desired amount of power. For the sake of consistency, the employee's role in influencing organizational climate will be developed from the standpoint of employees being a fairly organized group. This does not assume, however, that individual attitudes and behavior are unimportant and should be overlooked. Nor does it necessarily assume the presence of a union.

Even though climate has been defined as a summary perception which people have about an organization, it may be helpful to consider the influence of employees and management as separate groups that both play roles in determining the summary perception. Also, it should be recognized that many people who are in management positions will play different roles at various times. While everyone must be considered employees, those individuals fulfilling management roles will contribute to the climate by their behavior as managers and by their behavior as subordinates. Each role may take place within different subsystems or levels of the organization, but each role contributes to the climate of the entire system or the organization as a whole. There will be interaction between managers and subordinates within each of the components identified by James and Jones as being influential in the determination of organizational climate. While some subordinates may not always have formal input into each of the components, they are certainly affected by them and will therefore have some interface with management relating to:

1. Organizational context
2. Organizational structure
3. Process
4. Physical environment
5. Systems values and norms

Since, by virtue of its so-called prerogatives, management plays a dominant role in the establishment and maintenance of the organizational climate, the managerial contributions will be examined first.

The Role of Management in Establishing and Maintaining Organizational Climate

Management is responsible for the effective utilization of all resources. In order for management to successfully complete this mission it must be able to utilize the most important resource—human beings—in a manner that will allow personal satisfaction (as discussed in Chapter 4) while achieving organizational goals. This implies that any interchange between subordinates and management has the potential of lending something constructive to the organizational environment.

Of course, the attainment of goals is the best measure of effectiveness and is dependent upon the successful combination of all available resources. The degree that this has been done in the past will, in part, determine the organizational climate in the future. If managers can wisely use past experience as building blocks for the future, they will be providing a sound foundation for all members of the organization to work toward their own goals while attempting to attain the company objectives. As climate is to a large degree dependent upon the historical data of the organization and the interpersonal and interdepartmental relationships of the past, the existing internal impression of the organization can be traced back to a multitude of sources. But although an organization must build upon its history, it is important to consider how it can best continue to create and maintain a climate that it perceives as being the most compatible to its objectives and to its members.

It may be successfully argued that there exists an infinite variety of ways from which an organization may choose to accomplish this. One of the most effective would seem to be through an improved utilization of the human resources. In general terms, management can best improve the overall climate of the organization by seeking to make improvements in the five components identified by James and Jones.

Each subsystem (department) must make an effort toward improving its climate and efficiency so that the overall system can become more effective. This requires cooperation among all departments to bring about better definition of the roles of each department and how these roles can best be integrated to contribute to overall organizational success. Better integration of departmental functions will usually result in an improved organizational climate.

Good specific starting points for establishing or improving upon the existing climate are the personnel functions and leadership style. The processes of selection, placement, orientation, training, and, of course, the methods of supervision allow management ample opportunity to control the climate of the organization. The screening and selection of employees should be performed not only as an effort to obtain the needed skills for an organization, but also as a means of determining those candidates who would best fit the organization in terms of a "match" of personalities. This represents a means of maintaining a certain climate by restricting entry into the organization to those who appear to be compatible to the existing climate. The type of training that people are exposed to and the personal development procedure also can be indicative of an effort to promote a desired organizational climate.

In fact, management's control over the five components means that management has the ability to affect changes in climate through adjustments in any of the components. Given the nature of the make-up of an organization's climate, the real effect of any action taken by management can never be accurately predicted. However, management must take the initiative in improving the subordinate-manager relationship and the organizational climate, as their role in establishing a favorable climate is primarily action oriented while the employees' role is primarily one of reaction.

The Role of Employees in Influencing Organizational Climate

In the event of the existence of any unfavorable work conditions in an organization where the members of the work force have something less than perfect mobility, employees will try to bring about changes that will make their lot more endurable. They will do this insofar as they have the ability and power to in some way alter the existing conditions. This may mean an active exercise of the power that employees perceive themselves as having.

Employees may adopt any of several postures in their attempt to exert some measure of control over the work environment. These postures usually are manifestations of their attitudes concerning what they consider as being necessary to accomplish their objectives. Their behavior may range from complacency to belligerence. Those postures that are generally agreed upon as representing the gamut of employees' possible reactions to management include:

1. Cooperation
2. Accommodation
3. Conflict[8]

While there are differing degrees of these attitudes that may be displayed, these three positions are general classifications allowing for some distinction. They were originally applied in a labor relations context but are applicable to all levels of an organization's hierarchy. The adoption of a particular posture will be dependent upon the circumstances and will most likely vary according to the employees' interpretation of the situation. Of course, the level of the employees in the hierarchy will influence greatly the perceived action necessary to accomplish their objectives. Accompanying the difference in level will be differences in values. For instance, the higher employees are in the hierarchy, the more likely it is that their values will match those of management. In such circumstances a posture of conflict would be relatively rare. On the other hand, labor, especially if unionized, may believe the benefits to be gained from disagreement will make some amount of conflict worthwhile.

Cooperation.   That a cooperative posture by employees would have a positive effect on the climate of the organization is undeniable. By definition it implies some commonality in the goals of the organization and those of the employees. Although total cooperation is relatively rare, it is most likely to exist in an organization where the obstacles to the commonality of goals are few. In any case, the basis for an improved climate probably is to be found in management's manipulation of the five components of climate. If employees viewed management as influencing the climate in a favorable manner, there would most likely be a high degree of trust and confidence in management and the employees would, therefore, see no need to respond with any action other than cooperation in order to maintain a desirable climate.

Accommodation.   While on the surface accommodation may be difficult to differentiate from cooperation, the distinction seems to be in the motivating forces behind the two postures. The important factor in this type of posture is the mutual recognition and understanding of the symbiotic relationship that exists. Each party or entity is dependent upon the other. Thus, accommodation may be thought of more in terms of toleration rather than cooperation.

For most individuals this is not an attitude that can be successfully maintained for a long period of time. In other words, the accommodation relationship between a manager and subordinates will generally either improve or deteriorate further. The organizational climate will depend upon the degree to which the subordinates move toward cooperation or conflict in their reaction to some disturbance of the relationship. Naturally it is in the best interests of the organization if management takes some action to move the relationship toward one of cooperation. When there appears to be an accommodative climate in the organization or within any subsystem, it should serve as an indicator of the need for positive action by management. This positive action will probably be an adjustment in one or all of the five components of climate. For example, management may change the organizational structure and philosophy from a centralized to a decentralized orientation. Such a move would require more employee input and provide more decision-making prerogatives. This should increase the level of trust, improve morale, and in general be representative of a positive move by management to increase the level of cooperation within the organization.

Conflict.   In any formal relationship where there are leaders and followers, there is bound to be disagreement. When the parties are of nearly equal strength, the conflict generally ends in a relatively satisfactory compromise, but in a superior-subordinate relationship compromise is not always possible or practical. When there is conflict between a superior and subordinate, the parties are not of equal strength as peers would be. But even with the difference in formal power, a subordinate is capable of assuming a conflict posture at least in the short run. Generally, this kind of conflict is detrimental to organizational climate and could cause the climate to degenerate to an environment of hostility. Management, of course, wants to minimize the harmful effects of conflict and seek to take advantage of the possible positive benefits.

Whether or not conflict can be controlled depends upon the cause of the conflict. The issues which are the causes of conflicts can be broken down into substantive issues and emotional issues. Substantive issues stem from differing viewpoints about policies, organizational structure, operational practices, and role relationships.[9] Emotional issues are more personal in nature and involve feelings of distrust, rejection, fear, resentment and/or anger.[10] Since it is easier to control and to resolve conflicts caused by substantive issues, the emotional issues must be viewed as being the most detrimental to organizational climate.

Although it is not possible to completely eliminate conflict, it is possible for managers to create an environment or climate wherein conflict can be controlled so that there may actually be positive contributions to the existing climate. Among the possible values of conflict to the organizational climate are the following:

1. It may increase the motivation and energy available to do tasks required by the organization.

2. It may increase the innovativeness of individuals and the system because of the greater diversity of viewpoints and a heightened sense of necessity.

3. Each individual may develop a better understanding of his or her own position as conflict will force an articulation of personal views.

4. Each party may achieve greater awareness of his or her own identity.

5. Interpersonal conflict may help the parties to conflict manage their own internal conflicts.[11]

When managers make use of a goal-oriented system that emphasizes results, invite inputs from all members of the formal group, make use of people's ideas, and inspire feelings of trust and respect, an organizational climate has been created that allows the work group to benefit from the positive aspects of conflict.

Because of the ability of any employee to adopt one of the postures described above as an individual or as a group, it can be seen that the maintenance of a suitable organizational climate is not the sole responsibility of management. But the degree to which any one group of employees influences organizational climate is dependent to a great extent on the amount of power that group possesses.

A particular posture assumed by an individual in middle management may have an immediate impact upon subordinates and the climate of the department supervised, a more indirect effect upon the department's relationship with other departments and the climate of the division, and perhaps no influence at all upon the perceived organizational climate as a whole. However, if very influential members of top management or powerful groups within the organization were to change their attitudes and behavior, the organizational climate would be affected. The visibility and importance of the people concerned would attract the attention of other members of the organization and cause a perceived change in organizational climate.

MEASURING ORGANIZATIONAL CLIMATE

When asked to describe the climate of their organization, most people can provide a description based upon personal perception. Even though it is probably a very subjective view based upon criteria that are not especially relevant, it is correct in the eyes of that individual. If management is interested in determining what the climate is for certain departments or for the organization as a whole, it will be necessary to establish criteria and factors for analysis. Data can be gathered by interview, observation, questionnaire, or some combination of each. Perhaps the most economical and accurate method is the administering of a questionnaire.

Companies who regularly administer questionnaires to learn the attitudes of employees try to make the questionnaires as brief and as precise as possible. This means that there is usually fewer than thirty questions for employees to respond to. Keeping the number of questions relatively low assures a greater percentage of returned questionnaires and makes analysis much easier. Usually the questions are answered on some form of a scale which may vary from a one to five scale to a one to ten scale. The numerical scale is generally accompanied by descriptive terms for each point on the scale. Terms that are frequently used at opposite ends of the scale are "Never characteristic" and "Always characteristic" or "Strongly disagree" and "Strongly agree."[12] An example of the type of question and scale that might be used is presented below:[13]

My boss always gives me the opportunity to participate in decisions which affect me.

Never characteristic	Slightly characteristic	Sometimes characteristic	Considerably characteristic	Always characteristic
1	2	3	4	5

There are many questionnaires designed to measure climate. The dimensions measured will, of course, depend upon how climate is defined. Questions encompassing the components discussed earlier in the chapter would be a recognition that these are factors that are important in the determination of organizational climate. All questionnaires use slightly different terminology, but they are all very closely related in terms of concept and dimensions. For example, one questionnaire utilizes six dimensions:

1. Decision making
2. Warmth
3. Risk
4. Openness
5. Rewards
6. Structure[14]

Another makes use of seven dimensions:

1. Conformity
2. Responsibility
3. Standards
4. Rewards
5. Organizational clarity

6. Warmth and support
7. Leadership[15]

For the most part nearly all questionnaires purporting to measure organizational climate are quite similar. Of greater importance is the different ways in which management uses the results of any attempt to measure climate. Assuming that most management teams have some formal plans relating to where they want the organization to go and how they want it to get there, they must know where the organization is now. Once the climate of the organization is known, management can develop strategies on how to improve upon it so that operating goals may be more easily and realistically reached.

CHANGING ORGANIZATIONAL CLIMATE

The climate of an organization can be changed. If in the view of top management the effectiveness of the organization can be improved by an alteration in the climate, steps will be taken to bring about the desired change. An improvement in organizational climate may be accomplished by making adjustments in any or all of the components which influence climate. In most cases the changes must be initiated by top management in order to have the necessary impact upon organizational climate. For instance, a redesign of organizational structure, an adjustment in organizational goals, a change in communications flows, or an improved physical environment are among those decisions usually reserved for the upper level of management. Usually changes in climate seem to be gradual in nature rather than an overnight occurrence. Since climate is the manifestation of the attitudes of organizational members, it will take some time for a change to be reflected by the total organization. The time lag will encompass three phases:

1. Change in philosophy
2. Change in policies, rules, and procedures
3. Reaction of the human resources to the changes

The amount of time required from thinking through a change in philosophy to the reaction of people will be determined by the importance and magnitude of the change. Also important to the time lag and any appreciable change in climate is the manner in which the change is implemented.

Methods of change which do not allow for any employee input will probably cause the change to meet with some resistance. If an improvement in climate is sought, it is imperative that management initiate the necessary changes in a manner consistent with the climate that is sought. In other words, to make a climate more participative it would not be appropriate to use a dictate that "everyone will participate." Such an approach would probably bring about negative attitudes and behavior on the part of the employees. It should be remembered that any change in the behavior of either employees or management concerning one of the components of climate will not only alter the behavior of the other party but will create a new relationship based in part upon the old relationship. The action of one, therefore, will cause some type of reciprocal response on the part of the other group.

SUMMARY

While a precise definition of organizational climate may be lacking, this does not preclude its existence. As a reflection of the members' attitudes toward various aspects of the organization, climate is extremely important to the ultimate achievement of company goals and is, therefore, a concept that management can ill afford to ignore. Like many other elements of an organization, good organizational climate seems to become more important when it is missing.

The climate of a firm is subject to fluctuations which at times could be termed violent. Even a firm which has experienced a fairly stable environment for a relatively long period of time may suddenly find itself facing a situation that could possibly destroy the sound foundation of past relationships. Once destroyed, the firm may not be able to reestablish the type of organizational climate that was previously enjoyed. Consequently, it is far easier to maintain a good organizational climate than it is to establish one.

The reason for a particular climate within an organization is likely to be found by an examination of organizational context, organizational structure, process, physical environment, and systems values and norms. These components of climate are to be found within every organization. Some will be more important than others in certain organizations and/or in different situations. It takes considerable managerial experience and knowledge of the work environment to activate the appropriate combination of these components in establishing and maintaining a good organizational climate.

A good organizational climate is one which is conducive to meeting the objectives of the organization while allowing individuals to accomplish individual goals. This situation can occur only when there is some degree of compatibility between individual and organizational objectives. By the same token, this compatibility can exist only where the reciprocal effect can be said to have a measurable impact upon organizational climate. If there were no reciprocal effect, employees would have little influence on organizational climate and consequently would not be in a position to attempt to align personal and organizational goals.

When individuals have no input in the organization, they are most hesitant to make their personal goals mesh with organizational objectives. Thus, in the final analysis, the reciprocity of organizational climate is an important phenomenon in the labor-management relationship and may very well play a significant role in the overall success of the organization.

NOTES

1. Some of the material in this chapter is taken from an article by G. James Francis, "The Reciprocity of Organizational Climate," *SAM Advanced Management Journal* 38 (October 1973): 46–51.

2. R. W. White, The Abnormal Personality (New York: Ronald Press, 1948), p. 106.

3. G. A. Forehand and B. von H. Gilmer, "Environmental Variations in Studies of Organizational Behavior," *Psychological Bulletin* 62, No. 6 (1964): 362.

4. Benjamin Schneider and Robert A. Snyder, "Some Relationships between Job Satisfaction and Organizational Climate," *Journal of Applied Psychology* 60, No. 3 (1975): 318.

5. Lawrence R. James and Allan P. Jones, "Organizational Climate: A Review of Theory and Research," *Psychological Bulletin* 81 (December 1974): 1098.

6. R. E. Johannesson, "Job Satisfaction and Perceptually Measured Organizational Climate: Redundancy and Confusion," in *New Developments in Management and Organization Theory*, ed. M. W. Frey, Eastern Academy of Management, Proceedings of the Eighth Annual Conference (1971), p. 30.

7. Don Hellreigel and John W. Slocum, Jr., "Organizational Climate: Measures, Research and Contingencies," *Academy of Management Journal* 17 (June 1974): 277.

8. See Benjamin M. Selekman, Stephen H. Fuller, Thomas Kennedy, and John M. Baitsell, *Problems in Labor Relations* (New York: McGraw-Hill Book Co., 1964), pp. 5–7.

9. Richard E. Walton, Interpersonal Peacemaking: Confrontations and Third Party Consultations (Reading, Mass.: Addison-Wesley Publishing Co., 1969), p. 73.

10. Ibid.

11. Ibid., p. 5.

12. See Schneider and Snyder, "Some Relationships," p. 320.

13. Ibid.

14. See H. Kirk Downey, Don Hellriegel and John W. Slocum, Jr, "Congruence Between Individual Needs, Organizational Climate and Job Satisfaction and Performance," *Academy of Management Journal* 18 (March 1975): 150.

15. See STEVEN H. APPELBAUM, "The Organizational Climate Study: An Intervention Strategy to Change a Department," *University of Michigan Business Review* 28 (September 1976): 14–15.

QUESTIONS FOR THOUGHT AND DISCUSSION

1. Describe your perception of the organizational climate of the college or university you are now attending. How is the climate different at your school compared with another school with which you are familiar?

2. What seems to be the most important component in the determination of organizational climate? Support your answer.

3. Is the reciprocal effect a more viable concept within organizations that are participative in nature or within those that allow very little participation? Why?

4. Comment on the following statement: "Management plays the dominant role in determining organizational climate, but not necessarily the most important."

5. Why are emotional issues more difficult to deal with in the management of conflict than the substantive issues?

KEY TERMS

The student should be able to discuss the significance of these terms to the study of human behavior in the work environment.

Organizational climate
Components of climate
Organizational context
Organization structure
Organizational processes
Physical environment
Systems values and norms
Reciprocal effect
Cooperation

Accommodation
Conflict
Substantive issues
Emotional issues

CASE INCIDENT

Because of the lack of consistency of management throughout the various colleges and departments, the academic vice-president of a large, state-supported university circulated a letter to all deans and department heads advising them of the impending implementation of a goal-oriented management system for the entire university. After several training sessions and numerous attempts to deal with the resistance of many faculty to identifying work goals, the system was finally activated. Since the new system was something the management faculty of the College of Business taught in its courses and seminars, the chairperson suggested that all departmental members strive to make the department a model which other faculty members could look to as an example of goal-oriented management.

Although the organizational climate in the Department of Management could not be described as stimulating, it was fairly good as compared to other academic departments. It was hoped by the chairperson that the new system would rekindle some enthusiasm for departmental activities and create more feelings of commitment to the department and college. In keeping with his belief in faculty input concerning all major departmental decisions, the chairperson allowed the faculty to institute a new participative system to determine pay raises. Certain minimum and maximum limitations were set and the faculty as a whole would then determine how much of the available money for raises would go into a "pool" for cost-of-living increases and how much would be in the "pool" for merit increases. The chairperson would determine the exact amount of the merit portion of the raise to go to each deserving faculty member.

At the first faculty meeting called for the purpose of implementing the new participative system it was clear that faculty members would vote in a manner that would benefit them most. The limited budget presented to the group meant that only a few of the department's twelve members could receive a merit raise. Consequently, the majority voted to do away with the limitations of the distribution of the money into the two "pools" and to put all the money into one general pool to be distributed on a straight percentage basis. This meant all faculty members of the department would receive approximately a 6 percent raise.

Before this solution was reached the arguments for and against merit increases became less and less logical. Interpersonal conflicts during the participative process became more and more evident. Finally, when one of the highest paid members of the faculty argued against a merit increase by making personal references to faculty members who had spouses who worked (saying that they did not deserve as much of a raise irrespective of productivity) and by pointing out that he drove two old cars while others had newer vehicles, the department chairperson realized the system had failed. The climate of the department degenerated from one of cooperation to one of accommodation that at times bordered on conflict among the faculty members themselves. With morale and interpersonal relationships at an all-time low the chairperson was faced with trying to create a climate that was more conducive to productivity.

Questions for Discussion

1. Why did the participative system lead to a worsening of the climate within the department?

2. Was the cause of conflict in the department concerned with substantive issues or emotional issues? Explain.

3. What components of organizational climate appear to be the strongest contributors to the climate within the department?

4. What can be done to reestablish a climate that encourages cooperation and organizational efficiency?

6

The Presence of Stress in the Work Environment

LEARNING OBJECTIVES

Upon completion of this chapter, the student should be able to:

- Define job stress.
- Differentiate between organizational frustration and job stress.
- Discuss why success in business may not contribute to feelings of accomplishment, human worth, or self-acceptance.
- Describe how underutilization, work overload, insecurity, nonparticipation, job ambiguity, and job conflict affect the level of stress.
- Identify behaviors that are indicative of personality.
- Recognize symptoms of alcohol abuse and how to deal with alcoholism in the work environment.
- Identify drug abuses, estimate their cost to a company, and develop a workable rehabilitation program.
- Explain the costs to organizations caused by alcoholism and drug abuse.

We all know people who have the habit of pitting themselves against the clock. These people are usually ambitious, competitive, aggressive, and highly success-oriented individuals. They are likely to be individuals who try to control as many situations as possible and may succeed in all endeavors—even in a casual game of cards. Such people believe they can control almost everything and make anything happen that they wish. When problems or threats to their control emerge, they respond with an even greater intensity and often become more aggressive, frustrated, and stressful when their efforts to prevail fail. Even when they succeed, they may do so with great risk to their physical well-being.

People who have this intense desire to do well in everything, who feel impatient when people work slower than they would like, who have trouble relaxing, and generally who feel that there is not enough time in the day to get done what needs to be done are prime candidates for an early heart attack. Stress is the culprit. While some personality factors are seen to be linked with stress, some characteristics of jobs are just as much to blame. Work overload and work underload to many people are sources of endless frustration. Nonparticipation in company affairs and not feeling secure in the organization are other causes of stress in the work environment.

The first section of this chapter examines sources of stress in work and details how stress can be measured and eliminated. The latter part of the chapter explains how some people suffering from stress turn to alcohol or drugs, how supervisors can identify people who misuse alcohol and drugs, and how certain provisions for creating treatment programs can be implemented by an organization.

STRESS AND THE DESIRE TO SUCCEED

Many people aspire to executive positions that offer big salaries, power, and some degree of notoriety. The luxuries that would then be affordable and a life style that features a good deal of "wining and dining" other important people sound quite appealing. It is usually these more positive aspects of an executive's life that come to mind when employees think of how far they would like to advance within an organization. This positive view is perpetuated by managers who like to encourage their people to become motivated toward climbing the organizational hierarchy and performing in such a way as to be promotable. For some people aspiring to the top positions is quite appropriate. But it should be recognized that it isn't appropriate for everyone. Seldom does anyone take the time to think about some of the disadvantages that accompany top management positions.

The disadvantages include such things as the numbers of hours spent working or doing work-related activities for the organization, loss of privacy, less time spent with family and friends, less time to spend on hobbies and recreational activities, an almost total commitment to the organization and the job, and, of course, the inescapable burdens of responsibility and authority for making crucial decisions. But perhaps even more important than consideration of the disadvantages associated with executive positions is the question of whether or not the positive indicators of success really do anything to satisfy the perceived needs for success and achievement. It appears that people with accelerated achievement patterns who have acquired many of the symbols and amenities believed to accompany success have found that none of these symbols of success has really contributed to genuine feelings of accomplishment, human worth, or self-acceptance.[1]

This may in part explain why success seems to beget success. Besides the obvious reinforcement values, there may be the feeling that still more success may bring about the hoped for, but elusive, fulfillment of needs. Expectancies may be unrealistically high as a result of a deeply rooted need to achieve stemming from the childhood environment, the educational experience, and/or organizational training and development programs. It is therefore not surprising when people cling to delusions of grandeur until disillusion sets in in their mid-thirties. The result can be heart disease, alcoholism, or a variety of psychosomatic afflictions.[2] In many cases the causes of these illnesses can be traced to stress.

SOURCES OF STRESS IN THE WORK ENVIRONMENT

There are two broad categories of stress in the work environment:

1. Organizational frustration
2. Job stress

Frustration will influence a person to act aggressively or will instill a predisposition to aggress which is usually shown through anger. When people are frustrated in their organizational life, their first impulse is to "get back" at the company in some way. They will complain, criticize others, disobey rules and procedures, and even sabotage someone's work or plans. Job stress may be experienced when people become frustrated in trying to fulfill their job duties. Most feelings of job stress, however, are linked to job ambiguity or job conflict.

Organizational Frustration

People feel frustrated when they are blocked in achieving their goals. The normal response to being blocked is an attempt to "overcome" the barrier through some form of aggression. Three propositions about the frustration-aggression relationship have been developed:

1. The greater the frustrations, the greater the instinct to aggression
2. The stronger the motive being frustrated, the greater the frustration and the impulse to aggression
3. Aggression as a response to frustration increases with the number of frustrations up to a point and then it decreases[3]

The first two propositions are straightforward in saying that the more serious the frustrations, the more intense will be the aggression tendencies. The third proposition is more complex and implies that aggression tendencies increase as frustrations increase up to a certain point. After this point, people begin to expect frustration and this anticipation decreases the aggression tendencies. In other words, people become resigned to encountering problems and will "just not care" or seemingly give up. If people expect to be frustrated, their reactions will not be as intense as when they are "surprised" by frustration.

Think of one of your most frustrating work or school experiences. During the first several weeks on the job or at school, when you were really trying to do well, the frustrations were very irritating. The inconveniences and interferences were probably preventing you from doing the best possible job. However, over a longer period of time, you adjusted to the situation through a variety of ways and reduced the severity of the problems encountered. Apathy is a common means of lessening the impact of frustration. One researcher explains:

In general, expected frustrations produce less intense emotional reactions than do unanticipated frustrations. Two reasons are suggested: (1) through anticipating interference with his activity, the individual may alter his actions, or even his goals, so that he actually experiences less frustration; (2) expected frustrations may be judged as less severe.[4]

Some people learn to work around the sources of frustration or fight them directly while others simply give up and become resigned to experiencing frustration.

One attempt to learn about the ways people react to organizational frustration was carried out by asking people to agree or disagree with such statements as:

- "People act nasty to me at work."
- "I feel thwarted in my efforts to be creative."
- "Policies at work are not fair."
- "I often have problems doing my job because of the incompetence of others."

When individuals said they were frustrated, they behaved in the following ways:

1. Aggression—being nasty at work to someone not working for the employer
2. Sabotage—purposely damaged a valuable piece of property or equipment belonging to the employer
3. Wasted time—tried to look busy doing nothing
4. Hostility—said something derogatory about the boss to other people
5. Apathy—purposely did work incorrectly[5]

Organizational frustration can strongly influence the climate or personality of the organization. When people degrade each other, ignore the boss, think and talk about quitting, complain, destroy property, and act nasty to co-workers and to managers, the organizational climate will become defensive, blame-oriented, and nonsupportive.

If, after some time, organizations do not correct a frustrating situation, people will begin to behave in ways other than through acts of direct aggression. These nonaggressive responses to frustration are called adjustive reactions. Some of these adjustive reactions to frustration are described below with an example of each:

1. Compensation—A person devotes himself to a pursuit with increased vigor to make up for some feelings of real or imagined inadequacy. Example: a zealous, hard-working president of the Twenty-Five Year Club who has never advanced very far in the company.

2. Conversion—Emotional conflicts are expressed in muscular, sensory, or bodily symptoms of disability, malfunctioning, or pain. Example: a disability headache keeping a staff member off the job the day after a cherished project has been rejected.

3. Fantasy—Daydreaming or other forms of imaginative activity provide imagined satisfactions and an escape from reality. Example: an employee's daydreams of the day in the staff meeting when he corrects the boss's mistakes and is publicly acknowledged as the real leader of the company.

4. Projection—Individual protects himself from awareness of his own undesirable traits or unacceptable feelings by attributing them to others. Example: an unsuccessful person who, deep down, would like to block promotions of others in the organization and who continually feels that others are out to "get him."

5. Repression—Completely excluding from consciousness impulses, experiences, and feelings which are psychologically disturbing because they arouse the sense of guilt or anxiety. Example: a subordinate "forgetting" to tell his boss the circumstances of an embarrassing situation.[6]

We all use these adjustive reactions to "cope" in our day-to-day existence. A student receiving low grades may compensate for classroom inadequacy by being superior in other endeavors such as cultivating friendships or through athletics. A professor, notorious for being a generally poor teacher, compensates through an active publication record or through being active in student, university, or community services.

Job Stress

Job stress is much more specific than organizational frustration. Job stress takes basically two forms: job ambiguity and job conflict. Job ambiguity refers to the lack of clarity surrounding a person's job authority, responsibility, task demands, and work methods. If a job is ambiguous, the worker has unclear work goals, procedures, and responsibilities and may be uncertain about his or her authority. The person suffering from job ambiguity simply does not know what is expected in terms of job performance. Students may experience job ambiguity when they do not know how to study for a test.

Job conflict refers to the degree of incompatibility of expectations felt by a person on the job. In common sense terms, a person is caught in a decision quandary. A worker experiences job conflict when the worker must choose to do one thing over another and feels uneasy. For example, some staff employees may be reporting to the plant manager and to a staff manager with functional authority, each of whom wants the employee to follow specific orders. Each may ask the employee to do a different thing within the same time frame. The worker is in a dilemma about whose orders to follow. Another conflict arises when people are asked to perform duties for which they were not hired. Yet another example of conflict occurs when an individual is ordered to perform duties which seem unethical. If the duties are actually performed, the person may suffer from guilt feelings and depression from having sacrificed strongly held principles. On the other hand, if the employee elects to disobey the supervisor, he may be subjected to some form of punishment.

Measuring job stress. There is an accepted and well-tested method to measure the amount of job ambiguity and job conflict.

A fourteen item questionnaire has been devised which asks employees to respond on a seven point scale (1 = very true, 4 = neither true nor false, 7 = very false) about the extent to which they agree or disagree with statements such as the following:

1. I feel certain about how much authority I have.
2. I receive clear, planned goals and objectives for my job.
3. I know what my responsibilities are.
4. I receive a clear explanation of what has to be done in my work.[7]

Using this abbreviated version, if a worker has a total score between twenty-one and twenty-eight, the person has a job very high in ambiguity and literally does not understand why he was hired.

Job conflict is measured by eight questions, four of which are shown below. Workers are also asked to score each of their responses on a seven point scale (1 = very false, 4 = neither true nor false, and 7 = very true). Please notice that the scoring is the opposite of that used with job ambiguity.

5. I have to do things that should be done differently.
6. I receive an assignment without the manpower to complete it.
7. I receive incompatible requests from two or more people.
8. I have to buck a rule or policy in order to carry out an assignment.[8]

Overall scores between twenty-one and twenty-eight are very unfavorable and indicate that employees run into too many problems and interferences in performing their jobs.

All of us at one time or another have felt that "things ought to be done differently," "we don't have the manpower," or "we have to break rules to do our work well." These needless feelings of conflict, if persistent, will not only dampen a person's enthusiasm to do well but also will create a great deal of contempt toward the supervisor and the company. In fact, it has been found that the stressors which produce the most unhealthy behavior in individuals are the emotional aspects of the job.[9]

Reducing job stress.   Since ambiguity and conflict lead to such unfavorable consequences as fatigue, anxiety, and low confidence in supervisors and in the company, the cause of these problems must be determined. The question to be answered is: what factors or situations seem to create high levels of conflict and ambiguity? Basically, organizational weakness in two categories of factors—organizational principles and supportive leadership—can contribute to job stress. Conversely, good organizational principles and supportive leadership can serve to reduce and minimize the amount of job stress in the work environment (Figure 6.1).

Clear lines of authority, clearly defined jobs, and participative goal setting will insure that workers understand their own goals as well as those of the department and of the company. When there are clearly defined company, departmental, and personal goals, people will know what is expected of them in terms of duties, authority, and responsibility. Such human problems as aimlessness and anxiety will not be felt where there is effective goal setting and a clear chain of command.

The organizational principle prescribing that each worker should have only one supervisor prevents a situation where a worker must try to fulfill the expectations of two supervisors. Despite the absence of these dual reporting relationships on a company's organizational chart, an employee's efforts to appease as many people as possible sometimes results in several supervisors giving him orders.

The organizational principles of "responsibility equaling authority" and having "authority delegated as far down the line as possible" insure that people feel important and significant to the firm while guaranteeing that employees are able to carry out their responsibilities without interferences such as those involving overlapping authority. Many types of frustration and conflicts result from being delegated authority for the success of an activity and then having it undermined by the very person who delegated the authority in the first place. Employees must believe that delegated authority is authentic and genuine if full commitment is expected from the subordinates.

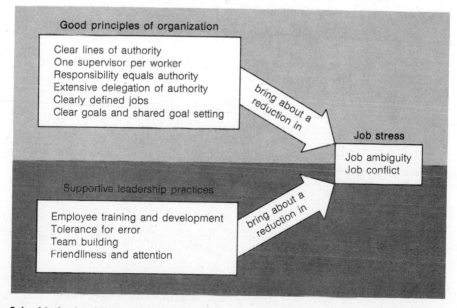

Figure 6.1   Methods of Reducing Job Stress

Source: Modified and adapted from John Rizzo, Richard House, and Sidney Lirtzman, "Role Conflict and Ambiguity in Complex Organizations," Administrative Science Quarterly 15 (June 1970): 150–63.

The supportive leadership practices such as concern for personal development, team building, and friendliness insure that the workers feel appreciated as human beings. When workers know that their feelings and interests are important to top level managers, they will be less likely to feel stressful when problems are encountered. When employees know that managers are concerned with their development and have some tolerance for error, they will be better able to work creatively with less tension than when the company is defensive, blame oriented, and discouraging.

Other sources of job stress. While job ambiguity and conflict are the most common sources of job stress, there are several others influencing the level of stress. These include underutilization, work overload, resource inadequacy, insecurity, and nonparticipation.

The effects of these sources of stress on various measures of physical and mental health, ranging from absenteeism to poor physical health, were studied for 1500 workers.[10] The investigators referred to the sources of stress as "strain indicators" and defined each as follows:

> **Work underload or underutilization:** too little to do or work tasks that are too easy and fail to tap the individual's capabilities.
>
> **Work overload:** too much to do or work tasks that are too difficult.
>
> **Resource inadequacy:** inadequate facts or resources to do the job.
>
> **Insecurity:** uncertainty about continued employment.
>
> **Nonparticipation:** lack of "say" in decisions that affect one's job.[11]

It was learned that job stress from the situations described above was significantly related to the following manifestations of poor mental health:

- Escapist thinking
- Depression
- Low self-esteem
- Low life and job satisfaction
- Low motivation to work
- Intentions to quit job
- Absenteeism

Nonparticipation and underutilization affected each and every measure of poor mental and physical health. The importance of providing room for employee participation cannot be overestimated. The opportunity to express opinions and suggestions and being creatively involved in designing policies and one's work environment prevent a worker from becoming frustrated. The opportunities for participation offer the worker a feeling of having "a way out" when conflict situations arise. Underutilization and nonparticipation operate almost hand-in-hand. When there are good opportunities for participation, there will tend to be effective utilization of human capabilities.

THE TYPE A STRESSFUL PERSONALITY

More Americans die of some form of heart disease, particularly arteriosclerosis or "hardening of the arteries," than from any other single cause. An estimated one to three million Americans had heart disease in 1975; of these, close to 675,000 will die of it, 175,000 of them before they reach 65.[12] Many of these people are working in good positions and die from stress-induced heart attacks in the prime years of their lives.

Not very long ago medical experts believed that heart attacks could be explained primarily by such factors as smoking, fatty foods, lack of exercise, and high blood pressure. However, research during the last decade has shown that the causes of these attacks are not as easily explained as once thought. Two groups of people can have identical diets, smoking habits, and exercise patterns but one group will experience a much higher incidence of heart disease than the other. What accounts for this difference? Many researchers now believe that a certain type of hard-driving, hurried, competitive, clock-watching personality is to blame. This competitive personality is technically called the Type A personality.[13] This person is often observed being irritable and anxious, tense in the presence of other workers, autocratic in working frustrations out on subordinates, absent, and alcoholic.

The Type A person is persistent, compulsive about work, oriented toward leadership and high achievement, and continually races against the clock. The Type A individual—male or female—always feels pressured for time and regularly reacts to frustration with hostility and anger.[14]

The opposite of the Type A is the Type B. This person has a genuinely easy and open manner and is not so preoccupied with success, achievement, or competition. There is overwhelming evidence that the Type A person may die of heart disease before the retirement years while the Type B person will enjoy a longer life.

The following questions are used by investigators to identify Type A and B people:

1. Since you began making your living did you or do you now go to night school to improve your chances of advancement?

2. When you play athletic or card games with friends, do you give it all your worth—is there fighting all the way? Do you play mainly to win or for the fun of it?

3. Are you a fast car driver? Does it irritate you to be held up by a car in front of you? Do you try to move him out of the way? Does your spouse usually try to slow you down?

4. Do you get impatient when you see something being done at home or at work slower than you think it should be done?

5. How much time do you spend on hobbies? Do you spend time with hobbies only when you have nothing more important to do?

6. Do you often try to get something else done, like calculating or reading trade material when eating alone? Or while in the bathroom?

7. Do you get irritated if you have to wait for a table in a restaurant? Do you wait? How about waiting in a bank line? Do you plan your eating out or going out to a bank so that you don't have to wait?

8. Do you often have the feeling that time is passing too quickly each day to get everything done that you want to? Does this sense of time urgency make you look at your watch often? Make you feel that you have to do everything in a hurry?[15]

The Type A person never seems to be able to get enough work done and when it is done, it probably does not seem done well enough. If you keep these ideas in mind, you should not have much difficulty in spotting Type A answers to the questions. Not only is the content of the answers important but so is the manner in which the questions are answered. When people are responding during personal interviews, the Type A individual will show certain motor signs such as impatience, rapid speech, and explosive accentuation. In short, Type A's will appear to be in a great hurry while the Type B's will be relaxed.

Some actual day-to-day behavior of Type A people has been identified by stress experts. Some of the extreme behaviors include the following:

The extreme Type A is the man who, while waiting to see the dentist, is on the telephone making business calls. He frequently sighs faintly between words. This is a deadly sign of emotional exhaustion.

He rarely goes to the doctor, and almost never to a psychiatrist—he does not feel he needs either.

Type A is often a little hard to get along with. His chuckle is rather grim. He does not drive people who work under him as hard as he drives himself, but he has little time to waste with them. He wants respect, not affection.

Type A, surprisingly, goes to bed earlier than Type B. He doesn't get much out of home life anyway, and might as well prepare for the day ahead with a good night's rest, whereas Type B will get interested in something and sit up late, or simply socialize.

Type A's have little time for exercise. When they do play golf, it is fast through, and on teams they can be difficult partners. . . . They never return to work a day or two late; they are more likely to be back early.

Often you can tell an A by the way he uses his body. His hands are slightly clenched. He may have a habit of tunelessly humming, or, while sitting, of jiggling a leg.
Says Friedman, "I have known A's who shave with two electric razors at once—one for each side of their face."[16]

Generally Type A people do not get the top level jobs because they are too compulsive, too noncreative, and too hurried in their decision making. Some observers have noted that some Type B top company executives also have become champion athletes who have mastered a good sense of perspective in responding to problems and opportunities. These people make it to the top, in part, because they are able to survive stress and, after they have made it, new challenges become stimuli rather than stress.[17]

THE ULTIMATE STRESS SOLUTION: CONFRONTING ONE'S INNERMOST SELF

Must high levels of achievement and ambition lead to physical or emotional breakdown? Our culture creates in us the idea that monetary or business success—and only such success—leads to self-acceptance and feelings of well-being. Being warmly accepted by people and having deep personal relationships are not always seen as measures of success. Our business schools endlessly promote the proposition that a high quality of life is felt by people in top level positions. There are two realistic problems with this idea:

1. There are very few good top level slots in managerial hierarchies.
2. It takes a long time to get to the top.

When it takes so much time and work to become a part of top management, why do executives commit suicide after reaching the top? According to two authorities, most people would ask "How could they? They had everything. They had material success; they had attained the pinnacle of success." The viewer would interpret the act in terms of personal unfulfilled needs, whether real or imagined.[18] However, in clinical interviews with many executives who were hospitalized with heart disease, the researchers discovered that these executives were unable to even vaguely define the "meaning of it all."[19] The patients, in other words, were not sure why they had worked so hard for so long.

The investigators asked whether "business achievement can ever become a truly self-fulfilling human experience." They feel it can only occur when executives come to terms with themselves and with the reasons behind their hard work. Business executives must ask if their managerial roles contribute positively to some issues of "ultimate reality," such as:

1. The sense of being a meaningful and valued human being
2. The sense of being a loved and loving person
3. Proof that you are a good, successful, husband or wife
4. The reassurance that you are a more acceptable son or daughter
5. Proof that your existence has contributed in some positive way to the existence of your fellow man[20]

By confronting these issues through introspection, a person can come to grips with his or her existence as an executive. In the words of Ogilvie and Porter, "in the moment of genuine inner reflection and the resultant self-criticism, we [the executives] are hard pressed in terms of continuing the charade."[21] (The charade refers to achieving for reasons other than those founded on well-defined and authentic reasons.)

OTHER SOLUTIONS

There are many different techniques being proposed to effectively deal with stress, ranging from bio-feedback to simple relaxation exercises. Most of them are seeking the results which Dr. Herbert Benson sees as the benefits to what he calls relaxation response:

1. Relieve fatigue and help you cope with anxieties
2. Relieve the stress that can lead to high blood pressure, hardening of the arteries, stroke, and heart attacks
3. Conserve the body's store of energy
4. Make you more alert, so you can focus on what is really important[22]

Basically, using a relaxation exercise involves just a few steps. A person should seek out a quiet and comfortable environment. Then the person closes the eyes, inhales deeply and exhales slowly. During the latter part of the exhale, the individual says a mantra—a soft-sounding word like "one." This procedure followed for about ten minutes has been found to reduce stress levels. Repeating these steps about three or four times during the work day is believed by Dr. Benson to be sufficient.

Unfortunately not everyone suffering from stress realizes it. Even those who may realize the impact stress is having upon them often turn to other, less acceptable means of dealing with it. In this regard alcohol and drugs serve as an escape from the pressures of a stressful environment.

ALCOHOLISM

A Disease with Many Causes and Costs

Although volumes of research have been published about the causes of alcoholism, we do not know what causes alcoholism for any one individual. No one factor can be credited as influencing one person in the same way that it affects some other person. At present, a good deal of evidence points to the following factors as being related to excessive drinking:

- Personal tension and job stress
- Organizational frustrations and blocked career ambitions
- Depression
- Absence of close personal relationships
- Guilt feelings
- Social rejection at work
- Genetic, chemical and mental disorders

Each of us may know several people who feel a great deal of tension, experience intense job stress, and are socially rejected by important social groups but who are not alcoholic or may not even drink. For this reason, some experts feel that alcoholism is caused mainly by hereditary or congenital factors, by a deficiency of specific nutrients, or by a brain pathology. Although these factors cannot be ruled out, there is insufficient reason to fix special causal powers to any genetic, chemical, or physiological factor in the cause of alcoholism.[23]

Alcoholism appears to have many causes and a host of disastrous consequences. We know that alcohol is a drug and any person who drinks enough over a period of time will develop alcoholism—meaning, at a minimum, a physical and/or psychological dependence on the drug. The addiction is so strong that the first step in the recovery program offered by Alcoholics Anonymous (AA) involves memorizing a resignation slogan

—"We admitted we were powerless over alcohol—that our lives had become unmanageable."

What is alcoholism and an alcoholic? These terms have been defined and redefined through the years in various ways. The following widely accepted definitions of alcoholism, the alcoholic, the problem drinker, and the heavy drinker are offered by the Conference Board on Alcoholism:

> **Alcoholism**—A chronic disease characterized by repeated excessive drinking, which interferes with the individual's health, interpersonal relations, or economic functioning.
>
> **Alcoholic**—An ill person suffering from alcoholism. His drinking is out of control and is self-destructive in many different ways, yet he views alcohol as a "sure cure" for all his problems.
>
> **Problem drinker**—An employee whose drinking affects his work adversely.
>
> **Heavy drinker**—An individual who repeatedly drinks greater than average amounts of alcohol in any form.[24]

Industry is not necessarily concerned with the heavy drinker until the heavy drinker turns into the problem drinker—one whose work is adversely affected by drinking. But even at that, alcoholism costs American business about 12.5 billion dollars a year.[25] This cost is paying for such job-related problems as absenteeism, sick leave, wasted time and ruined materials, medical services, accidents, and premature death. The damage done by excessive drinking is startling. Some of these depressing findings include:

- Each alcoholic worker costs a firm over $2500 in unnecessary extras.
- Alcoholic workers are 2½ times as likely to be absent as their fellow employees.
- Compared to other employees, 12.8 percent of alcoholic workers are disabled for 30 days or more a year (6.5 percent for other workers).
- Thirty-six million work days are lost due to excessive drinking.
- The accident rate for alcoholic workers is 3.6 times that of fellow workers.
- Alcoholic workers have twice the rate of heart disease, three times the incidence of digestive and muscular problems, as nonalcoholic workers, and twice the incidence of high blood pressure.
- Alcoholic workers collect over three times the amount of sickness payment as other employees.[26]

Even given these statistics, James S. Kemper, Jr., President of Kemper Insurance Companies and a reformed alcoholic, believes that some companies are underestimating the extent of alcoholism.

It seems to me that today's employers, who say they have no problem drinkers in their organization, are not unlike the employed alcoholic who insists he or she has no problem with alcohol. Neither is facing the realities of the situation. They are alike, too, in that both are paying a heavy and needless penalty for their illusions.[27]

Identifying the Alcoholic Employee

The alcoholic employee is usually able to remain on the job for several years after the initial onset of alcoholism. This is accomplished by some very inventive ways of camouflaging excessive drinking and unsatisfactory work habits. Although alcoholic workers have developed camouflage into a fine art, there are certain patterns of behavior indicative of excessive drinking of which supervisors should be aware. Since job requirements and the available opportunities for hiding alcoholism vary among jobs, there may also be some different alcoholic behaviors demonstrated in the work environment. These differences are probably most distinguishable between the broadly defined white-collar and blue-collar workers. Some signs of alcoholism among white-collar workers include:

1. Avoiding boss and associates or becoming grandiose or belligerent
2. Swings in work pace become more pronounced and more frequent
3. Excuses for work deficiencies become elaborate and often bizarre
4. Severe financial difficulties
5. Frequent use of breath purifiers to cover drinking during working hours
6. Increased nervousness, gastric upsets, and insomnia problems[28]

Since it is more socially acceptable today for production workers to exhibit their drinking, both on and off the job, there are particular clues indicating their alcoholism. Some of these are:

1. Personal appearance occasionally sloppy and showing signs of hangover on the job
2. Lapses and carelessness become more frequent, occasionally causing damage to equipment or material or creating a safety hazard
3. Increased trips to water cooler and taking other rest breaks
4. Reporting for work intoxicated or drinking on the job
5. Marked increase in nervousness and occasional hand tremors
6. Marked increase in hospital-medical-surgical claims, often involving off-the-job accidents, gastric disorder and conditions commonly associated with lack of proper diet[29]

Alcoholic workers rate hangovers on the job, drinking before work, absenteeism, and nervousness as the four symptoms most indicative of alcoholism. When supervisors were asked to rank the four most prevalent signs of alcoholism, they included leaving the work area temporarily, drinking at lunch, red eyes, and mood changes after lunch.[30]

Programs to Reduce Alcoholism

Companies that have real alcoholism programs, as distinguished from those that consist of distributing a pamphlet on alcoholism once a year, have a recovery rate of 60–80 percent.[31] For example, the following results of programs to aid recovery from alcoholism have been reported:

Allis-Chalmers states that their absentee rate was slashed from 8 percent to 3 percent and the discharge rate was reduced from 95 percent to 8 percent amounting to savings of some $80,000 per year.

Consolidated Edison reports that 60 percent of those treated were successfully rehabilitated and absenteeism was reduced from an average of fourteen days to four days per year.

Minnesota Mining has disclosed that 80 percent of their alcoholic workers are either recovered or controlled to the point where noticeable and marked improvement in attendance, productivity and family and community relationships now exists.[32]

Typically, the ingredients of a good alcoholism control program involve the following elements:

1. The formal establishment of a written company policy on alcoholism
2. The applicability of the program to workers at all levels
3. The training of supervisory personnel and shop stewards in working with written guidance and policies
4. The availability of advice about the available treatment modalities
5. Full and equal participative support by unions where they are involved
6. A clear understanding that if work performance does not improve or if treatment is not accepted or followed, the person's job could be in jeopardy

The formal establishment of a written company policy is needed to insure that every worker clearly understands that the company is genuinely concerned about the plight of the alcoholic worker. A statement of company policy should include reference to the ideas that:

1. Alcoholism is a disease that can be successfully treated

2. Each worker will be treated confidentially
3. No one will be forced to accept treatment under the firm's program if the person shows evidence of solving the problem by some other means

Since about one-half of all employed alcoholics are supervisors, managers, or executives, it is important that people in these positions have the opportunity to participate. People in these positions will also be key figures in the implementation of the company's alcoholism control program. They need to be trained in understanding the purposes of the program, in the background of alcoholism, and in identifying the problem drinker. Once the excessive drinker has been identified, the person will probably be sent to either the firm's medical department or to the personnel department for counseling and for further referral.

The immediate supervisor should be prepared to explain the alternative methods of treatment available to the alcoholic. Not only must the supervisor know what to say but what not to say. The supervisor must not try to diagnose the problem, moralize about drinking, or be sympathetic because the drinker is an expert at minimizing the value of that approach.

Union support for the total rehabilitation program will be crucial for its success. A union can help a great deal by issuing its own policy statement consistent with that of the company. This statement should emphasize the protection of employee rights, the assurance of uniform and fair policy administration for everyone, and the assurance that job security, seniority, wages, benefits and promotion opportunities will not be jeopardized by a request for treatment.

To summarize, the effectiveness of an alcoholic control program hinges upon:

1. The early identification of a probable drinking problem
2. The supervisor's discussion with the problem drinker in trying to persuade the person of the necessity to start a treatment program
3. The cooperation of the labor union, if any, with the goal of reestablishing the person as a productive and healthy human being
4. The referral to an appropriate treatment facility

According to Mr. William Dunkin, Assistant Director of Labor Management Services at the National Council on Alcoholism, employee programs are the best way to treat alcoholism because of the employee's motivation to keep his job.[33] The costs associated with treatment of alcoholics and problem drinkers seem to be minimal in terms of any cost-benefit analysis. One small company estimated that its 102 problem drinkers were costing the firm $100,650 annually, but a successful program to treat these workers cost $11,400 a year.[34] Of this total, $4,000 a year went to a part-time trained employee counselor. Two hours a week of a physician's time cost $3,000 annually. Administration of the program consumed 10 percent of the time of a personnel department member, valued at $2,000 a year. The time spent by 100 supervisors was valued at $2,400 a year.[35] According to one consultant on alcoholism control programs, a company will spend 35 to 50 cents per month per employee to finance an effective treatment program.[36]

IDENTIFYING DRUG ABUSERS

Generally, people take drugs while at work not to induce pleasure, but rather to reduce displeasure. Displeasure may have many causes, some of which the worker brings from home, and some of which are caused by the organization. Regardless of the cause, supportive and effective companies realize that most human problems can be successfully treated, provided a problem is identified in its early stages and referral is made to an appropriate treatment program. This underlying philosophy should be followed, whether the problem is one of physical, mental, or emotional illness or one of alcoholism or drug abuse. Regardless of the specific problem and its causes, employers should be concerned about workers with health or behavioral problems that result in excessive tardiness, absenteeism, and deteriorating job efficiency. As with alcoholism, supervisors must only be concerned with drug usage as it might be influencing unsatisfactory job performance.

To some extent, the symptoms of drug abuse are similar to those related to alcoholism. Some common signs of drug misuse include:

- Slurred or incoherent speech
- Dilated eyes
- Uncontrollable laughter or crying
- The general appearance of excessive drinking without the smell of alcohol
- An unsteady walk
- Lack of dexterity

Although there are many other clues given by the drug abuser, depending on the type of drug used, the end result is always the same: the person is probably unfit for work. Only when the person appears unfit for work or his or her condition is affecting performance should the person be confronted by the immediate supervisor.

Drugs Used by Workers

As mentioned earlier, the symptoms of drug misuse will vary depending on which drug is used. However, there are enough similarities in the symptoms that it is difficult for an untrained layperson to identify what kind of drug has been taken. It is possible though for supervisors to receive enough information in a brief workshop to be knowledgeable enough to deal with drug problems if they occur. One of the first things generally covered in such a session is a discussion of the four major categories of drugs and common behaviors related to the misuse of the drugs.

Stimulants. Stimulants act on the central nervous system and are often used to keep people awake. The most used is caffeine, which is found in coffee, tea, and some soft drinks. The most misused are amphetamines. Cocaine, usually referred to as "coke," is a stimulant that is similar to amphetamines. It is sniffed or injected with the result being a strong stimulation of the central nervous system. Generally the stimulants produce increased activity, irritability, nervousness, excitation, talkativeness, dilated pupils, and the ability to go without sleep for long periods of time. Stimulants are often referred to as "bennies," "pep pills," "speed," "meth," "crystal," "greenies," "oranges," and "dexies."

Depressants. Depressants, many of which are barbiturates, also affect the central nervous system but are used to induce sleep or act as a sedative or tranquilizer. They are prescribed by doctors to treat anxiety and high blood pressure as well as for the treatment of some forms of mental disorders. Barbiturates create a physical and psychological dependence and when usage stops, a person may experience a lack of muscular coordination similar to epileptic seizures. A supervisor may be able to spot a barbiturate abuser by such signs as staggering or stumbling, falling asleep on the job, appearing disoriented, slurred speech, difficulty concentrating, and extreme passivity. Slang terms for depressants include "goof balls," "goofers," "barbs," "yellow jackets," "yellows," "blues," "blue birds," "pinks," "reds," and "rainbows."

Narcotics. Narcotics are a family of drugs which induce sleep and stupors and relieve pain. The four most common narcotics are opium, morphine, heroin, and codeine. These drugs depress the central nervous system to produce a marked reduction in sensitivity to pain, create drowsiness and sleep, and reduce physical activity. A narcotic abuser may have symptoms of excessive yawning, running eyes and nose, sweating, muscle twitching, hot and cold flashes, vomiting and diarrhea, increases in breathing rate and blood pressure and a loss of appetite for normal meals while preferring candy and sweet snacks. Slang terms for narcotics include "H," "horse," "junk," "smack," "sugar," "M," and "hop."

Hallucinogens.   Hallucinogens are so named because they produce hallucinations or illusions of the various senses. When experiencing a hallucination or illusion, a person's ability to perceive is based, not upon objective reality, but upon a distorted one. Usually, hallucinogens distort or intensify the user's sense of perception and lessen the ability to discriminate between fact and fantasy. The user's judgments of direction, distance, and objectivity are generally out of proportion. A hallucinogen abuser has such symptoms as dilated pupils, eye sensitivity to light, exhilaration, and the tendency to sit or recline quietly in a trancelike state. The person may experience nausea, chills, flashes, sweating, and hand trembling. Hallucinogens include marijuana, LSD, DMT, STP, peyote, mescaline, and morning glory seeds. Some of the slang terms used to describe various hallucinogens are "pot," "tea," "grass," "Mary Jane," "acid," "Blue Cheer," "Lucy in the Sky with Diamonds," "businessman's special," "syndicate acid," "buttons," and "seeds."

Who Uses What

Marijuana, tranquilizers, barbiturates, and amphetamines are the most common types of drugs taken by employees across all job categories. Research shows that there is some difference between the types of drugs used by people in different occupational categories. In one large study of 1,692,000 employees in the "professional, technical and managerial" group, tranquilizers, barbiturates and marijuana were the most popular drugs.[37] The most frequently used illegal drug was marijuana with about 21 percent of its regular users reporting smoking it at work. A regular user in this study was interpreted as someone who takes a drug at least six times a month. Barbiturates and marijuana each had about 50,000 regular users.[38]

The types of drugs used by the clerical and white-collar workers (1,422,000 people studied) were about the same as for the professional-managerial group, although the number of users per category differed in some ways.[39] The clerical and white-collar workers used tranquilizers—100,000 regular users—much more heavily than the professional-managerial category. The white-collar group had a lower use of barbiturates but a much higher use of heroine (9,000 regular users). Thirty-five percent of the regular marijuana users in the white-collar category said they used the drug at work.

Marijuana is also the most heavily used illegal drug by skilled and semi-skilled workers. Of a sample of 2,421,000, there were 86,000 who claimed to be regular users of marijuana, and it is used at work by 22 percent of its regular users.[40] Tranquilizers are the second most frequently taken drug by this group, with barbiturates third in usage.

Many more scientific investigations are needed to clarify the frequency of drug abuse and its costs to industry and to the quality of human existence. There are no well-developed figures for the costs of drug abuse. Estimates range from a conservative $10 billion upwards to $17 billion. This figure includes the costs related to lost productivity due to tardiness, absenteeism, poor performance, and treatment and prevention programs.

An Effective Drug Treatment Program

Many companies seem to have the attitude "if you catch the drug abuser, fire him." Although this "remedy" saves a lot of people time and trouble, it is neither humane nor effective in curbing abuse. Drug abuse, like most other forms of disease, is treatable, and many companies have developed formal policies to attack the disease. In most respects, programs for drug abuse parallel those for alcohol abuse. Typically, a drug program will include these steps:

- *Step 1.* Establish a committee consisting of equal representation from management and labor, including a representative from the medical department, if one exists.
- *Step 2.* Develop a policy statement expressing the philosophy of the company toward problems affecting job performance.
- *Step 3.* If there is a union, develop a joint labor/management policy statement which recognizes that drug abuse can lead to serious health and behavior problems affecting many areas of a person's life.
- *Step 4.* Define and train supervisors in appropriate drug control skills.[41]

Supervisors must monitor the rehabilitation of their subordinates as they progress in the treatment program. If the employees fail to respond, performance remains unsatisfactory, or there are relapses, decisions must be made regarding the workers' tenure. To insure consistency of discipline, some supervisors may be helped by asking themselves, "What action is consistent with the way the situation would be handled if it were some other critical disorder affecting the workers' job behavior?" When job performance is being affected by alcoholism or drug abuse, there is a strong tendency to be severe in disciplinary actions. Supervisors and members of the committee should consider how the workers would be treated if poor job performance was being caused by some more socially acceptable disease like tuberculosis or advanced arthritis.

Cures and treatments for alcoholism and drug abuse would be easier to find if the exact causes of these diseases were known. One of the causes is, no doubt, stress stemming from the work environment. All organizations must become more aware of people who are susceptible to stress-related diseases in terms of selection, job placement, and performance expectations. Programs on how to deal with the stressors in the work environment, as well as more formal efforts to cure and control alcoholism and drug abuse, will hopefully become more common in the near future.

SUMMARY

Stress in the work environment can be separated into two categories: organizational frustration and job stress. While most job stress is linked to job ambiguity or job conflict, other sources of stress include work overload and underload, resource inadequacy, insecurity and nonparticipation. Two broad factors influencing the levels of ambiguity and conflict are: (1) how well a firm is following certain good principles of organization and (2) how well supportive leadership practices are displayed by supervisors and managers.

A person feels frustrated when he or she is blocked in achieving a goal. When people are frustrated in their organizational life, their first impulse is to "get back" at the company in some way. They will complain, criticize others, disobey rules and procedures, and even sabotage someone's work or plans.

High levels of stress have been linked to heart disease. The people who seem most susceptible appear to be those described as Type A personalities. The Type A person is competitive, hard-driving, and aggressive. The Type B personality, on the other hand, is more open and not so preoccupied with success, achievement, or competition. These people are able to react to challenges as stimuli rather than stress. One remedy for stress suggests that people confront their innermost selves and examine their personal values. The competitive business manager is asked to question whether the managerial role contributes positively to perceived needs and a feeling of self-worth. Bio-feedback and relaxation response are other treatments frequently used to combat stress.

Alcoholism and drug abuse are seen by some as an escape from stressful situations. Together they cost industry over $20 billion a year in wasted materials, absenteeism, accidents, premature death, and rehabilitation programs. However, the costs of good rehabilitation programs have been found to be extremely low when compared with the costs of allowing alcoholism or drug abuse to go unattended. From a cost/benefit analysis standpoint, as well as from the humanistic considerations, it pays management to help employees deal more effectively with stress and the damaging escapes from stress such as alcohol and drug abuse.

NOTES

1. Bruce C. Ogilvie and Albert Porter, "Business Careers as Treadmill to Oblivion," *Human Resource Management* 13 (Fall 1974): 17.

2. Ibid., 15.

3. L. Berkowitz, *Aggression: A Social Psychological Analysis* (New York: McGraw-Hill, 1962), p. 72.

4. Ibid.

5. Paul E. Spector, "Relationship of Organizational Frustration with Reported Behavioral Reactions of Employees," *Journal of Applied Psychology* 60, No. 5 (1975), 635–7.

6. Partial list of adjustive reactions from Timothy Costello and Sheldon Zalkind, *Psychology in Administration: A Research Orientation* (Englewood Cliffs, New Jersey: Prentice-Hall, 1963), pp. 148–9. Reprinted by permission of Prentice-Hall, Inc., Englewood Cliffs, New Jersey.

7. John Rizzo, Robert House and Sidney Lirtzman, "Role Conflict and Ambiguity in Complex Organizations," *Administrative Science Quarterly* 15 (June 1970): 150–63.

8. Ibid.

9. Alan A. McLean, "Job Stress and the Psychosocial Pressures of Change," *Personnel* (January–February 1976): 41.

10. Bruce Margolis, W. Kroes and R. Quinn, "Job Stress: An Unlisted Occupational Hazard," *Journal of Occupational Medicine* 16, No. 10 (1974): 659–61.

11. Ibid., p. 660.

12. David C. Glass, "Stress, Competition and Heart Attacks," *Psychology Today* (December 1975): 57.

13. Meyer Friedman and Ray Rosenman, *Type A Behavior and Your Heart* (New York: Alfred A. Knopf, 1974).

14. "Executives: Taut, Tense, Cracking Up," *Duns Review* (March 1969): 55.

15. From *Type A Behavior and Your Heart*, by Meyer Friedman, M.D. and Ray H. Rosenman, M.D. Copyright © 1974 by Meyer Friedman. Reprinted by permission of Alfred A. Knopf, Inc. Pp. 100–2.

16. Taken from Walter McQuade and Ann Aikman, *Stress: What It Is* (New York: Bantam Books, 1974), pp. 223–33. (They excerpted some work of the Western Collaborative Group Study, which included Drs. Friedman and Rosenman among others.)

17. "Stress Has No Gender," *Business Week*, 15 November 1976, pp. 73–6.

18. Ogilvie and Porter, "Business Careers as Treadmills to Oblivion," p. 17.

19. Ibid.

20. Ibid., p. 18.

21. Ibid.

22. HERBERT BENSON, *The Relaxation Response* (New York: Morrow Press, 1976), appendix.

23. For an excellent overall discussion of alcoholism, see JOSEPH FOLLMAN, *Alcoholics and Business* (New York: American Management Association, 1976).

24. Ibid., pp. 29–30.

25. Ibid., p. 82.

26. Ibid.

27. Statement found in KEN A. ROUSE, *What to Do about the Employee with a Drinking Problem*, Long Grove, Ill., Kemper Insurance Company, no. XD180418 (September 1976).

28. *Detour Alcoholism Ahead*, Long Grove, Ill., Kemper Insurance Company, no. XD1840-6 (September 1976), pp. 8–12.

29. Ibid.

30. H. M. TRICE, "New Light on Identifying the Alcoholic Employee," *Personnel* (September–October 1964): 17–24.

31. "Business Dries Up Its Alcoholics," *Business Week* Nov. 11, 1972, p. 168.

32. ROUSE, "What to Do about the Employee with a Drinking Problem," p. 2.

33. ROGER RICKLEFFS, "Drinkers at Work," *Wall Street Journal*, 1 December 1975, p. 1.

34. FOLLMAN, *Alcoholics and Business*, p. 140.

35. Ibid.

36. Ibid.

37. CARL D. CHAMBERS and RICHARD HECKMAN, *Employee Drug Abuse* (Boston, Mass.: Cahners Books, 1972), p. 149.

38. Ibid.

39. Ibid., p. 150.

40. Ibid., p. 151.

41. For an excellent example of a formal policy detailing a joint labor/management alcoholism and drug control program, see the Ontario Federation of Labor/Addiction Research Foundation *Joint Guidelines for the Establishment of Employee Assistance Programs* (Employee Assistance Task Force, 33 Russell Street, Toronto, Ontario, N55251). The discussions in this chapter were strongly influenced by this and Western Electric Company's program.

QUESTIONS FOR THOUGHT AND DISCUSSION

1. Comment on the quotation "business achievement can never become a truly self-fulfilling human experience."

2. Turn back to the beginning of the chapter where "organizational frustration" was discussed. Think of your own work or school experiences and offer two examples of each of the three propositions about the frustration-aggression relationship.

3. Refer to the "measuring job stress" section of this chapter. Answer the eight questions regarding job ambiguity and job conflict on a 1 to 7 point scale. Discuss how your work situation could be improved, based on your unfavorable answers to these questions.

4. Reproduce the Figure titled "Methods of reducing job stress" and score your present work organization (or a past work experience) on a 10 point scale with 1 meaning a very unfavorable score while 10 means a very favorable score. List your suggestions for improving your organization where it scored poorly.

5. Please reread the descriptions of the Type A personality in the chapter. List as many of the behavior characteristics demonstrated by a Type A person personally known by you as you can. In what ways could this Type A individual alter his or her mode of behavior in order to reduce the chances of stress and heart disease?

6. If you have the occasion to work with or know a problem drinker, comment on the clues indicating alcoholism or heavy drinking outlined in this chapter. Are there others?

7. Suggest how a program to prevent drug abuse in the work environment should be designed and implemented.

8. What effect(s) might the decriminalization of marijuana have on employees, managers, and the overall work environment of an organization?

KEY TERMS

The student should be able to discuss the significance of these terms to the study of human behavior in the work environment.

Job stress

Organizational frustration

Adjustive reactions

Job ambiguity

Job conflict

Work overload

Resource inadequacy

Work underload

Insecurity

Nonparticipation

Type A personality

Type B personality

Confronting the innermost self

Alcoholism

Alcoholic

Problem drinker

Heavy drinker

Stimulants

Depressants

Narcotics

Hallucinogens

CASE INCIDENT

Jack Femmerman, as you remember from Chapter 3, is the president of a medium-sized insurance company with over 4,000 employees. In the Chapter 3 case incident he was thinking about redesigning secretarial jobs so as to upgrade skill variety, autonomy, closure, and performance feedback for the secretaries. In the ensuing months, an experiment was conducted with the secretarial jobs in one division of the company. The purpose was to offer workers greater job responsibility and authority, more opportunities for growth and development, and a greater diversity of job experiences. Scores on the *Job Characteristics Questionnaire* improved favorably about three points per question.

The president is now concerned with improving the quality-of-life experienced by the plethora of middle managers. The consultant hired by Jack Femmerman for the job redesign program has, with the help of a clinical psychologist, interviewed 40 middle managers during a three week period. They found a high incidence of adjustive reactions to frustration such as compensation, conversion, projection, and repression. The middle managers were also asked to complete a job stress questionnaire which is shown below along with their scores (1 means very true while 7 means very false).

The Job Stress Questionnaire

	AVERAGE SCORES
On Job Ambiguity	
1. I feel certain about how much authority I have.	6
2. I receive clear, planned goals and objectives.	5
3. I know what my responsibilities are.	7
4. I receive a clear explanation of what has to be done in my work.	5
On Job Conflict	
5. I have to do things that should be done differently.	2
6. I receive an assignment without the manpower to complete it.	4
7. I receive incompatible requests from two or more people.	1
8. I have to buck a rule or policy in order to carry out an assignment.	3

All three people, Jack and the two outside experts, view these average scores as reflecting a very poor work environment. All areas of job ambiguity and conflict need to be improved.

Along with the questionnaire on job stress, the psychologist learned many things about how the company operated. Since the chain of command was not clear, some workers were reporting to two rather than one supervisor. The organization was autocratic with little opportunity for participation among the middle and lower level managers. These managers, in their interviews with the psychologist, reported that many jurisdictional disputes were precipitated by the absence of realistic job descriptions. There were job descriptions but they were outdated. Being an autocratic organization, the level of team building, friendliness, and attention paid to subordinate managers was minimal. Lip service was given to employee training and development. Employees could be reimbursed for job-related college courses only if they strongly argued their case and completed several long bureaucratic forms.

Questions for Discussion

1. Outline a program on how to reduce the high level of job ambiguity in this company. Think about the factors which need to be studied.
2. Outline a program to reduce the high level of job conflict in this company. As with question 1, think about the issues or topics which need to be examined.

PART FOUR

UNDERSTANDING MOTIVATED BEHAVIOR

Every manager would like to have a group of highly motivated subordinates. However, not all managers would define motivated behavior in the same way. Some would see motivated behavior as a drive to satisfy needs. Others might perceive it as a response to rewards. Of course, the way in which any supervisor interprets motivated behavior will in large degree determine how that manager elects to stimulate greater motivation.

This problem as well as others stemming from the topic of motivation will be addressed in the next three chapters. The motivation of people in the work environment is probably one of the more popular subjects of seminars, workshops, and books, but yet it remains as one of the least understood. Too often a simplistic approach is adopted that relies upon the needs concept or the old carrot and stick methods. The following chapters will demonstrate the highly complex nature of motivated behavior by offering several definitions and schools of thought and examining some of the more popular theories. As in the preceding chapters, there will be an effort to focus upon reality when dealing with the myths and controversies of motivation. The reader should make note of how the elements of the work environment covered thus far in the book affect motivated behavior and how an individual's philosophy of management helps shape an approach to the understanding and development of motivated behavior.

7

Human Needs
and Motivation

LEARNING OBJECTIVES

Upon completion of this chapter, the student should be able to:

- Explain the influences of a philosophy of management on motivational techniques.
- Demonstrate why the term motivation should be considered as a process governing choices made by people.
- Describe why employee choices on such actions as attendance, performance, self-training, and creativity should be considered as being motivated.
- Identify and critique several human needs considered important in motivation.
- Understand what it means to become self-actualized.
- Explain the importance of several motives such as competence, power, achievement, and affiliation, as well as the significance of work for top level managers.
- Explain why a manager can demonstrate power and concern for people at the same time.
- Identify jobs which do not motivate and ways to upgrade a job's motivational impact.

Managers are typically told that part of their job is the motivation of subordinates. Thus some managers attempt to "motivate" their people by providing incentives, by giving various kinds of rewards, by creating competitive situations, and by making threats. But many management theorists and practitioners claim that such activities do not motivate employees. In fact these approaches are really nothing more than sophisticated carrot-and-stick methods of getting people to work. Manipulating people by offering bribes is hardly motivational in nature. At issue is the question, is it possible to motivate others?

From a technical perspective the answer is "no," it is not possible for one person to motivate another. As will be explained later in the chapter, motivation comes from within an individual. There is a certain force within each of us that is described as drive or motivation, which would be most difficult to transfer to someone else. However, it is within the manager's capabilities to control and manage the work environment and the conditions of employment in such a way as to allow people to become motivated. Therefore, the terms which refer to motivating others in one way or another are actually misnomers, but such phrases have become part of the management jargon simply because they are easier to say than "we are going to create an organizational climate within which workers can become motivated." Technically, what is commonly referred to as motivation is actually a crude attempt at behavior modification or changing behavior through the use of positive reinforcement and punishment—the topic of the next chapter.

Everyone will respond to external stimuli or reinforcers in different ways. Managers must find what turns people on and causes them to want to work and to become more goal oriented. In this chapter we will present various approaches to how managers can work to enhance the goal-directed or choice dimensions of employee behavior that is referred to as motivated behavior. We will begin by examining what motivation is and what is meant by motivated behavior.

MOTIVATION DEFINED

The concept of motivation has only recently been studied as a unique or distinct psychological process. It has been difficult to separate behavior referred to as motivated from that associated with the emotional, perceptual, learning and thinking processes. However, English and American educational psychologists in the 1880s began to write about voluntary action and propensity to act. Sully in 1884 discussed a "moving force, stimulus, or motive which precedes a behavior or an act."[1] A slightly expanded definition was offered by M. R. Jones (known as the Father of Modern Psychology) who maintained that motivation is concerned with "how behavior gets started, is energized, is sustained, is directed, is stopped, and what kind of subjective reaction is present in the organism while all this is going on."[2]

Industrial psychologists have been somewhat more definitive. One well-known industrial psychologist defines motivation as "a process governing choices, made by persons or lower organisms, among alternative forms of voluntary activity."[3] Another definition suggests that an individual's motivation has to do with

1. The direction of a person's behavior, or what one chooses to do when presented with a number of possible alternatives
2. The amplitude, or strength, of the response (i.e., effort) once the choice is made
3. The persistence of the behavior, or how long the person continues with it.[4]

Although psychologists may attach different meanings to the term motivation, there is less disagreement about the term motive. A widely accepted explanation of the term defines motive as an internal factor that:

arouses, directs, and integrates a person's behavior. It is not observed directly but inferred from his behavior or simply assumed to exist in order to explain his behavior. Motivation is distinguished from all other factors that also influence behavior, such as the past experience of the person, his physical capabilities, and the environmental situation in which he finds himself, although these other factors may influence his motivation.[5]

Motives, such as the need for power, achievement, and affiliation, will be discussed later in this chapter. For now it should be recognized that a motive is a single factor that gets a person started in the motivational process. The term motivation is much larger in meaning and refers, again, to how a person's behavior "is started, is sustained, is directed, and is stopped."

EMPLOYEE CHOICES ARE MOTIVATED

Many of the definitions of motivated behavior contain phrases like "workers make choices" or "individuals take voluntary action." At the outset, it is perhaps clearer to talk in terms of the choices people make about the work situation (or choice behavior) rather than to talk about motivated worker behavior. We will learn that the choices made by people in the work environment are motivated. The level of job performance is only one of many concerns of managers who must seek to enhance employee motivation.

Choice behaviors subsume many activities of individuals regarding their relationship with work. In industry, employee choice behaviors refer to decisions directed toward the following:

1. Occupational preference
2. Occupational choice
3. Organizational choice
4. Job attendance
5. Job performance
6. Self-training
7. Creativity
8. Spontaneity
9. Job termination

When employees consider any one of the nine areas, they may choose among several alternative courses of action. Each course of action is associated with both costs and benefits. Generally, people will choose the alternative that (1) is perceived to be reasonably attainable, and (2) is perceived to be linked to the most satisfying rewards. For example, a person may have two occupational preferences, becoming a physician or an accountant. Although being a physician is the most preferred occupation to this person, the person's subjective feeling is that the discipline required for the long preparation period to be a physician is too demanding. Therefore, the person chooses to be an accountant—the occupational choice.

When a person wakes up in the morning, the individual has a choice to make regarding job attendance. The person can be on time, be late, or not even show up at all. The individual will compare the costs and benefits for each behavior. The decision to be at work on time is a choice behavior, therefore, it is motivated behavior. The decision to be creative at work is a choice to be made by some workers. Being creative when possible is motivated behavior. The decision to expend a little extra effort for self-training is a decision many workers confront frequently. The decision to improve abilities through self-training is motivated behavior. Each decision or choice can be examined using this abbreviated version of the expectancy theory which will be fully discussed later in the chapter.

THE HIERARCHY OF NEEDS AND MOTIVATION

Unfulfilled Needs as Motivating Factors

Many students are familiar with the popular hierarchy of needs theory of Abraham Maslow which was briefly discussed in Chapter 1. The theory says that human behavior is influenced by a set of needs,[6] and that an unsatisfied need motivates while a satisfied need does not. The needs are arranged in a hierarchy of "prepotency," meaning as a person fulfills a lower need the next higher need becomes important in directing the person's behavior. The hierarchy is shown below:

- Level 1—Physiological (food, air, water, sleep, sex)
- Level 2—Safety and security (both physiological and psychological, shelter, housing, economic security)
- Level 3—Belonging and social (friendships, group memberships)
- Level 4—Esteem and status (self-respect, recognition, achievement, dignity, accomplishment)
- Level 5—Self-realization or -actualization ("becoming all that one can")

Although the hierarchy of needs theory is well known to managers and is one of the most popular theories in business textbooks, caution should be exercised in attempting to understand and predict the motivations of employees with the hierarchy concept. The popularity of the need hierarchy can be attributed to the apparent ease of understanding the model as well as to its simple and logical appearance. However, Maslow developed the hierarchy from his clinical work with neurotics. Maslow has written:

My work on motivations came from the clinic, from a study of neurotic people. The carry-over of this theory to the industrial situation has some support from industrial studies, but certainly I would like to see a lot more studies of this kind before feeling finally convinced that this carry-over from the study of neurosis to the study of labor in factories is legitimate.[7]

Several studies of the type Maslow refers to above have been completed and they generally do not support the hierarchy of needs theory. One report found no support for the theory while finding data contradicting Maslow's dictum "a satisfied need is not a motivator."[8] The report found in studying 49 managers at A.T. & T. that there was a tendency for need satisfaction to be positively correlated with need importance. This means, as a person satisfies a need, the need becomes more intense or activated. For example, as a person begins to satisfy the social need, the social need does not become less important but more important.

Another study involving 187 managers from two different organizations found very little support for the theory that needs exist in a multi-level hierarchy and proposed a simple two-level hierarchy consisting of the physiological needs on one level and all other needs in no particular order on the other.[9]

The most recent test of the hierarchy did find support for the existence of the need categories. A research team developed a new questionnaire and administered it to 602 accountants and 290 engineers.[10] They discovered that these people did have the following categories of needs: safety, social, esteem, autonomy (need for independence), and self-actualization. This study did not investigate the relationship among need categories but simply and thoroughly examined the very important question, "Do specific need categories even exist in people or is there an absence of need patterns?"

In summary, the Maslow hierarchy, as well as the others, is of minimal value in understanding and predicting employee work behaviors. The hierarchy concepts fail to address the fundamental questions and issues in motivation theory regarding the direction of behavior, the amplitude of responses and the persistence of the behavior. At best, need theories suggest that people have various needs and in some way seek to fulfill these needs. Need hierarchies have been used to explain and to understand motivated behaviors ex post facto. This type of application is not of great value to practicing managers who need to predict employee behavior in order to direct human effort effectively.

Again, one should be reminded of the original intent of Maslow's research. The desire of behaviorists to find a foundation for motivational theory that could be applied in the work environment led to some abuses and generalization of Maslow's theory. For instance, the belief that self-actualization is an end state of "becoming all that one is capable of becoming" is misleading. The following note on self-actualization explains what Maslow meant when he referred to the highest order of needs.

A Note on How to Self-Actualize

The term self-actualization has become a "buzz" word in the management literature. Yet neither its meaning or the process of self-actualization has been well understood. This is particularly true in regards to the application of the self-actualization idea to the work situation. Since Abraham Maslow feels that being self-actualized represents the highest level of human development, it seems important to briefly quote Maslow on the "how" behind this important human process:

First, self-actualization means experiencing fully, vividly, selflessly, with full concentration and total absorption. . . .

Second, let us think of life as a process of choices, one after another. . . . To make the growth choice instead of the fear choice a dozen times a day is to move a dozen times a day toward self-actualization.

Third, self-actualization involves letting the self emerge. Most of us . . . listen not to ourselves but to . . . the voice of the Establishment, of the Elders, of authority, or of tradition.

Fourth, when in doubt, be honest rather than not. . . .

Fifth, self-actualization is not only an end state, but also the process of actualizing one's potentialities at any time, in any amount. . . .

Sixth, seeking peak experiences which are transient moments of self-actualization. . . .

Seventh, involves identifying defenses, and after defenses have been identified, it means finding the courage to give them up. . . .[11]

SELF-ESTEEM MOTIVATION

While Maslow's hierarchy is of minimal value in predicting behavior, the needs concept is of value to managers in terms of recognizing behavior patterns. This is especially true when employees are not given the opportunity to experience any self-esteem.

For example, under conditions of managerial disrespect and domination, subordinates will try to regain a sense of self-respect. The need for self-respect is a strong motivator in most people. A dictatorial, autocratic manager, according to Maslow, "outrages the dignity of the worker. He fights back in order to restore his dignity and self-esteem, actively with hostility and vandalism and the like, or passively as a slave does, with all sorts of underhanded, sly and secretly vicious countermeasures."[12]

If interviews were to be obtained from people working under domineering Theory X managers about what they dislike, they would list such things as:

- Being manipulated
- Being pushed around
- Fear of reprisals
- Threats
- Unappreciated
- Not respected

- Laughed at
- Given orders
- Controlled
- Not taken seriously[13]

Most of us have felt in these ways at one time or another. Also, at some times in our work experiences we have met managers who try to take positive steps to insure people have dignity and self-esteem. Such managerial techniques as participation, job enrichment, management by objectives, and democratic supervision are steps in the right direction for building employee self-esteem.

How can managers treat subordinates so that they will have high self-esteem? People psychologically need the following experiences to have high self-esteem:

- To have control over one's own fate
- To determine one's movements
- To expect success
- To be active rather than passive
- To be a person rather than a thing
- To be self-starting
- To have others acknowledge one's capabilities fairly[14]

THE COMPETENCE MOTIVE

Closely aligned with the self-esteem need is the need to be competent. One responsibility of any manager or supervisor is to insure that the work environment assists rather than hinders people in doing what they were hired to do. A feeling of competence gives workers a sense of efficacy or, more simply, a feeling of self-confidence. This mastery of job responsibilities has been discovered to be an important factor affecting the level of both work and life satisfaction.

A psychologist has offered a convincing argument that the striving to be competent or effective in dealing with the environment is a significant, innate (or inborn) motivating force.[15] Individuals will strive to become effective in interacting with the environment for no obvious reason other than to master or control it. As the writer has said:

The instinct to master has an aim—to exercise and develop the ego functions—and it follows hedonic principles by yielding "primary pleasure" when efficient action enables the individual to control and alter his environment.[16]

The motivational implication for practicing managers, therefore, is to organize and utilize people in such a way that workers can apply all their abilities and skills to their job. In other words, a manager must structure or design a work situation so that workers can use their valued abilities, skills, and knowledge in becoming competent in the job they were hired to do, without having to dilute their resources with time-consuming, meaningless interruptions, interferences, and conflicts. Blocking a worker's performance is the second most important cause of job stress. Not knowing what a job entails (lack of clarity) is the first most important source of job stress.

Related to the idea of job structure is Henri Fayol's idea of order. (Fayol is called the Father of Management.) This principle directs managers to "have a place for everything and everything in its place."[17] Each person in an organization should have a position and should operate from only that position; similarly, all support materials should be in a certain place. In this way, the expenditure of effort can be fully directed toward being competent. A manager using the concept of competence and the concept of order to insure that subordinates are effective would do the following:

1. Place the right person in the right job.
2. Make sure the person clearly understands the job responsibilities, work methods, and procedures. This will increase job clarity.
3. Remove or minimize meaningless activities so that the person may allocate all energies toward becoming task competent. This will reduce the many sources of job conflict.
4. Provide for increased job responsibilities as the person demonstrates mastery over the present job. This will insure that the employee experiences growth.

When managers do these things, they are creating a positive work climate. Their philosophies of management are being activated in a manner that provides an organizational climate in which employees are more likely to exhibit motivated behavior.

THE CLIMATE FOR MOTIVATION: THE "BIG PICTURE"

In Chapter 5, the topic of organizational climate was discussed. We said that climate refers to an organization's personality. Organizations, being entities in their own right, have personalities ranging from being very suppressive and autocratic on one hand, to being very encouraging, supportive, and democratic on the other. Climates are greatly influenced by the thoughts and actions of the people at the very top. Managers have certain assumptions about how people relate to work and subsequently develop policies and practices from these assumptions. The managers' assumptions about people and the resulting policies and practices which organize and direct employees are referred to as a "philosophy of management." It is called the "big picture" of motivation because the philosophy of management used by the very top executives will have a great impact on the one-on-one, superior-subordinate motivational techniques tried in the lower levels of organizations.

As an example of managerial philosophies, let us use a classroom situation: Would a mathematics teacher organize, lead, and influence the motivation of students in the fifth grade and in the eleventh grade in the same way? Probably not. The teacher would make different assumptions about such characteristics as willingness to learn, ability, knowledge of mathematical concepts, and discipline between the two groups of students. These assumptions lead to a set of different behaviors in the processes of organizing, "motivating," and leading. These assumptions and behaviors reflect the teacher's philosophy of managing a classroom.

The climate serves to set boundaries and constraints containing the possible range of behavior which can be reasonably demonstrated by people within the organization. We will learn that a particular style of influencing worker motivation, which is effective in certain organizational climates, would be inappropriate in other organizational climates.

Table 7.1 shows three philosophies of management along with some typical policies associated with each. The first philosophy draws from the traditional Theory X model[18] (introduced in Chapter 1), where managers' behaviors are based upon these assumptions about their subordinates:

1. They dislike work
2. They care more about pay than the work they do
3. They are not creative or self-directed

These assumptions about subordinates pave the way for actual managerial behavior in terms of policies and procedures. When a manager believes in the assumptions of the traditional model, the manager can be expected to develop policies that are based upon the following:

1. The major management job is to closely supervise subordinates.
2. The manager must break whole jobs down into simple, short-cycle, repetitive tasks.
3. The manager must detail easy-to-follow work procedures, since employees dislike work and are not very bright in the first place.

TABLE 7.1   Three Philosophies of Management

TRADITIONAL MODEL	HUMAN RELATIONS MODEL	HUMAN RESOURCES MODEL
Assumptions 1. Work is inherently distasteful to most people. 2. What workers do is less important than what they earn for doing it 3. Few want or can handle work which requires creativity, self-direction, or self-control	*Assumptions* 1. People want to feel useful and important 2. People desire to belong and to be recognized as individuals 3. These needs are more important than money in motivating people to work.	*Assumptions* 1. Work is not inherently distasteful. People want to contribute to meaningful goals which they have helped establish 2. Most people can exercise far more creative, responsible self-direction and self-control than their present jobs demand
Policies 1. The manager's basic task is to closely supervise and control his subordinates 2. He must break tasks down into simple, repetitive, easily learned operations 3. He must establish detailed work routines and procedures and enforce these firmly but fairly	*Policies* 1. The manager's basic task is to make each worker feel useful and important 2. He should keep his subordinates informed and listen to their objections to his plans 3. The manager should allow his subordinates to exercise some self-direction and self-control on routine matters	*Policies* 1. The manager's basic task is to make use of his "untapped" human resources 2. He must create an environment in which all members may contribute to the limits of their ability 3. He must encourage full participation on important matters, continually broadening subordinate self-direction and control
Expectations 1. People can tolerate work if the pay is decent and the boss is fair 2. If tasks are simple enough and people are closely controlled they will produce up to standard	*Expectations* 1. Sharing information with subordinates and involving them in routine decisions will satisfy their basic needs to belong and to feel important 2. Satisfying these needs will improve morale and reduce resistance to formal authority; subordinates will "willingly cooperate"	*Expectations* 1. Expanding subordinate influence, self-direction, and self-control will lead to direct improvements in operating efficiency 2. Work satisfaction may improve as a "by-product" of subordinates making full use of their resources

Source: Raymond E. Miles, Theories of Management, Implications For Organizational Behavior and Development, *McGraw-Hill, New York, 1975, p. 35. Copyright © 1975 McGraw-Hill Book Company. Used with permission of McGraw-Hill Book Company.*

After these types of policies are developed for the subordinates, the manager will be able to expect certain forms of behavior from the employees. For example, a manager can expect people to "produce up to standard" when jobs are designed to be simple, repetitive, and programmed. Since people are assumed to dislike work and to be nonself-directed in the traditional model, managers can be expected to attempt to influence subordinates with coercion, fear, and the threat of punishment.

The second philosophy of management is called the human relations model. This model, like the traditional model, has the managers remaining in control of subordinates in their dealings. The needs of the organization are still tantamount to the needs of people. But, unlike the traditional model, the human relations model suggests that managers attempt to fulfill a variety of other needs of subordinates in addition to their monetary needs. The assumptions in the human relations model in Table 7.1 lead a manager to create these types of policies:

1. The manager should try to make each worker feel important
2. The manager should keep people informed
3. The manager should allow some worker participation, at least on routine matters

The human relations model suggests that managers attempt to improve subordinates' motivations through participative practices of a limited nature. This philosophy acknowledges that workers want to be recognized and appreciated in the minds of their superiors.

The third philosophy of management is called the human resources model. This philosophy places strong emphasis on the needs of people rather than just on the needs of the organization. Unlike the human relations model, this model draws on the "self-actualization" view of human nature which says that one goal of living is to "become all that one can become." Since it is assumed that people like to work and like to be creative, self-directing, and self-motivating, a manager is likely to establish these types of policies:

1. The manager's major task is to use people's untapped resources
2. The manager should create and nurture an encouraging and supportive work environment
3. The manager must encourage full participation so as to develop subordinates' abilities to be self-managing.

Some readers may not at first see a difference between the human relations and the human resources models. At the very least there is an attitudinal difference.[19] In the human relations model, the bottom-line reasons why managers employ democratic practices such as employee participation are to increase job satisfaction and to decrease resistance to formal authority. In the human resources model, managers employ participative practices not to increase worker commitment to higher authority, but rather to heighten their subordinates' sense of competence as well as their productivity. The philosophies and purposes of the two models are somewhat different. The human relations model emphasizes the satisfaction of basic needs and the reduction of resistance to authority, while the human resources model emphasizes an approach which appeals to the higher level needs of the individual and allows more self-direction and self-control in the performance of the job. Thus the human resources model is more compatible with the creation of a climate that permits the individual to satisfy higher level needs while performing the job.

Once the top level managers have selected and demonstrated their philosophy of management through the policies they create, the subordinate managers will do several things. First, the subordinate managers will try to confirm which management philosophy is being used by observing the managerial processes. Table 7.2 shows the influences of each managerial philosophy on the managerial processes of leadership, motivation, decision making, goal setting, communication, and controlling.

Secondly, after the subordinate managers ascertain their supervisors' philosophies of management and subsequently confirm this philosophy, they will try, in most cases, to model the way they carry out management processes after that of their superiors. In other words, the lower level managers will tend to copy the style of their superiors. They do this for several reasons:

1. They might assume the superior's behavior is correct
2. They think it is safer emulating their superior's style
3. Since superiors usually control the reward system, it is better—in the thinking of subordinates—to look and act like "one of the boys."

When a manager believes in the traditional philosophy, the manager will behave in the following ways:

1. Will not show much confidence in subordinates
2. Will use fear and threats of punishment to try to instill motivation
3. Will make most of the decisions singly rather than participatively
4. Will set goals for subordinates
5. Will not develop lines for upward communication
6. Will audit subordinates' performances rather than having subordinates correct their own performance

TABLE 7.2   The Influence of Management Philosophies on Management Processes

	TRADITIONAL MODEL	HUMAN RELATIONS MODEL	HUMAN RESOURCES MODEL
Nature of Leadership			
a. How much confidence and trust is shown in subordinates?	Virtually none	Some	A great deal
Nature of Motivation			
a. Where is responsibility for achieving firm's goals?	Mostly at top	Top and middle	At all levels
Character of Decision Making			
a. At what levels are decisions made?	Mostly at top	Policy at top, some delegation	Throughout, but well integrated
Nature of Goals			
a. How are organizational goals established?	Orders issued	Orders, some comments invited	By group action
Nature of Communication			
a. What is the usual direction of information flow?	Downward	Mostly downward	Down, up and sideways
Nature of Control			
a. How concentrated are review and control functions?	Very highly at top	Quite highly at top	Widely shared

Source: Modified and adapted from Rensis Likert, The Human Organization *(New York: McGraw-Hill, 1967), Table 3–1. Copyright © 1967 McGraw-Hill Book Co. Used with permission of McGraw-Hill Book Company.*

When a manager subscribes to the human relations philosophy, we can expect to see these behaviors:

1. Some trust in subordinates
2. Delegation to some extent when the problem is of a routine nature
3. Communication mainly through orders
4. The main source of control is with the manager with some subordinate self-control on routine matters

While the actual behavior of managers toward subordinates under the human relations model is generally better than under the traditional model, there is an even greater employee orientation with the human resources philosophy. A manager can be expected to:

1. Show a great deal of trust in subordinates
2. Encourage subordinates' motivation through giving them a great deal of involvement in their work decisions
3. Allow subordinates a great deal of decision-making and goal-setting activity
4. Share the task of correcting substandard performance with their subordinates

The particular philosophy of a manager or a management team will thus determine how the organization will attempt to encourage motivated behavior. A traditional approach would usually rely on extrinsic factors in an attempt to reinforce acceptable behavior. People embracing either the human relations or human resources philosophy would probably seek to utilize intrinsic means of motivation to bring about job satisfaction.

FACTORS WITHIN THE JOB AND MOTIVATION

The Two-Factor Theory

The so-called two-factor theory or the motivation-hygiene theory developed by Frederick Herzberg and his associates[20] in the late 1950s has attracted considerable attention and has also been subjected to a great deal of critical research. Herzberg et al. were interested in isolating the factors that tended to contribute to job satisfaction and job dissatisfaction and to different levels of task performance.

According to the two-factor theory, the primary determinants of job satisfaction are within the job and are called the intrinsic, content, or motivating factors. These factors include achievement, recognition, the work itself, responsibility, and advancement.[21] The primary determinants of job dissatisfaction are outside of the job itself and are called the hygiene, context, or dissatisfaction factors. The hygiene factors are company policy and administration, supervision, salary, interpersonal relations with co-workers and working conditions.[22] According to the theory, the hygiene factors can usually only dissatisfy if they are not present in sufficient amounts. At best, they can bring an individual to a neutral point (no job dissatisfaction) where the motivating factors can provide job satisfaction and increased motivation.

A critical-incident type of interview (story telling) was used to gather comments from 203 engineers and accountants on which factors made them feel exceptionally good or exceptionally bad about their jobs. Herzberg found that the hygiene factors tended to be recalled by the participants as contributing to bad or dissatisfying jobs while the motivating factors contributed to good or satisfying jobs. In analyzing the original Herzberg data, an opponent of the theory found the research methodology to be biased toward the results obtained:

. . . good critical incidents were dominated by reference to intrinsic aspects of the job (motivators), while bad critical incidents were dominated by reference to extrinsic factors (hygienes), . . . this tendency was quite marked; in the reports of good critical incidents, motivators were alluded to almost four times as frequently as hygienes (78 percent vs. 22 percent), whereas in bad critical incidents, hygienes were mentioned about twice as frequently as motivators (64 percent vs. 36 percent).[23]

Although the participants reported that satisfaction with the motivators leads to increased job performance, there is only very weak evidence that the motivators affect performance in the manner described by Herzberg. Another opponent of the two-factor theory feels there is much more data on the determinants of satisfaction than on performance:

Unfortunately, Herzberg et al. did not develop any theoretical concepts to explain why job factors should affect performance. . . . Thus, in the strictest sense of the term, it is not a theory of motivation at all; rather it is a theory primarily concerned with explaining the determinants of job satisfaction and dissatisfaction.[24]

After approximately ten years of research and experience with the theory, R. J. House and L. A. Wigdor summarized the findings of several research efforts.

1. A given job factor can cause job satisfaction for one person and job dissatisfaction for another. Some factors partially determining

whether a given factor will be a source of satisfaction or dissatisfaction include: job level, age, sex, formal education, and culture.

2. A given factor can cause job satisfaction and dissatisfaction in the same sample of workers.

3. Intrinsic or motivator factors are more important to both satisfying and dissatisfying job events.

4. The Herzberg theory is an oversimplification of the relationships between motivation and satisfaction, and the sources of job satisfaction and dissatisfaction.[25]

They also pointed out several sources of error contained in Herzberg's methodology and theory development. First, the critical-incident interviewing technique may elicit the use of defense mechanisms on the part of the participants. For example, when the job is satisfying, people will normally take the credit to enhance their feelings of self-esteem and blame others or factors outside of their control when dissatisfied. Second, the objectivity of the coding procedures is suspect when the intended responses by the participants require interpretation by the researcher. The objectivity could have been improved through having the respondents do the necessary rating and evaluating.

Perhaps one of the more stinging negative summaries of the two-factor theory was offered by another team of researchers:

> It seems that the evidence is now sufficient to lay the two-factor theory to rest, and we hope it may be buried peaceably. We believe that it is important that it be done so that researchers will address themselves to studying the full complexity of human motivation, rather than continuing to allow the direction of motivational research or actual administrative decisions to be dictated by the seductive simplicity of the two-factor theory.[26]

Although many well-known researchers now consider the two-factor theory suspect, one must give credit to the theory for stimulating new and ambitious attitudinal investigations. Additionally, as we will see in the next chapter, Herzberg's idea on the motivational potential associated with job designs may be correct but for the wrong reasons.

Activation Theory

Why do we frequently observe employees at all organizational levels engaging in the following activities or behaviors?

1. Restlessness

2. Changing posture

3. Taking unauthorized breaks

4. Stretching

5. Daydreaming

6. Engaging in horseplay

7. Feeling irritable

8. Performing poorly and having poor attitudes

As suggested earlier in the chapter many experts believe that the job itself is the strongest motivating factor for most people. Unfortunately, over a period of time the job may fail to stimulate the employee sufficiently to maintain a comfortable level of arousal, attention, or alertness. The brain stimulation level provided by the job may become so low that an employee not only experiences boredom but also lacks muscular coordination and experiences a decrease in hearing and sight. These consequences of tedious work may contribute to poor task performance and poor work attitudes as depicted in Figure 7.1. The opposite situation may occur when a worker is in the very early stages of training. In such instances the job stimulation level may be too high causing the worker to experience anxiety, loss of muscular coordination, and general confusion.[27]

Activation theory is a neuropsychological approach to understanding long-term employee behavior toward routine work. Activation theory

. . . anticipates any number of behavioral outcomes in tasks which require the constant repetition of a limited number of responses to stimulation which is

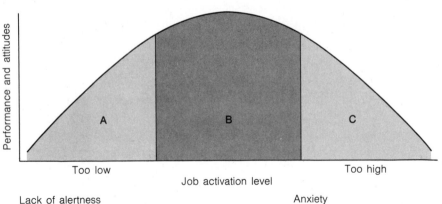

Figure 7.1 Expected Consequences of Low and High Job Activation Levels. Area A, job stimulation too low, job enrichment needed; Area B, job stimulation compatible with worker; Area C, job too high in stimulation, job redesign needed.

configuratively simple and temporally unvarying. . . . As the individual becomes familiar with surroundings and learns the responses required in the repetitive task, a decline in activation level is expected.[28]

It is important to realize that all work tends to become routine or repetitive after the job has been learned and practiced over a period of time. Some jobs become routine sooner than others because of the limited variety and the absence of difficulty of the tasks performed. Repetitive jobs are not inherently boring and monotonous. Boredom is a perceived phenomenon rooted in the individual's interest and perception of job characteristics. This means that the same job may be stimulating to one person while boring to another.

Each individual desires a particular level of stimulation where that person can function best; this level is called the characteristic activation norm. Some workers function best under complex and stressful situations while others function best under more structured and less stressful situations. When a job fails to provide adequate brain stimulation, a worker seeks ways to increase stimulation to the level of the characteristic norm.

Additional cortical stimulation resulting from thoughts of an anticipated hunting trip or the recall of a recent encounter with a sexual partner may offset a decline in activation level. The individual may increase . . . stimulation and thus sustain activation level by stretching, alternating position, or otherwise varying position at the task site. Leaving to visit the water fountain, another department, or the rest room not only increases . . . stimulation but results in greater stimulus variation.[29]

Other nonproductive behaviors such as social conversations, complex group relationships, gambling, and horseplay also introduce variation that serves to reduce the degree of monotony in the work environment.

If patterns of nonproductive activity are observed, managers should consider enriching jobs through job redesign—the topic covered in Chapter 3. But it should be pointed out that even enriched jobs may become boring after they have been learned and practiced over a period of time. Perceptive managers continually think in terms of job redesign since they know that the stimulation provided by a job will decrease with job experience.

REWARDS AND MOTIVATION

In the beginning of the chapter we mentioned that the term motivated behavior in industry subsumes several choices on the part of individuals. Once again, the choice behaviors to which we refer include:

1. Occupational preference
2. Occupational choice
3. Organizational choice
4. Job attendance
5. Job performance
6. Self-training
7. Creativity
8. Spontaneity
9. Job termination

For each of the above actions the employee will make a choice between alternatives. Alternatives for job attendance include arriving at work on time, being late, or being absent altogether. Alternatives for levels of job performance include performing substandard, standard, or above standard. Each employee develops alternatives—consciously or unconsciously—for each of the nine choice-decision areas.

Victor Vroom suggests that employee choice behaviors can be best understood through an expectancy theory where motivation is the product of expectancy, instrumentality, and valence.[30] In general terms, expectancy refers to a person's feelings of being able or not able to do something. For example, one reason students are in school is because they expect that they can perform satisfactorily if they study enough. Instrumentality refers to the relationship of an action and the result or outcome. Another reason students are in school is because they believe that a higher education will be instrumental in securing a good job. Valence refers to a person's feelings regarding the value and importance of the outcomes associated with one's efforts. Students also believe that obtaining a good job is an important goal to obtain.

Employees develop or think about alternatives for each of the nine choice areas. According to the expectancy theory people will select alternatives that are believed to be both attainable and highly rewarding. It should be remembered that the costs of attainment are balanced against the rewards linked with each alternative. Workers may choose to behave creatively on the job because they believe they can be creative if they want to be and valued and important rewards are linked with being creative. Likewise, people may select particular occupations because they believe that they can be successful in those occupations, and valued and important rewards are associated with being successful in the occupations.

It is essential to understand that the rewards may take many forms. Work itself, pay, promotion, supervisory style, co-worker interaction, and working conditions are common sources of rewards. One of management's more challenging tasks is to match workers with rewards they value.

THE COMPLETE MOTIVATIONAL MODEL

Many of the motivational ideas in this chapter have been integrated into a model developed by Lyman Porter and Edward Lawler.[31] As shown in Figure 7.2, performance is influenced by a person's effort and abilities. A person may exhibit a great amount of effort but perform very poorly if the individual does not have a satisfactory level of ability. Similarly, a person may have a great deal of ability but perform poorly if the individual does not try hard enough.

Intrinsic and extrinsic rewards are seen as consequences of perform-ance. The broken line means that there may not be a clear, direct relation-ship. That is, a person may perform well but be rewarded poorly. This situation is very common in industry since techniques of linking rewards to performance are not well developed with the exception of a few jobs such as that of a commissioned salesman. To briefly review, intrinsic rewards refer to positive feelings workers give themselves for performing well in the job itself. Feelings of mastery, competence, personal achieve-ment, dignity, and self-esteem are examples of intrinsic rewards. Extrinsic rewards come from the environment in which a job is performed. Pay, fringe benefits, and supervisory praise are some extrinsic rewards. One task of managers in using this as well as other models, is to find out which rewards are important to their subordinates. It makes no sense to reward a person highly for good performance with a reward of no value to the individual.

Satisfaction is a consequence of how equitable a person perceives the rewards given for performance. In Chapter 9, we will learn that work-ers compare what they receive from a job and what they put into their jobs with other people performing similar jobs. Satisfaction is felt when the

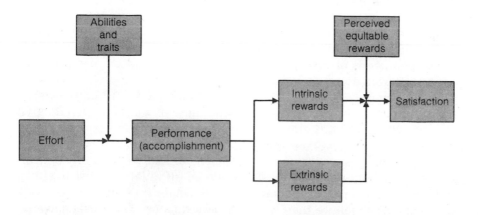

Figure 7.2 The New Motivational Model

Source: Modified and adapted from Lyman W. Porter and Edward E. Lawler, III, Managerial Attitudes and Performance *(Homewood, Ill.: Richard D. Irwin, Inc., 1968), p. 17.*

balance between effort expended and reward granted seems fair to the worker compared with the efforts and rewards of other workers in the same category.

The model in Figure 7.2 represents one work cycle. For example, picture a student writing a term paper. The student expends high effort and has adequate abilities and understands how to conduct a thorough library search. Performance on the term paper should be high. Imagine that the student receives a grade of C on the well-written and factually correct paper. Satisfaction with the reward (the grade of C) will probably be low. The resulting dissatisfaction will affect the value of reward and perceived effort-reward probability on the next work cycle (term paper). If the student believed that high effort was expended on the first assignment and associates the grade with working at maximum ability, it is questionable whether similar effort will be expended on the next paper. However, an argument can be advanced that the grade received may spur higher effort if the student believes that trying harder will lead to a valued higher grade.

As mentioned earlier, rewards come in many forms. Some workers value co-worker interaction as an important reward from work; others consider interaction with a supervisor as a more important reward. The guiding principles for properly rewarding workers to increase job effort are:

1. Tie valued and important rewards to performance.
2. Reward high performance better than low performance and make these rewards visible to all to see.

The first principle directs managers to reward workers with something of value to them. Some workers would rather have time-off or an extended vacation rather than a salary increase or bonus. Other workers perform effectively only to have favorable supervisory attention directed toward them. Still others work hard only to feel a sense of efficacy or competence from doing a good job.

A manager must not only reward workers with valued rewards but must insure that workers associate these rewards with effective task performance. The timing or schedule of rewards is important—the dictum of "rewarding workers immediately after they perform well" is supported by a wealth of psychological evidence. Industry commonly distributes year-end bonuses with the intention of stimulating worker effort. What seems to occur is that employees associate the bonus more with job attendance or tenure than with job performance. The closer rewards can be linked to performance, the more effect the rewards will have on task effort.

The second principle suggests that the ineffective workers acknowledge that the effective workers are being rewarded handsomely. Only in this way will the ineffective worker clearly realize that rewards are actually tied to performance in the organization. A common error in organizations involves the inequitable distribution of a blanket salary or "across the board" increase or bonus. For instance, in a secretarial pool of eight employees, three are high performers, three are average, and two are poor performers. A blanket salary increase (not a cost-of-living increase) is awarded to all eight secretaries. Equity theory would predict that the high performing secretaries will reduce both work quality and work quantity in order to attain equity and to reduce tension caused by feelings of underpayment. The task performance of the average and poor performers will be reinforced, resulting in continued poor performance because behavior which is reinforced tends to be repeated.

It is important, of course, to know what "motivators" people are most interested in. What is valued by a particular individual is dependent upon the motives that are directing that person's behavior. Everyone has some mixture of the motives identified in the chapter:

- The need to achieve
- The affiliation need
- The need for power

However, it appears that effective managers and leaders have motives that are somewhat unique.

MOTIVES AND MANAGERIAL BEHAVIOR

What is it that motivates managers to become successful in running a large organization? Among other things it is their need to have an impact, to be strong, and to influence the behavior of others for the organizational good. What separates good managers from poor managers is the "need for power" according to Dr. David McClelland, a recognized expert on the power motive.[32]

What they need is a special kind of power. It is not dictatorial, nor is it power for personal aggrandizement. It is not a crude kind of power, or power used impulsively. It can be referred to as altruistic power, meaning the power to influence people for the good of the organization for which they work. It also may be called socialized power, meaning power which is tempered by a large dose of self-control, and perspective.

When a large number of executives are grouped according to their success in running large, complex corporations, the profile of the effective manager looks like this:

The top managers of a company must possess a high need for power, that is, a concern for influencing people. However, this need must be disciplined and controlled so that it is directed toward the benefit of the institution as a whole and not toward the manager's personal aggrandizement. Moreover, the top manager's need for power ought to be greater than his need for being liked by people.[33]

A good manager is not primarily motivated by the need for affiliation. The affiliation need refers to the desire to be liked and accepted by other people. People with a strong affiliation need do not typically do well in management positions. To maintain a high morale and a productive environment, policies must be applied universally and consistently. A manager concerned with developing friendly relationships may make too many "exceptions to the rule" for certain subordinates, thereby upsetting subordinates not receiving special favors. A manager motivated by the affiliation need may create poor teamwork and low morale. This, of course, would be inadvertent, as such an individual would not purposefully do anything to upset the relationships in the work group. It would occur most likely because of the failure of the manager to focus on the task to be accomplished.

Likewise, the need for achievement is not extreme among effective managers. The need for achievement means a desire to do things better and to attain personal accomplishments. Good salesmen and successful entrepreneurs, for example, are high in the need to achieve. This is understandable since people high in this need try to do things better themselves and want constant feedback on their performance to see how well they are working. While good managers may be high in the need to achieve, it is usually not greatly out of balance when compared to the power and affiliation motives.

A manager with an unusually high need to achieve would probably be characterized by the inability to delegate authority. Managers are required to get things done with and through other people. They must delegate authority. The manager must get others to do things through influence or through persuasion. By definition, then, one aspect of a manager's job is to help others perform their jobs better, rather than trying to better perform the many short-term projects alone.

A mature, self-controlled need for power will help create a good manager who

helps subordinates feel strong and responsible, who rewards them properly for good performance, and who sees that things are organized in such a way that subordinates feel they know what they should be doing. Above all, managers should foster among others a strong sense of team spirit, of pride in working as part of a particular team. If a manager creates and encourages this spirit, his subordinate(s) certainly should perform better.[34]

In Chapter 11, the topic of leadership styles will be discussed. In that chapter, you will learn that the actions of managers can be measured along two dimensions—a concern for people and a concern for production or output. A strong power need combined with a weak need for affiliation does not conflict with being people-oriented or democratic toward subordinates. Power is a motive while being people-oriented is a behavior or an action. Motives are internal; behavior is external. In the words of David McClelland,

Management is an influence game. Some proponents of democratic management seem to have forgotten this fact, urging managers to be primarily concerned with people's human needs, rather than with helping them to get things done.[35]

Effective managers, in their efforts to influence subordinates to get work done, express their strong power needs in democratic, people-oriented ways. Research on power in organizations indicates that the managers who were strong in power needs were also rated strong on the people-oriented supervisory style by their own subordinates.

SUMMARY

Motivation is defined as "a process governing choices, made by persons or lower organisms, among alternative forms of voluntary activity." As such, motivation is concerned with (1) the direction of behavior, or what a person chooses to do when presented with a number of possible alternatives, (2) the amplitude, or strength, of the effect once the choice is made, and (3) the persistence of the behavior, or how long the person continues with it. Choice behavior refers to decisions directed toward occupational preference, choices, organizational choices, job attendance, self-training, creativity, spontaneity, and job termination.

Almost all workers are motivated to have a high level of self-esteem in the work situation. Often, when a person is not in a work situation providing high self-esteem, the person will be "fighting back"—actively or passively, like a slave—with all sorts of sly countermeasures. People do not want to be pushed around, misunderstood, unappreciated, mistreated, controlled, or laughed at. All these things cause low self-esteem. The individual does want to expect success, to be active, to be respected, to exercise self-control, and to be self-starting.

Factors within the job (intrinsic factors) are usually effective motivators and can help awaken the urge to accomplish and to be self-starting. Such factors include feelings of achievement, recognition, and responsibility among others. These feelings sometimes "surprise" workers and in so doing inspire and encourage high motivation. Jobs not providing for intrinsic motivation are low in "cultivation" or stimulation. Some form of job redesign is suggested for this type of job.

Whether or not management will spend the time and money redesigning jobs is in part dependent upon their overall managerial philosophy. Three philosophies of management were discussed along with their implications on motivational styles. The three philosophies include the traditional, human relations, and human resources models. Each of these philosophies influence the climate for motivation, which is caused in part by the thoughts and actions of the managers at the very top of organizations. These managers will have certain assumptions about how people relate to work and subsequently develop policies and practices from these assumptions. The "motivating climate" will have a strong impact upon the one-on-one motivational techniques tried in the lower levels of organizations.

The new motivational model includes many of the earlier theories of motivation examined in the chapter. The direction of influence in this model is as follows: effort → performance → reward → satisfaction. The factors of effort and level of ability influence performance. Rewards can be either intrinsic or extrinsic and should be closely linked to performance. Satisfaction with rewards is moderated by a person's perception of equity of rewards.

This chapter has suggested that high task performance results when (1) Employees are able to use their valued abilities and skills in becoming task competent; (2) Employees perceive valued and equitable rewards to be linked to task performance; and (3) Employees acknowledge a differential reward system based on performance within the organization.

Finally, it should be remembered that the power motive is important to effective managers. This need is not for dictatorial power or crude, impulsive power, but rather socialized power, and the power to influence people for the sake of the organization. While some balance of motives is usually present within most individuals, a high need for power seems to be critical to a person's ability to function as a manager.

NOTES

1. J. Sully, *Outlines of Psychology* (New York: D. Appleton and Co., 1884).

2. M. R. Jones, *Nebraska Symposium on Motivation* (Lincoln, Neb.: University of Nebraska Press, 1955), p. viii.

3. V. Vroom, *Work and Motivation* (New York: John Wiley and Sons, 1964), p. 30.

4. J. P. Campbell, M. D. Dunnette, E. E. Lawler, and K. E. Weick, *Managerial Behavior, Performance, and Effectiveness* (New York: McGraw-Hill, 1970), p. 340.

5. E. J. Murry, *Motivation and Emotion* (Englewood Cliffs, N.J.: Prentice-Hall, 1964), p. 7.

6. A. Maslow, *Motivation and Personality* (New York: Harper and Row, 1954), pp. 91–2.

7. A. Maslow, *Eupsychian Management* (Homewood, Ill.: Richard D. Irwin, 1965), p. 55.

8. D. T. Hall and K. Nougaim, "An Examination of Maslow's Need Hierarchy in an Organizational Setting," *Organizational Behavior and Human Performance* 3 (February 1968): 12–35.

9. E. E. Lawler III and J. Suttle, "A Causal Correlation Test of the Need-Hierarchy Concept," *Organizational Behavior and Human Performance* 7 (April 1972): 265–87.

10. Vance Mitchell and Pravin Moudgill, "Measurement of Maslow's Need Hierarchy," *Organizational Behavior and Human Performance* 16 (August 1976): 334–49.

11. Abraham H. Maslow, "Self-Actualization and Beyond," in *Challenges in Humanistic Psychology*, James Bugental, ed. (New York: McGraw-Hill, 1967), pp. 279–86.

12. Maslow, *Eupsychian Management*, pp. 44–5.

13. Ibid.

14. Ibid.

15. Robert W. White, "Motivation Reconsidered: The Concept of Competence," *Psychological Bulletin* 66 (September 1959): 297–333.

16. Ibid., p. 316.

17. Henri Fayol, *General and Industrial Management* (London: Sir Isaac Pitman and Sons, 1949), pp. 19–42, reprinted in Harwood Merrill, ed., *Classics in Management* (New York: AMA, 1960), pp. 217–41.

18. See Douglas McGregor, *The Human Side of Enterprise* (New York: McGraw-Hill, 1960).

19. For a more complete discussion, see Raymond Miles, *Theories of Organization Implications for Organizational Behavior and Development* (New York: McGraw-Hill, 1975), pp. 31–47.

20. F. Herzberg, B. Mausner, and B. B. Snyderman, *The Motivation to Work* (New York: John Wiley, 1959).

21. Ibid., p. 80.

22. Ibid.

23. N. King, "Clarification and Evaluation of the Two-Factor Theory of Job Satisfaction," *Psychological Bulletin* 74 (July 1970): 20.

24. E. E. Lawler III, *Pay and Organizational Effectiveness* (New York: McGraw-Hill, 1970), p. 98.

25. R. J. House and L. A. Wigdor, "Herzberg's Dual-Factor Theory of Job Satisfaction and Motivation: A Review of the Evidence and a Criticism," *Personnel Psychology* 20 (Winter 1967): 388.

26. M. D. DUNNETTE, J. P. CAMPBELL, and M. D. HAKEL, "Factors Contributing to Job Satisfaction and Dissatisfaction in Six Occupational Groups," *Organizational Behavior and Human Performance* 2 (May 1967): 173.

27. This discussion of activation theory was strongly influenced by an outstanding article by WILLIAM SCOTT, "Activation Theory and Job Design," *Organizational Behavior and Human Performance* 1 (August 1966): 3–30.

28. Ibid., p. 15.

29. Ibid.

30. VROOM, *Work and Motivation.*

31. LYMAN W. PORTER and EDWARD E. LAWLER, III, *Managerial Attitudes and Performance* (Homewood, Ill.: Richard D. Irwin, 1968).

32. Much of this section on the power, achievement, and affiliation motives was influenced by DAVID MCCLELLAND, "Power Is the Great Motivator," *Harvard Business Review* 54 (March–April 1976): 100–110.

33. Ibid., p. 101.

34. Ibid., p. 102.

35. Ibid., p. 105.

QUESTIONS FOR THOUGHT AND DISCUSSION

1. The chapter identified three philosophies of management which can influence a company's motivational climate. Think about a job you have had or presently occupy and identify your manager's philosophy as traditional, human relations, or human resources. Why did the manager use that philosophy? In what ways did the manager carry out the management processes?

2. Many choices made by employees are thought to be motivated. Select three of the nine choices identified in this chapter and explain why you would consider the choices motivated.

3. In what ways do you fulfill the social and esteem levels of needs at work or in school?

4. A section of this chapter dicussed "how to self-actualize." Think of and list one personal example for each of the seven steps of how you have self-actualized at work or in school.

5. Effective managers are said to be motivated by a strong power motive. This motive is expressed in behavior which is nondictatorial and nonimpulsive. Subordinates of a manager with a strong power motive report that the manager is people-oriented rather than output-oriented. Discuss how a manager can have a strong power motive and still be people-oriented.

KEY TERMS

The student should be able to discuss the significance of these terms to the study of human behavior in the work environment.

Motivational climate
Philosophy of management
Traditional model
Human relations model
Human resources model
Management processes
Motivation
Motive
Choice behavior
Hierarchy of needs
Self-actualization
Competence motive

Power motive
Affiliation need
Achievement need
Two-factor theory
Hygiene factors
Intrinsic factors
Activation theory
Expectancy theory
Expectancy
Instrumentality
Valence
Perceived equitable rewards

CASE INCIDENT

Jack Femmerman, the president of a mid-Atlantic insurance company employing more than 4,000 people, is concerned about the level of motivation demonstrated by his 180 upper and middle level managers. Like the secretaries and clerks who were discussed in earlier chapters, the managers are doing dependable work but unenthusiastically. Some managers have left the company in recent years. During their exit interviews with Jim Donway, Vice-President of Personnel, they mentioned a host of reasons for their departures. Notable among the issues mentioned were low opportunity for personal growth and development, average self-esteem, moderate feelings of accomplishment, and feelings of low authority.

The 180 managers are responsible for performing the traditional tasks usually done by managers. These tasks include training and developing workers, selecting and utilizing manpower, giving explicit or general directions, helping workers with job problems, providing feedback, establishing a work climate, securing support and services from outside the unit, making plans for the future, setting performance goals, coordinating work flow and so on.

An outside consultant was engaged to try to determine the motivational climate since the climate puts constraints on the types of motivational efforts that can be used. The consultant administered two survey questionnaires. These questionnaires were based upon the classifications of philosophies of management as shown in Tables 7.1 and 7.2 of this chapter. The results showed overwhelmingly that the management people in this company subscribe to the traditional philosophy of management. One hundred and thirty believe in the traditional assumptions about people; 36 believe in the human relations assumptions; and only 14 believe in the human resource assumptions.

To confirm if these philosophies of management were being applied to actual procedure, the consultant examined the processes by which managers did their jobs. The consultant found that the assumptions were carrying over to actual behavior and procedures. One hundred and twenty-five of the 130 managers subscribing to the traditional assumptions were, in fact, behaving toward subordinates in a fashion consistent with the traditional model. Forty top managers were actually behaving in a manner supportive of the human relations philosophies and 15 exhibited behavior based upon assumptions of the human resources model.

Questions for Discussion

1. Should these managers' behaviors be changed?

2. How can these top level managers be changed in terms of behavior so that they can come closer to behaving in a manner consistent with the human resources model? Should their beliefs (assumptions) be changed before trying to change their behavior?

3. Pick one of the motivational theories discussed in this chapter and detail a program whereby the managers would not only be more motivated themselves but would also be able to motivate their own subordinate managers.

8

Goal Setting and Reinforcement

LEARNING OBJECTIVES

Upon completion of this chapter, the student should be able to:

- Differentiate reinforcement ideas about motivation from the traditional motivation theories.
- Discuss the many different types of rewards other than money.
- Explain why reinforcement experts believe that human behavior is caused by a person's environment rather than being caused by the person's needs and interests.
- Distinguish between negative reinforcement and punishment.
- Discuss the four basic operations in reinforcement theory.
- Discuss the different schedules for giving positive reinforcement.

All people like to know they are doing a good job. By telling a subordinate that the worker did a good job a manager is providing reinforcement. This form of a compliment is known as reinforcement in that it causes the individual to want to repeat the performance or behavior that brought about the compliment or reward. Receiving a reward is satisfying; not receiving a reward or being punished is dissatisfying. People tend to repeat actions that are satisfying and not repeat actions that are dissatisfying. This seemingly simple and obvious idea is called the "Law of Effect" or the principle of reinforcement. It is the fundamental principle behind behavior modification.

Today organizational behavior modification (OB Mod) is being used as a process to make inappropriate worker behavior less likely to occur and to make appropriate worker behavior more likely to occur. A worker's behavior is usually interpreted as being appropriate when the person:

1. Arrives at work on time
2. Produces high quality work
3. Produces a high quantity of work
4. Works safely
5. Works creatively
6. Works compatibly with supervisors and co-workers

When these standards of on-the-job behavior are met, the worker is rewarded so that the good behavior will probably be repeated. The reward or reinforcement is directly dependent upon worker behavior. This contingency approach to reinforcement is essentially an "if-then" situation. "If" there is good performance, "then" there will be a good reward.

In this chapter some methods of externally modifying worker behavior will be discussed. "Externally" means that the explanation of the "why" of employee behavior is attributed to factors outside the individual rather than inside. External factors are in the form of organizational rewards and punishment. Organizational behavior modification relies upon this externally oriented reinforcement theory while traditional motivation theories assert that the causes of worker behavior reside within the person in the form of needs, desires, and motives. Behavior modification also differs from traditional motivational ideas covered in the last chapter in that more attention is paid to:

1. What the best reward is for a particular person
2. How often and under what circumstances rewards should be given to a worker.

This chapter presents the groundwork for the use of behavior modification in organizations.

REINFORCEMENT THEORY VERSUS
TRADITIONAL MOTIVATION THEORIES

In Chapter 7 we discussed Maslow's hierarchy of needs and Herzberg's two-factor theory. In what ways does reinforcement theory differ from these traditional motivation ideas? As shown in Figure 8.1 the traditional motivational theories place importance on a person's needs, motives, and personality as the causes of behavior. Reinforcement theory does not credit these internal states as influences on the way people behave. To reinforcement theorists, behavior is a function of its consequences or rewards. Mental activities such as thinking and evaluating are not important to reinforcement theorists. According to B. F. Skinner

The organism [the person] is irrelevant either as the site of physiological processes or as the locus of mentalistic activities. I don't believe the organism contributes anything to these overall relationships beyond the fact that it is the behavior of an organism we are studying. . . . The organism is simply mediating the relationship between the forces acting upon it and its own output.[1]

In Figure 8.1, the reinforcement model shows that rewards precede and follow worker behaviors. This illustrates the key role of rewards in OB Mod. Since behavior is a function of its consequence (the rewards or lack of rewards), managers seeking to influence employee behaviors need

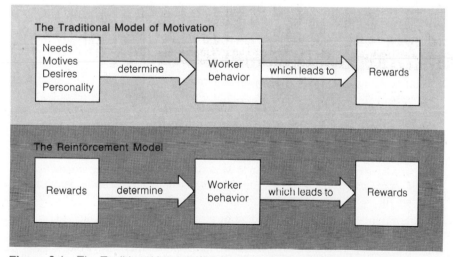

Figure 8.1   The Traditional Model of Motivation and the Reinforcement Model

only to evaluate whether a given reward is creating the desired behavior. As pointed out by the preceding quote, B. F. Skinner has suggested that the thinking activities of employees are not really important in motivating workers. To him, managers need only concern themselves with the behavior of their subordinates that is observable and measurable.

BEHAVIOR MODIFICATION TERMS

The terms used in behavior modification are fairly technical and specific. Several definitions are provided below.

The Law of Effect (as defined by E. L. Thorndike)—Of several responses made to the same situation, those which are accompanied or closely followed by satisfaction [reinforcement] . . . will be more likely to recur; those which are accompanied or closely followed by discomfort [punishment] . . . will be less likely to occur.[2]

A stimulus—Anything that influences worker behavior. In terms of reinforcement theory all stimuli are found outside of the worker in the environment. Common stimuli in the organization include the work itself, pay, supervision, co-workers, and working conditions. Rewards are stimuli because they influence worker behavior.

A reward—Something granted the worker as a consequence of behavior. Although not necessarily a positive reinforcer, a reward is a positive reinforcer when it makes good behavior reoccur.

A positive reinforcer—Tends to make good worker behavior likely to occur in the future. Typical positive reinforcers include meaningful work, people-oriented supervision, incentive pay, pay increments, and favorable attention given by supervisors and co-workers.

A negative reinforcer—A consequence of worker behavior that, when removed, increases the likelihood of good behavior. Therefore, negative reinforcement is like positive reinforcement in that both increase the likelihood of good behavior. But unlike the giving of rewards as positive reinforcement, something is taken away from the worker. Punishment or the threat of punishment is withdrawn when a worker behaves in the desired manner. A worker will have to act in an appropriate manner or be punished. One expert says that negative reinforcement "is really a form of social blackmail because the worker will have to behave in a certain way or be punished."[3] For example, a worker is negatively reinforced when arriving to work on time prevents a reprimand from a supervisor. When the reprimand is not given, there has been negative reinforcement.

Punishment—Either the withholding of a reward or the application of an unpleasant or painful stimulus in order to stop an inappropriate behavior. Withholding a reward or inducing pain are the two forms punishment may take. A supervisory reprimand directed to a person for arriving late for work (the behavior) will be punishment if it stops the worker from being late again. However, it may not cause a person to behave properly. It simply stops an undesired worker behavior. For example, suppose a worker strongly dislikes the organization. This discontent may take many forms. The person may complain, be late for work, disobey supervisory orders, disturb co-workers, damage machines, produce inferior products and so on. Punishing only one of these bad behaviors may bring about a change concerning that particular behavior but will do nothing about the other behaviors exhibited because of the discontent.

Extinction—Tends to make any form of worker behavior less likely to occur again because the behavior is neither rewarded nor punished. There is a neutral outcome or consequence. Ordinarily extinction is used as a replacement for punishment to stop undesirable behavior. The idea is that a person will, in time, learn that some actions do not "pay off" and will begin to act in ways that do have pleasant consequences. For example, children often cry to get the attention of parents. When parents pay no attention to crying, the crying will, in time, stop because parental attention is not given. Crying becomes "extinct" because it does not work.

It is important to understand that an individual does not have to be aware or conscious of a specific positive or negative reinforcer for that reinforcer to be effective. The individual merely knows that acting in a certain way leads to pleasure or to displeasure. However, it is the role of managers and supervisors to know exactly what stimuli (rewards) bring about good worker behavior.

Most behavior modification activities in organizations involve the use of either positive or negative reinforcement. A summary of the four basic operations in reinforcement theory is provided below:

1. If a *positive reinforcer* is given to a worker after an appropriate behavior, the result is positive reinforcement.

2. If a *positive reinforcer* is withdrawn after an inappropriate behavior, the result is punishment.

3. If a *negative reinforcer* is given to a worker after an inappropriate behavior, the result is punishment.

4. If a *negative reinforcer* is withdrawn after an appropriate behavior, the result is negative reinforcement.[4]

Giving a positive reinforcer or withdrawing a negative reinforcer usually result in making good worker behavior more likely to occur in the future. Withdrawing a positive reinforcer or giving a negative reinforcer result in making undesirable worker behavior less likely to occur.

Attempts to improve behavior depend upon the timing of the reward as much as the reward itself. Giving a child a gift two weeks after the child behaved outstandingly will be of no reinforcement value. The child simply does not know why the reward is being given. Similarly, in the work environment, praising an employee four or five weeks after the worker's superior performance will not have much effect. In the next section we will discuss the various ways of administering positive reinforcement.

IDENTIFYING POSITIVE REINFORCERS

To identify and use positive reinforcers a manager must:

1. Identify the appropriate worker behaviors (good attendance, working safely, etc.) to be improved or maintained
2. Identify the reward that a worker wants from each type of good behavior
3. Give a worker the reward only if the person demonstrates the appropriate behavior

The same reward may be reinforcing to one person but not to another. One worker (X) may value a money bonus for superior performance while another worker (Y) would prefer an extra day of vacation. Giving worker Y a money bonus for superior job performance will not be satisfying. Therefore, the worker may avoid repeating the superior performance because a valued reward did not result. On the other hand, worker X will be reinforced when the money bonus is given for superior performance. This person values money and wants more. If worker X knows receiving money is related to good performance, this person will tend to continue to work hard as long as money is important.

Table 8.1 lists numerous kinds of positive reinforcers that can be used in organizations.

The student may observe that the same factor, for example, supervision, may be reinforcing to different people for different reasons. For one person, people-oriented supervision may be reinforcing because it induces feelings of recognition and approval. For another person, the same style of supervision may be reinforcing because of the feelings of friendship or security it brings.

Positive reinforcement must be applied on a person-by-person basis. One way to identify positive reinforcers is to ask employees what is reinforcing. A supervisor may ask, "If your job performance improves, how do you want to be rewarded?" This question will elicit some kind of answer about what the worker wants in the way of reward. However, research has shown that there is a tendency for workers to respond to that kind of questioning with what will please the supervisor. For example, the worker may tell the supervisor that more job responsibility and opportunity to

TABLE 8.1   Some Positive Reinforcers Found in Organizations

Performing the work itself induces:
feelings of growth and development
feelings of accomplishment
feelings of achievement
feelings of worthwhile accomplishment

Receiving pay induces:
feelings of self-assurance
feelings of reduced anxiety
feelings of independence
feelings of self-esteem

Receiving a promotion induces:
feelings of status
feelings of recognition
feelings of accomplishment and achievement
feelings of self-esteem

Receiving considerable, people-oriented supervision induces:
feelings of friendship
feelings of self-esteem
feelings of security
feelings of recognition and approval

Interacting well with co-workers induces:
feelings of friendship
feelings of security
feelings of belonging
feelings of prestige

Other, "contrived," on-the-job rewards include:
commendations
trophies
company car
wall plaques
club privileges
private office
redecorated office
access to important company information

participate in decision making would be rewarding. This kind of answer is socially acceptable, that is, very American and compatible with the Protestant work ethic. The worker may have a hard time saying, "I'll improve my performance only when I get paid more." For many people this type of reply is difficult to offer because they sense that, generally, managers would prefer workers to work hard for the sense of accomplishment and achievement (intrinsic rewards) rather than for money (extrinsic reward).

Another way of identifying positive reinforcers has been designed that asks employees to respond to statements on a questionnaire. Fourteen statements in the 20 item questionnaire measure the contingency relationship between behavior and a supportive or rewarding organizational response. After studying workers' replies, a manager will know the rewards the subordinates see as reinforcing. Generally, the list of possible rewards closely reflects those found in Table 8.1. The 14 statements used to isolate positive reinforcers (supportive responses) are presented below:

In your opinion what is the probability that . . .

1. Your supervisor would personally pay you a compliment if you did outstanding work.

2. Your supervisor would lend a sympathetic ear if you had a complaint.

3. You will eventually go as far as you would like to go in this company if your work is consistently above average.

4. You would be promoted if your work was better than others who were otherwise equally qualified.

5. Your supervisor would help you get a transfer if you asked for one.

6. Your supervisor's boss or others in higher management would know about it if your work was outstanding.

7. Your supervisor's recommendation for a pay increase for you would be consistent with his evaluation of your performance.

8. Your supervisor would show a great deal of interest if you suggested a new and better way of doing things.

9. You would receive special recognition if your work performance was especially good.

10. Your supervisor would do all he could to help you if you were having problems in your work.

11. Your supervisor's evaluation of your performance would be in agreement with your own evaluation of your performance.

12. Your next pay increase will be consistent with the amount recommended by your supervisor.

13. Your supervisor would encourage you to do better if your performance was unacceptable but well below what you are capable of doing.

14. You would be promoted within the next two years if your work was consistently better than the work of others in your department.[5]

For each statement a worker selects one of six replies:

1. One hundred percent certain
2. Very probable
3. Fairly probable
4. Uncertain
5. Fairly improbable
6. Very improbable

Responses of "100 percent certain" and "very probable" identify positive reinforcers that appear to be in use, while the lower responses identify factors that are not being used to reinforce workers. Management could use such an approach to measure the difference in the perceived uses of reinforcers between managers and subordinates. By studying the answer patterns to this or similar questionnaires, managers should be able to apply positive reinforcement more systematically.

Another good method of identifying positive reinforcers has been developed by Fred Luthans and Robert Kreitner and asks people to choose rewards they feel will be reinforcing. This approach is called the self-selection technique; the respondents match possible reinforcers to appropriate behaviors. For example, a worker may choose the reinforcer of supervisory friendship to match the appropriate behavior of submitting a useful suggestion. Incomplete statements are used to reflect the contingency relationship between a behavior and a reward. For example, "If I ask for a transfer then _____."[6] After the worker completes the questionnaire, a manager is able to identify the positive reinforcers that workers believe are contingent upon certain appropriate behaviors. The investigators described a similar procedure that was used to improve classroom performance of problem children. Each child selected the reward most preferred from a "reinforcement menu." Under this system, they found

. . . children start working for rewards they desire, not rewards the teacher arbitrarily thinks they desire or should desire. A reinforcement menu typically involves items such as playtime away from the task, recess, and favorite curricular and extracurricular activites. Importantly, all reinforcers are given contingent (dependent) upon the achievement of desirable performance criteria. If a student properly completes an assigned activity, then he/she gets to pick a desired reward from the menu. This technique has proven successful for many teachers.[7]

It is important that the student understands exactly what the assigned activities are, as well as the rewards that could be expected from the successful completion of the assignments. Likewise, in organizations, it is crucial that the employees clearly understand what they have to do to receive the specific positive reinforcement. Workers must be able to anticipate receiving a particular reinforcer after a particular appropriate behavior.

REINFORCEMENT SCHEDULES

It is not enough just to identify the positive reinforcer for an individual. The use made of the reinforcer, even if it is the correct one, is critical. For instance, the employee who values money must be given the reinforcement (money) at the appropriate time. The worker must feel that the money bonus is being given for good performance and not for anything else. Research with animals suggests that a five-tenths of a second time lag between performance and reward is outstanding, in that the animal clearly knows that a specific reward follows a specific action, performance, or accomplishment that elicited the reward. While the time lag for human beings is somewhat longer, rewards such as supervisory recognition and praise should be given to a person immediately following good behavior, but not necessarily after every good behavior.

The timing and frequency of rewards in behavior modification is referred to as a schedule of reinforcement. Rewards can be given continuously or intermittently (off-and-on). A continuous reinforcement schedule is one where rewards are given for every appropriate behavior. The applause given to a professional tennis player after each good shot represents a continuous reinforcement schedule. An intermittent schedule refers to one where rewards are not given for each desirable behavior. A weekly paycheck received by an employee on Friday does not reinforce every good behavior during the previous five days. To reinforcement experts, this paycheck simply reinforces the behavior of going to work on Fridays and picking up the envelope containing the check.

Continuous Reinforcement

Suppose a worker "turns over a new leaf" and starts arriving at work on time and the supervisor wants this new behavior to continue. What should the supervisor do? Give praise every time the worker arrives on time? Every other day? Every week?

If the positive reinforcer (praise) is awarded to the worker every time the worker arrives on time, that behavior is being continuously reinforced. As shown in Table 8.2 continuous reinforcement brings about appropriate worker behavior when it follows every response. That is, the worker will arrive for work on time only when praise is given every time. Once the supervisor forgets to give praise, the worker's punctuality will drastically decrease.

Examples of continuous reinforcement schedules can easily be found in our daily lives. We are continuously reinforced when we know rewards will follow every good behavior. Some examples of continuous reinforced behavior include:

- Knowing that a candy bar will be obtained after putting money in a machine and pulling a knob
- Knowing that a pay bonus will follow every sale
- Knowing that teacher approval will follow every worthwhile comment by a student

In all these examples an individual can predict when a positive reinforcer will be given. Although continuous reinforcement results in a steady rate of performance as long as reinforcement continues to follow every response, the positive reinforcer may lose its power as a reward over time. Another disadvantage of continuous reinforcement is that the person receiving the reward may simply get tired of it.

Intermittent Reinforcement

Table 8.2 shows that there are four methods of intermittent reinforcement:

- Fixed ratio
- Variable ratio
- Fixed interval
- Variable interval

With the ratio schedules, behavior is reinforced after a particular number of good worker behaviors. With the interval schedules, reinforcement is based upon the passage of time.

Fixed ratio reinforcement. Fixed ratio reinforcement produces a high rate of response which is vigorous and steady. An individual is reinforced after a certain number of appropriate behaviors. The piece-rate pay method is an example of this type of schedule. Under that kind of system a worker must produce, for example, ten chairs before receiving a pay bonus.

Variable ratio reinforcement. The variable ratio schedule produces the strongest rate of desired behavior of all the schedules. Many reinforcement theorists believe that this schedule represents the best way to rein-

TABLE 8.2   Schedules of Reinforcement

Schedule	Description	Effects on Responding
Continuous (CRF)	Reinforcer follows every response.	(1) Steady high rate of performance as long as reinforcement continues to follow every response. (2) High frequency of reinforcement may lead to early satiation. (3) Behavior weakens rapidly (undergoes extinction) when reinforcers are withheld. (4) Appropriate for newly emitted, unstable, or low-frequency responses.
Intermittent	Reinforcer does not follow every response.	(1) Capable of producing high frequencies of responding. (2) Low frequency of reinforcement precludes early satiation. (3) Appropriate for stable or high-frequency responses.
Fixed ratio (FR)	A fixed number of responses must be emitted before reinforcement occurs.	(1) A fixed ratio of 1:1 (reinforcement occurs after every response) is the same as a continuous schedule. (2) Tends to produce a high rate of response which is vigorous and steady.

continued

force individuals. With a variable ratio schedule of reinforcement a worker is surprised by the presentation of the reward. The reward occurs randomly after an unspecified number of responses. The randomness means that the individual cannot predict when the reward will be given. Furthermore, the person may behave appropriately a large number of times without being rewarded. When the positive reinforcer does occur, the worker, in effect, is surprised and highly stimulated. Some examples of variable ratio reinforcement include:

TABLE 8.2   Schedules of Reinforcement (cont.)

Schedule	Description	Effects on Responding
Intermittent (cont.)		
Variable ratio (VR)	A varying or random number of responses must be emitted before reinforcement occurs.	(1) Capable of producing a high rate of response which is vigorous, steady, and resistant to extinction.
Fixed interval (FI)	The first response after a specific period of time has elapsed is reinforced.	(1) Produces an uneven response pattern varying from a very slow, unenergetic response immediately following reinforcement to a very fast, vigorous response immediately preceding reinforcement.
Variable interval (VI)	The first response after varying or random periods of time have elapsed is reinforced.	(1) Tends to produce a high rate of response which is vigorous, steady, and resistant to extinction.

Source: Fred Luthans and Robert Kreitner, Organizational Behavior Modification *(Glenview, Ill.: Scott, Foresman and Co., 1975), p. 51. Copyright © 1975 by Scott, Foresman and Company. Reprinted by permission.*

- Receiving special approval in terms of attention and compliments
- The surprise of winning in a lottery
- The surprise of winning with a slot machine
- The surprise of hitting a perfect tennis shot
- The surprise of hitting a perfect golf shot
- The surprise of winning at bingo
- Feelings of achievement from doing good work
- Feelings of self-fulfillment from doing good work
- Feelings of development and accomplishment from doing good work

People will sit for hours playing bingo or slot machines with the hope of winning (receiving reinforcement). Winning occurs very randomly and only after an unspecified number of responses. After winning, the player returns to the robotlike actions that produced the reward. A study of the behavior of people in Las Vegas casinos would indeed substantiate the impact of the variable ratio reinforcement schedule.

The last three examples in the list refer to positive reinforcers received by the workers as a result of good performance on a job. People having fairly high standards for themselves may actually be rewarded by the formal system on a continuous basis but they may perform well enough to meet their own demanding standards only on certain occasions. The intrinsic rewards would therefore be given on a variable ratio basis. The Herzberg two-factor theory of motivation discussed in Chapter 7 is pertinent here. The motivating or intrinsic factors in the theory included achievement, accomplishment, recognition, responsibility, growth, and development. Workers give themselves these rewards on a variable ratio schedule for satisfactorily performing a task. Reinforcement theorists are constantly seeking ways to create jobs that reinforce the workers with intrinsic rewards. Such managerial practices as job enlargement, job enrichment, and job rotation provide for these types of rewards.

Hitting a perfect shot (appropriate behavior) in tennis or golf often leads to increased participation in the sport. The individual is seeking to duplicate the swing that produced the reinforcement (a feeling of accomplishment). Advanced players seem to get better and better because they receive more reinforcement than do players not so advanced. Beginners in most athletic activities receive little reinforcement from performing the tasks because there are very few rewards from poor performance. Diligence, not reinforcement, keeps the beginner going. But one must be aware of *why* the individual is involved in the activity in the first place. For the individual who is playing tennis purely for the recreational benefits and/or for the physical exercise, the activity itself, done rightly or wrongly, will provide satisfaction. Thus, in some cases the activity can be reinforcing despite the level of performance.

Fixed interval reinforcement. Fixed interval reinforcement produces behavior ranging from very slow to very energetic. Behavior is reinforced only after a certain period of time. A weekly, biweekly, or monthly paycheck represents a fixed interval schedule. Although an individual may consistently work properly, the worker is only reinforced after the passage of a certain period of time. Thus, a large number of good behaviors are not reinforced. It has been suggested that many compensation programs actually reinforce bad worker behaviors. Walter Nord, an authority in this field, stated:

Often, means of compensation, especially fringe benefits, have the unanticipated consequence of reinforcing the wrong responses. Current programs of sick pay, recreation programs, employee lounges, work breaks, and numerous other personnel programs all have one point in common. They all reward the employee for not working or for staying away from the job. . . . An employer who relies on them should realize what behavior he is developing by establishing these costly programs.[8]

As mentioned earlier, a weekly paycheck only reinforces the act of going to work and picking up the pay envelope on payday.

Variable interval reinforcement. Variable interval reinforcement produces high rates of desirable behavior, which is strong and resistant to extinction. On an interval schedule the positive reinforcer is presented after the passage of time. Being variable as well as interval means that the positive reinforcer is presented to a worker after a random period of time has elapsed. The worker cannot predict when reinforcement will be given because the time periods between reinforcement vary a great deal. A supervisor can give reinforcement on a variable interval schedule by pleasantly visiting with the worker without prior notice, when the time periods between visits are different. For example, during one week the supervisor visits with the worker two times and then visits only once during the next week.

PUNISHMENT

To change worker behavior managers should use positive reinforcement or extinction rather than punishment. Extinction should be used before punishment to remove undesirable or inappropriate worker behaviors. Too many bad side effects may result from punishment. In almost all circumstances punishment just isn't worth the risks. The effective use of punishment occurs so rarely that no research findings are available that show any successful, long-term applications of punishment. Although punishment may stop undesired behavior, will good behavior automatically occur next? Even if punishment does stop an undesirable behavior, are the numerous bad side effects worth it? The answer appears to be no to both questions.

Punishment, as defined earlier, refers to either the withholding of a reward or the application of an unpleasant or painful stimulus in order to stop an inappropriate behavior. In our culture, punishment is the most frequently used method in attempting to change behavior. Perhaps this is a result of our need to experience a sense of fairness or equity. Our belief in "an eye for an eye" influences most of us to punish, or desire the punishment of, others. Several of the bad side effects from punishment are outlined below:

1. Punishment leads to more punishment.   Often punishment is a positive reinforcer to the one who gives the punishment. For example, when a supervisor criticizes a worker for poor performance, the poor performance will temporarily stop. This temporary stopping of poor performance is pleasant to the supervisor and could, therefore, promote further use of negative criticism. The supervisor may also get reinforcement from the visible display of power that punishment provides.

2. The threat of punishment must always be present.   "If the cat is away, the mice will play." When the supervisor is the main source of punishment for subordinates, the subordinates will tend to behave properly only when the supervisor is present.

3. Punishment does not bring about good work behavior, it only temporarily stops bad behavior from reoccurring.   However, if the next most likely behavior is an appropriate one in a person's response hierarchy, punishment may elicit a good behavior. Here, the problem is knowing a person's response hierarchy.

4. Punishment leads to fear, psychological tension, and anxiety which may interfere with the worker's desire to behave properly.   Both manual and cognitive skills are adversely affected by anxiety and fear. After being punished, a worker may actually want to behave properly but this desire could be short-circuited by the person's attention to fears. It is difficult to pay close attention to more than one activity.

5. Punishment may cause a punished worker to avoid or counterattack the punisher.   Just as the supervisor punishes the worker for inappropriate behavior, the worker may punish the supervisor for causing displeasure. This may be done by sabotage or "malicious obedience." For example, malicious obedience occurs when a subordinate carries out the orders of a superior exactly as they were given, even though the orders were incorrect or incomplete.

6. Punishment may become a positive reinforcer for the punished person.   Some people identify more closely with the informal work group than with the organization. In many informal groups negative recognition and attention from management results in peer group acclaim and support. Causing trouble for management brings formal punishment to a member of an informal group, but punishment in this case may actually function as a positive reinforcer as the individual gets various kinds of rewards from the informal group for upsetting management.

   Thus, it is clear that punishment has many bad side effects. However, as we all know, punishment in organizations will continue to exist. There are some worker actions that are so harmful and damaging that punishment should be used.

If punishment must exist, it should be combined with positive reinforcement. If a dose of positive reinforcement is added, many of the undesirable side effects will not occur. Luthans and Kreitner suggest that

the major advantage of the punishment/positive reinforcement strategy is that it avoids putting pressure on the punished person and backing him/her into a corner. The opportunity to behave in positively reinforced alternative ways acts as a safety valve. As a result, the undesirable side effect of emotional responding (fear, anxiety, anger) is minimized. The major strength of punishment, an ability to immediately terminate a response, is retained while the major advantages are, to some extent, neutralized.[9]

If punishment is necessary, the manager should try to inform the punished person exactly what the individual may do to receive positive reinforcement, that is, he should offer alternative ways to behave and specify the rewards attached to good behavior. The crucial point to remember is to explain the alternative good behaviors and their accompanying rewards.

Let's say a worker is producing substandard products. Punishing the worker could generate several undesirable side effects. The worker might feel boxed-in, fearful, and anxious. An approach that combined punishment and positive reinforcement would lessen the likelihood of the bad side effects. Berating the person's job performance could easily be followed with an explanation of how the product should be assembled. The supervisor should also point out the favorable consequences from proper job performance. These may include upgraded job responsibility, a pay bonus, or even the possibility of training new employees in assembling the product. If such an approach was used, the worker would have been both punished and reinforced at the same time. The individual would then understand what leads to punishment and to pleasure and would not feel boxed-in by the supervisor. The worker would see a reason for performing well.

SUMMARY

A reward for one person may not be a reward for another. Rewards most commonly available from organizations are related to the work itself, supervision, pay and fringe benefits, co-workers, and promotions.

Behavior modification attempts to make good or appropriate worker behavior more likely to occur in the future through the application of reinforcement theory. Reinforcement theory attributes the cause of worker behavior to things external to the person. Traditional motivational theories attribute the cause of worker behavior to forces within the person in the form of needs, desires, feelings, and the like. Subjective and personal factors as these play no important role in reinforcement ideas.

Positive reinforcers and negative reinforcers make appropriate worker behaviors more likely to occur in the future. Extinction and punishment make inappropriate worker behaviors less likely to occur in the future.

The application of positive reinforcement is the best way to improve worker behavior in organizations. Positive reinforcement may be administered on the following schedules: fixed ratio, variable ratio, fixed interval, and variable interval. Giving rewards on the interval schedules is based on the passage of time. Rewards given on a ratio schedule follow a number of appropriate worker responses. The variable ratio schedule is the strongest way to reinforce behavior. Workers, in effect, are surprised by the rewards. The work itself can be designed to include a host of positive reinforcers. Workers performing their job satisfactorily give themselves reinforcers such as feelings of achievement, accomplishment, growth, and development. The motivating or intrinsic factors in the Herzberg two-factor theory can be designed into the work people perform.

Positive reinforcers are found not only in the work itself but also in pay, supervision, promotions, and co-worker interaction. Managers can identify existing and potential positive reinforcers by administering either of the two self-report questionnaires described in the chapter.

Punishment decreases the frequency of inappropriate worker behaviors, but, unfortunately, a large number of undesirable side effects are related to the use of punishment. These side effects may be eliminated when punishment is combined with positive reinforcement. By using this approach the worker can see the advantage of performing well.

NOTES

1. R. I. Evans, *Skinner: The Man and His Idea* (New York: E. P. Dutton, 1968), pp. 22–3.

2. E. I. Thorndike, Animal Intelligence (New York: Macmillan, 1911), p. 243.

3. Fred Luthans, *Organizational Behavior* (New York: McGraw-Hill, 1977), p. 294.

4. W. W. Wenrich, *A Primer on Behavior Modification* (New York: Brooks/Cole Publishing Co., 1970), p. 53.

5. H. J. Reitz, "Managerial Attitudes and Perceived Contingencies Between Performance and Organizational Responses," *Academy of Management Proceedings* (Atlanta, Georgia: The Academy of Management, 1971), pp. 227–38.

6. Fred Luthans and Robert Kreitner, *Organizational Behavior Modification* (Glenview, Ill.: Scott, Foresman, and Co., 1975), p. 97.

7. Ibid.

8. Walter Nord, "Beyond the Teaching Machine," *Organizational Behavior and Human Performance* 14 (1969): 275–401.

9. Luthans and Kreitner, *Organizational Behavior Modification*, p. 127.

QUESTIONS FOR THOUGHT AND DISCUSSION

1. A list of "appropriate" worker behaviors was presented at the outset of the chapter. Think about your last two work experiences and add as many other appropriate worker behaviors as you can. In addition, comment on the reward, if any, which was tied to or linked with each appropriate behavior.

2. Comment on the following quotation of the popular reinforcement psychologist B. F. Skinner. "The organism (person) is irrelevant either as the site of physiological processes or as the locus of mentalistic activities. I don't believe the organism contributes anything to these overall relationships beyond the fact that it is the behavior of an organism we are studying. . . . The organism is simply mediating the relationship between the forces acting upon it and its own output."

3. Think of at least five examples of the "law of effect" in your own experiences, work or otherwise. The law is defined thus: "Of several responses made to the same situation, those which are accompanied or closely followed by satisfaction (reinforcement) . . . will be more likely to reoccur; those which are accompanied or closely followed by discomfort (punishment) . . . will be less likely to occur."

4. Place numbers from 1 through 14 down the left margin of a piece of paper. Turn to the fourteen reinforcement statements presented in this chapter. Using a past or present job, decide on how certain you are of each statement. Then, across from each number, put one of six replies: (1) 100 percent certain; (2) very probable; (3) fairly probable; (4) uncertain; (5) fairly improbable; and (6) very improbable. Interpret what your answers to the Reitz questions mean.

5. In what ways could a job you have or have had be redesigned to capitalize on variable ratio reinforcement? (Some students may be helped by briefly reviewing Chapter 3 on job design.)

KEY TERMS

The student should be able to discuss the significance of these terms to the study of human behavior in the work environment.

Law of effect	Continuous reinforcement
Stimulus	Fixed ratio reinforcement
Reward	Variable ratio reinforcement
Positive reinforcement	Fixed interval reinforcement

Negative reinforcement
Extinction
Punishment

Variable interval reinforcement
Self-selection questionnaire
The punishment dilemma

CASE INCIDENT

Jack Femmerman, as you will recall from three previous case incidents, is the president of a medium-sized, full-line insurance company employing 4,800 people. The management consultant retained by this company is training the sales managers in reinforcement techniques with the hope that the salespersons will not only be more satisfied with supervision and with the company as a whole but also with themselves.

The consultant administered the Luthans and Kreitner "self-selection" questionnaire to six hundred salespersons. This questionnaire, as described in the chapter, requires a person to choose a reinforcer to match an appropriate behavior. For example, a worker may choose the reinforcer of supervisory friendship to match the appropriate behavior of submitting a useful suggestion. After the worker completes the questionnaire, a manager is able to identify the positive reinforcers that workers believe are contingent on certain appropriate behaviors. It is crucial that the employees clearly understand what they have to do to receive the specific routine reinforcement. In this case, the salespersons must be able to anticipate receiving a particular reinforcer after a particular appropriate behavior.

After the six hundred questionnaires were completed by the salespersons, the consultant tallied the responses to see what answers were given most frequently. The responses for some sample items are shown below and should be interpreted as the most frequently mentioned response for that question.

Most Frequent Responses to Sample Items from the Self-Selection Questionnaire

Performance	*Consequence*

If *I increase sales by 20 percent,* then I will get a raise.

If *I add nine new accounts per week,* then I will be complimented by my supervisor.

If I do my job better than usual, then *I expect a promotion.*

If my work is outstanding, then *I expect a merit pay raise and maybe a promotion.*

If *I am a top performer,* then I will be formally recognized by top management.

If I save the company some money, then *I should share in the savings.*

The tasks remaining for the consultant and the president are to not only understand the meanings of the responses, but also to decide which of the five schedules of reinforcement is most useful for eliciting each appropriate behavior on the self-selection questionnaire.

Question for Discussion

Decide which of the five schedules of reinforcement would be best for bringing about each good behavior on the sample items of the self-selection questionnaire. Be as specific as you can in outlining such factors as number of times performance must occur, frequency of rewards, and so forth.

9

The Relationship of Money and Motivation

LEARNING OBJECTIVES

Upon completion of this chapter the student should be able to:

- Identify and discuss the human needs most likely to be satisfied by money.
- Contrast the two conflicting views of money as a source of motivation.
- Discuss the importance of a referent other or comparison person to an individual's pay satisfaction.
- Describe the determinants of pay satisfaction.
- Identify the causes of pay dissatisfaction.
- Recognize how people behave when they are dissatisfied with their pay.
- Explain when money can be used to motivate and when money should not be used to motivate.
- Compare the advantages and limitations of group and individual incentive programs.

"Money isn't the only thing that interests me, but it's way ahead of whatever is in second place." Usually such a statement is made jokingly, but it
may hold a good deal of truth for some people. While some theorists, such
as Frederick Herzberg, do not believe money acts as a motivator, there is a
sizable portion of the working population who may disagree with that. In
fact, money is a very potent reinforcer of behavior because it can mean so
many different things to different people. From an organizational standpoint, pay is used not only in return for services rendered but also as a
means to attract, hold, and enhance employee motivation toward objectives of the organization. Pay does seem to have a strong influence on
attracting job applicants to an organization. The higher-paying companies
ordinarily attract more applicants and more qualified applicants than do
the lower-paying companies in the same industry.

To some people, pay is a way of attaining social status. To others pay
is a form of recognition. To most people pay is what determines their
standard of living. Pay is also important in holding or keeping workers in
the company as it is an important part of job satisfaction. Likewise, pay
can be an important source of motivation when the amount of pay an
individual receives is tied to the person's job performance. Yes, money
has many varied but interrelated roles in our society. This chapter will
examine some of the various roles of money and how it can influence the
motivational level of employees, as well as discussing the causes and
consequences of pay satisfaction and dissatisfaction.

RESEARCH ON PAY

Only fairly recently have researchers seriously studied the causes and
consequences of pay satisfaction and dissatisfaction, although there was
some earlier research that touched upon the subject.

Frederick Taylor, the father of scientific management, was the first to
seriously study and write about the importance of pay. Around 1900

Taylor observed a worker who, after working hard for twelve hours lifting and moving pig iron, would run twelve miles up a mountain to work on his cabin. From this and other observations, Taylor came to believe that this extra energy could easily be channeled into the job. He felt that employees would work harder only when they were paid for doing so and when they clearly realized that pay was tied to performance. Taylor devised ways of measuring worker output and paying workers on how much they produced rather than how long they worked.

We learned in Chapter 7 that the Hawthorne studies focused attention upon human behavior in the work environment. The emphasis was on the intrinsic aspects of work and the conditions that contributed to productivity and satisfaction. Elton Mayo (the research leader) discovered that co-worker interaction and other social processes accounted for differences in satisfaction and motivation.[1] Pay was not found to be an important factor.

In 1959, Frederick Herzberg popularized the two-factor theory, discussed in Chapter 7, that contended pay was a hygiene or maintenance factor and was not important in inspiring the will to work. Pay was not found to have significant potential for increasing worker motivation.[2] In fact, the Herzberg study found that pay ranked sixth in importance behind the five factors presented below:

1. Job security
2. Job interest
3. Opportunity for advancement
4. The company and management
5. Intrinsic job factors (feelings of growth/accomplishment)[3]

Because of the impact of the Mayo and Herzberg studies, behavioral scientists believed for several decades that pay did not have a strong influence on worker behavior. However, the controversial Herzberg findings caused a good deal of interest in the role of pay. Consequently much of what we now understand on the subject of pay can be credited to the stimulation provided by the Herzberg study. Some of the more recent research results will be presented throughout this chapter.

PAY AND THE SATISFACTION OF NEEDS

Although pay is better able to satisfy some needs more than other needs, pay does have the potential to satisfy all needs to a certain extent. Pay satisfies or fulfills a need when the person believes that pay is instrumental (helpful) in satisfying the need. When a need is perceived to be un-

satisfied and when the worker believes that pay will be useful in satisfying the need, pay is important. This may be true of almost any need.
Physiological needs, for example, may be satisfied by the purchase of
food, clothing, and shelter. By buying housing in particular, more than
one need is satisfied. While the individual may claim the need to be
satisfied is physiological when buying a house, there are also elements of
security, social and esteem (ego) needs being satisfied. Thus, money has
the ability to help satisfy human needs at several levels. Even if the relationship of money and need satisfaction is not direct, the capacity to buy
that which will satisfy a need makes money instrumental to need satisfaction.

   If, in the past, pay has been useful in satisfying a particular need, pay
will probably retain its rewarding properties. If, on the other hand, pay
has not been useful in satisfying a particular need, pay will not have any
special rewarding value. The importance of what money can do and how
pay is generally perceived may go back to one's childhood. When children are told that they can not have the bicycles which they want so
badly because "we cannot afford it" or because "it costs too much," they
learn very early what money can do. Such children probably think, "if we
had more money I could have the bike." Having the bike would bring
happiness so having money becomes equated with happiness. Or similarly, the fact that the bicycle couldn't be bought may lead to the belief that
the shortage of money causes unhappiness. Regardless of what money
does in fact do in terms of providing happiness, the point is that such an
experience may have influenced all of us in the way in which we perceive
the importance of money. The example of the bike points out another way
money is related to need satisfaction—it seems to be more important to
those who don't have it.

MONEY AS A MEASURING STICK

It is quite possible to satisfy some needs in an absolute sense while others
must be satisfied on a relative basis. This implies that a comparison takes
place with how other people are satisfying those particular needs. A
majority of people in the United States make enough money to live on. Yet
most people seem always to want or need more money. This apparent
contradiction can be explained by what people think they need to live the
way they want to live. Items that were once considered luxury items are
now viewed as necessities. People can satisfy physiological needs and
security needs by living in rather spartan conditions. But would this do
anything toward meeting esteem needs? Probably not. So even when
lower level needs are satisfied, people often think they need to meet other
needs by "keeping up with the Joneses." Keeping up usually takes more

money, but it is an outward sign of success. Money has provided a measurement of success that is visible to all.

Money allows people to buy material things that are important to them. But an even more important role of money to a large segment of the population is the fact that it does represent a common measuring stick. Even though salary and wage comparisons which cross industry lines are not very accurate or necessarily fair, they are a common practice. On an informal basis people seem to like to compare their earnings with others. The amount of money earned is, after all, the only general standard for comparison that all people can identify with. For example, individuals working at Ace Manufacturing have their performances measured by a boss who is evaluating in terms of the performance appraisal system in use at Ace Manufacturing. Those workers working for Whistle's Incorporated are under an entirely different appraisal system doing a different type of job in a different industry. The only way for people to have some idea about their relative contribution, then, is to compare the one thing they have in common—pay. Nearly all of us have someone with whom we compare ourselves. This other person can be very important to our level of job satisfaction.

THE REFERENT OTHER IN PAY COMPARISONS

As was explained in Chapter 4 the comparison person whom we use to measure our success is known as a referent other. A referent other is a person with whom we are comparing our inputs and outcomes. Most writing on this subject suggests that individuals may compare their pay with someone outside of the organization or within, or with peers, subordinates, or superiors.

One study of 228 managers found mixed results. Table 9.1 shows that lower-middle managers tended to compare their pay with people outside of the company (35 percent). Middle managers mainly compared their pay with people on a lower level within the company. Lower level managers (first-line supervisors) were divided with regard to referent others. While 35 percent selected a peer within the organization, another 35 percent chose a referent other from outside of the company.[4]

Table 9.2 identifies referent others based upon educational level. One obvious trend is that people with higher levels of education are more likely to choose a referent other from outside the company. Conversely, the lower the education the more likely it is that an individual will make pay comparisons with a peer in the same company.

It has also been discovered that pay dissatisfaction can be better understood by knowing the relative pay position rather than the absolute pay position. Highly paid workers in a low-paying company reported

TABLE 9.1   Choice of Reference Group as a Function of Management Level (Percent of first choice)

| | CHOICE OF REFERENCE GROUP | | | | |
| | Outside company | | | Within company | |
	Higher level	Same level	Lower level	All outside choices	N
Middle management	12	12	41	35	(17)
Lower-middle management	17	20	10	53	(70)
Lower management	16	34	15	35	(134)

Source: I. R. Andrews and Mildred M. Henry, "Management Attitudes Toward Pay," Industrial Relations *3, No. 1 (1963): 31.*

TABLE 9.2   Choice of Reference Group as a Function of Education (Percent of first choice)

| | CHOICE OF REFERENCE GROUP | | | | |
| | Within company | | | Outside company | |
	Higher level	Same level	Lower level	All outside choices	N
Some high school	29	43	21	7	(11)
High school degree	5	45	21	29	(38)
Some college	18	31	14	37	(49)
Business college	15	35	5	45	(20)
College degree	19	21	12	48	(58)
Postgraduate	12	12	20	56	(41)

Source: I. R. Andrews and Mildred M. Henry, "Management Attitudes Toward Pay," Industrial Relations *3, No. 1 (1963): 32.*

more pay dissatisfaction than medium-paid workers in a high-paying company. According to the researchers, "a good relative pay position within a company did not compensate for an inadequate pay level taken within a broader context."[5]

EQUITY THEORY: THE EFFECTS OF OVERPAYMENT AND UNDERPAYMENT

One-fourth of the secretaries in a secretarial pool are high performers while one-fourth are poor performers. All the secretaries receive exactly the same pay raise. Which group of secretaries will change their work quality and quantity, and why? A professor in a business class requires term papers from the students. One student spends four weeks researching and carefully writing an excellent paper while a friend only spends two days on the entire paper, research and all. The first student has evaluated the friend's paper and is sure it is clearly inferior. Both receive a grade of A on their papers. Which student will adjust the effort on the next paper, in what direction, and why?

We learned in Chapter 4 that equity theory investigates the effects of wage inequity—overpayment or underpayment—on work quality, work quantity and on work attitudes. Inequity has been defined as follows:

Inequity exists for a Person whenever he perceives that the ratio of his outcomes to inputs and the ratio of Other's outcomes to Other's inputs are unequal.
This may happen either (a) when he and Other are in a direct exchange relationship or (b) when both are in an exchange relationship with a third party and the Person compares himself to Other.[6]

Equity or inequity is a perceived phenomenon. Whether equity or inequity exists for a person is determined by a social comparison and may have little to do with factual information. If a person perceives something as being real, it is real to that individual regardless of what the situation may be. Again, a person will compare what is put into and received from a job with the efforts and rewards of a comparison person as illustrated below:

		Comparison Person
Person		
	compared with	
Inputs		Inputs
Outputs		Outputs

If the ratios are unequal, the person will be motivated to remove or to reduce the discrepancy causing the uncomfortable state of tension now existing. For example, if one feels underpaid, one way to feel better is to change either work quality or quantity.

Figures 9.1 and 9.2 show the various ways workers can behave to attain perceived equity. Workers can reduce work quantity and quality to "get even" when they are paid by the hour and feel underpaid. In those rare situations when employees feel overpaid on an hourly rate basis, employees could reduce the inequity by improving work quality and increasing work quantity. In a piece-rate situation, quantity will actually decrease with a perceived overpayment in order to "protect" the standards; however, quality should increase. When underpayment is perceived on a piece-rate system, quantity will go up as the worker attempts to make

	HOURLY RATE SITUATION	PIECE-RATE SITUATION
Overpayment	↑	↓
Underpayment	↓	↑

Figure 9.1   Effects of Inequitable Payment on Work Quantity

	HOURLY RATE SITUATION	PIECE-RATE SITUATION
Overpayment	↑	↑
Underpayment	↓	↓

Figure 9.2   Effects of Inequitable Payment on Work Quality

Source: Edward Lawler, III, Pay and Organizational Effectiveness: A Psychological View *(New York: McGraw-Hill, 1971), p. 95.*

more money, but quality will likely suffer because of the attempt to produce more pieces.

Other remedies for reducing tension caused by underpayment include:

1. Leaving the company
2. Changing the comparison person
3. Changing one's perception of personal inputs and outputs
4. Changing the perception of the referent other's inputs and outputs

The purpose of these tension remedies is to make the two ratios equal. Regardless of the technique used to resolve feelings of inequity, the end goal is to achieve a feeling of pay equity and fairness.

THE CAUSES OF PAY SATISFACTION AND DISSATISFACTION

It is not known exactly why people are satisfied or dissatisfied with their pay. Most of the published research on the topic of satisfaction cannot identify cause-and-effect relationships. We do know what factors are related to pay satisfaction and will attempt to put these factors in some manageable framework.

As mentioned earlier in the chapter, people may be satisfied in an absolute sense until they make comparisons. However, the tendency of most people is to make comparisons almost continually concerning nearly all parts of their lives. While eating in a restaurant, diners formulate an opinion or feeling about the quality of the food and service. While taking a college course, students develop a feeling about the quality of the course. When on a date, couples even develop a feeling about the quality of the dating experience. How do these feelings or evaluations develop? People compare one experience with other experiences—either real or imagined. In the dinner situation, the quality and service of one restaurant is compared with that of another and with preconceived standards. Likewise, the quality of one college course is compared with another. Moreover, the comparison process does not have to be a conscious one.

Workers' feelings about pay result from their comparisons of what is put into the job (inputs) and what is gotten out of the job (outcomes) with the inputs and outcomes of some referent other. Does this mean that everyone wants more money? Perhaps not, if they feel they must earn it. But it is not unusual for an individual to feel underpaid. In fact some employers repeatedly say that they do not want anyone working for them who thinks they are paid enough. The logic behind such reasoning is that the employers want people who believe they have a lot to offer and believe they contribute more than they are paid to contribute. If employees feel they are paid what they are worth, then it is questionable if they are even worth that much. Such an attitude of being very satisfied with pay may indicate a satisfaction with the quantity and quality of work. Few employers want employees who are not willing to put forth a little more effort or accept a greater challenge. These are generalizations, of course, and there are undoubtedly many exceptions, but the value placed upon one's work by the individual may given an idea of what that work is really worth. This assumes a desire to continually improve and the belief that what one has to offer is indeed expanding. It does not necessarily hold true of people who are just riding along with union demands for more with no relative increase in productivity.

As shown in Figure 9.3, there are several input factors and outcome factors. The most important input is performance, while the most important outcome is pay. Basically, if the amount of pay that workers think should be received matches the amount actually received, pay equity exists. Under the situation of pay equity, as shown in Figure 9.3, workers are satisfied with their pay. Pay dissatisfaction is experienced when the amount of pay received is less than the amount that workers think should be received.

The model shows that it is the perceptions of reality which really matter, rather than reality per se. A problem occurs when employees attempt to perceive the inputs and outcomes of the referent other. There is a human tendency to underestimate the performance of others and to overestimate the pay of others. As a consequence, workers are more dissatisfied with their own pay than they would be if these perceptual errors did not occur.

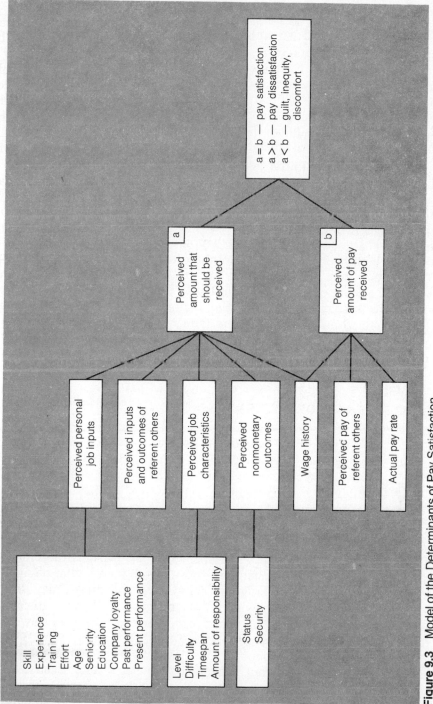

Figure 9.3 Model of the Determinants of Pay Satisfaction

Source: Edward Lawler, III, Pay and Organizational Effectiveness: A Psychological View (New York: McGraw-Hill, 1971), p. 215.

There seems to be no easy solution for this problem. Many companies have policies that forbid the open discussion of salaries. If all salaries were known, there of course would be no problem of overestimating the pay of others, but there seems to be no effective way of measuring and comparing the performances and contributions of each individual in an organization. The difficulties that may arise as a result of making salaries and performance levels available to all organizational members may actually be worse than the problems associated with estimating the pay and performance of others.

Most public employees, for example, have their pay published in a local newspaper or at the very least it is a matter of public record. At some universities where professors' salaries are published, the morale and motivational levels of many professors are at low points for the year when their pay is printed in the paper. When employees of any kind feel they have done a good job and notice they have received smaller raises than others who they feel have done nothing, there are bound to be problems. The impact upon morale and motivation is devastating and may last for several weeks or months. It is hard to say which problem is more severe, estimating the pay of others or actually knowing. This is a dilemma which as yet has had no suitable answers. The fact that the relative amount of pay can stir such emotions and cause such problems further points out the importance most people attach to it.

THE CONSEQUENCES OF PAY DISSATISFACTION

After following the pay comparison process described above, an individual may become dissatisfied with the pay received. As Figure 9.4 shows, pay dissatisfaction leads to two major consequences:

1. The desire for more pay
2. A lowered attractiveness of the job

The model suggests that pay dissatisfaction may lead to absenteeism, turnover, overall job dissatisfaction, and a search for a higher-paying job. Some actions, such as striking and submitting grievances, may directly satisfy the desire for more pay and, thus, may reduce pay dissatisfaction. When engaging in these behaviors the worker has chosen to stay in the organization and fight it out.

One serious consequence of pay dissatisfaction is when people decide not to stay and fight it out. When people become very dissatisfied and believe they can better their position and pay by going elsewhere, they frequently quit their jobs. In some cases the turnover may actually be

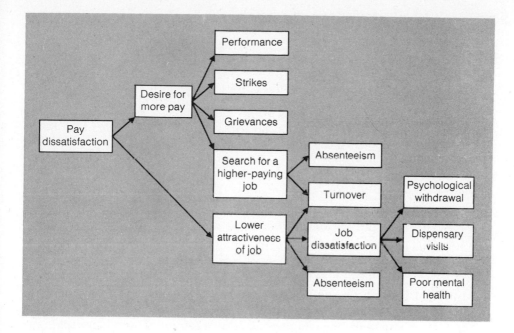

Figure 9.4 Model of the Consequences of Pay Dissatisfaction

Source: Edward Lawler, III, Pay and Organizational Effectiveness: A Psychological View *(New York: McGraw-Hill, 1971), p. 233.*

welcomed, but many times a good employee with years of valuable experience is lost. A phenomenon that is true of all organizations, private and public, is that a good employee is more valuable to another organization than to the present employer. Or, at least another organization is willing to pay more for that employee. For example, let's assume that Betty Blow feels she deserves a bigger raise than she received. Her boss, Jane Doe, agrees but claims she just can't do it. Both parties become increasingly defensive and the battle comes down to "the principle of the thing." Betty says that unless she gets that meager $200 she feels she deserves, she will quit. Jane silently agrees that Betty is worth it, but she just cannot allow such a thing to happen or other people will think they can pull the same thing. The precedent is just too dangerous. Betty quits and goes to a competitor where she receives $2,000 more per year. Jane is forced to find a replacement and has to pay someone with very little experience $1,000 more than Betty was paid. The $200 Betty asked for then looks cheap compared with the $1,000 and the lack of experience.

This is a very real situation. People can often better their pay by "jumping" to other companies. The company that loses a good employee frequently has to pay even more to get a new, less qualified person. Perhaps the answer lies in using a more behavioral approach in the management of people as much as in the level of pay.

PAY AS A WORK-RELATED REWARD

Most people who work will look to the rewards associated with the job when considering job satisfaction. Rewards from working may be related to one of many work role factors. An employee's overall behavior and commitment to the organization are influenced by:

- Rewards from the work itself
- Rewards from the supervisor
- Rewards from pay and fringe benefits
- Rewards from promotional opportunities
- Rewards from interacting with co-workers

The most important reward for one person may not be the most important reward for another. While many recent college graduates look for jobs offering rewards from the work itself and promotional opportunities, others seek jobs where good co-worker and supervisory relationships are available. Some people simply seek the highest paying job without any apparent concern for any other reward factors.

It should be apparent to all managers that if they are going to treat pay as a work-related reward, they should know how their employees respond to it. A frequently told story about a youth who got a job at a manufacturing plant illustrates how money is important in different ways to people. The young man was habitually absent on Fridays. After giving warnings and finally a written notice that allowed the worker one more chance before being fired, the foreman decided to have a talk with him. In response to the question, "Why do you consistently work four days a week?" the young man replied, "Because I can't make enough in three days." For him the money from his paycheck afforded a certain lifestyle. The maintenance of that lifestyle was what was really important to him. The additional money earned by working one more day a week was not needed, so he did not feel compelled to work on Fridays.

In short, if a manager is to develop a useful reward system the rewards must be valued by the subordinates. If the rewards are valued, they will reinforce behavior and provide a tool to be used in enhancing the motivation of people.

USING MONEY TO INCREASE MOTIVATION

There are several work role factors that can be used to influence a worker's motivation. The work itself, supervision, pay, promotional opportunities, and co-worker interaction all may contribute to upgrading a worker's performance. Using pay as a motivational tool requires managers to have a good understanding of the conditions in the work situation which may favor or prohibit the use of money as a significant force. Several of the limitations are presented below:

1. Do not use pay to increase motivation when the level of trust between the workers and managers is low or marginal.

2. Do not use pay to increase motivation when a worker's job performance is difficult to measure. To improve motivation with money, pay must be closely tied to a good measure of worker output.

3. Do not use pay to enhance motivation when large pay rewards cannot be given to the best workers. Small pay rewards are not very powerful motivators. Workers quickly get used to small and medium-sized pay rewards. This means that large pay rewards are generally needed to stimulate workers.[7]

There are also certain forces and values within people which can determine the ability of pay to increase motivation. One expert on pay contends that:

1. Employees must attach a very high value to pay. Workers concerned with satisfying social and self-actualization needs do not value pay as much as those who are concerned with security and esteem needs.

2. Employees must believe that good performance does in fact lead to high pay. Individuals will not be motivated by money when money rewards are not given to them for superior performance.

3. Employees must believe that their job performance reflects to a large extent how hard they are trying. Some jobs are machine paced, like many assembly line jobs, which prevents workers from significantly upgrading their performance by themselves.

4. Employees must see that superior performance is related to more positive consequences than negative consequences. Superior workers are sometimes ostracized from the work group. This obviously is a negative consequence of good performance. Feelings of recognition, achievement, and acceptance are positive consequences of superior performance.[8]

When, in the judgment of managers, conditions favor using pay as a motivational tool, the next step is the selection of an acceptable method of administering a reward system. Basically, pay rewards may be administered in two ways:

1. Through wage/salary rewards (pay raises)
2. Through giving bonuses

A salary reward increases the base pay of a worker. If the worker was earning six hundred dollars monthly, the worker may, following the increase, be earning seven hundred dollars a month. Pay raises are usually permanent whereas superior performance may be just temporary. Changes in base pay or salary may, therefore, be more appropriate when the worker has some change in responsibilities.

From a motivational standpoint a bonus is a more effective method of rewarding outstanding performance. It is closely tied to performance and is only given when the worker demonstrates superior work performance. Some companies have bonuses that range from a few hundred dollars to five thousand dollars or more. Most bonuses are given shortly after the performance that earned it so that there is a very strong reinforcement of desirable behavior. This pairing of performance followed closely by reinforcement will do a great deal to assure that the performance will be repeated.

A good performance measure is required if pay is to be used to motivate people. Generally performance measures based upon productivity are much better than measures based upon superior ratings. Productivity rates can be quantified and are factual in nature. From that standpoint, it is easier for workers to have trust and confidence in productivity ratings than in the subjective judgments of supervisors.

Perhaps the most crucial factor affecting the success of using pay to increase motivation is the worker's belief that pay is tied to performance. The best way to insure that workers believe that their pay is tied to their performance is to offer individual bonus rewards based on productivity performance measures. When productivity measures are not available, select the next best performance measure but try to use an individual plan when possible.

A listing of the advantages and disadvantages of individual and organizational incentives is shown in Table 9.3. This table shows that group and plantwide plans have more basic advantages and fewer basic limitations than the individual plans. Although this is true in terms of numbers, the significance of the advantages associated with the group and plantwide programs are not as important as those associated with the individual plans. By the same token, the disadvantage of the group and plantwide incentive systems (of not rewarding each employee according to individual productivity) is more damaging motivationally than those cited for individual incentive plans. That is to say, when the individual

TABLE 9.3 A Comparison between Individual Incentives and Group Incentives

Items of Comparison	Incentives	
	Individual	Group and Plant Wide
Basic Characteristics	Rewards are based on individual performance in number of units produced per hour.	Rewards are based on group performance in number of dollars saved or increased (in profits, sales values, production value added by manufacturer, or prime costs).
	Performance (output) needs to be within the direct control of the individual.	Performance is often only indirectly controlled by employees.
	The industrial engineer usually determines performance standards.	A committee is most likely used to determine performance standards.
	Rewards are forthcoming every pay period.	Rewards are forthcoming on a monthly, quarterly, semiannual, or annual basis.
	Encourages individuality and competition.	Encourages teamwork and unity.
	Relies heavily on monetary rewards.	May have nonfinancial as well as financial rewards.
Basic Advantages	Appeals to individualists.	Motivates large numbers of employees.
	Rewards employees in direct proportion to their productivity.	Useful on a wide variety of tasks.
	Provides fairly accurate cost data for estimating job costs.	Draws employee and firm goals together.
		Can include all employees in firm.
		Administrative costs are minimal.
		Does not resist technological change.
		Employees cooperate in solving problems that arise.
		Provides continuous opportunities for employees to be constructive and to satisfy many of their needs.

continued

TABLE 9.3 (continued)

Items of Comparison	Incentives	
	Individual	*Group and Plant Wide*
Basic Limitations	Rarely includes all employees. Restricted to mass-produced, relatively simple operations. Causes a number of grievances. Has been limited to physical output. Not very adaptable to high-quality jobs. Difficult to get agreement on job standards. Employees do not cooperate in policing system. Extra records and costs are incurred. Difficult to maintain over the long run.	Does not reward each employee according to his exact productivity.

Source: Herbert G. Zollitsch and Adolph Langsner, Wage and Salary Administration *(Dallas, Texas: South-Western Publishing Co., 1970), p. 605.*

incentive plans work, they work very well. On the other hand, when the group and organizational plans work, they have low to average effects on increasing the motivation of the workers. The task of each manager is to choose between salary or bonus rewards and between individual, group, or organization pay plans to suit the particular situation. Some compromises may have to be made. Nevertheless, given time, a carefully designed program of paying people for performance will develop a highly satisfied and motivated work force. In the long run, employee turnover will be centered only among the poor performers when people are paid for performance. The poor or marginal performers will simply not earn enough money to satisfy their needs. The high performance workers will stay in the organization when they feel their performance is rewarded appropriately. Unless, of course, they are lured away by some other organization that offers even better rewards.

CAFETERIA COMPENSATION

A recent innovation in pay administration is referred to as a cafeteria or smorgasbord approach. It is so named because the employee is allowed to select a combination of fringe benefits. Such plans allocate a sum of money to the employee that is equal to the total of the wage or salary plus the fringe benefits for the individual. Based on the total compensation costs, an employee may choose to receive more compensation in salary or may elect to get more of certain benefits. Everyone places different values on pay increases, sabbatical leaves, extra vacation days, insurance, medical care, and the like. A young unmarried worker may prefer more vacation time and more cash-on-hand. Older workers may want greater retirement benefits. By recognizing this, and trying to better meet the needs of employees in terms of compensation, the organization can optimize the value of the labor cost dollar.

At this time, the cafeteria plan is experimental. It does require a good deal of flexibility within a compensation department because of the administrative problems that exist when everyone is selecting a different combination of pay and benefits. It would seem that some type of plan that would offer a limited number of alternatives giving various mixes of benefits would be a logical approach.

The greatest benefit of any cafeteria plan is the fact that for once all employees would be fully informed about their compensation. Employees would be motivated to learn more about their compensation system as they would have to make a decision on the combination of benefits. Pay dissatisfaction is influenced by several perceptions, one of which is the amount of compensation actually received. Perceptions of pay will improve once workers know the actual value of their compensation package. In addition, if management is going to use pay as a motivational device, this plan has a greater chance of increasing the motivation of people as it can be designed to more closely meet the needs of the individual than any other plan.

SUMMARY

Pay is the return for services rendered to an organization. Pay, as part of the total compensation package, is thought to attract workers to an organization, hold them in the organization, and influence them toward personal and organizational goals.

Presently, money is believed to strongly influence employee satisfaction and motivation to work. Pay becomes important when the worker believes that money can be helpful in satisfying unfulfilled needs. Money has the potential for satisfying all needs but usually does more to meet esteem, security, and physiological needs than social and self-actualization needs.

Pay dissatisfaction occurs when employees perceive a difference between the amount received and the amount that should be received. An employee's perception of the amount that should be received is strongly influenced by the performance and pay of the referent other. The referent other may be a peer, superior, or a subordinate and may be employed in the same company or in another. There is a tendency for people with higher educational attainment to compare their pay with persons in companies outside of their own.

Equity theory explains how employees change work quality and quantity due to feelings of underpayment or overpayment. They seek to resolve feelings of inequity in order to feel that they have been treated fairly and equitably in pay matters.

For pay to motivate workers, several conditions must exist: (1) workers must attach a high value to pay; (2) employees must believe that good performance does in fact lead to higher pay; (3) employees must believe that their performance reflects to a large extent how hard they are trying; and (4) employees must see that superior performance is related to more positive consequences than negative. Bonus incentive plans are much more effective in tying pay to performance than are salary increases.

From a motivational standpoint, individual incentive plans are more effective than group incentive plans. While both approaches have several advantages and disadvantages, it is the task of a manager to know which plans best suits a particular situation.

A fairly recent innovation in pay administration allows employees to select the combination of fringe benefits they believe to be the most useful. This cafeteria approach provides workers the opportunity to create their own reward system and helps the organization optimize the value of the investment put into employees.

NOTES

1. E. J. ROETHLISBERGER and W. J. DICKSON, *Management and the Worker* (Cambridge, Mass.: Harvard University Press, 1939).

2. FREDERICK HERZBERG, B. MAUSNER, and BARBARA SNYDERMAN, *The Motivation to Work* (New York: John Wiley and Sons, 1959).

3. Ibid.

4. I. R. ANDREWS and MILDRED M. HENRY, "Management Attitudes Toward Pay," *Industrial Relations* 3, No. 1 (1963): 28–36.

5. Ibid.

6. J. S. ADAMS, "Injustice in Social Exchange," in *Advances in Experimental Social Psychology*, Vol. 2, ed. L. Berkowitz (New York: The Academic Press, 1965), p. 280.

7. See EDWARD LAWLER, III, *Pay and Organizational Effectiveness: A Psychological View* (New York: McGraw-Hill, 1971), Chapter 9.
8. Ibid.

QUESTIONS FOR THOUGHT AND DISCUSSION

1. How does money become important? What human needs does it fulfill? How important is money to white-collar workers? To blue-collar workers?

2. Why does research on the various effects of pay have such a short history?

3. List the last two jobs you have held. Now, please identify the person or persons with whom you compared your pay as well as your performance. Lastly, comment on your level of pay satisfaction in each case and how the referent other influenced your pay satisfaction. (Students who have not been previously employed can make the comparison based upon different college classes. Grades can be treated as the equivalent of pay.)

4. Turn to the model of the consequences of pay dissatisfaction. Think of two of the past work (or school) experiences where you felt underpaid and identify the consequences of pay dissatisfaction you demonstrated. Add other consequences of dissatisfaction if necessary.

5. Many companies give lip service to the ideas of influencing worker motivation with money. Drawing from the constraints or limitations presented in the latter part of this chapter, offer your opinions on the practicality of an average firm trying to use money as a motivational tool.

KEY TERMS

The student should be able to discuss the significance of these terms to the study of human behavior in the work environment.

Referent other	Determinants of pay satisfaction
Equity theory	Pay dissatisfaction
Wage inequity	Consequences of pay dissatisfaction
Pay satisfaction	Cafeteria compensation

CASE INCIDENT

The Mid-Texas Oil Company is a relatively small oil company employing about 400 people. A good proportion of its people are scientists with various training, such as geologists, physicists, engineers, and the like. There are seven other firms in Texas specializing in the same kind of work as the Mid-Texas Oil Company.

Rodney Stiff, President of Mid-Texas, has been informed by Carol Jones, the Vice-President of Personnel, that the scientists are unhappy about their pay. Rodney Stiff does not understand how the unfavorable pay attitude has developed since the company is paying the scientists 6 percent to 11 percent higher than even the top-paying firms in the industry. The president and vice-president of personnel have examined the validity of the survey questionnaire originally used to gather the satisfaction data and confirmed its validity and reliability. The survey program also measured the level of work, promotion, supervision and co-worker satisfactions. All of these indices of satisfaction showed a good state of affairs.

A management consultant was retained to study the possible reasons for the low pay satisfaction. The consultant interviewed forty of the scientists as well as twenty middle and upper managers and found that they were genuinely dissatisfied with their salaries. This means the people believed that they should receive more than the pay they actually received. During the interviews the consultant learned several things. First, surprisingly, the personnel interviewed did not compare their pay with their peers, supervisors, or subordinates. Second, the employees did not know they were being paid higher than the employees in the seven other firms in the industry. Third, the scientists were comparing their pay with people outside of their industry as well as outside of their company. The referent others were generally higher paid people doing nonscientific work in a variety of other industries.

Adding to the dilemma facing Rodney Stiff, Carol Jones and the consultant, the employees did not demonstrate any behavioral consequences often linked with pay dissatisfaction. That is, the workers did not search for higher paying jobs, did not lower job performance, were not absent from work any more than normal, were not tardy, and did not quit.

However, the workers were perceived by Carol Jones as apathetic and listless. She attributed these feelings to pay dissatisfaction. She believed that the scientists should be high in pay satisfaction and suggested to Stiff and the consultant that "we manage the pay comparison phenomenon."

Questions for Discussion

1. In your opinion were the scientists really dissatisfied with their pay?

2. Since the scientists and managers were being paid higher than their industry's average, how can Mid-Texas Oil insure that in the future the employees compare their pay internally with peers, superiors, and subordinates or with people holding similar jobs in another company? Use the key terms to organize your answer.

PART FIVE

LEADERSHIP AND HUMAN BEHAVIOR IN THE WORK ENVIRONMENT

A leadership style is usually an expression of an individual's managerial philosophy. The way a manager displays and applies this philosophy is dependent upon his or her ability to communicate. Generally, people will have a communication style that is supportive of their leadership style. Chapter 10 discusses the communication process by pointing out some of the more common barriers to communication and how they may be minimized. The chapter emphasizes the dynamics of the communication process and how the link between leader and follower may be strengthened through better communications.

The remaining three chapters of this part demonstrate that the process of leadership is extremely critical to the success of any group. An effective leader has the ability to lead the group to the accomplishment of group or organizational goals in a manner that is consistent with the situational requirements. This means that an appropriate leadership style will vary with the situation. The style that is most appropriate for getting the work done in one situation may be ineffective in different circumstances.

Just as leadership style varies with the situation so will the amount of group participation. There are many factors to consider in deciding how much participation is desirable. This is especially true when using a team problem-solving approach. Leaders are thus required to be able to read the situation and to utilize techniques that are compatible with the situation. The most difficult element of the situation to know and to predict is human behavior. Therefore, the leader must know something about the people and their needs, what motivates them, what stresses they are under, and how the job and work environment impacts upon them.

10

Communications in the Work Environment

LEARNING OBJECTIVES

Upon completion of this chapter the student should be able to:

- Define the communication process.
- Identify barriers to communications.
- Take steps to overcome barriers to communications.
- Explain the role of management in developing and maintaining a good communication flow.
- Show the relationship of communication factors to organizational goals.
- Describe how a supportive level of communication is important to the leadership process.
- Contrast the differing nature and content of upward and downward communications.
- Recognize the role of the informal network.
- Discuss the relationship of formal and informal communications.

"What we have here is a failure to communicate." This well-known quote from the movie *Cool Hand Luke* points out the cause of many misunderstandings and conflicts. The failure to communicate is perhaps cited more often than any other single reason as a contributor to poor interpersonal relations. Surely we all can't be so poor in our communication efforts that we unknowingly but continuously contribute to interpersonal problems. Wrong! Many individuals either create problems or add fuel to existing ones because of inept communications. Since it is assumed that communication problems or shortcomings are not interjected purposefully, it would follow that such problems are due to either a lack of knowledge of proper communications or carelessness in the communications process. Before we can appreciate the nature and the impact of communication shortcomings on the work environment, we must first better understand the communication process.

THE COMMUNICATION PROCESS

The process of one individual communicating with another is something with which we are all familiar. It has been part of our lives since birth. We all have experienced the various methods of sending and receiving messages. Even before we had command of the spoken or written word, we managed to communicate. We were quite capable as babies at informing our parents what pleased us and when we felt we needed something. Generally we used our capacity to express ourselves, without yet being able to talk, to inform others that we were uncomfortable, hungry, or in need of attention. Thus, most all of us were practitioners of body language and other communicative processes long before we had ever heard of the various techniques of communication.

If we were so successful as babies and young children in communicating our desires, why do we seem to blunder so often now as adults? The answer rests in the different kinds of relationships we experience. As babies the communication process was mainly a one-sided affair. An explanation from Mother as to why a bottle was not ready for us at the exact moment we awoke did little to satisfy the perceived need for food at that moment in time. Today as adults it is unfortunate that some people continue to view communications with the same selfish one-sidedness as they did as children.

Communication is much more than sending a message. Many times we send a message and wrongly assume that its intent is understood. This mistake occurs primarily because of our failure to recognize the other person's perception. If all people viewed things in the same manner as the sender of a message, there would be little chance of misunderstanding. However, since each individual has a different perception, each indi-

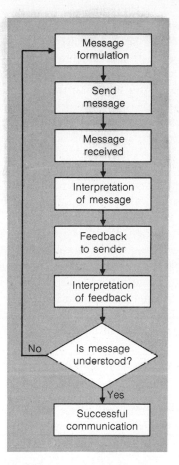

Figure 10.1   Communication Process

vidual will interpret the message in terms of his or her own particular situation. An otherwise simple message can be interpreted in as many different ways as there are individuals receiving the message.

The communication process must, therefore, be recognized in total—not just as the sending of the message. Figure 10.1 demonstrates the complete process in flow-chart form. Successful communication involves formulating the message, sending the message, receiving the message, interpreting the message, and understanding the message. The figure represents the steps that must be completed for successful communication, but it does not demonstrate where breakdowns may occur to disrupt communication. There may be breakdowns or reasons for breakdowns at any step of the process. Faulty message formulation or the manner in which the message is delivered could interrupt the successful transmission of a message. Understanding is, of course, the most troublesome part of the communication process. There are probably always some perceptual barriers that prevent complete understanding of a message, but after feedback from the receiver, the sender may be satisfied as to an appropriate level of communications. Again, the individual's perception will influence the way the feedback is interpreted, but if there seems to be a misunderstanding the sender may repeat the message using different words, analogies, and symbols until the receiver provides the kind of feedback that informs the sender that there is understanding of the message. The ultimate responsibility for communication rests with the sender of a message, not the receiver.[1]

Feedback may not always be voluntary. The sender of the message may feel it necessary to ask questions or encourage the receiver to ask questions to ascertain the level of comprehension. Facial expressions, actions, body language, or verbal (oral) responses are types of feedback that the sender must be able to interpret. Since the interpretation of the feedback is done by the sender of the message, the decision as to the necessity of repeating the message is most often left to the initiator of the communication. This means that the interpretation of feedback is one of the most critical, but most ignored, steps in the communication process. A person who is a good communicator will not only be aware of feedback but will constantly seek feedback for an indication of understanding.

METHODS OF COMMUNICATING

The most often used and abused method of communicating is the spoken word. A recent study indicates that even in organizations where the written word is emphasized in giving orders to subordinates, oral communications are still used more frequently. In fact, 70 percent of the 465 respondents to the study stated that 75 percent of the assignments given to them by their superiors were given by oral communications.[2]

The term "communications" typically conjures up an image of two people engaged in conversation. It is within these one-on-one relationships that we experience most of our communication efforts. But oral communications may also involve small groups of people or very large groups. Most managers must have the capacity to speak successfully to groups of people as well as being able to communicate on a one-on-one basis.

The written word is generally believed to be the second most used means of communicating. Books, newspapers, magazines, reports, memos, letters, and signs confront us with literally thousands of words daily. Each attempt at communicating through the written word represents what is thought by the writer of the message to be the best choice of words to transfer information to the reader. The "best choice," of course, depends upon the reason for the message. One might expect a difference in the choice of words in a letter written to a friend and in a business letter informing a client of an overdue bill. Also the language used in a popular novel is quite different from that used in writing a legal case brief. Since the audience for the written word may oftentimes be a very diverse group in terms of education and background, the writer of material to be read widely by the population must be most careful of the reading level. Conversely, the manager of a work unit has a very narrow and well-defined audience which has a similar perspective in terms of the organizational environment. The fact that messages written to such a group in what is believed by the manager to be very clear and concise terminology are frequently misinterpreted serves to point out the complex nature of the communication process.

Pictures, images, and symbols are also attempts to communicate. Other art forms such as dancing, sculptures, and music likewise represent communication of ideas, thoughts, and feelings through media with some aesthetic value. While artistic offerings are among the most misunderstood methods of communicating, they are the most prized. Even though the intent of the artist may be completely misunderstood by the general populace, the art itself is appreciated for its aesthetic appeal. This is unique to this method of communication. Seldom would a manager hear a subordinate say, "I really don't know what you are trying to tell me or what you expect of me, but you certainly have a beautiful vocabulary."

The use of symbols to communicate is becoming more common today. Within manufacturing plants symbols on multi-colored signs are being used to warn of hazardous equipment, hard-hat areas, and no smoking areas, and to identify particular operations. The use of symbols on signs provides information quickly and easily with minimal possibilities of misinterpretation. For example, in traffic control where language can be a barrier the adoption of international symbols to inform motorists of hazards and regulations minimizes the chance of misunderstanding.

Other nonverbal means of communicating include facial expressions, gestures, and body language. The interpretation of the latter has become so sophisticated in terms of analyzing body movements that an individual can supposedly tell what another really means when communicating. Speakers can even favorably influence the opinion of their audience through the use of more open body positions.[3] Certain postures are indicative of defensiveness, openness, hostility, and nearly every mood or emotion of which human beings are capable. As with other types of communication, however, it is wise to seek additional feedback to make sure one's interpretation of body language is correct.

Telecommunications will soon become a reality in the business world. The various electronic devices that will be utilized will surely facilitate the communication process between individuals who are physically far removed from one another. It will be possible to talk face-to-face with business associates regardless of distance and to participate in nationwide meetings without leaving the office.[4] Such sophisticated advances in the transmission process, however, will still not rid communication attempts of barriers that tend to impede and inhibit the transferal of information. Ridding the communication process of the human-oriented problems presents much more of a challenge than overcoming those which are mechanically oriented.

BARRIERS TO COMMUNICATIONS

Barriers to communications exist in many different forms and are to be found in nearly all environments. A barrier to communications is anything that interferes with the transmittal, reception, or understanding of a message. This applies to the feedback process as much as to the sending of a message. These interferences are frequently referred to as "noise."[5] While a literal translation of the word noise is appropriate when applied to barriers, a broader definition is more useful. Noise in this instance is meant to include all kinds of interference. For example, when two young students are talking on a busy street corner, the distraction of a feared teacher walking by represents "noise" in their communication process just as the din of heavy traffic is also "noise."

Semantic Differences

According to *Webster's Seventh New Collegiate Dictionary,* semantics is the study of meanings of words. The fact that words may have different meanings to different people adds to the chance that any communication attempt may be misunderstood. In some cases the connotation is unclear to the receiver of the message. A manager may forget that for an employee to understand the words given, the employee must know the manager's purpose in using them.[6] Trying to interpret the sender's words from the sender's perspective requires more knowledge of the manager than most subordinates have.

Some semantical problems may be due to differences in background such as the region of the country or ethnic neighborhood in which an individual was reared. Whatever the reason, it is clear that words may be interpreted differently by different people. The following conversation between two men in a small town in Florida illustrates a semantic difference. One man who is approximately twenty-five years of age is reading the paper. The older gentleman, about sixty-five years old, is sitting next to the younger man and whittling. The conversation begins with a comment from the younger man:

Younger Man: Well, it's about that time of year. The Yankees are coming south next week.

Older Man: Yup. I reckon you're right. I just wish they'd stay where they belong.

Younger Man: What do you mean by that?

Older Man: Why can't they stay up north and do their hell raisin' there?

Younger Man: It's too cold. They've got to get in shape.

Older Man: Drinkin' beer and sleepin' on the beach ain't my idea of gettin' in shape.

Younger Man: Where did you ever hear such a thing?

Older Man: It hits the papers every year. Can't keep a thing like that quiet, you know.

Younger Man: I doubt that Billy Martin would stand for that kind of behavior. He just wouldn't allow it.

Older Man: I wouldn't know about Billy Martin, but Billy Graham sure has done his best to stop such goings on.

Obviously, throughout the abbreviated conversation, the two men were talking about different things. The older man, when he heard the "Yankees" were coming south, understood the message to mean that the college students from the north were beginning their annual spring migration. The younger man was, of course, talking about the New York Yankee baseball team. While the example is somewhat exaggerated, it does demonstrate how the different interpretation of one word can influence the entire conversation, even though that word was never used again.

As words are simply symbols used to convey information, it is quite likely that these symbols convey the meaning most familiar to the receiver. The manner in which certain words or phrases are interpreted is often due to individual perception.

Perceptual Bias

Perceptual bias is a major barrier to communications in that it can act as a contributor to almost every other barrier. Each person's background and experiences influence the way in which that individual will view things. This unique way in which a person views the world is known as perception. Seldom will two people have backgrounds so similar that their viewpoints will be consistently the same. However, when two people are very close, their ability to communicate is so exceptional that they seldom even speak in complete sentences. Facial expressions, body language, and the use of certain words will frequently be all that is needed to transfer information from one close friend to another. This, of course, is possible due to a high degree of compatibility between the individuals.

But so many factors contribute to one's perception or viewpoint that any variance in one factor can be enough to cause perceptual differences. For example, two young trainees with nearly identical backgrounds in terms of economic status, education, religion, and families may have quite a different perception when it comes to communicating within the business organization. While both have degrees in marketing, one pursued a career in sales and the other decided upon advertising. Even though they are in the same division, when reading a memo or receiving various communiques, the new employees will interpret the message in terms of their own particular interests.

The position a person holds, the company worked for, economic status, geographic location, and other physical and psychological factors determine the perceptual bias for individuals. This bias, or set, will influence how people view things and even what they expect to see or hear. These perceptual differences become important when they represent barriers to effective communications. Perhaps the most obvious example within any organization is the differences that exist between labor and management. The fact that the relationship is often referred to by terms such as "us" and "them" is usually a strong indication that there are perceptual differences.

Perceptual differences are not limited to just widely diverse groups such as labor and management. From one level of management to the next there may be very pronounced differences in perception of job-related duties. One study using a random sample of 989 manufacturing firms in the Midwest having fifty or more employees found that the perception of the level of authority of the first-line supervisor (foreman) differed greatly between the foreman and the next level superior.[7] Out of a total of 39 situations described for the respondents, which required a response as to whether or not the foreman had the authority to handle the situation, the mean and median number of disagreements was 19.7. In other words, in the decision-making situations presented to the respondents there was a fifty-fifty chance that the foreman and the superior would disagree on the amount of authority the foreman had to take some action.

Perceptual Distortion and Stereotyping

Another perceptual problem that interferes with communication is perceptual distortion. Since people always select a perception that matches their self-concept, it is possible for individuals to distort information that conflicts with their self-image so that it will match their beliefs.[8] This process of purposely distorting a message so that it is more compatible with one's beliefs is known as perceptual distortion.

On occasion individuals will disregard information about particular people or groups in order to support prior beliefs about those people. This type of perceptual distortion is known as stereotyping. Because of pre-conceived ideas about certain groups of people, individuals may some-times see all people in a group as being the same. Using information gained in an isolated incident and applying it to all situations or people perceived to be the same as those who were directly involved is stereo-typing.

The typical college campus offers an excellent example of stereotypes. Certain majors, fraternities, and sororities will usually be stereotyped by others. Engineers are seen as being very good in math and generally so specialized that they are not "well-rounded." Fraternity members are commonly referred to as "animals" and not given much credit for possessing any intellect. Sorority members are characterized as being solely concerned with fashion and social affairs. Likewise profes-sors must live with the stigma of being "a little weird" and extremely absentminded.

When employees allow stereotyping to interfere with communica-tions, they are really evaluating the source of a message instead of the message itself. For example, the intent may be completely missed or the message ignored because it came from the personnel department, "and you know how credible those people are."

Emotional States

This barrier is particularly difficult to overcome because the emotional state of an individual is causing the breakdown, not a shortcoming in the process itself. When a person is terribly depressed, everything sounds bad and a pessimistic view will take precedence. Conversely, when someone is in an extremely good mood, everything sounds good and it is easy to be optimistic. Adding to the problems associated with this barrier is the tendency of an emotion to be self-perpetuating and contagious. In other words, within a human being depression tends to beget depression. It is often easier to fall further into the depths of depression than it is to pull oneself out of it.

An emotion also can be contagious to others. Effective speakers can use this contagious aspect of emotionalism to great advantage. Adolf Hitler was a master of this technique, as are many successful salespeople, comedians, and actors. Although this emotionalism may occur at inop-portune moments, it is a part of the communication process that can be used in either a positive or negative manner.

The fact that emotionalism not only interferes with the communica-tion process but is also self-perpetuating, contagious, and inopportune in terms of timing can be shown by an example. One which nearly all of us have witnessed or have been part of as children usually takes place in church or at other fairly organized and solemn occasions. When one child sees, hears, or imagines something funny, pains are taken to suppress laughter. This just makes matters worse. The friend witnessing this aborted attempt to hold back laughter finds that to be terribly funny. From then on they reinforce one another's behavior and literally everything becomes funny. This emotional condition usually continues until threatening behavior from parents or other authority figures puts a stop to it.

Past Relationships

Past relationships cause people to have certain expectations concerning the behavior of others. When these expectations are not met, the individuals find themselves operating on different wavelengths. If, for example, employees have become accustomed to an autocratic approach from their boss, an attempt toward democratic leadership may be ignored because it does not coincide with their expectations.[9] A sincere effort on the part of a supervisor to become more participative may not be accepted because it does not match past behavior. It is therefore viewed as behavior that is out of character and hence not "real" and not to be taken seriously.

Managers who have not had successful dealings in the past with their subordinates may find it difficult to establish a more favorable relationship for future endeavors. It is hard to overcome the problems or perceived problems of the past. Comments such as, "The boss didn't tell me the truth the last time, why should I believe things are different now?" are frequently heard. Even though a past mistake may have been unintentional, if the subordinate believes it was purposeful, it becomes a very real and pressing issue.

The manager of a work unit must constantly seek to establish a climate of mutual credibility and respect. This means bringing disagreements and petty differences into the open so they may be put to rest before they are allowed to cause the relationship to degenerate. Candor, sincerity, and encouragement of open communications can be among the best weapons for overcoming problems of the past. Such an approach also provides a strong foundation on which to build the present and future relationship.

Timing

Timing of a message can add or detract from the value of the communication. A poorly timed release of a notice to install new equipment in a manufacturing plant, for example, can present a very formidable barrier to employee understanding. When such a message occurs during a business downturn, employees will interpret the meaning in negative terms.

"Knowing" that automated machinery is going to take over their jobs, people will quit prematurely in order to begin the search for other employment. This example has been all too real for several organizations. With more attention given to the timing and the content of the communique, needless personnel turnover could have been eliminated.

A message that would be very appropriate at one point in time could prove very inappropriate at another time. The perception of the receiver is often the determining factor. This makes a manager's ability to feel empathy with subordinates important not only for content but timing as well.

Geographical Distance

Distance between people creates a physical barrier that limits the frequency and means of communicating. This can be true even when people are located within the same plant. Although they may be separated by less than a city block, the physical distance between two individuals can be exaggerated by the presence of organizational lines, differing operating philosophies, and, of course, a buffer of people. Even a small difference in physical location can be as formidable a barrier as when two people are in different sales offices. This becomes even more true when individuals are working within different functional areas.

With an increase in geographical distance separating sender and receiver there is generally a greater chance for distortion or misunderstanding. Part of the case for distance being a barrier is the limited direct personal contact. There is understandably less chance for feedback to help clarify communications. In addition, frequency of contact is limited. Usually communications will improve the greater the frequency of contacts. While there are exceptions, people will become accustomed to one another's methods of communicating and each other's perceptual set.

Filter Problem

As children most of us played a game in which a message was started by one child who whispered it to the person next to him. The message was quickly passed from one child to the next until it finally reached the last one in the circle. At this point the message as received was told to all and the initiator of the message was asked to divulge the original message. The difference usually caused wild outbreaks of laughter. Why and how the message became so garbled was not important; the outcome was important.

The game described depicts a communication barrier known as the filter problem. Just as in the game, it seems the more people a message must pass through the greater the likelihood of it being changed. While people like to add their own interpretation and opinion to information passed through them, there does not have to be a purposeful attempt to change the message in order for distortion to occur. Even when a communique flows through the organizational channels unencumbered with rumors and other additions or deletions, the chances are that it will be changed slightly somewhere in its conveyance. Unlike in the children's game, the possible reasons for breakdown are important. Analysis of the media used, the channels followed, and of course the points at which the change appeared to take place are necessary to deal with the filter problem.

Minimizing Barriers

While it is very unlikely that the various barriers to communications can be completely eliminated, they can be minimized. The methods available for reducing the impact of the barriers make use of a combination of communication basics. The following basics of successful communications offer little in the way of originality but serve as a reminder of those things which can be done to improve communication efforts.

Listen.   Both sender and receiver should be fully aware of what the other person is trying to communicate and should concentrate on listening as if a summary of the remarks was going to be required. The listener should always be evaluating the message.

Seek feedback.   Questions should be encouraged. It is important to utilize all sources of possible feedback: formal, informal, and accidental. Body language can reflect reactions of listeners and should be treated as an important source of feedback.

Interpret feedback and respond.   The correct response to feedback is in part a function of the correctness of the interpretation of the feedback. Recognition of the need indicated by the feedback and being able to satisfy that need is a characteristic of an effective communicator.

Build credibility.   Words should be backed up with action. This is the one sure method of building credibility. Many times the superior-subordinate relationship suffers from poor credibility. Promises made and not kept and failure to complete a job on time after assurances that it would be done with time to spare are but two examples of actions that contribute to poor credibility. In order for both superiors and subordinates to build their credibility, there must be an understood reciprocal agreement to be honest and forthright in communicating and to make an effort to live up to what is said.

Use empathy.   Being able to project oneself into the other person's situation will help a speaker or listener be more cognizant of the other person's feelings. This ability to be sensitive to another's perception will greatly enhance the communication process by minimizing those barriers resulting from people's differing perceptual sets.

Be candid and straightforward.   When delivering a message the chances of it being misunderstood can be minimized by being direct and straightforward, making use of simple language. By avoiding the use of words that may cause confusion, some semantical difficulties can be eliminated.

Vary media.   Overuse of one particular method of communicating may rob it of effectiveness. By changing media from time to time a high degree of awareness to the message itself can be maintained. When a mimeographed memo is distributed to all employees to inform them of the mundane and "administrivia," chances are that the use of that means to communicate a message of import will cause the audience to ignore it. Since the receiving audience has become accustomed to having nothing important on the mimeographed sheets, many people will not even read them before filing them in the "circular file."

Reiterate.   A certain amount of repetition is often needed. This is especially true when managers find themselves involved in training employees. By rewording an instruction slightly and saying the same thing in a different way, managers can improve the degree of understanding through an effective use of reiteration. In fact, repetition also has been used very effectively in mass communication efforts. Results of a study on the use of repetition in advertising show that similar rather than identical messages could have an immediate impact upon people's attitudes. The same information presented in a new context with different phrasing appears to be very efficient in helping to change attitudes.[10] Appropriate utilization of repetition depends upon timing and the manner in which the message is delivered. It will probably do little good to repeat the message over and over in exactly the same terms. If the listener did not understand something the second or third time, there is only a remote chance that it will be understood after further repetitions. The use of analogies and examples can be a very meaningful way of applying effective reiteration.

While the above information is by no means a comprehensive coverage of barriers and methods to minimize them, this discussion is representative of the problems and techniques common to most all levels of communications. The next section will deal more specifically with the communication efforts within the hierarchical structure.

THE ROLE OF MANAGEMENT IN ORGANIZATIONAL COMMUNICATIONS

Organizational communications consist of all formal communications within the established networks and structure of an organization. All possible media that can be used to transmit information should be considered as being part of the organizational communications effort. This effort is functional in nature in that either directly or indirectly all formal organizational communications should contribute something to goal achievement.

Organizational communications can, therefore, be defined in terms of purpose, operational procedure, and structure.[11] The purpose of organizational communications is to help in the achievement of organizational goals. Operational procedures include:

- The utilization of communication networks
- The adoption of communication policies
- The implementation of the policies[12]

The structural elements of organizational communications comprise:

- The organization unit (department, division, etc.)
- The functional communication networks (formal organizational relationships)
- Communication activities[13]

Figure 10.2 demonstrates the relationship of the communication factors and organizational goals. In order for the communications to be as effective as possible, management must be able to relate organizational goals to all members of the organization, develop operating procedures for the communication system, and develop an appropriate structure within which the system can operate. While the policies on communications are developed by top management, middle managers and first-line supervisors must be the activators.

Filtering of Communications

The major responsibility for communications within any department rests with the manager of that work unit. How well managers actually fulfill this responsibility, however, is not always something for which they can take sole credit or blame. Good communication in an organization is dependent upon all members of the organization. Ultimately top management is responsible for the company's communication flow. Manage-

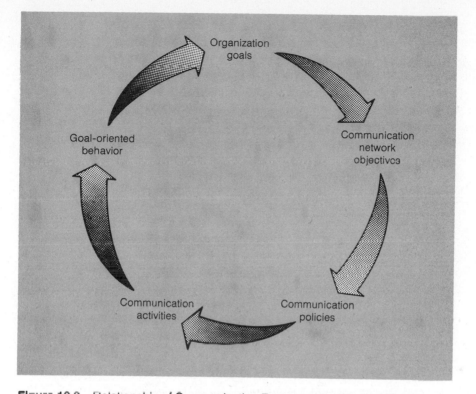

Figure 10.2 Relationship of Communication Factors to Organization Goals

From Howard H. Greenbaum, "The Audit of Organizational Communication," Academy of Management Journal *17 (December 1974): 743.*

rial philosophy, leadership styles, policies, and organizational structure are among those factors that will affect the flow. Since philosophies, attitudes, and leadership styles filter from the top down, the upper levels of management tend to influence all levels of management regarding these factors. As these elements contribute to the overall organizational climate and hence the supportive level of communications, the importance of top management's impact can clearly be seen.

Individual managers will interpret top management's intentions and expectations and strive to fulfill them in the process of carrying out the departmental objectives. Each lower level manager's interpretation of top management's desires is usually based upon the immediate superior's interpretation. Herein is one of the most critical filter problems in an organization. All managers serve as information centers—if not for the entire organization at least to the people within their respective departments. A slight misinterpretation at one level will have a chain reaction type of effect. Figure 10.3 demonstrates how the chain reaction is likely to be worsened as a message travels down through the hierarchy. Given the chance of some misinterpretation at each level and the fact that each interpretation of top management's intent is based upon that of the im-

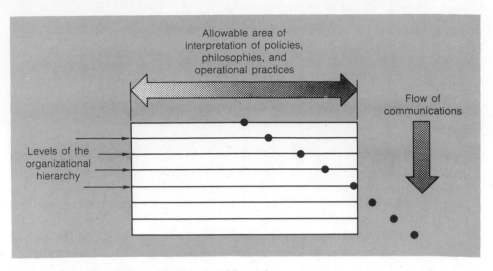

Figure 10.3 The Filtering Problem in a Hierarchy

mediate superior, the deviation at the lower levels will become exaggerated. The result is similar to that of the old "crack the whip" game. Those at the end of the communications chain have suffered more from the cumulative actions of the complete chain than those at the top.

The two vertical lines in Figure 10.3 represent the allowable area of interpretation—there usually is some flexibility in interpreting top management policies and philosophies within certain limits. In the situation presented by Figure 10.3 the dots represent a person who is a receiver, interpreter, and sender of a message coming from top management. The alignment of the dots serves to indicate the degree of correctness in the interpretation of the message. As the message goes through each organizational level the errors in interpretation cause further distortion. With each successive interpretation being based upon a previous misinterpretation, the allowable limits are soon violated and top management's expectations are not met. Since the real activation of a message may not be carried out until the middle to lower levels of the hierarchy, the misinterpretation at higher levels may not be realized until the point of application of the message at the lower level. By that time the difference between what was intended and what was actually done has been exaggerated by organizational distance.

Supportive Levels of Communications

The supportive level of communications is the level that is consistent with the leadership style and managerial philosophy. In other words, the degree of openness in communications is a reflection of the leadership style. It can be said that there is actually a communication style that accompanies each leadership style. Inconsistencies between the two in the work environment are glaring. As will be discussed in Chapter 11, autocratic managers would not generally be individuals who would encourage open communications. By the same token managers who outwardly advocated participative management would not be consistent if they did not encourage open communications. For any leadership style to be successful, there must be a supportive level of communications.

Managers who genuinely believe in their leadership styles will have little trouble in adopting a supportive level of communications. It is possible that just a desire to exhibit a certain type of leadership style will be enough to appreciably change the effectiveness of communications within a department. For example, if managers appear more open and accessible to subordinates, the subordinates will perceive a greater acceptance of ideas and other input. Over time this perception of openness will be tested. If input is accepted or at least considered by the manager, the climate will become increasingly more participative in nature. This is the opportunity for a manager to build credibility by backing up words with actions. However, even in very participative environments most formal communications will still be flowing downward.

Downward Communications

It is not difficult to initiate downward communications. However, it is difficult, because of the various barriers, to have the same message transmitted correctly through several organizational levels. More organizations should be concerned with facilitating the downward flow before moving into highly participative programs requiring a good deal of upward flow. If communications are consistently misunderstood in the downward flow, chances are the upward movement of information will not be appreciably better.

Despite a good deal of literature citing the negative aspects of downward communications, downward communication flow is necessary in all organizations. It cannot be eliminated. Even when participative programs are installed, the emphasis should be upon improving the flow in both directions, not cutting back on the downward flow. If anything, the downward flow should probably be improved in terms of both quantity and quality. It is the nature of the content of the information being sent downward that should change. More feedback in terms of praise, needed corrections, company and departmental goals, and results needs to be communicated rather than directives and unilateral decisions.

Realistically, downward communications are necessary in order for an organization to function properly. Therefore, when used with regard to the flow of information, "downward" is not a derogatory word. For some reason it has come to be associated with autocratic and paternalistic management. This should be true only of a certain kind of downward communications. Unfortunately, in a good deal of management literature the useful elements are overlooked in order to exaggerate the negative. It seems the phrase "downward communications" is similar to the word "snakes." Most people immediately think of the "bad" kind instead of the kind that are good. It is important to remember that it is the purpose for which the downward communication flow is used that makes it either a significant contributor or significant detractor to organizational goals.

Upward Communications

Management theorists Katz and Kahn have identified four kinds of job-related information that subordinates may volunteer or be required to communicate upward:

1. Performance and problems of the assigned job
2. Fellow employees and their problems
3. Organizational procedures and policies
4. Tasks to be performed[14]

Other kinds of upward communications include suggestion boxes, the "open-door policy," and group meetings sometimes referred to as "coffee with the boss." Since more attention is being given organizational development now than in the past, many companies are utilizing survey feedback techniques (questionnaires) and other sophisticated methods to improve upon the upward communication flow. Some of the other innovative techniques include a system whereby employees can question or discuss anonymously any job-related problem with a responsible company official by telephone or in writing, and the use of teams of volunteer, nonmanagement employees to work on company time to find solutions to company problems.[15] No doubt there are other equally creative and effective means of improving upon upward communications, but the above may be considered as representative of the attempts that are ongoing in industry today.

While downward communications are not bad in themselves, the absence of upward communications may cause them to look bad. Just as in a conversation, if the communication process is to be effective it must be two-way. Even in the most one-sided communication, there is a certain element of feedback from the listener. Only the most callous of persons can ignore the feedback as part of the two-way flow. However, in some cases organization management seems to possess such a callous attitude. Feedback in the form of slowdowns, grievances, absenteeism, and tardiness is an attempt on the part of the workers to communicate with management. They are providing a warning that something is wrong.

Managements that do not recognize this kind of feedback are doomed to failure. Those that do recognize it will seek more information and encourage an ongoing interchange to attempt to find a workable solution to the problem causing such negative feedback.

Management must constantly be aware of new ways to increase the upward flow of information as there are so many possible barriers to slow or discourage such communication efforts. It appears that the one best way to accomplish an upward communication flow is to develop an organizational climate that invites employee input and provides no deterrents to participation. When such a climate exists, there will be an ongoing dialogue that will be a true example of a two-way flow.

The upward flow of information is much more prone to breakdown than is the downward. Given the usual differences in message content between the two, the greater likelihood of distortion in the upward flow is not too surprising. Downward-directed messages are usually directives from superiors and are accepted at face value while upward-directed messages consist of information from subordinates which will often attempt to maximize their own gains.[16] Distortion is therefore more likely to occur in upward flows because of the tendency of the sender to maximize data that emphasizes strengths and minimize data that demonstrates weaknesses. It should also be noted that the risks taken when distorting messages are much greater in downward than upward communications. Most people will be hesitant to add or delete information from downward directives. Failure to carry out a directive could possibly cost individuals their jobs or at the very least bring about a reprimand. A distortion in upward communications is not so likely to cause such repercussions. The risk involved with exaggeration appears to be minimal, with a greater possible payoff. There is always the possibility that the boss may see the subordinate in a more favorable light as the result of some upward-directed information. Consequently, people who receive upward communications are more likely to take the message "with a grain of salt." This phenomenon, known as counter-biasing, appears to be one of the reasons for some distortion in upward communications. Research data have shown that upward-directed information that is unfavorable to the subordinate is perceived to be more accurate than that which is favorable.[17]

Being so delicate in nature, upward communications do require continual nurturing and cultivation. The success of an upward communication flow will be partially dependent upon the nature and the success of downward communication flow. From an employee's viewpoint the expression of organizational climate from management comes in the form of downward communications. The manner in which a message is delivered from the top down, the content of the message, and the degree to which inputs are encouraged will have a direct bearing on the amount and the quality of upward communications. However, the degree to which employees respond favorably to such encouragement is in part dependent upon interpersonal factors. The most critical of these factors appears to be trust. The more trust an employee has in his superior the greater the openness of communications between the two.[18] While this is undoubtedly true of any personal relationship, the nature of the superior-subordinate interface makes reciprocal trust even more important in establishing a genuine two-way flow of communications.

Lateral Communications

Communications between people on the same organizational level are known as lateral or horizontal communications. They often cut across organizational lines and are interdepartmental in nature. This cutting across organizational lines was referred to by Henri Fayol as the gangplank concept.[19] It does away with the necessity of channeling messages through each person's superior and thus makes the communications effort much faster and more efficient. The purpose of a horizontal flow of information is to coordinate departmental and individual work efforts so they are compatible and contribute to the achievement of organizational objectives. A good lateral communication flow will also prevent duplication of effort, will help identify problems in the system, and keep people informed regarding the locale of specialized expertise. Lateral communications can provide decision makers with the necessary information upon which to base their decisions. As the timeliness of most decisions is a critical factor, no manager can realistically depend solely upon the vertical communication system to provide all of the information needed at the time it is needed.[20]

In fact, many of the interdepartmental communications that are referred to as lateral are diagonal. Even though one person may appear higher on the organizational structure than another person from a different department, there are no direct authority lines, so they can communicate as if they were on the same level. The relationship will depend on how well they know one another, how often they work together, and the relative power of their departments.

A sometimes critical factor in determining lateral relationships is the line-staff distinction. In some organizations the distinction is very noticeable and in others it is inconsequential. When either line or staff is dominant, lateral communications appear to be something other than lateral. For example, in a corporation where the line people have the power, a personnel officer (staff) trying to promote a training program may seem subservient to a line manager on the same level. In fact, in some instances a line manager who is below a staff manager in terms of the hierarchy may have more organizational influence than the staff manager. Communications between the two will reflect this difference in perceived organizational power.

It is best that such power differences in line and staff not be emphasized. If lateral communications are to bring about the hoped for coordination among various departments, there is no place for displays of power. When one department is clearly more powerful than another on the same level and chooses to dominate it, communications are lateral in terms of formal description only. In practice another artificial organizational level has been added by the superior-subordinate relationship that exists between the departments.

INFORMAL COMMUNICATIONS

The organizational structure provides a formal communication network. There is a path for the flow of communications vertically and horizontally. However, there are communications within an organization which do not necessarily follow the formal paths. These informal communication networks may take several different forms but all may be considered as part of the "grapevine."

Even though the grapevine is an informal network, it is amazingly fast and frequently very accurate. In fact, recent research has found that between 75 and 95 percent of the information carried on a grapevine is correct.[21] It is therefore much more than a rumor mill. It serves to supplement formal communications. An astute management team will try to use the grapevine to good advantage. One of the best ways to do so is to provide information that is desired by the employees. When people do not receive the information they believe they should have, the grapevine has a tendency to carry an "unofficial" version that soon becomes accepted as fact. If the grapevine is unusually active, it is generally believed to be an indication of inadequate formal communications. However, results of research concerning the relationship between formal and informal communications do not completely support this belief. In fact, in organizations which have a communication flow that is characteristically vertical in nature, the activity of the informal network appears to be independent of the formal communications effort.[22] The relationship between formal horizontal communications and informal communications was found to be much stronger. It seems that increased peer contact and the informal lateral flow of communication do away with the need to even schedule formal meetings.[23]

Informal communications will, of course, cut across formal departmental lines and informal groups. Consequently, the grapevine can be viewed as a "super network of informal communications." In fact, the grapevine can even transcend individual company structures. It is not unknown for information from grapevines to be passed along to an employee's family members who in turn may introduce the message, provided it is of some interest, into other informal networks. The grapevine may become so efficient at bypassing certain groups or individuals that the employee's family may hear the latest information before the employee. Flows of information or networks within the grapevine may be very convoluted with seemingly little reason for the existing paths. There are, however, usually very good reasons why the messages flow the way they do.

Even when considering the round about network of the grapevine, its efficiency and speed are to be envied by the formal network. Because of its efficiency, speed, and ability to reach nearly every single employee, the potential disruptive power of the grapevine cannot go unnoticed. For some reason messages that are perceived as being bad news and those that shock people seem to spread most rapidly through the grapevine. Managers should be very concerned with the manner in which the grapevine works so that they might be better prepared to "plug into" the informal network from time to time in order to prevent the spread of possibly harmful rumors. It appears to be one of the best ways to effectively communicate with employees. The grapevine has the potential to assist organizational communications if it is cultivated in the proper way. After all, how often can management afford to say, "what we have here is a failure to communicate?"

SUMMARY

Every manager in an organization is an information center. This is especially true with respect to the people who work for and with a particular manager. Each manager is thus a critical link in the upward, downward, and lateral flows of communications.

As the communication process is a part of all interpersonal relationships, a breakdown at any point in the process can lead to misunderstanding and even conflict. While the total process involves formulating a message, sending of the message, receiving the message, interpretation of the message, feedback, and interpretation of feedback, the process cannot be considered complete until there is an understanding of the message by the receiver. The sender must be the judge of the level of understanding by the receiver through the use of feedback.

Perhaps one of the best ways to improve individual communication efforts is to be aware of the various barriers that interfere with the transfer and understanding of a message. Most barriers are related in some way to the different perceptions of sender and receiver. As all individuals will interpret a message in terms of their particular positions and/or interests, the potential for miscommunication is quite high.

By attempting to follow a few basic guidelines, barriers to communications can be minimized. Managers and employees should (1) listen more attentively, (2) utilize feedback, (3) build credibility, (4) try to empathize, (5) be candid, (6) vary the use of media, and (7) use repetition to advantage.

A manager's communication effort must be compatible with and supportive of the leadership style used. Generally there will be a high degree of consistency as the leadership style of a manager must be manifested by some form of communications with subordinates. However, an inconsistency between that which is espoused and that which is practiced usually is due to the inability of the manager to successfully adopt a supportive level of communications. Since the performance of a manager is so dependent upon the ability to communicate, neither the individual nor the organization can afford frequent usage of the quote, "what we have here is a failure to communicate."

NOTES

1. Arthur W. Combs, Donald L. Avila, and William W. Purkey, *Helping Relationships: Basic Concepts for the Helping Professions* (Boston: Allyn & Bacon, Inc., 1974), p. 253.

2. Marshall H. Brenner and Norman B. Sigband, "Organizational Communication—An Analysis Based on Empirical Data," *Academy of Management Journal* 16 (June 1973): 325.

3. Hugh McGinley, Richard LeFevre, and Pat McGinley, "The Influence of a Communicator's Body Position on Opinion Change in Others," *Journal of Personality and Social Psychology* 31, No. 4 (1975): 689.

4. E. Bryan Carne, "Telecommunications: Its Impact on Business," *Harvard Business Review* 50 (July–August 1972): 125.

5. Harold J. Leavitt, *Managerial Psychology*, 2nd ed. (Chicago: University of Chicago Press, 1964), p. 139.

6. Phillip Lewis, *Organizational Communications: The Essence of Effective Management* (Columbus, Ohio: Grid, Inc., 1975), p. 73.

7. Bradford B. Boyd and J. Michael Jensen, "Perceptions of the First-Line Supervisor's Authority: A Study in Superior-Subordinate Communications," *Academy of Management Journal* 15 (September 1972): 334.

8. Lewis, *Organizational Communications*, p. 58.

9. See Bette Ann Stead, "Berlo's Communication Process Model as Applied to the Behavioral Theories of Maslow, Herzberg, and McGregor," *Academy of Management Journal* 15 (September 1972): 389–93.

10. J. Lee McCullough and Thomas M. Ostrom, "Repetition of Highly Similar Messages and Attitude Change," *Journal of Applied Psychology* 59, No. 3 (1974): 397.

11. Howard H. Greenbaum, "The Audit of Organizational Communication," *Academy of Management Journal* 17 (December 1977): 740.

12. Ibid.

13. Ibid.

14. D. Katz and R. Kahn, *The Social Psychology of Organizations* (New York: John Wiley & Sons, 1966), p. 245.

15. Bruce Harriman, "Up and Down the Communication Ladder," *Harvard Business Review* 52 (September–October 1974): 147–8.

16. Lyle Sussman, "Perceived Message Distortion or You Can Fool Some of the Supervisors Some of the Time," *Personnel Journal* 53 (September 1974): 681.

17. Ibid., pp. 679–82.

18. See Karlene H. Roberts and Charles A. Reilly, III, "Failures in Upward Communication in Organizations: Three Possible Culprits," *Academy of Management Journal* 17 (June 1974): 205–15.

19. See Henri Fayol, *General and Industrial Management*, trans. Constance Storrs (London: Sir Isaac Pitman & Sons, 1949), p. 35.

20. M. Blaine Lee and William L. Zwerman, "Developing a Facilitation System for Horizontal and Diagonal Communications in Organizations," *Personnel Journal* 54 (July 1975): 401.

21. Keith Davis, "The Care and Cultivation of the Corporate Grapevine," *Dun's*, July 1973.

22. Cora Bagley Marrett, Jerald Hage, and Michael Aiken, "Communication and Satisfaction in Organizations," *Human Relations* 28, No. 7 (1975): 619.

23. Ibid.

QUESTIONS FOR THOUGHT AND DISCUSSION

1. Even in organizations where written communications are encouraged and emphasized, 75 percent of the assignments are given by oral communications. Why do you think that written explanations of orders are avoided?

2. Is the written message better than an oral communication for transmitting work orders? Explain.

3. Suggest some ways of getting people to use more written communications.

4. Give at least two examples of instances when a common barrier to communications has caused some misunderstanding within the work or school environment.

5. Why must a manager's communication style support his leadership style? From an employee's perception what makes a communication and leadership style compatible?

6. Explain the concept of counter-biasing in upward communications.

KEY TERMS

The student should be able to discuss the significance of these terms to the study of human behavior in the work environment.

Communication process

Feedback

Barriers to communications

Semantics

Perceptual bias

Stereotyping

Filter problem

Empathy

Organizational communications

Supportive level of communication

Downward communications

Upward communications

Counter-biasing

Lateral communications

Informal communications

CASE INCIDENT

After twenty-five years as manager of the same state agency things were not going well for J. J. Weems. His performance record was mediocre at best although he was once considered one of the best managers in the state government. Other agencies were envious of the collection of talent he had somehow recruited. But it seemed he could no longer identify with his subordinates. They viewed J. J. as being overly critical, loud and obnoxious, and unable to adjust successfully to any changes. Although most people respected him for what he had accomplished and for his knowledge of the agency, those who had worked for him were in agreement that his practices of criticizing employees in front of others and shouting directions when his orders were not carried out precisely were unprofessional and embarrassing.

The eight department managers under J. J. Weems were asked to participate in an organizational climate survey being administered to all state agencies. Results of the survey indicated a poor working relationship between the superior and subordinates with very little management support offered to the employees. Especially critical, however, was the employees' perceptions of successful communications. All aspects of downward communications were viewed as poor. There was also felt to be no upward communications because of Weems' refusal to listen and accept any ideas other than his own.

When J. J. Weems was given the results of the survey he called a meeting of his eight department managers to discuss the stated problems of communications. His remarks were as follows:

"First of all, I'd like to say that it is apparent to me that none of you know what is involved with being the director of this agency. I will admit to being partly to blame for this problem, real or imagined. I apparently haven't spent enough time with many of you explaining in detail how everyone's job is interrelated. We are a team and we must function as a cohesive unit. When we pull against one another, we aren't going to accomplish our objectives. I can assure you that I will put forth a greater effort to meet our objectives and I will try to correct these problems that you apparently believe exist. As a first step to correct the situation I have called the State Personnel Director about a communications seminar. He has agreed to let all of you attend a seminar that will be conducted the first and second Saturdays of next month. I will send you the details as soon as I receive them. If anyone else has any suggestions on how to solve this problem let's hear them."

After a long silent pause he continued: "Well, good. I think you'll find the seminar will be of great benefit to all of you. Remember the staff meeting Friday morning. Thanks for coming."

With that J. J. turned and left the room. The bewildered department managers immediately began discussing ways to get their message to J. J. without being subjected to his vindictiveness.

Questions for Discussion

1. What barriers to communications seem to exist in this agency?
2. Can these barriers be overcome? Explain.
3. How can the department managers provide J. J. with input? Is there any way to open up the line of communications?
4. Will J. J. Weems' suggestion help solve the problem?

11

Leadership Styles

LEARNING OBJECTIVES

Upon completion of this chapter the student should be able to:

- Describe the nature of the leadership process.
- Differentiate between leading and directing.
- Explain how an employee orientation and a task orientation influence leadership behavior.
- Demonstrate how the Managerial Grid® is used.
- Relate the significance of a leadership style continuum.
- Compare the major classifications of leadership styles.
- Define leadership consistency.
- Discuss the determinants of leadership style.
- Explain contingency management and the path-goal theory of leadership.

The "follow me, men" type of leader frequently depicted in movies, television series, and novels has created an unfortunate stereotype of leaders. Consequently, when asked to describe a good leader, many people will rely upon the image with which they are the most familiar. The strong, dominant, take-charge sort of person is believed by many to be the type of individual who is best qualified to lead. Because of the nature of the problems in the movies or adventure stories where the stars are cast in leadership roles, the situation usually calls for someone who will take command. But there are many other situations where the same type of behavior may constitute an overreaction and a leader may fail. In other words there is a need for different kinds of leadership for different situations. The stereotyped strong, outgoing leader is not always effective. Providing the right kind of leadership at the right time requires much more than a willingness to assume command.

The leadership abilities of a manager are very important skills which must be learned and practiced in order to achieve organizational objectives consistently. A successful manager in the modern industrial environment usually does not become successful by relying solely upon so-called natural leadership characteristics or charisma. This, of course, implies that leadership is more complex than being able to depend upon one's natural talents. Indeed, there is a great deal to learn about the nature of leadership. Why can one individual give a directive that is willingly followed while another person can give the same command and cause rebellion? What are the elements in an environment that allow for one leadership style and will not accommodate another? In this chapter we will discuss the nature of the leadership process, leadership styles, and the variables which interact to determine style and success.

THE NATURE OF THE LEADERSHIP PROCESS

Leadership is needed within a group to:

1. Help define the mission of the group
2. Help create an environment in which group members can become committed to the objectives of the group
3. Serve as an interpreter of messages and behavior of other groups and individuals who may have some influence on the group
4. Coordinate the activities of group members to insure compatible and consistent efforts toward goal achievement
5. Provide needed resources for the group

The process of leadership is a manifestation of management philosophy. Past experience, education, environment, and the organizational climate within which the leader works all contribute to the formulation of a management philosophy. When translated into economic terminology, management philosophy is essentially the leader's views and beliefs concerning what is managerially the most economical and efficient utilization and allocation of all resources. In this instance the phrase "economical and efficient utilization" applies not only to short-term actions that may be financially the most rewarding but also to the long-run impact. An autocratic or unilateral approach may save time and money in the short-run, but the behavioral repercussions will probably prevent it from being efficient or economical in the long-run.

In general terms then, the leadership process is an action orientation designed to bring about group commitment to and accomplishment of group goals. By carrying out the process of leadership individuals of necessity set themselves apart from regular group membership. While still a member of the group, the leader is a very special member of the group. Within formal organizations the leader cannot enjoy the luxury of a free and unstructured relationship with other group members. As leader the demands for consistency of treatment and fairness create a situation in which nonpreferential behavior must be exhibited. To have more than a professional relationship with subordinates is very difficult and usually invites charges of favoritism.

The manner in which managers relate to subordinates and makes decisions is influenced greatly by their managerial philosophies. There will be times, however, when an action by a leader is not indicative of managerial philosophy. In such cases the situation and all of the variables within it may literally dictate a particular kind of action. Being able to read and interpret a situation is an important element of the leadership process. On many occasions coaches or participants in athletic events have used the phrase "we are not going to worry about our opponents; we're just going to go out and play our own game." This is fine if the team can overwhelm its opponent to the extent that everything goes its way, but this is seldom the case. Really astute leaders have the ability to adapt to the situation. If the situation calls for a rather subtle approach, the leader who "sticks with the game plan" and comes on too strong may make a grievous error. This capacity to meet the situation with the appropriate action is but one of the qualities which seems to distinguish true leadership from a more simplistic form of directing.

LEADERSHIP VERSUS DIRECTING

The functions or fundamentals of management are commonly referred to as:

- Planning
- Organizing

- Directing
- Controlling
- Staffing.

Questions of where one begins and the other ends, as well as more controversial issues, have been associated with the various functions since they became an accepted part of management language. In recent years, however, the directing function has come under heavy criticism. In fact, many authors and experts in the field of management have replaced the word "directing" with "motivating" or "leading." While this does not change the general meaning or objective of the directing function, the implied method of achieving that objective is changed. It is the negative connotation frequently given directing that has caused the term to fall into disrepute. The word directing seems to give the impression of an autocratic approach. To direct or give commands is generally understood to be unilateral, with very little or no participation from the followers. The change in terminology allows for a more flexible interpretation of what has been known as the directing function.

The directing or leading of employees will have an impact upon their attitudes. If the leadership style does not meet their expectancies, the employees' satisfaction may be less than desirable. In this regard authoritarian supervision will increase job dissatisfaction among employees who desire some independence in decision making. When leaders must consistently rely upon the use of rules and threats, they are not functioning as true leaders. It takes more talent to lead people than it does to direct people. Anyone can give orders and bark out commands. Provided one has the formal authority to enforce the directives, it is not difficult to perform the role of a dictator. However, it takes a good deal of ability and knowledge of people to be able to lead people. Leaders must be able to help followers work toward achievement of individual objectives while striving to accomplish organizational objectives.

Within an organizational context the failure to work toward the achievement of either organizational or individual objectives probably is indicative of a manager who is something less than a successful leader of employees. Organizational objectives receive the attention of managers because it is recognized that they must be met for organizational survival. But, if they are met while individual objectives are ignored, it could prove a costly mistake.

To be a leader in the true sense of the word is not always easy. An autocratic or authoritarian approach assumes little concern for the well-being or motivation of the subordinates. A leader must always be concerned about the followers as individual human beings. Establishing and maintaining an organizational climate in which people can become motivated and seeking to make individual and organizational goals compatible are much more challenging than just the direction of people. While there is a time and place for autocratic management, in the long-run it is not an acceptable mode of operation for most managers in modern organizations.

LEADERSHIP BEHAVIOR ORIENTATION

Leadership behavior can be broken into two broad but distinct kinds of orientation:

- Employee (relationship) orientation
- Task (production) orientation

A leader who has an employee or relationship orientation is very concerned about the human element. In fact, it is possible that a supervisor can be so concerned with the human element that productivity is sacrificed. Such a supervisor would probably not allow anything to interfere with the interpersonal relationships within the group.

A manager who has a task or production orientation is more concerned with levels of productivity. If such a leader was to be extreme in this orientation, human beings would be viewed as just another resource to be used to increase the rate of productivity. Realistically though, one orientation is usually at least partially offset by the presence of some of the other orientation within the individual. This orientation mix will depend upon a number of things such as personality, the nature of the job, the situational environment and so on. As demonstrated by Blake and Mouton's Managerial Grid® (Figure 11.1), it is possible for a person to be high in both orientations or high in one and low in the other or low in both.[1]

A leader who is a 9,1 on the grid is extremely task-oriented and allows the human element to "interfere to a minimum degree." Such a manager would maximize production by exercising power and authority and achieving control over people through coercion.[2] Conversely a leader who is a 1,9 on the grid is highly employee-oriented to the point that the task, indeed the reason for the job, is forgotten. The maintenance of a "comfortable friendly organization atmosphere" is more important than the task or purpose of the organization. Such an individual might "give the company away."

There are, of course, managers who do just enough to maintain organization membership. A person who would be low in concern for both production and people would be classified as a 1,1. A 5,5, while getting adequate performance from subordinates, maintains the morale of the

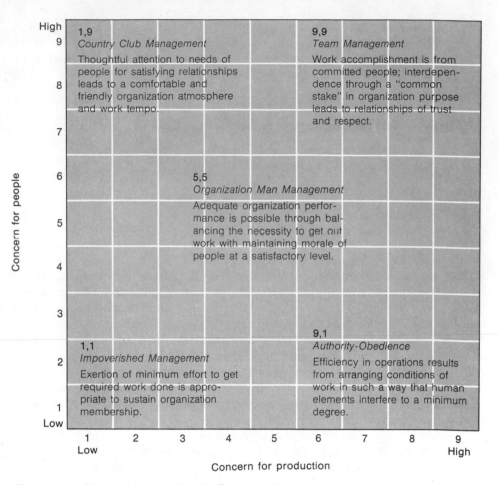

Figure 11.1 The New Managerial Grid®

Source: Robert R. Blake and Jane Srygley Mouton, The New Managerial Grid *(Houston: Gulf Publishing Company, 1978), p. 11. Copyright © 1978, Gulf Publishing Co. Reproduced by permission.*

people at a "satisfactory level." Such an individual is referred to as an "organization man" type of manager. Because of the high value placed upon maintaining the status quo, Blake and Mouton have labeled this a "go-along-to-get-along" approach. A 9,9 or any person falling somewhere in the upper right-hand quadrant would have not only a high task orientation but also a high employee orientation. This style of managing is goal-oriented and emphasizes results through participation, involvement, commitment, and conflict solving.[3]

Good managers and effective leaders will have an integration of high levels of both production and people orientations. There is no quantitative formula that is guaranteed to always be best, such as a sixty-forty, seventy-thirty, or a fifty-fifty mix. The formula that is best is the one that works most effectively for the individual in a particular situation.

A LEADERSHIP CONTINUUM

The two leadership orientations can be broken down further into several different leadership styles. The leadership continuum represented in Figure 11.2 uses the task and employee orientations and the styles identified by Rensis Likert to demonstrate the range of possible leadership or management patterns. While it may be argued that there should actually be a continuum for each of the orientations, Figure 10.2 illustrates the blending of the orientations. Nearly all leaders can be said to have a mixture of task and employee orientations with one of the orientations dominating their particular leadership style. Task orientation is the strongest at the extreme left side of the continuum and becomes less dominant moving to the right. By the same token the strongest employee orientation is at the far right and decreases in strength moving to the left on the continuum.

The four leadership styles identified in Figure 11.2 are useful in that they imply the amount of employee participation or input into the decision-making process. System 1, exploitative and authoritative, is a form of management that exploits subordinates. It is primarily an autocratic approach that is characterized by its unilateral nature. While not all autocrats are necessarily dictatorial, their decisions are made with very little or no participation from subordinates. In many instances autocratic leaders assert themselves and fully utilize their power and authority in an attempt to hide their weaknesses and areas of incompetency. By establishing a strong position that creates an environment of unquestioning obedience the leader is less likely to have weaknesses exposed.

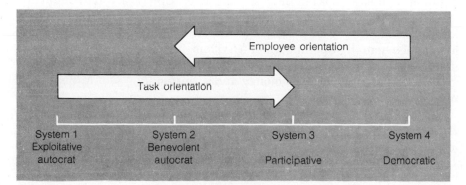

Figure 11.2   A Continuum for Leadership Styles

Modified and Adapted from Rensis Likert, The Human Organization *(New York: McGraw-Hill, 1967), p. 4.*

Moving left to right each succeeding style involves more employee orientation and hence more employee participation. The System 2 pattern of management, benevolent authoritative, is one which is basically paternalistic. A manager who exhibits tendencies toward paternalism is one who utilizes a "parent to child" approach when talking with subordinates. The condescending attitude is generally accompanied by the belief that the subordinates must be told precisely what to do. In many cases there may be some employee input, but participation is still greatly limited.

One factor that distinguishes the System 2 approach from System 1 is the presence of some employee orientation. Even though a System 2 approach is predominantly task-oriented, most paternalistic companies and managers seem to have at least some concern for their employees. If members of such an organization perform as expected by top management, they will be rewarded. But in the event of a less than satisfactory performance, punishment is used in much the same way as an autocrat would administer it. The rewards may not always serve to reinforce employee behavior as they are usually oriented toward maintaining the status quo.

The next point on the continuum, System 3, implies still more participation and employee input. Subordinates will usually be consulted for their ideas and input, and managers will try to implement them when possible. In most participative systems, the participation of the subordinates does not imply a specific commitment to utilize the input. The manager still has the final authority and may elect to use or not to use the employees' ideas. However, it should be remembered that the more often the employees' opinions are ignored, the less likely it is that they will continue to want to provide input.

The extreme right of the continuum represents a democratic posture. This leadership style implies a complete trust in the subordinates' active role in the decision-making process. Employee input is always sought and decisions are made through group processes. While this is an ideal situation in which employees are highly committed and motivated, organizations which actually operate under a System 4 leadership style are few in number. It is a worthwhile goal to work toward achieving a System 4 organization as operating efficiency and group morale would be greatly increased.

Each of the styles identified along the continuum represents a range within which elements of that leadership style are present. It is quite possible for there to be an overlap as most leadership styles are difficult to classify. To interpret styles as being specific points on the continuum implies a sophistication in identification of leadership styles that simply does not exist. Such an interpretation gives an illusion of the ability to accurately distinguish managerial behavioral characteristics and quantify them precisely.

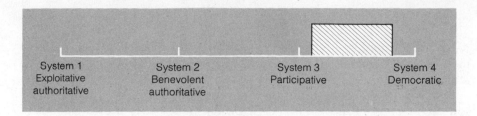

Figure 11.3   Range of a Leadership Style

Seldom will an individual be clearly one particular kind of leader all the time without demonstrating characteristics of other styles. A good leader will change style to meet the situation. Most managers, however, will identify themselves as being a certain kind of leader, i.e., "I am a democratic leader." But not many will add qualifying remarks. Actually people who manage other people operate within a given range for the everyday occurrences. Thus, when managers say they are democratic, they are probably located on the right side of the continuum, and they use some form of participative or democratic management. Usually such a leader would be placed on the continuum in the range illustrated in Figure 11.3. A range represents the effective boundaries or parameters within which the leader activates a leadership style, depending upon the particular situation. Each situation will have slightly different variables. These variables will require an appropriate adjustment on the part of a manager. While the leadership style, guided by managerial philosophy, will not differ greatly, some of the techniques utilized can be somewhat different. For instance, it may be simply a matter of giving a little more or a little less guidance to subordinates. The basic style has not been altered drastically by a subtle difference in implementation.

Leadership Consistency

One of the most often heard maxims of good management is that a manager must be consistent. Does this mean a manager finds one particular leadership style and applies it in all situations? No! Consistency in leadership style refers to the fact that a good manager will use the same style and techniques in *like situations*. This means that managers may still be quite consistent in approach even though they have been autocratic on occasion and displayed tendencies toward a participative approach at other times. For example, if a decision has to be made in a very short time span and the failure to make that decision could prove costly to the organization, managers have no time to gather and analyze employee input. The shortness of time dictates a unilateral decision. On the other hand, a decision that does not seem all that critical to the organization may be handled with very little or no managerial input. A decision as to where and when to hold the departmental Christmas party (assuming it is after work hours) may be best left to the department members. The manager may find a laissez faire (or "hands off") posture quite appropriate for the situation.

While these examples do seem to represent opposite kinds of behavior, such changes in leadership style do not necessarily indicate a lack of consistency. Some leadership styles may be far removed from one another on the continuum, but are appropriate for a particular manager to use in a particular situation. In this respect a leadership continuum is best used to indicate that most leaders possess some degree of overlap in their leadership styles. The true leadership style of an individual may be best expressed in terms of a range on the continuum. The differences that exist in participative approaches may be a matter of degrees. Some leaders will seem to utilize more elements of a participative or democratic approach than others. The situation will be a major determinant of the pragmatic range of leadership style.

Leadership Style and Employee Commitment

When employees are made to feel an important part of the organization, they will have more of a commitment to their work, their superiors, and the organization as a whole than when they feel ignored. Since the relationship with one's superior is one of the more critical variables in influencing employee commitment, a manager's leadership style is very important in determining how an individual feels about the organization.

A security consultant recently made an interesting correlation between leadership styles and the employee theft rate. There is an indication that certain leadership styles lower employee morale and may cause more internal theft. In organizations where an exploitive and authoritative (autocratic) system was in use and threats and punishment were used extensively, 70–90 percent of all employees stole from the company. Similarly, a benevolent authoritative or paternalistic style resulted in 60–70 percent employee theft. Where subordinates were allowed to participate in managerial decisions the theft rate was between 30–45 percent. The most dramatic difference occurred when decision making was widespread throughout the organization and employees were highly motivated to participate. In this type of system the employee theft rate dropped to 3 percent or less.[4]

Employees obviously respond very directly to the leadership style of their boss. It is difficult to explain why employees steal from an employer, but in cases where employees do not feel they are justly treated, they may simply rationalize their actions by reasoning, "they owe it to me" or "I deserve it; I am not rewarded in any other way." It must be remembered that the act of physically stealing something from the company involves a certain element of risk with rather severe punishment being possible. If employees are willing to assume such a risk, and apparently they are in autocratic systems, what will they do in terms of stealing time? Extended coffee breaks, longer lunch hours, and other more imaginative means of wasting time can be practiced rather easily. Stealing time is not difficult to do and the risks are considerably less frightening. Thus it would seem that leadership style does have a significant impact upon the productivity level and profitability of an organization. Not only is physical output related to leadership style, but so are the potential losses through employee theft and the stealing of time. A challenge to good managers is to harness the creativity that employees sometimes use to beat the system and use it in working toward the achievement of organizational and personal objectives.

DETERMINANTS OF LEADERSHIP STYLE

The determinants of leadership style are to be found within the leader, the followers, and the situation. Technically speaking, the leader and the followers could be included as being part of the situation. In most leadership literature, however, they are treated separately. The situation is generally viewed as including all environmental factors other than the leader and the followers. A brief discussion of the elements present within each of these three major variables should provide some insight into the evolution of an individual's leadership style.

Factors within the Leader

The leader brings to the current situation many "givens" which influence the choice of an appropriate leadership style. Such things as level of education, amount and kinds of training, work experience, management philosophy, interpersonal skills, native intelligence, personal need structure, and personality will help shape a person's approach to leadership. In some instances such personal factors will not only influence the particular leadership style that is chosen, but they also will help determine the effectiveness of the individual in the role of leader. If the personal characteristics and experience seem to indicate a need for an autocratic approach and the subordinates perceive a different approach as being appropriate, the leader probably will not be very effective.

The nature of the leader's personal system of needs is a determinant of the leadership style employed.[5] As all employees carry out their jobs, they knowingly or unknowingly (subconsciously) are doing the tasks at hand in a way which will satisfy personal needs as well as satisfy organizational needs. Personality is important not only in determining personal needs but also in serving as a fairly accurate predictor of leadership style.

Personality characteristics such as a willingness to take responsibility for actions, self-confidence, preference for making one's own decisions, enthusiasm, and a realistic outlook on life seem to be indicative of a superior who will use a leadership style that is highly reinforcing to subordinates.[6] However, those leaders who make use of negative sanctions appear to be uninhibited and outgoing, suspicious, opinionated, deliberate in their thinking, and shrewd.[7] Ironically researchers are looking to personality characteristics as predictors of leadership style at a time when the "trait theory" of leadership has fallen into disfavor. Although trait theory is concerned with identifying people as potential leaders who have characteristics or traits in common with successful leaders, current research is using these characteristics to predict and study the leadership style of people already in leadership positions.

Recent research seems to indicate that some of the differences in personal needs between men and women can reflect upon their leadership styles. In one study examining the needs of leaders, it was found that the male respondents credited their leadership styles to the satisfaction of the needs for prestige and personal growth, while the women associated their leadership styles with the opportunity to develop close friends.[8] Although the results of particular research studies will probably vary, the fact is that all members of an organization carry out their jobs as leaders and subordinates in a manner that will best satisfy their own unique system of needs.

The Role of Followers

Most individuals, who must at times be followers, have a certain set of personal characteristics which affect their expectancies related to the leadership provided. Just as with the leader, the level of education, amount and kinds of training, work experience, management philosophy, interpersonal skills, native intelligence, personal need structure, and personality contribute to expectancies of subordinates. Studying these employee factors can help the leader decide which kind of leadership style will produce the best results. For example, employees with a high level of education or a lot of work experience can usually be expected to respond more favorably to a participative form of management than to an autocratic one. Such employees will accept responsibility more readily and will usually be more capable of giving usable input than those with lesser degrees of education and experience.

Other factors, such as the nature of the employee's job and level within the hierarchy, are also important to the manager in selecting a leadership style. For example, scientists are generally allowed more freedom and are given more of a chance to participate in management decisions than are people who are performing common labor. It should also be noted that although jobs may be on a comparable level, they may require different kinds of leadership. One would expect at least slightly different approaches to be utilized in the supervision of salespeople and accountants. In this case, the nature of the job the employees perform will be important in the selection of a leadership style. Salespeople may require a managerial approach that allows considerable freedom and provides a good deal of feedback and positive reinforcement. Supervisors of accountants, on the other hand, must be more concerned with detail and consequently be somewhat more task-oriented.

Situational Factors

Within the situation are a number of factors that interact with those of the leader and followers. All three sets of factors are closely related. In fact, in some cases the categorizing of a variable as belonging to the situation or the leader or the followers may be an arbitrary assignment. An example could be the nature of the employee's job. It could be interpreted by many as being a part of the situation just as easily as including it as a factor of subordinates. Some managers may have a method whereby factors are consistently sorted into one of the three categories. This may be a formal or informal process. However, it is not the categorization itself that is important to a good manager. It is the consideration of all possible factors that could be significant to the selection of a leadership style that is important.

One of the more critical situational factors is time. Time, it is often said, is money. Failure to make use of time in the best possible way can indeed be expensive. Time is not a commodity that can be stockpiled, so a unit of time that is lost is lost forever. Managers must keep this in mind when determining how to handle a particular problem. It is not unusual for time to be the most important element in choosing a leadership style. Some decisions must be made within a very short span of time. Regardless of all other factors, if there is no time for participatory methods, a unilateral decision must be made. When the leader has the luxury of having a fairly long period of time in which to make a decision, there is an opportunity to seek the input of subordinates, peers, and superiors.

The amount of money involved in a decision is also an extremely important consideration. How much will a mistake cost? Could the money be used elsewhere more economically? Ironically the monetary impact can lead managers in different directions in terms of leadership styles. When large sums of money are at stake, some managers will undoubtedly reason that the decision is too important to entrust it to others. Conversely, many managers will want to get as much input as possible. These approaches are not necessarily on opposite ends of the continuum since in most cases the final decision will not be one that is participatory in nature. Although input is received, the difference lies in the fact that the information is gathered to enable the manager to make the decision.

Other situational factors include such things as the need for consistency, the acceptance by subordinates of a manager's decision, the amount of control exercised by top management, organizational relationships, the total impact of the decision, and the amount of stress in the situation. The greater the need for consistency, the more likely it is that some form of centralized or unilateral decision will be made. The greater the need for acceptance of a manager's decision, the more participation will be allowed. Conversely, the more centralized an organization, the less likely it is that a participative approach will be used.

Organizational relationships have to do with the power structure, the tendencies of top management and the immediate superior, the lateral relationships, and the extent to which a systems approach or some particular decision-making process is being utilized. Also the identification of where, how, and when a decision will have an impact upon various units of the organization can be said to be closely aligned to organizational relationships in making a situational analysis.

Finally, it should be recognized that all situations that call for a decision to be made present some form of stress for someone. The pressures associated with making a decision are not limited to just the decision maker, as those who have input and those who must live with the results of a decision could also experience some stress. Seldom will a situation affect two people in exactly the same manner, so it is difficult to predict how the presence of stress will influence different leaders. However, a recent study has shown that as situational stress increases, leaders who have an employee orientation tend to become more employee-oriented and those who have a task orientation become more task-oriented.[9] That is, those people who operate under a good deal of situational stress will rely heavily upon those methods that they feel most comfortable with and that apparently have worked best for them in the past.

CONTINGENCY MANAGEMENT

The contingency approach to leadership recognizes there are variables other than leader behavior to consider when evaluating leadership effectiveness. Specifically, contingency theory is based upon the belief that the correlation between leader behavior and the criteria to determine leader effectiveness is dependent upon the situation variables. In contrast noncontingency theories of leadership assume a relationship between leader behavior and the criteria for determining leader effectiveness without considering any contingency (situational) variables.[10]

Perhaps one of the better known noncontingency theories of leadership is McGregor's Theory Y.[11] It is a noncontingency approach in that it does not explicitly acknowledge a relationship between situational variables, leader behavior, and leader effectiveness criteria. It does assume, however, that there is a correlation between leader behavior, which for Theory Y would be an employee orientation, and the criteria to determine leader effectiveness such as group performance, absence of conflict, employee satisfaction, interpersonal relationships, or other appropriate measures.

The Contingency Model of Leadership Effectiveness

While there are several slightly different definitions of contingency management, the contingency model set forth by Fred E. Fiedler seems to be one of the most influential contributions to leadership theory.[12] In the model Fiedler describes leader effectiveness in terms of the favorableness of the situation for the leader. Favorableness is defined by Fiedler as the amount of power and influence a leader has in a particular situation. A situation that is either very favorable to the leader or very unfavorable will be handled most effectively by a task-oriented leader. The employee-oriented leader will be most effective in situations that are moderately favorable or moderately unfavorable.

One result of Fiedler's research has been the finding that some leaders perform very well in certain situations while others do better in different kinds of situations. This would suggest that the selection process for managerial positions is extremely critical, as no one individual can be equally effective in all situations. In addition, the contingency approach of focusing attention upon the situational variables has some important implications for leadership training. Instead of concentrating training efforts on changing the leader, perhaps the leader should be trained in situational analysis and in methods of making situations more favorable to the leader.[13] There will undoubtedly be continued research in the future as many scholars believe contingency management can be the means to unify management theories.

The Path-Goal Theory of Leadership

The path-goal theory of leadership is essentially a contingency approach. It was originally advanced by Basil Georgopolous, Gerald Mahoney, and Nyle Jones, Jr.,[14] and subsequently modified by Robert House.[15] The modification offered by House was the introduction of the situational variables, making it a contingency theory of leadership.

The theory with its modifications is concerned with the function of the leader in the achievement of subordinate goals and the paths that the subordinates can take for goal achievement, rewards, and personal job satisfaction.[16] According to the theory, the leader's function is to provide personal rewards to subordinates for goal attainment and make the rewards more attainable by defining the path to the rewards, reducing the obstacles to goal attainment, and making more job satisfaction possible. If the relationship of the path and the goal can be clearly established in the minds of subordinates, they will be motivated to follow the recommended path of motion in expectation of receiving the rewards. Where jobs are rather unstructured, managers should take steps to provide structure and thus reduce role ambiguity. Informing people about what is expected of them and the rewards associated with job performance will tend to have a positive influence on motivation. However, if employees are already well aware of the paths they are supposed to be taking, the attempts of the manager to further structure the jobs or to clarify path-goal relationships will likely be detrimental to employee satisfaction.

From a practical managerial viewpoint, the path-goal theory makes sense. If managers define a work-related goal, point out the path to follow for goal accomplishment, and inform people of the rewards associated with goal achievement, it would seem that most people would be motivated to perform at a satisfactory level. When goals are achieved and employee expectations are met the positive reinforcement would encourage a repeat of the job performance that earned the rewards. By the same token, when tasks are not well defined, the manager should provide more task structure and minimize role ambiguity to increase the opportunity for personal job satisfaction.

Recent research findings on path-goal theory appear to indicate that the situational variables may be even more important than originally thought. Studies with samples varying from machine operators to military officers have had somewhat different results. The variance in the results has been reported to be a result of the level and the nature of the jobs in the samples and the failure of the theory to fully consider the personal characteristics of the leaders and the subordinates.[17] These findings serve to further emphasize the importance of situational analysis and the inclusion by the leader of all variables when making a decision as to the best way to lead subordinates toward goal achievement.

SUMMARY

The leader of any group performs a number of activities which are designed to help the group meet its objectives in a manner that the leader has determined as appropriate. An individual who is carrying out the leadership process is seldom allowed a full and unstructured relationship with members of the group. This is but one of the limitations placed upon a leader who is responsible for administering policies, rules and regulations in an equitable way.

Nearly all leaders have some blend of employee and task orientation in their leadership styles. If task orientation is more closely aligned to their managerial philosophies, their leadership styles will be on the left half of the continuum (see Figure 11.2). If, on the other hand, a leader is influenced more by an employee orientation, the leadership style will probably be on the right side of the continuum, demonstrating a greater concern for the people supervised.

Good leaders recognize when a situation calls for a particular kind of action. Thus, it is possible for an individual to be autocratic in one situation and to be democratic in another. This is not necessarily indicative of leadership inconsistency. Consistency in leadership styles means using a similar style in like situations. It does not mean that one particular style should be used for all situations. Recognizing the factors within the situation, within the followers, and, of course, within the individual leader is extremely important in the selection of a leadership style. Being able, then, to adjust leadership styles while meeting the organizational and group goals to the greatest possible extent will mark the presence of an individual who could truly be said to be a "leader for all seasons."

NOTES

1. See ROBERT R. BLAKE and JANE S. MOUTON, *The Managerial Grid* (Houston: Gulf Publishing Company, 1964).

2. ROBERT R. BLAKE and JANE S. MOUTON, *The New Managerial Grid* (Houston: Gulf Publishing Company, 1978), p. 12.

3. Ibid., pp. 2–4.

4. "Security Pulse," *Protection Management*, November 1, 1974, p. 9.

5. DONALD L. HELMICH and PAUL E. ERZEN, "Leadership Style and Leader Needs," *Academy of Management Journal* 18 (June 1975): 401.

6. BERNARD L. HINTON and JEFFREY C. BARROW, "Personality Correlates of the Reinforcement Propensities of Leaders," *Personnel Psychology* 29 (Spring 1976): 65.

7. Ibid.

8. HELMICH and ERZEN, "Leadership Style," p. 401.

9. L. LARSON and K. ROWLAND, "Stress and Leader Behavior," *Academy of Management Proceedings*, 32nd Annual Meeting (1973): 188.

10. ABRAHAM K. KORMAN, "On the Development of Contingency Theories of Leadership: Some Methodological Considerations and a Possible Alternative," *Journal of Applied Psychology* 58, No. 3 (1973): 384.

11. See DOUGLAS MCGREGOR, *The Human Side of Enterprise* (New York: McGraw-Hill, 1960).

12. See FRED E. FIEDLER, "A Contingency Model of Leadership Effectiveness," in *Advances in Experimental Social Psychology*, ed. L. Berkowitz, vol. I (New York: Academic Press, 1964); and FRED E. FIEDLER, *A Theory of Leadership Effectiveness* (New York: McGraw-Hill, 1967).

13. See FRED E. FIEDLER, "Predicting the Effects of Leadership, Training and Experience from the Contingency Model," *Journal of Applied Psychology* 56 (1972): 114–9; and FRED E. FIEDLER, "How Do You Make Leaders More Effective? New Answers to an Old Puzzle," *Organizational Dynamics*, Autumn 1972, pp. 3–18.

14. See BASIL S. GEORGOPOLOUS, GERALD M. MAHONEY, and NYLE W. JONES, JR., "A Path-Goal Approach to Productivity," *Journal of Applied Psychology* 41 (1957): 345–53.

15. See ROBERT J. HOUSE, "A Path-Goal Theory of Leader Effectiveness," *Administrative Science Quarterly* 16 (1971): 323–4.

16. Ibid.

17. See R. HOUSE and G. DESSLER, "The Path-Goal Theory of Leadership: Some Post Hoc and A Priori Tests," in *Contingency Approaches to Leadership*, ed. J. G. Hunt and L. L. Larson (Carbondale, Ill.: Southern Illinois University Press, 1974), pp. 29–55; JOHN E. STINSON and THOMAS W. JOHNSON, "The Path-Goal Theory of Leadership: A Partial Test and Suggested Refinement," *Academy of Management Journal* 18 (June 1975): 242–52; and H. KIRK DOWNEY, JOHN E. SHERIDAN, and JOHN W. SLOCUM, JR., "Analysis of Relationships Among Leader Behavior, Subordinate Job Performance and Satisfaction: A Path-Goal Approach," *Academy of Management Journal* 18 (June 1975): 253–62.

QUESTIONS FOR THOUGHT AND DISCUSSION

1. Is there really a difference between leading people and directing them? Support your answer.

2. If a task orientation is productive in the short-run, why isn't it equally effective over a longer period of time?

3. Give specific examples of leaders who could be classified as System 1 and System 2 leaders. What are the differences in behavior between System 1 and 2 leaders?

4. How is it possible for leaders to be consistent and yet utilize a contingency approach?

5. Analyze your leadership style. When in leadership situations are you task- or human-oriented? How much emphasis do you put on goal accomplishment? How do you support your followers? Where would you be located on the managerial grid?

6. Analyze the leadership style of two different people you have worked for (on the job or in school, i.e., a coach, an instructor, etc.). What characteristics did they display that were most indicative of their leadership style?

KEY TERMS

The student should be able to discuss the significance of these terms to the study of human behavior in the work environment.

Leadership processes
Directing
Employee-oriented behavior
Task-oriented behavior
Managerial Grid®
Organization man
Exploitive autocrat (System 1)

Benevolent autocrat (System 2)
Participative (System 3)
Democratic (System 4)
Leadership consistency
Situational factors
Contingency management
Path-goal theory

CASE INCIDENT

The Reno, Nevada, plant of the Jerricho-May Company was about to be closed. For the last two years the manufacturing plant had been losing money. At first it was thought that the conditions of the economy were to blame, but during the last year the demand for the automatic irrigation system being made at the Reno plant had been very strong and the plant was simply not able to keep up with the orders. In such a strong market the executives at the corporate headquarters in Phoenix concluded that the continued losses were due to a poorly motivated and ill-trained work force. The only alternative was to close the plant and move the operations to another plant in Arizona that had been doing similar work.

Before the plant was closed Wallis Hives, an employee relations manager at headquarters, asked permission to use the plant for some leadership research. The permission was granted as the lame duck operation would continue for at least another eight months. Employees would not be notified of the planned closing until three months before the scheduled shutdown.

While starting her research on leadership styles, Wallis learned through the grapevine that the plant manager was not liked or respected by the plant personnel. S. H. Rider, the plant manager, was referred to as "the Hitler of the sprinklers," "Napoleon," and other even less complimentary terms. While S. H. was known at corporate headquarters as a conservative and traditional type of manager, they had no idea until then that he was so disliked.

After spending one week at the plant and conducting numerous interviews, Wallis found that S. H. was indeed very autocratic and very jealous of his authority. His two assistants, Jack and Ben, were affectionately referred to as "Space" and "Tubby" by the people in the plant. They were viewed as "yes-men" and were not given much credit for being able to do anything without having direct orders from S. H.

Wallis learned that nearly all the department heads were also somewhat autocratic in their leadership styles. Most, however, expressed a feeling of uncomfortableness with that approach but felt they had no other choice because of the demands placed upon them. Wallis could see that the plant had some potentially good managers but they were never given the chance to manage. In addition, the work force in her opinion was also quite capable and had all the skills necessary to perform their tasks efficiently. The high rate of scrap loss, waste, and reprocessed items just did not make sense. She concluded that there was an extreme lack of motivation on the part of everyone throughout the plant due to the leadership style exhibited by the top levels of management at the plant. Surprisingly, the plant had never been unionized.

Wallis arranged a meeting with the vice-president of employee relations, the vice-president of manufacturing, and the president of the corporation to present them with a plan which she believed could save the plant. The proposal was primarily a plan for changing the climate of the plant through changes in leadership style of managers to allow more involvement in decision making by the employees.

Questions for Discussion

1. Could such a plan really work? What are the major obstacles to overcome?

2. What variables must be considered when selecting an appropriate leadership style?

3. If you were a member of Wallis's staff, what would you suggest for possible inclusion in the proposal? Why would your suggestions be needed to insure success of the plan?

4. Could a plan to change leadership styles throughout the plant be effectively implemented with S. H. and his staff remaining in their positions?

12

Participative Management: Real and Imagined

LEARNING OBJECTIVES

Upon completion of this chapter the student should be able to:

- Explain the concept of participative management.
- Identify the participation characteristics displayed by participative leaders.
- Discuss the results of a participative management approach.
- Describe the varying degrees of participation in terms of the manager's use of authority.
- Explain management by objectives.
- Contrast decentralized and centralized organizational structures.
- Define pseudoparticipation.
- Identify the limitations on participation and discuss how they may be overcome.

In recent years participative management has become one of those "buzz phrases" that seem to denote current interest in a management technique. Even within organizations where real employee participation in management decisions is seldom seen, the words "participative management" can be heard with disturbing frequency. The fact that the phrase is overused and applied to situations where it really does not exist can be credited to exposure to the current literature and an attempt to display the use of jargon that appears to be "in" at the moment. Such misusage is generally a fairly good indication that a particular approach or concept is popular. However, the abuses in the application of the terminology should not detract from the value of the concept. Participative management is, after all, not only a popular approach but also a pragmatic one that can show positive results in terms of profits and employee satisfaction.

THE CONCEPT OF PARTICIPATIVE MANAGEMENT

Participative management is not a specific technique but rather a concept of management that advocates employees having a voice in the decision-making process. In a study to determine how 318 executives viewed participative management, Larry Greiner found that despite the rather abstract concept of participation there was a high level of agreement as to the characteristics of a participative approach.[1] No matter what

RANK		AVERAGE SCALE RATING
1.	Gives subordinates a share in decision making	6.08
2.	Keeps subordinates informed of the true situation, good or bad, under all circumstances	5.69
3.	Stays aware of the state of the organization's morale and does everything possible to make it high	5.45
4.	Is easily approachable	5.38
5.	Counsels, trains, and develops subordinates	5.34
6.	Communicates effectively with subordinates	5.22
7.	Shows thoughtfulness and consideration of others	5.19
8.	Is willing to make changes in ways of doing things	4.96
9.	Is willing to support subordinates even when they make mistakes	4.92
10.	Expresses appreciation when a subordinate does a good job	4.80

Figure 12.1   The Ten Highest Participation Characteristics

Source: Larry E. Greiner, "What Managers Think of Participative Leadership," Harvard Business Review *51 (March–April 1973): 114.*

their particular managerial techniques, most of the respondents viewed certain elements as always being present before participative leadership exists. As shown in Figure 12.1, the act of allowing subordinates to share in decision making was ranked the highest among ten participation characteristics. The 6.08 rating given this characteristic of participation is an average of responses where 7 was equal to high participation and 1 equal to low participation.[2]

As can be seen by the nature of the characteristics listed in Figure 12.1, the basis of the participative concept is more involvement of employees in the management functions. These characteristics are important elements in the success of a participative style of leadership and can be related to the discussion of determinants of leadership style in the preceding chapter. The participation characteristics represent subordinate expectancies and also indicate what a manager must do to be successful in a participative approach. The ability to incorporate these characteristics into a leadership style would create an environment that would reinforce employee involvement and encourage further participation.

With increased participation of subordinates it is hoped that the following results will occur:

1. The manager will be free of some of the less important tasks and thus will be able to spend more time on more important matters
2. The employees will be provided valuable experiences in decision making, better preparing them for higher level jobs
3. The quality of the decisions will be increased as the decision making is moved closer to the point of impact of the decision
4. When employees have a vested interest in a decision, they will do their utmost to see that the decision is carried out in the best possible manner.

Of course, the key to any successful participative method is the people of the organization. If the members of an organization have the will to make it work and if the organizational climate encourages such a system, it will work. In most cases it is better to have a decision that is something less than ideal but that is supported by the employees than to have a decision that "looks good on paper" and does not have the backing of the employees.

DEVELOPING GROUP PARTICIPATION

Developing group participation is not always easily accomplished. In the initial stages of a participative system, the actual involvement of the personnel will depend upon past relationships. It will be most difficult to overcome a long-standing management philosophy that has been either autocratic or paternalistic in nature. The manager's relationship (be it good or bad) that has been established with the subordinates will surely carry over into the new system to some degree. This relationship appears to be very important to the successful introduction of a participative system, as the effective sharing of decision making depends upon the manner in which the participative approach is applied.[3] In order for the new approach to be workable and believable the manager must forsake the authoritative methods relied upon under the old system. There is no question that it will take time to establish a new kind of relationship with subordinates, but with a gradual improvement in credibility will come an improvement in group performance and satisfaction.

Equal Opportunity

One of the critical issues of a participatory system is who is allowed to participate. Should everyone have an equal opportunity to supply input or must there be limitations? This is a complex problem when it comes to the actual involvement of the personnel within one group. Many management experts would argue that everyone must be treated the same. This is generally a good rule to follow but like every other rule it, too, has exceptions.

Not everyone is motivated to advance within organizations. By the same token, not everyone wishes to take part in the decision-making process. This is fine and is to be expected within any organization. However, it is one thing to be given an opportunity to provide input, even if that opportunity is rejected, and quite another to be ignored when others are solicited for their suggestions. Even those people who do not wish to take part in decision making will usually appreciate the chance to turn it down. Indeed, the chance to turn down any kind of an opportunity may be viewed by some as being more important than the opportunity itself.

In one organization of about twenty-five hundred employees there was one particular managerial job that seemed to open up with a good deal of regularity. Each time the position was vacant top management offered the job to John, a long-time employee with considerable managerial experience. Even though the job would have given John an increase in salary, a larger staff, and generally better work conditions, he turned the job down every time it was offered. Each of the three times he rejected the opportunity John cited the reason as being "I just don't want the hassle." When the job became open again two years later, it was offered to and accepted by a younger man who lacked experience but seemed to possess a good deal of enthusiasm. John was irate. A colleague, trying to calm John down, said, "John, you know you didn't want that job anyway. You already have turned it down three times." Reluctantly, John agreed but quickly added, "But they could have at least asked me."

Just as in the above example, there will be people who do not really want to participate or take advantage of an opportunity. But when it appears that the decision has been made for them by someone else, they may become quite upset. There is some appeal to an individual's ego when he or she is solicited for input or given the opportunity for an important job. In most cases it takes very little additional time to extend the opportunities to everyone and the payoff in morale will prove worth the time spent.

Methods of Solicitation

When developing group participation another important factor is how the input is solicited. Many times the method of solicitation will indicate the importance that management attaches to the employees' contributions. The manager may present the group with a problem and ask for suggestions, direct questions concerning a particular problem may be asked, or a proposed solution may be presented with critique invited. Some managers may take the problem on an individual basis to each employee, seeking opinions. This method may be indicative of the treatment of a problem deemed critical by some managers. On the other hand, the more important issues may be presented by some to the subordinates as a group. Each manager will have a means of getting employee input that is believed to be the best way of getting valuable contributions for that situation.

In any case, the approach used will be determined by the manager's philosophy of participation. Managers who believe everyone should be involved will present the opportunity for input in a way that even those employees who they consider the least capable can take part. Others will direct their message to the "average," while some will believe that it must be aimed at only the most capable employees. In the latter case the reasoning is that this is the group of employees who typically wants to be involved and are the ones who will provide the most useful input. Whatever the philosophy, the manager must remember to offer a chance at real participation and give employees the opportunity to contribute to the organizational effort and to grow as members of the management team.

DEGREES OF PARTICIPATION

Robert Tannenbaum and Warren H. Schmidt developed a continuum of leadership behavior which is most useful in demonstrating the degrees of participation. The continuum presented in Figure 12.2 shows different combinations of the use of managerial authority and freedom of subordinates in the decision-making process.

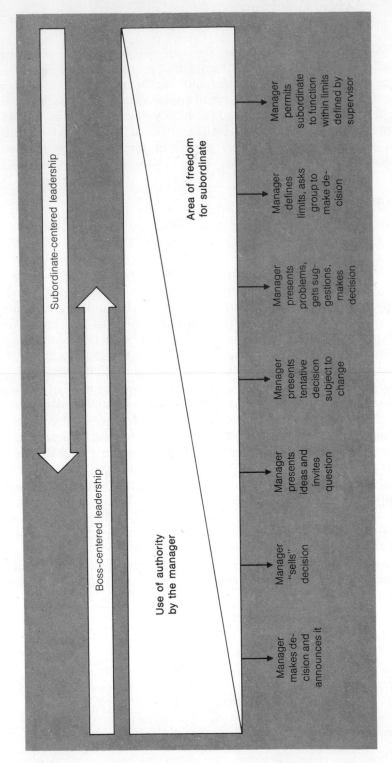

Figure 12.2 Continuum of Leadership Behavior

Source: Robert Tannenbaum and Warren H. Schmidt, "How to Choose a Leadership Pattern," Harvard Business Review 36 (March–April 1958): 96.

An important aspect of the Tannenbaum and Schmidt continuum is the implied utilization of situational analysis. In other words, good leaders will interpret the situation and apply the most appropriate leadership style. Although managers may tend to favor particular leadership styles, they will seldom limit themselves to one leadership style all the time. Successful managers have the ability to adapt their styles of leadership to fit the situation.

Again, referring to Tannenbaum and Schmidt's leadership continuum, the phrase "use of authority by the manager" is critical. The word "use" is the key word. Moving from the left to the right on the continuum the actual use of authority by the manager decreases, and the degree of freedom for subordinates increases. The ultimate authority remains unchanged; the manager has simply chosen not to make use of all the power that rests with the office. By delegating some of the authority for use by the subordinates, the manager has allowed the subordinates some degree of freedom in the decision-making process. Even though the authority is delegated, neither the actual power of the office nor the effective power of the person is diminished. In fact, the manager's effective authority could actually be increased because others perceive managers who share their power to have more power.

Although some managers may seem to satisfy the requirements of the right side of the continuum, they may not really belong there. The continuum assumes that managers are genuinely interested in getting subordinates involved in the decision-making process. Managers who are insincere regarding employee participation cannot realistically be located on the right side of the continuum. For example, even though a superior may define limits and ask the group to make the decision (second point from the right on the continuum), this action is not necessarily representative of subordinate-centered leadership. The limits may be defined in a manner that will actually restrict employee freedom. In this regard, although the manager has used a leadership style described as being on the right end of the continuum, there has not been real employee participation. The manager has ignored the criteria for locating on the right of the continuum—subordinate-centered leadership—and is therefore practicing nothing more than pseudoparticipation.

AUTHORITY AND PARTICIPATION

There are many people who believe that if they delegate or share their authority, this sharing in some way detracts from the amount of power that they possess. Managers who believe this are most hesitant to delegate and typically do all they can to hoard authority. In practice, however, the opposite assumption appears to be true.

Mason Haire has conducted research which suggests that the more authority managers delegate, the more others believe them to have.[4] These research findings support what would be referred to as "common sense" in other situations. For example, if we know two individuals to be wealthy people but have no real idea as to how to distinguish who possesses the most money, we would rely on indicators that are the most evident to us. If one was quite stingy and the other was a philanthropist, we would be inclined to think the one who shares with others was the richer person. Even though it may not be true, the one who shares generally will be perceived as having more. So it is with authority.

TECHNIQUES OF PARTICIPATIVE MANAGEMENT

The actual methods of getting people involved in decision making are limited in number only by the imaginations of managers. This is true because of the many "hybrid" forms of participative management that have been developed exclusively for particular organizations. Although this is as it should be, the discussion that follows will be limited to those techniques which provide the foundation for most participative systems.

Management by Objectives

Management by objectives (MBO) has been referred to as a managerial philosophy, a supervisory technique, a method of performance appraisal, and various other descriptive phrases that make it sound like the "cure-all elixir" for an ailing management process. It is more appropriately defined as a managerial system that is based upon the philosophy of participative management. As a management system it lends itself to a flexibility in application that allows MBO to be almost anything a manager wants it to be. As such it really amounts to a "managerial lifestyle."

MBO (which was referred to as management by results) was originally expounded upon as a viable approach to management by Peter Drucker in 1954 in *Practice of Management.*[5] In recent years MBO has been popularized by George Odiorne, who is probably recognized as its leading advocate.[6]

While there are many instances cited as being successful applications of MBO, there are, unfortunately, many failures as well. Generally speaking when failures do occur it has been because of the presence of at least one or more of the limiting factors to be discussed later in this chapter and/or trying to use a recipe or a cookbook approach for MBO's implementation.

One of the advantages of MBO is that it can be adjusted to fit the needs of the organization. In addition, the setting of objectives for employees is done in such a manner as to make organizational and individual objectives as compatible as possible. Most MBO efforts are centered upon the mutual setting of goals and the measurement of performance related to those goals. There are five elements that seem to be basic to the installation of MBO:

1. Effective goal setting and planning by top levels of the managerial hierarchy
2. Organizational commitment to this approach
3. Mutual goal setting
4. Frequent performance review
5. Some degree of freedom in developing means for the achievement of objectives[7]

The above mentioned elements seem to be representative of those mentioned by most explanations of MBO. For each individual, the process of setting work-oriented objectives in conjunction with one's superior is the step which lays the groundwork for the remaining steps. After there is agreement on these objectives and organizational objectives have been communicated, there is then a basis for conducting performance appraisals. Periodic feedback (usually quarterly) is given by the manager to the individual, pointing out areas of strength and areas that need improvement. If the objectives have been too ambitious, they may be adjusted downward or in some cases there may be a need to make the objectives more challenging. The important aspect of the performance appraisal and review is that the employee has actually had some say in the development and implementation of performance standards. Employees are thus involved with comparing their actual output with the preconceived standards they have helped set. This serves to place the emphasis on output and makes MBO a very results-oriented system. In such a system the results of the work effort become recognized as important, and attention is appropriately shifted from the activity or means of accomplishing objectives to the actual output.

Perhaps the greatest problem facing managers who are operating under an MBO system is the method of determining rewards. Work objectives may be set according to the job or to the individual. When set according to the job, the job description provides the major source of information and thus the objectives of people holding the same job in an organization would not vary to any great extent. However, many MBO systems advocate setting objectives according to the individual's strengths and weaknesses, likes and dislikes. Here is where the reward problems become difficult. Who should be rewarded more—the person who sets low objectives and meets them or the individual who sets very high objectives and does not attain them? There is no best answer to this question. One answer may be implied, however, by a comparison of actual outcomes. Results of research would seem to indicate that performance is generally better by those who set more challenging goals.[8]

Depending upon its application, MBO can do a great deal toward increasing the quality of communications and improving the motivational level of the employees, while improving employee performance and increasing efficiency. All of this, however, hinges upon what could be the most critical element in the successful implementation of MBO—*real employee participation*. One of the aspects of MBO, which makes it especially attractive as a device for increasing workers' personal involvement, is that employees have input at virtually every stage of the job. They are mutually setting objectives with their superiors (planning), they, of course, are performing the job, and they are playing a role in their own performance appraisals. In this manner, MBO provides an opportunity for employee participation that contributes to the growth and development of the individual and to the improved operation of the organization.

Decentralization

Decentralization is actually an organizational technique and, like MBO, in order to be successful it should be treated as a managerial philosophy. The basic philosophy of decentralization is to spread the decision making among more people within the organization. In contrast to a centralized structure, the decentralized structure is wider and has fewer levels in the hierarchy. This implies a broader span of control than the tall, narrow structure of a centralized organization.

Basically the differences in the centralized and decentralized structures are the number of levels in the hierarchy and the number of positions on a given level. The centralized structure will usually have more levels than the decentralized. Thus, centralized organizations are referred to as being tall. Decentralized structures generally have fewer levels but more positions per level than the centralized. Hence the decentralized organization is wider and flatter. These differences are illustrated in Figures 12.3 and 12.4. Figure 12.3 points out what is meant by the level of a hierarchy. Each box represents a position within the organization.

Figure 12.4 uses a hypothetical example of two organizations having the same number of employees. One organization, utilizing the centralized structure, has ten levels and an average of five positions per level. The decentralized structure of the other organization has five levels with an average of ten positions per level. While the numbers used are perhaps understated (especially for number of positions per level), the illustration graphically demonstrates the concept of tall and flat structures.

As a managerial philosophy, decentralization is the process of moving decision-making authority and responsibility further down the

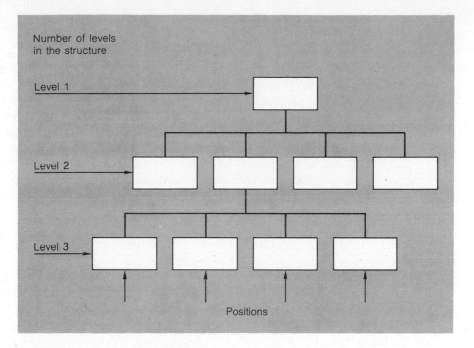

Figure 12.3   Levels of a Hierarchy

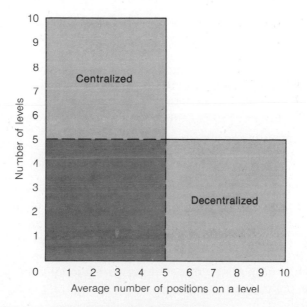

Figure 12.4   Tall versus Flat Organizational Structures

hierarchy. Delegation of authority becomes the critical factor of a good decentralized system. For the individual this usually means being thrust into a "sink or swim" situation earlier in one's career than would be true in a centralized organization. The individual who thrives on more job independence would probably adapt very well to such a situation. Participation in the decision-making process is a way of life for employees in decentralized organizations. A definite advantage for this type of managerial system is the broader range of experience and training (in a practical sense) of the employees. Because the workers become more actively involved in the decision-making process, they are more likely to have a vested interest in the decisions and, therefore, more likely to carry them to a successful conclusion. In addition, the more individuals are exposed to decision-making situations, the better those people are prepared to handdle them.

Among the disadvantages of decentralization are the expense of training managers (formal training and the expense of mistakes) and the absence of uniformity of action when uniformity is desirable. From a behavioral standpoint, there are individuals who would be uncomfortable in a decentralized system. Such individuals would probably not be all that interested in climbing the organization ladder and would really not care to be burdened with additional responsibility. However, when top management is committed to the idea of more employee participation and when managers and employees are well trained, a decentralized structure can work extremely well. Companies such as Sears, Roebuck and Company; General Motors; and DuPont have used a decentralized approach to great advantage.[9]

Other Participative Management Techniques

Many other methods to gain employee participation are being used quite successfully. A number of them are based on one of the following:

1. Democratic management (usually a misnomer as far as application)
2. Consultative management
3. Varying forms of management by committee.

There are also some people who view participative management as having its foundation in suggestion systems and use such systems as the framework for their managerial approach. In any case, the goals of any system designed to allow employee participation in the management process are all closely related. The active involvement of the employees will lead to a firmer commitment to organizational goals with mutual benefits to the organization and to the individual being the result.

PSEUDOPARTICIPATION

One of the practices of some managers who are operating under the banner of participative management has caused charges of manipulation to be leveled at behavioralists and, in particular, at the study of human behavior in the work environment. This practice is what can be referred to as pseudoparticipation. By deceiving subordinates into believing that they have actually had some input into a decision when, in fact, they have none, some managers believe that they have achieved "the best of all possible worlds." The employees *think* that they have participated, which is the most important element of the scheme, and the managers have activated the decisions that they personally wanted. Of course, this procedure may work with no one being the wiser; however, if the subordinates learn of the deception, the managers have lost their credibility and are no longer effective leaders.

There are a number of ways in which pseudoparticipation has been implemented. The following two examples are representative of how some individuals have abused the authority of their positions by misleading, indeed by manipulating, the people of their departments or organizations. It should be added that such an approach is seldom successful, and even where it appears to have worked, the chance of discovery grows with time.

Pseudoparticipation—Example #1.   A large state institution announced that a system of management by objectives (MBO) would be implemented in order to give all levels of employees a greater voice in planning and setting their own standards of performance. The employees would actually be setting the goals of the organization as objectives set at each level would be carried upward to the next level and so on. It appeared to be a bottoms-up type of management set within an MBO framework. In reality only those goals that fit the preconceived plans of top management were selected. This would have been fine if the employees had understood the ground rules. As it was, the size of the organization (approximately two thousand employees) assured the initial success of this approach. With all employees stating personal goals and suggesting organizational goals, the odds were in favor of top management that some people would state objectives which would match almost identically the preconceived notions for objectives of top management.

Pseudoparticipation—Example #2.   Pseudoparticipation has also been used in the selection of leaders. An example frequently cited is the choosing of a new department head by secret ballot. Once the list of candidates is narrowed to two or three, the individual with the responsibility of administering the election will ask for a secret ballot vote. Once all ballots have been gathered, the plant manager (president, etc.) announces the new head of the sales department to be Sally Snow. The management representative typically congratulates Sally Snow and the people of the sales department for electing such an outstanding salesperson and leader.

When small groups of people of the sales department get together over coffee breaks or lunch, the conversation may go something like this:

Employee #1: What do you think of Sally Snow as a department head?

Employee #2: Well, if she is what the majority want then I can live with her, but I sure didn't vote for her.

Employee #1: I didn't either. She's a good salesperson, but she knows nothing about managing people.

Employee #3: I would rather have seen John Doe get it. He seems to be really interested in people as individuals.

Employee #4: Well, one thing for sure, Sally Snow isn't. We're just something to improve her sales record.

After a few conversations like this among several groups of sales representatives, someone is going to ask "Who voted for Sally Snow anyway?" When it is remembered that the final vote was never made public in order to avoid any embarrassment to the candidates, it may become obvious to all members of the department that the selection of the new department head was not made by the department personnel but by the management. It amounted to nothing more than an appointment.

This type of pseudoparticipation could be most successful from a management viewpoint, if the people involved in the so-called goal setting or election were geographically separated and/or had limited communications with one another on an informal basis. Without the continual interchange that is prevalent among employees within close proximity, the deception would take longer to discover and could possibly go undetected. However, in most situations the employees would find out within a relatively short time period, destroying any possible benefits management may have believed were being gained by taking such action.

These are isolated instances of pseudoparticipation in today's organizations and are not indicative of most participative management attempts. There are, of course, degrees of pseudoparticipation in use by managers who really are not capable of leading under a participative style of management. These types of managers are generally hesitant to delegate true authority, are probably a little unsure of their relationships with their subordinates, and seldom have much knowledge of their employees' abilities or aspirations. In short, practitioners of pseudoparticipation are not good managers.

LIMITS ON PARTICIPATION

From a pragmatic standpoint, the limits on participation are going to depend upon two elements:

- The organization's managerial philosophy
- The factors present in the situation

It would be nearly impossible to implement a successful participative system from the middle management level on down if such a system were contrary to top management's beliefs. Despite a growing emphasis upon executive development workshops, seminars and continuing education, perhaps the most widely used and most successful form of development of management talent has been emulation. In other words, if individuals believe their superiors are successful, they will adopt a management style that is quite similar. Thus, the difficulty of implementing a participative system at the middle management level without top management's support is compounded. First, from an operational standpoint, a diversity of managerial systems within one organization could only contribute to confusion and inefficiency. Second, the likelihood of subordinates installing and practicing a mangerial philosophy that is not compatible with their immediate superiors' is slim indeed. Third, from an individual's viewpoint, it would be most frustrating to be caught in the middle, reporting to a "benevolent autocrat" and then attempting to be a democratic leader to one's subordinates.

The situational parameters that would limit the extent of participation are essentially those discussed under situational analysis in Chapter 11. The factors having special relevance and that could possibly limit the success of a participative management attempt are presented below with a brief suggestion as to how these limitations may be offset:

Time.   When operating under time constraints, the manager may have to rely upon a more autocratic approach. It should be noted that even in a successful participative system it may become necessary at times to utilize an autocratic approach. It is hoped that such situations require only a temporary shift in managerial orientation.

The Managerial System.   Participative management will not work effectively in all organizations or under all conditions. Some organizations will have a structure or policies that are not compatible with a participatory approach. In such companies any changes that occur seem to happen over a period of time with changes in personnel philosophy and make a movement to participative management evolutionary in nature rather than revolutionary. Overnight results cannot be expected.

Subordinates.   The training and background of subordinates will also determine the degree to which they are capable of taking an active role in the management process. Education, development, and supervisory techniques can help subordinates become more active in the decision-making process by helping them become better prepared to participate and by reinforcing their efforts to take part in management activities.

Expense.   Participative methods are expensive in their initial stages of implementation. Cost in terms of time and mistakes can be quite high. Many times management may be willing to initially absorb a high cost in order to reap the benefits in the long-run. A cost/benefit analysis or an ROI (return on investment) study will usually demonstrate the economic feasibility of a participative approach.

Need for Consistency.   The greater the need for a high degree of consistency in decision making, the more likely there is to be some centralized form of management system. When the need for consistency is not so critical, participative management is more feasible. With proper training, development, and delegation of authority there does not have to be any deterioration in the consistency of decisions. Consistency should be stressed in terms of the high quality of decisions and not in terms of approach or methodology.

Managers must remember that leadership is a function of the situation, the leader and the led, and give careful attention to each of these variables when deciding upon the most appropriate action to be taken. Since these are truly variables in the literal sense, adjustments in the management process must be made accordingly. Nearly all the variables mentioned that could limit the success of a participative approach can be offset by appropriate management action. In this regard, a good manager works within the situational limitations and uses them as a guide for effective management.

SUMMARY

One of the assumptions underlying participative management is that individuals who have played a role in making a decision will be more likely to be committed to that decision and to the organization. The benefits to be gained from allowing subordinates to actively make input into the management process are both tangible and intangible. The pay-off is not always immediate, but in the long-run some very real progress is usually noted that can be measured in dollars and time saved. In addition the training of subordinates with on-the-job experience makes those employees more valuable to the organization and better prepares them for promotions within the hierarchy. An indirect benefit of allowing subordinates a more active role is the feelings of greater self-worth on the part of individuals because of a perceived increase in their contributions to the organizational effort.

Managerial philosophy, organizational climate, time and money are a few of the factors which separately or in combination limit the extent to which a participative management technique can be successfully implemented. In the presence of such limitations, some members of the management team may try to overcome the obvious barriers by forcing the issue. Such an attempt at participative management is futile. The limitations must first be minimized and a favorable organizational climate must be established for a successful participatory system. If management fails to do this, pseudoparticipation may be the result.

When managers are unwilling to delegate authority, no true participation can take place. Those who choose to hold onto their authority do not fully understand the nature of the managerial task or the objectives of delegation. However, the reasons for success or failure of a management system can seldom rest with only one of the variables. In the final analysis the success of a participative approach is dependent upon the appropriate combination of the elements which determine leadership style. In other words, the success of participative management is a function of the situation, the leader, and the led.

NOTES

1. Larry E. Greiner, "What Managers Think of Participative Leadership," *Harvard Business Review* 51 (March–April 1973): 113.

2. Ibid.

3. Michael R. Cooper and Michael T. Wood, "Effects of Member Participation and Commitment in Group Decision Making on Influence, Satisfaction, and Decision Riskiness," *Journal of Applied Psychology* 59, No. 2 (1974): 133.

4. See Mason Haire, *Psychology in Management* (New York: McGraw-Hill, 1964).

5. Peter Drucker, *Practice of Management* (New York: Harper, 1954).

6. See George S. Odiorne, *MBO* (New York: Pitman Publishing Corp., 1965); George S. Odiorne, *Training by Objectives* (New York: The MacMillan Company, 1970); and George S. Odiorne, *Personnel Administration by Objectives* (Homewood, Ill.: Richard D. Irwin, Inc., 1971).

7. Stephen J. Carroll, Jr., and Henry L. Tosi, Jr., *Management by Objectives* (New York: The MacMillan Company, 1973), p. 3.

8. See Gary P. Latham and Gary A. Yukl, "Effects of Assigned and Participative Goal Setting on Performance and Job Satisfaction," *Journal of*

Applied Psychology 61, No. 2 (1976): 166–71 for a review of goal setting and employee performance.

9. See ALFRED D. CHANDLER, JR., *Strategy and Structure* (Garden City, N.J.: Doubleday and Company, 1966) for a detailed study of decentralization in large scale corporations.

QUESTIONS FOR THOUGHT AND DISCUSSION

1. Is participative management synonymous with democratic management?

2. How does a manager benefit from a participative approach?

3. Can the value of participative management ever be expressed in dollars and cents?

4. Does a manager automatically forfeit some authority when subordinates are allowed to take part in the decision-making process? Why or why not?

5. It is often said that MBO may be as participative (or nonparticipative) as a manager wants it to be. Do you agree?

6. Have you ever been exposed to a case of pseudoparticipation? Describe the situation, pointing out where the leader failed to exercise good leadership practices.

7. Why is a decentralized structure better suited for participative techniques than one which is centralized?

KEY TERMS

The student should be able to discuss the significance of these terms to the study of human behavior in the work environment.

Participative management	Management by objectives
Degrees of participation	Decentralization
Continuum of leadership behavior	Centralization
Use of authority	Pseudoparticipation
Delegation of authority	

CASE INCIDENT

Joe McMahon and Mark Broman were becoming increasingly concerned about their plant's slipping safety record and the almost casual attitude of the workers toward safety and productivity levels. The plant manager, Joe, understandably wanted to cut down on the accidents and increase the output. Mark, the personnel director, was in charge of the safety program and believed the expensive compensation payments could be reduced if there was some way to gain more employee commitment to the company. They discussed the situation and decided to invite Jim French, a management consultant, to help the Ebax Company with its problem.

After the consultant's initial tour of the foundry operation which made railroad switching devices ("frogs"), railroad wheels, and other smaller products, the plant manager suggested to him: "What we would like you to do, Jim, is to motivate those workers you saw out there." Jim explained that even if that were possible, he didn't believe he himself would work as hard as the people in the plant given the current work environment. It was later decided that the best approach to take was to train the foremen in management skills and present them with alternative leadership styles that might be more effective than the autocratic methods being used. They all believed this was the best approach for improving the climate of the plant.

Over the next year training was conducted for the foremen; their immediate superior, the superintendent; and most of the other administrative members of the organization. Results of a participative style of leadership were being noticed in all operating units but one. This one department had made no appreciable production gains and had the worst safety record in the plant. Joe, Mark, and Jim were at a loss as to what to try next in order to turn things around for the department. The foreman of the department was an employee of over thirty years tenure who still relied upon physical strength to "handle" personnel problems.

On the consultant's next trip to the plant he was met by the "beaming" superintendent who explained that he had finally convinced the problem foreman to adapt to the company's preferred participative leadership style. Being both surprised and happy with this news, Jim asked how this change in heart had been accomplished. "Very easy," was the superintendent's reply, "I told him this was his last chance to shape up. He of course didn't take kindly to the suggestion and offered to help me out of his department. Well, it was then that I decided to demonstrate to him just how wrong he was."

"What did you do? Show him his safety record again?" asked Jim.

"Nope, I knocked him over a three foot high stack of wheels. He's going to be a good participative manager now."

Questions for Discussion

1. In light of the improvements made by the other departments why would a foreman resist changing his leadership style?

2. How can a change in leadership style (from autocratic to a more participative style) lead to more employee commitment?

3. Can a participative system be implemented by autocratic means? Why or why not?

13

Leadership and Effective Group Performance

LEARNING OBJECTIVES

Upon completion of this chapter, the student should be able to:

- Discuss the importance of leadership to group problem solving.
- Describe the nature of the relationship between leaders and group members.
- Distinguish between interacting and noninteracting group problem-solving processes.
- Enumerate the guidelines for the use of committees.
- Explain the jury technique.
- Contrast brainstorming and nominal grouping.
- Explain the Delphi technique and its advantages.
- Recognize how informal groups can assist in the achievement of formal organizational objectives.

Leadership is common to all group activity. Regardless of the purpose of a group, someone will usually assume a position of leadership to help keep the group moving toward the accomplishment of its objectives. The qualities of leadership are recognized and rewarded in informal groups and formal organizations alike.

Within any organization there are formal and informal relationships. While informal groups cannot always be controlled with formal authority, they can certainly be influenced by various elements of the formal organization. Knowing how to reach informal groups is a prerequisite for managers today. In some instances this ability to work with and through informal groups will distinguish the good managers from the average ones.

There are formal groups that managers must work with as well. Of course, the immediate work group is the one with which the manager will have the most contact. A good behavioral approach to management is perhaps even more of a challenge in a one-to-a-group situation than on a one-to-one basis. In an effort to meet the challenges of managing various groups' behaviors and achieving better performance, this chapter will examine the symbiotic relationship of leader and follower, the use of interacting and noninteracting groups in problem solving, and the soliciting of cooperation from informal groups.

LEADER AND FOLLOWERS:
A SYMBIOTIC RELATIONSHIP

In biology the term symbiosis is used to describe a mutually beneficial relationship between two dissimilar organisms. While the leader and the followers are not dissimilar organisms, their roles are dissimilar, and, when both roles are fulfilled, there can be a mutually beneficial relationship. In most cases, a group requires some organization and some leadership to provide unity of direction. Likewise, leaders are dependent upon the group for the implementation of plans. In other words, a successful group, formal or informal, has recognized the importance of the various roles of the individuals and exhibits a successful coordination of the roles.

A term used frequently to describe this cooperative action is synergism. Where synergism exists, the cooperation between two separate groups or enitities is such that the outcome of the cooperative effort is greater than the outcome had each group or entity worked independently. In work groups where roles are clearly defined and there is appropriate delegation, a cooperative team effort is necessary if the output is to increase at a greater rate than the input. If there is such an increase as a result of the teamwork, a synergistic relationship can be said to be in existence. In order to reach this level of cooperation the group would need to display a great deal of trust and confidence in the supervisor (leader) and vice versa. This mutuality implies a symbiotic relationship where each party is in some way dependent upon the other.

Of course these explanations are "word games" to a certain extent, but the point is: There is a very special relationship between leader and followers. The roles of each must be clearly understood by everyone. Even then there will be difficulties because of the numerous human variables that come into play. The relationships in the work environment that are truly synergistic and symbiotic are ideal and something to continually strive for. It is a responsibility of the leader to convey, through words and action, the nature of the relationship that should exist within the work unit. Only by possessing much knowledge about the members of the group and the objectives and the function of the leadership role can a manager accomplish this task.

GROUP PROBLEM SOLVING: GENERAL PROCEDURES

The factors discussed in Chapter 11 regarding the determination of leadership style also apply when a manager is working with a group. Factors within the leader, the followers, and the situation must ultimately be translated into action by the leader. After the forces within these three variables have been considered, the leader or manager must make a decision as to what approach is needed for the particular situation at hand. Generally, this decision will be made in relation to a general problem-solving procedure. Not all managers will consciously think about the problem-solving process in a step-by-step manner, but they will make a decision using a framework with which they are comfortable. Some will utilize the traditional problem-solving methodology that follows:

- Step 1—Define the problem
- Step 2—Identify the constraints
- Step 3—Generate alternatives

- Step 4—Select the best alternative and supplement it
- Step 5—Follow up

Managers using this framework as an approach to making a decision will relate their perceptions of the situation to the framework in terms of deciding how much participation is appropriate. For example, a manager who sees the possibility of some, but not total, group participation may decide to define the problem for the group and allow them to identify the constraints and generate the alternatives. The manager, who feels ultimately responsible for the decision, will then select what seems to be the best alternative.

The degree to which groups are involved can thus be related to the number of steps in the problem-solving approach that they are asked to participate in. There are, of course, degrees of involvement at each step but the number of steps that the group participates in does serve as a general indication of the amount of overall group participation. This is one way a manager's preference for use of authority (as demonstrated in the previous chapter in Figure 12.2) can be clearly seen.

The role of any group will be dependent upon the leader or manager's view of how involved the group should be. A group may be used at any or all steps in the problem-solving process. When managers believe a situation that calls for a decision is one which could best be handled by a participative approach, there must be a decision as to whether the participation should be in the form of individual input or as a group working as a team. Once a team approach has been decided upon, then it must be determined if the group can contribute more through an interacting or noninteracting approach. Some of the specific techniques of interacting and noninteracting groups, as well as some of the advantages and disadvantages of each, will be examined in this chapter.

PROBLEM SOLVING IN INTERACTING GROUPS

When people talk about group problem solving, it is usually assumed that the group is a traditionally structured, interacting group. The typical group process is generally perceived as hearing ideas or suggestions from the group, discussing the ideas, and then making a decision through some voting procedure. Some groups will be very loosely organized and have very few real operating procedures, while others will adhere to a fairly rigid format. The following discussion will include general approaches of three such groups:

- Committees
- The jury technique
- Brainstorming.

Management by Committee

It has been facetiously said that a camel is a horse put together by a committee. The statement clearly exhibits the feelings of many people about the effectiveness of committees. All of us have probably had some experience serving on a committee or working with one. The inefficiencies are indeed there, but could better leadership enable management to maximize the contributions of a committee? Without a doubt the answer is YES! Simply put, there are times and situations when committees can be most useful just as there are times and situations when they will do little more than waste time.

Some of the faults that committees are accused of—being time consuming, self-perpetuating, and a body of compromises—can, in most cases, be blamed upon poor management. Many times the reasons for such inefficiencies can be found in the purpose of the committee. If management fails to clearly define the role and responsibilities of the committee, there will indeed be a great deal of time wasted. Management must indicate what the role of the committee is relative to the problem-solving framework. The committee members should be told if they are to be involved with defining the problem, generating alternatives, or selecting the best alternative. In this regard, it appears that committees can be used to greatest advantage in the generation of alternatives.

Committees do have the advantage of eliciting the different viewpoints of the members. In addition, each member will have slightly different talents to contribute to the group. The key to successful committee usage becomes the management of the committee as a group. A leader or chairperson will have to be able to conduct a committee meeting so that everyone has an opportunity to provide input, but no one has the opportunity to dominate the meeting. Another one of the challenges of managing a committee is keeping everyone fairly objective. A common complaint directed toward many committees is that each member is there to represent a particular department or interest and will, therefore, be more concerned with supporting, defending, and protecting that particular group than with the achievement of the objectives of the committee. This kind of behavior is also what leads to unproductive compromises.

Because of the disadvantages generally associated with committees, there have been many suggestions and rules made about how to take advantage of the positive contributions that committees can make. Some of the suggested guidelines for use in the management of committees are:

1. Do not put a committee in a decision-making capacity.

2. Use a committee as an advisory body to make recommendations.

3. Have the committee be directly responsible to a member of management who is in a position to weigh the alternatives and recommendations of a committee and make a decision.

4. Be sure the committee has a specific objective or responsibility.

5. Define the committee's role so that everyone on the committee understands the mission of the committee and has a feel for his or her role.

6. Make serving on a committee a rewarding rather than a punishing experience.

To gain a real benefit from committees, managers must take the above points into consideration. Although the committee is the most used interacting group approach, it is also the most abused. Usually committees are given rather vague and general objectives. Ironically, those interacting groups that have abided by the rules set forth for committees by management are referred to as being something different from committees. The jury technique is an example of such a distinction.

The Jury Technique

The jury technique utilizes an interacting group that is distinguished by its structured approach. The "jury" is limited to no more than twelve people. After the manager who has ultimate authority over the particular problem at hand has identified those people who are immediately involved with the problem, the problem-solving procedure is ready to begin. Steps to be followed in the process are outlined and the participants are invited to the session. Participants are encouraged to bring all information and data they have regarding the problem to the problem-solving session.

The conduct of the actual session may vary according to the leader's ideas as to the most effective format. Generally the approach will be similar to the one suggested by Donald W. Devine:

- The group leader presents the problem to the group with background information.
- Each participant is given the opportunity to relate to the group what he or she knows about the problem.
- Members of the "jury" are allowed to ask open-ended questions of each individual after his or her statements concerning the problem.
- The problem is then redefined if necessary.
- The group is broken into small work groups of two to three members to develop pragmatic solutions.
- The efforts of the small work groups are consolidated into an overall definition of the problem and the plan of action to be implemented.
- Each individual then assumes responsibility for various actions and reports on progress at the next meeting of the group.[1]

While the jury technique is not terribly innovative, it does provide a framework for group problem solving that can be most useful. It is an example of a commitment to use group input in every step of the problem-solving process. This in itself means that the technique has limited application within most formal organizations. When the jury technique is used, consolidating the efforts of the small work groups into a workable report presents perhaps the biggest obstacle to success. But if the leader has successfully guided the discussion before breaking down into the small groups, the parameters for solving the problem should be narrow enough to allow a good deal of consistency and comparability in the proposed solutions. In contrast to the rather confining parameters necessary for the jury technique, brainstorming and other idea-generation methods need to minimize the restrictions on the group process.

Brainstorming

Brainstorming and its various modifications have been used in many different problem-solving situations. It is perhaps most frequently used to generate ideas or alternative solutions to problems, but it can be used effectively for any of the first three steps in the problem-solving process. Innovative thinking is encouraged by a group leader who tries to develop a creative environment for participants in the session. This is done by the leader's approach in conducting the session. Setting very wide parameters for the group to work within, emphasizing creativity, allowing participants to build upon one another's ideas, and disallowing criticism or negative feedback during the generation of ideas are ways in which the leader can provide the group with an effective environment for brainstorming. Ideas are usually not discussed in detail until the idea generation has ceased. When no member of the group can add anything to the recorded list of ideas or come up with any new suggestions, the generation phase has ended. Duplications are identified and discussion of the pragmatics of the ideas can begin. The time allowed will be dependent upon the group and the leader.

There is no definite requirement for the size of a brainstorming group. Perhaps the most critical variable is whether or not the group is to be an interacting group or a noninteracting (nominal) group. According to a recent study, increasing the size of interacting groups adds very little to the performance of the group while increasing nominal group size increases performance significantly.[2] It should be remembered that the larger an interacting group is, the more limited the participation of any one member of the group will be. For interacting groups, therefore, it appears to be better to limit them to a group size of three to seven members. Nominal groups seem to be able to function best when the group size ranges from six to twelve.

Like any other group approach to problem solving, brainstorming is an attempt to better utilize the human resources of an organization. By seeking input from more people in a less confining environment, it is hoped that more creative problem solving may be accomplished. While it is quite possible that some individuals will work better by themselves, the exchange of ideas in an open forum can serve as a catalyst to build upon individual thinking. An effective leader will seek to utilize several different approaches to ascertain which works best for a particular kind of situation. In some cases a nominal or noninteracting group similar to the ones explained below may be most useful.

PROBLEM SOLVING
IN NONINTERACTING GROUPS

As mentioned earlier, group decision making is generally a process of compromise. The compromise is seen as the easiest way to overcome differences of group members. Because of the difficulty of resolving the differing opinions, the compromise decision emerges as the "best" one the group can make although it may actually be unproductive. Two techniques are currently being used to overcome some of the traditional weaknesses of group and committee problem solving that lead to such unproductive compromises. The Delphi technique and nominal grouping both make use of group input without interaction of group members. All members of the group have an opportunity to provide input and the group cannot be dominated by one or two particularly strong personalities.

The Delphi Technique

The Delphi technique was developed by the Rand Corporation in the early 1950s for use in planning and forecasting. It offers the advantage of collecting and tabulating individuals' opinions without the usual interchange and debate of the group process. In its original application, experts from a variety of backgrounds were used for technical forecasting.

Typically, the individuals involved are not aware of the identification of the other people who are participating. Everyone fills out a series of questionnaires on an independent basis. After the questionnaires have been tabulated, the participants, referred to as the panel, receive feedback that includes data from all members of the panel. Only facts are presented in the feedback, with no opinions or supporting statements accompanying the data. If more information concerning the problem or issue at hand is needed by any participant, it is provided. Another round of questionnaires or interviews is then administered and the feedback is once again provided to all panel members. This process is continued until there seems to be significant agreement. If some disagreement still exists, it is usually explained in the final report which presents the results of the process. Differences that are clearly removed from the position of general agreement of the panel are usually due to applying different assumptions or misinterpreting data.

Among the major advantages of the Delphi technique are:

1. Identities of the panel members are unknown to one another, eliminating bias.
2. There is no ego involvement in defending an idea or estimate.
3. The halo effect is minimized as a highly regarded panel member cannot influence others with his or her response because of anonymity.
4. There is no need to meet as a group, thus the usual confrontation of interacting groups is avoided.
5. Panel members can contribute regardless of geographical location.
6. There is no limitation as to the size of panel.[3]

Of course there are disadvantages as well. Most, however, have to do with how the panel of experts is made up and do not necessarily reflect directly on the process itself. Among those limitations most frequently mentioned are:

1. The possibility of poor panel selection
2. Occasional low panel motivation
3. Length of time to analyze data and complete the process[4]

The most damaging criticism is probably the amount of time involved. But most managers would willingly sacrifice time in order to obtain better solutions and avoid the compromise situations of interacting groups. While the Delphi technique is not usually used for routine types of problems, it can be effectively used for planning and for situations involving a certain amount of risk or uncertainty. Like brainstorming, it is probably most effectively used in the first three steps of the problem-solving process.

Nominal Grouping

Another technique for problem solving in noninteracting groups is known as nominal grouping. It offers some of the same advantages as the Delphi technique but is more closely akin to traditional group structuring. Unlike the Delphi technique, the nominal approach allows people to be part of a group but there is no interaction among the members of the group. Since the control of interaction is not inherent in the process as in the Delphi approach, it requires a very strong leader who can encourage individual creativity and prevent defense of ideas. In other words nominal grouping seeks to maximize individual contributions and minimize interaction among members of the group.

Nominal grouping can be used to identify and define problems, identify constraints and priorities, develop alternative solutions, and select the best solution. The uses and outcomes are somewhat similar to brainstorming but the process itself is conducted within a fairly rigid set of rules. Most nominal groups are from ten to twelve members but they may be as small as five or six. The leader asks each person in the group to make a list of the possible answers to the question or statement posed by the leader. The question may be something like "What is the major cause in the decline of sales in our southern region?" Each group member then develops a list of the possible major causes of the decline in sales. The leader asks each member to contribute one of the items from the list and the participant gives the item with no explanation as to why it should be included. Under no circumstances does the leader allow any discussion at this point. Participants continue to give their ideas one at a time until their lists have been exhausted. As the ideas are given, each one is recorded by the leader on a chalkboard or flip chart where all members can see them. After the cumulative list has been completed, the participants are given a few minutes to study the list. Duplicates are eliminated by a vote of the group, but there is still no discussion or defense of items. Next the group is asked to rank the items on the list or to select the top five or some similar procedure to establish priorities. A common practice is to allow each member a vote for first place, one for second and so on with points being allocated according to how an item is ranked. For example, a first place vote may count five points and a second place vote, four points. The group leader then totals the points and identifies the priority of the items. Items ranked as the most important, perhaps the top three, are then discussed. After the discussion the leader is responsible for summarizing the group findings and feelings as indicated by the ranking and the discussion.

The advantages of such an approach are similar to those of the Delphi technique. Although the number of participants is limited in any one group, there is the possibility of running several groups simultaneously. Comparisons of findings can be very useful. There are several ways in which nominal grouping can be used and modified to meet an organization's needs.[5] However, there seems to be two critical variables that may determine the success of a nominal session when compared to an interacting group:

1. The participants' knowledge of the facts that are the object of the fact-finding task
2. The participants' willingness to communicate.[6]

WORKING WITH INFORMAL GROUPS

Up to this point the discussion of group problem solving has been concerned with organized attempts within specifically formed formal groups. Managers must also be aware of the potential within informal groups for solving problems and how that potential can be tapped.

As discussed in Chapter 2, informal groups are an integral part of all formal organizations. Even though their existence is primarily for providing various satisfactions to members, informal groups can also assist in the achievement of formal organizational objectives. The effective leader will recognize the possible contributions of informal groups and will solicit their cooperation.

Informal groups serve as training grounds for leaders in the groups to practice their leadership skills. Since these leaders have a very strong influence on group members, managers should make a special effort to identify them. Many times gaining the cooperation of an informal group leader is synonymous with gaining the cooperation of the informal group itself. By identifying informal leaders and soliciting their input and cooperation, the manager has a greater chance of reaching the level of group performance desired.

A point often overlooked in discussions of the influence of informal groups on production is that they may discourage too low of an output as well as discouraging the "rate buster." In any case, group norms and values do help to regulate production. Whether the production is regulated to assure a certain minimum level or to establish a maximum level depends upon the degree to which the formal objectives coincide with the values and norms of the informal group.

An important mechanism linking the formal and informal organizations is the informal reward system.[7] People who are respected for their job skills and performance may be rewarded in the informal group with status. However, this is true only if the group values the possession and exercise of outstanding skills. Management must, therefore, seek the cooperation of informal groups to make the basis for formal and informal rewards as compatible as possible. A posture of cooperation on the part of management, supported by an effort to get input from the informal group, will improve upon the likelihood of linking the formal and informal groups in a positive way. At the very least, management should attempt to create an environment in which informal groups will not feel compelled to base rewards on behavior that is detrimental to the formal organization.

In many instances cohesion of informal groups has been found to contribute to greater productivity, lower absenteeism, higher job satisfaction, and lower turnover rates.[8] While managers should avoid attempting to break up informal groups, it is ironic that pressure and/or attacks from outside sources actually cause an informal group to become more cohesive. Perhaps the best way for management to encourage stronger group cohesiveness rests with the creation, development, and maintenance of a work climate that encourages teamwork and cooperation. Job design and the proximity of work stations, as well as the work conditions themselves, can be arranged in a manner that will create and maintain a climate within which individuals can become part of a more cohesive, informal group.

When a favorable climate for the formal organization is developed, there is a better chance that the climate of the informal group will also be favorable. The values and norms of the informal group will reflect the group's perception of the formal organization and the work environment. A favorable perception of the formal organization will usually result in group norms that are more compatible with the objectives of management. While complete compatibility probably cannot be reached, any improvement in the attitude of informal groups toward the formal organization will prove worthwhile. In fact, the informal group climate can change the attitudes of individual members and will also influence a group member's behavior regardless of his or her own attitude.[9]

SUMMARY

Regardless of the purpose of a group there will usually be someone who will assume the leadership role. The leader will keep the group moving as a unit toward goal accomplishment. To achieve goals requires teamwork and cooperation of all members of a group. This mutuality of leader and followers implies a symbiotic relationship wherein each party is in some way dependent upon the other.

A manager's perception of the situation and the factors within the subordinates and the manager will be the major determinants of group involvement in the decision-making process. The amount of participation a group will be allowed can usually be related to the steps in the problem-solving methodology. As a general rule, the number of steps the group is involved in is a good indication of overall group participation.

On many occasions managers will use some form of group problem solving to maximize input and to arrive at a solution that will better satisfy the people involved. Group problem solving techniques may be interacting or noninteracting in nature. Interacting groups encourage interchange among group members. Committees, the jury technique, and brainstorming are examples of interacting groups.

Noninteracting groups try to take advantage of the number of people involved by getting contributions from all members. Individual input is solicited without the interaction of the individuals within the group. The Delphi technique and nominal grouping are two approaches to noninteracting group problem solving. Generally speaking, the productivity of noninteracting groups will increase with their size. The opposite appears to be true of interacting groups, as a large group tends to limit the participation of any one member of the group.

Besides being able to use formal groups for problem solving, leaders must also have the ability to work with informal groups. Since the values and norms of an informal group will probably reflect the group's perception of the formal organization, the development of a favorable climate for the formal organization will have an impact on the informal group. A good work climate, a posture of cooperation on the part of management, and an effort to solicit the input and cooperation of informal groups will improve upon the likelihood of linking the formal and informal groups in a positive way.

NOTES

1. DONALD W. DEVINE, "The Jury Technique: Will the Real Problem Please Stand Up," *Personnel*, September–October 1976, pp. 27–8.

2. THOMAS J. BOUCHARD, JR., JEAN BARSALOUX, and GAIL DRAUDEN, "Brainstorming Procedure, Group Size, and Sex as Determinants of the Problem-Solving Effectiveness of Groups and Individuals," *Journal of Applied Psychology* 59, No. 2 (1974): 138.

3. RICHARD J. TERSINE and WALTER E. RIGGS, "The Delphi Technique: A Long-Range Planning Tool," *Business Horizons*, April 1976, pp. 51–2.

4. Ibid., p. 55.

5. See THOMAS J. BOUCHARD and MELANA HARE, "Size, Performance and Potential in Brainstorming Groups," *Journal of Applied Psychology* 54 (1970): 51–5; and ANDREW VAN DE VEN and ANDRE L. DELBECQ, "Nominal Versus Interacting Group Processes for Committee Decision-Making Effectiveness," *Academy of Management Journal* 14, No. 2 (1971): 203–12.

6. THAD B. GREEN, "An Empirical Analysis of Nominal and Interacting Groups," *Academy of Management Journal* 18, No. 1 (1975): 72.

7. PETER M. BLAU and W. RICHARD SCOTT, *Formal Organizations: A Comparative Approach* (Scranton, Pa.: Chandler Publishing Co., 1962), p. 94.

8. Ibid., pp. 95–6.

9. Ibid., p. 101.

QUESTIONS FOR THOUGHT AND DISCUSSION

1. The term "synergistic" was used to describe a cooperative relationship between two entities. How can the leadership style of a manager contribute to synergism between the manager and subordinates?

2. Under what circumstances will a committee approach be most successful in problem solving?

3. A group of people with divergent backgrounds and talents is asked to work together on a project requiring: (1) an initial statement of objectives, and (2) the determination of the best way to meet the most important objective. As the leader of the group, what techniques would you utilize? (Assume that the group will not be able to meet together during the formulation of objectives stage but will meet as a group to determine the approach to meet the selected objective.)

4. How can informal groups be used to assist in the decision making process of the formal organization?

KEY TERMS

The student should be able to discuss the significance of these terms to the study of human behavior in the work environment.

Symbiosis
Interacting groups
Noninteracting groups
Management by committee
Jury technique

Brainstorming
Delphi technique
Nominal grouping
Informal reward system
Group cohesiveness

CASE INCIDENT

Middleton, Iowa, is an urban community of approximately thirty thousand people. The community is operated under a city manager form of government and recently underwent its first major administrative change in twelve years. Due to ill health, Daniel Keller, who had occupied the position of city manager for that twelve year period, was stepping down. Replacing him was an experienced administrator, Diane Armstrong. Diane Armstrong had been involved in municipal government for eight years. She had served as Director of Public Works in Waterloo, Iowa, for three years. Next, she had taken a position as an assistant city manager in Des Moines, Iowa. She held the position for five years and once described her experience in Des Moines by saying, "I learned more about city management while there than I ever knew existed."

Diane Armstrong's first official act as the new city manager was to call together the heads of all the major departments in the city. She told the supervisors that she had no major changes in mind at the moment but that she would like to see some type of report about what each department was doing and had accomplished over the last three years. Diane was surprised to see expressions of shock on many of the faces in the room. Finally one of the department heads, Mary Walton, spoke up: "I'm not sure that we know what you mean, Ms. Armstrong. We all do our jobs and we don't get too many bad reports. Speaking for my staff, when we do get a complaint we get right to it and try to straighten the matter out."

Diane interrupted: "But have you accomplished what you set out to accomplish? What is it that your department is trying to do?"

Again there was silence in the room. Then slowly, one by one, the department heads began to respond to Diane's question.

The police chief stated that his men did their best to hold crime in Middleton down to a minimum. The supervisor of the Sanitation Department said that his department made sure that all refuse was picked up from each home in the city at least twice a week and from each business firm about three times a week. In addition, he stated that his men were responsible for maintaining the cleanliness in the downtown area.

"Now just a minute! We're responsible for the streets when the sewers overflow," stated Bob Henry, Supervisor of the Sewer Department.

"You know I think each of you guys is misleading Ms. Armstrong," said Charles Fifer. "My men in the Street Department maintain those streets year around. It's not very often that your men have to get out and work on the city streets, downtown or elsewhere."

"The hell we don't, Charley!"

At this point Diane Armstrong interrupted. "I really don't think we need to argue about these things now. From everything I can see, things look pretty shipshape to me. Why not write up your reports and then let's see if we can get a clearer picture of the responsibilities of each department. If we're going to serve the people of Middleton in the next one, three, or five years then we'll have to know exactly who is responsible for what and what each of us hopes to accomplish for the community."

Each of the supervisors nodded in agreement. But they knew they had a difficult task before them. After all, no one had ever asked them before to "write down" what they were doing and what their goals were. They each knew that already.

At the end of the week, all of the reports had been turned in, and it was agreed that everyone would meet again on the following Tuesday morning. Diane Armstrong took the reports home to read them over the weekend. On Tuesday morning she handed a sheet of paper to each department supervisor at the meeting. On the paper was a list of observations made by the new city manager.

Observations on Some Problem Areas

1. There seems to be considerable overlap of work done in various departments.
2. All but two departments have turned in requests for more employees, but personnel expenses exceed regional averages for a town of Middleton's size.
3. The programs of some departments seem to be in conflict with those of other departments. For example, last month the Fire Department conducted a "clean-out-your-attic" campaign. However, complaints were received by the city because some trash left on the curbs was not picked up for up to ten days. The delay was due to the fact that last month the Sanitation Department initiated a preventive maintenance program on all trash pickup vehicles. This program resulted in having one of the three main trucks out of action each of three subsequent weeks.
4. Turnover has been as high as 200 percent for some departments and no lower than 50 percent in any other department for the last three years.
5. Hiring policies are not uniform between departments.
6. City workers recently filed to have a union election even though wages were raised the maximum percentage allowed by law.
7. Promotion presently is based on a seniority/merit system. However, most supervisors agree that seniority is most important since merit cannot be easily measured.
8. Citizen complaints about service were down last year. This was attributed largely to "long overdue" improvements in the city water system.

Questions for Discussion

1. At this point what kind of leadership style should Ms. Armstrong use?
2. Can a group problem-solving approach be used effectively? If so, for what problem areas could it be applied most advantageously?
3. If Ms. Armstrong were to use a group problem-solving method, would you recommend an interacting or noninteracting method? Explain.

Case Contributor: Don White, Associate Professor of Management, University of Arkansas.

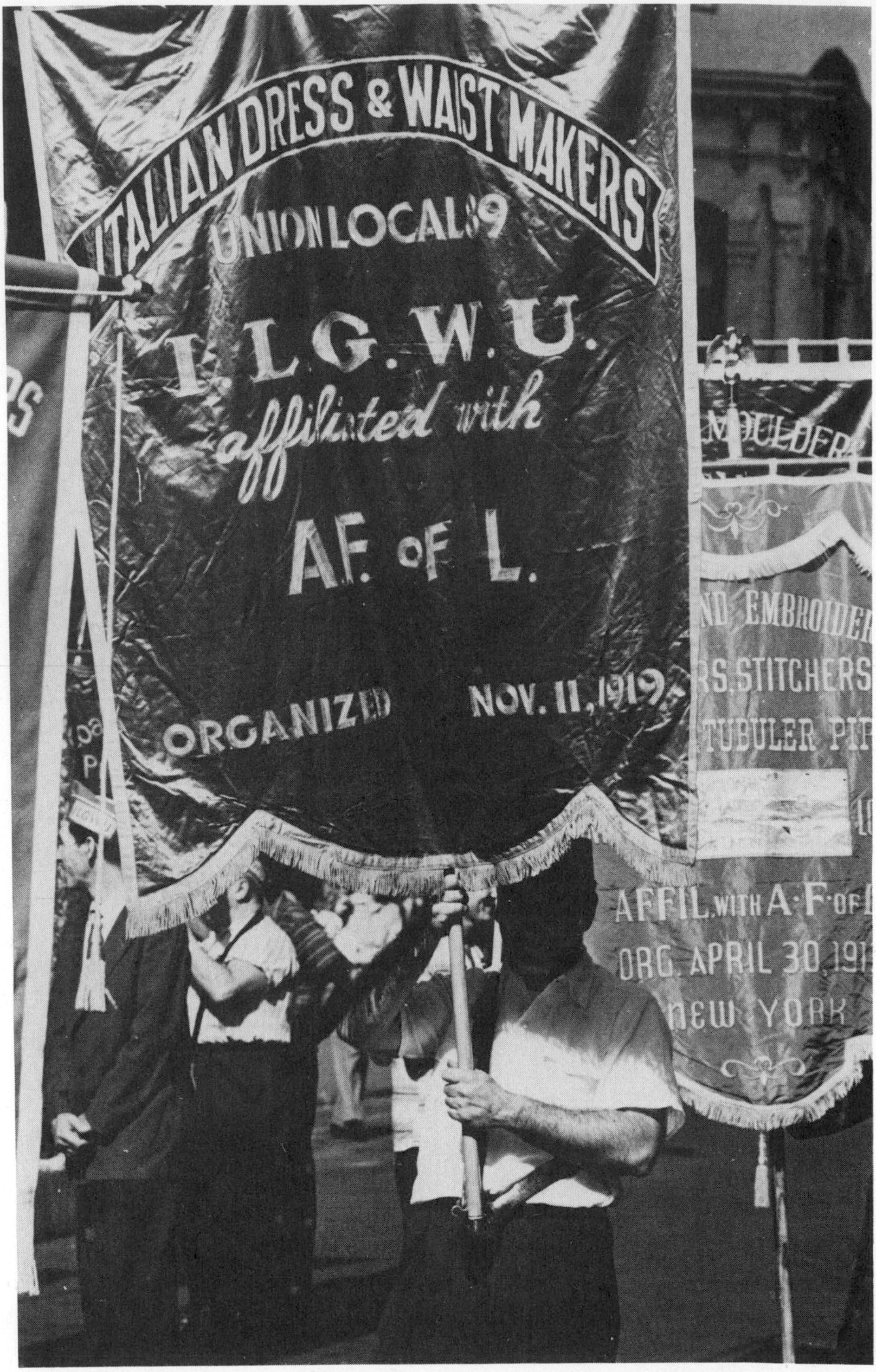
ITALIAN DRESS & WAIST MAKERS
UNION LOCAL 89
I.L.G.W.U.
affiliated with
A.F. OF L.
ORGANIZED NOV. 11, 1919
AFFIL. WITH A·F·OF
NEW YORK

PART SIX

SPECIAL GROUPS AND THEIR INFLUENCE ON BEHAVIOR IN THE WORK ENVIRONMENT

One of the greatest influences upon human behavior in the work environment is the group or groups with which a person identifies. While the groups included in this section may have some of the same characteristics of the informal groups discussed in Chapter 2, they are treated more as classifications or general categories of employees that present management with special problems. There may be informal groups within any one of these special groups discussed in the next three chapters. The main concern of these chapters is to examine how some of the major identifiable groups impact upon individual member behavior and upon managerial behavior.

One of these special groups is known as knowledge resources, which consist of people such as lawyers, cost accountants, researchers, and engineers. Besides occupationally oriented groups, an individual may be influenced by a group wherein the common link to other members is race or gender. Still another type of special group in which a person may hold formal membership is the labor union. Union membership means belonging to two formal organizations within the same work environment. The following chapters discuss these special groups, which are usually present within most organizations, in terms of how they influence the behavior of the people identifying with them and the special problems they create from a managerial perspective.

14

Knowledge Resources

LEARNING OBJECTIVES

Upon completion of this chapter the student should be able to:

- Explain the term "knowledge resources."
- Distinguish between professional, technical, and managerial occupations.
- Discuss the rapid increase of knowledge workers in the work force.
- Differentiate between a cosmopolitan orientation and a local orientation.
- Explain the dual ladder concept.
- Provide reasons why scientists and engineers do not have the same opportunities for advancement as those with a business background.
- Describe what is necessary to create a scientific environment for scientists.
- Discuss how to improve upon knowledge workers' motivation and productivity.
- Explain how matrix project management is used.

In the process of moving from an agrarian society to one that is industrially oriented the nature of the work force has undergone some rather drastic changes. A developed economy requires more professionals, managers, and technicians and proportionately fewer people possessing manual skills. Consequently more people are spending more time in becoming formally educated. When these people with baccalaureate and graduate degrees become part of the work force, they join the fastest growing segment of workers in America. These highly educated workers, who are paid for putting knowledge to work rather than for manual skill or strength, are called knowledge resources and are now the largest single group in the work force.[1] Knowledge resources (or knowledge workers) have thus become the major element of many organizations. There is a great diversity in the nature of the training and the jobs of knowledge resources, and these differences have caused considerable managerial problems. Perhaps the first step in dealing with these differences is to learn more about knowledge resources.

THE NATURE OF KNOWLEDGE RESOURCES

The employment of professionals, managers, and technicians in industry is increasing at a much more rapid rate than is total employment. In fact, during the period from 1973 through April of 1975 total employment actually declined while professional and technical workers grew in number. During a time when total employment dropped by about 323,000, the employment of professional and technical workers grew by approximately 839,000.[2]

In Table 14.1 it can be seen that during the first half of 1978 white-collar employment grew by almost two million. Included in the category of professional and technical workers are such occupations as lawyers, doctors, professors, accountants, engineers, and a wide range of scientists and technicians.

One of the major reasons for the rapid increase in the employment of engineers and scientists has been the emphasis placed upon research and development. Part of this growth can also be attributed to socio-political trends that have prevailed in the past decade. For example, the concern that society in general has expressed about ecological issues has contributed greatly to the hiring of more scientists by industrial and governmental organizations alike. As laws covering pollution continue to be passed and enforced, the numbers of scientists and engineers will continue to grow. The impact of this recent growth in scientific employment is more widespread than the growth of the '50s and '60s. In the previous two

TABLE 14.1 White-Collar Workers in the United States

OCCUPATION	EMPLOYMENT[1]		
	1976	*1977*	*1978*[2]
Professional and technical and kindred workers	13,329	13,980	14,307
Managers and administrators, except farm	9,315	9,915	10,084
Salesworkers	5,497	5,773	5,901
Clerical workers	15,558	16,549	16,672

[1] Numbers in thousands
[2] First six months of 1978

Source: Adapted from U.S. Department of Labor, Bureau of Labor Statistics, Monthly Labor Review, *101 (August 1978): Table 1, p. 4 and* Monthly Labor Review, *101 (October 1978): Table 3, p. 69.*

decades scientists tended to be concentrated in a few industries. Today the distribution is much more widespread throughout all industries.

In some industries the scientific contribution is literally the lifeblood of organizations. Without a continual effort to improve upon existing products, enterprises in a highly innovative industry would not survive. The aerospace industry and the electronics industry are examples of the importance of a continued research effort. In these high technology industries, the competitive edge will go to the innovative leader. To be a leader requires a great deal of capital and, of course, the appropriate blend of scientific talent and production capabilities. However, in order to receive the maximum benefits of such a blend there must be the best possible utilization of the scientific resources. This requires more than the usual managerial knowledge and capabilities, as scientists must be considered unique employees.

The managers and administrators referred to in Table 14.1 are those people in organizational hierarchies of both private and public organizations who have managerial prerogatives and responsibilities. Considering that this group is made up of people practicing the same profession— management—the total employment figures are very impressive. This is not to say that the backgrounds and education of all managers and administrators are the same, for they certainly are not. But regardless of past training or experience, they are all involved with the management of things and/or people. These managers may be involved in sales, production, accounting, research, or any one of thousands of different occupations. They are knowledge resources who are pursuing managerial careers within some specialty.

OCCUPATIONAL LOYALTY VERSUS
ORGANIZATIONAL LOYALTY

One of the characteristics of modern day organizations that has been spawned by the emphasis placed upon specialized knowledge is the growing percentage of employees who possess more loyalty to their occupations than to the organization. As people spend longer in preparing for occupations, and as their training becomes more and more specialized, this trend toward occupational loyalty appears inevitable. There are indications that this trend is spreading to nearly all occupations found within the hierarchy of an organization.

Alvin W. Gouldner uses the terms "cosmopolitan" and "local" to describe the difference in the locus of loyalty.[3] People who are considered cosmopolitans rate the recognition received from peers in their profession or occupation to be of greater importance than organizational recognition. Such individuals will usually view an organization as a means or a vehicle to help them in achieving their professional goals. Typically, cosmopolitans will seek employment with organizations that allow them a good deal of freedom in pursuing professional objectives. When organizations seem to have too many barriers that restrict the cosmopolitans from practicing their professions, they will seek another organization that will better serve as a vehicle in the accomplishment of professional goals.

Locals will generally be oriented more to the organization for which they work. Recognition coming from the formal reward system is more important to the locals than occupational recognition. Therefore, loyalty is centered with the organization as advancement in the hierarchy is quite important to locals. Locals are sometimes said to be "place bound" in that they are either bound to the organization or the geographical location. Cosmopolitans, on the other hand, are more likely to be "career bound" and will move frequently in order to better their careers. Knowledge resources are more likely to be cosmopolitans than locals in their orientation.

The norms of the two groups are quite different. While locals conform to norms stressing the organizational value system, cosmopolitans are much more tolerant of individual differences. The following group norms are typical of most cosmopolitans:

- Support originality, allow eccentricity and communication openness
- Seek high quality independent effort and full participation in group effort
- Seek integrative decisions through analysis and creative compromise[4]

Since group norms are a manifestation of the knowledge workers' inclinations toward creativeness and autonomy, management must implement leadership and reward systems that will be compatible with these standards. In many cases some of the motivators that are usually relied upon in the corporate structure may not be appropriate for certain knowledge resources. For example, research scientists are usually not as motivated by the possibility of promotion as professional managers would be.

PROMOTION OF KNOWLEDGE RESOURCES

Promotion for managers and administrators seems to be among the more valued motivators. Progression in the hierarchy is generally a common objective for these types of knowledge workers, but those falling in the categories of professional, technical, and kindred workers do not have the same motivation as managers. In fact they do not have the same opportunities for promotion.

People within professional occupations such as lawyers and accountants are frequently viewed as being in somewhat the same category as the technically trained research scientists and engineers. However, accountants and lawyers are afforded a much better overview of organizational operations and are thus considered to have a high potential for promotion into more responsible staff or line positions in top management. This promotion usually takes place within the normal hierarchy and represents an opportunity to make decisions having a direct impact upon operations. In addition, accountants and lawyers will be more likely to possess educational backgrounds and experience that is somewhat compatible with other members of the management team.

Scientists and engineers, on the other hand, are seldom given the same opportunity for advancement within the hierarchy for several reasons:

1. Their training is not oriented toward business operations.
2. They are more or less isolated from the operational activities of other departments.
3. Their experience within the organization is usually not geared to supervision and decision making.
4. Most scientists have a low regard for the utility of time, giving higher priority to the potential outcome of the research.

There are exceptions to this, but for the most part scientists and engineers must be viewed as operating within an environment which is science-oriented and not always conducive to promotion within the managerial ranks.

Because of scientists' intense interests in their own endeavors, few of them display much enthusiasm about promotional opportunities. Promotion in the normal sense (an upward move in the hierarchy) would probably mean sacrificing the creative research aspects of the job for administrative duties. This, of course, is unacceptable to most scientists, so there must be some other incentives connected with the formal organization, in addition to the inherent qualities of the research.

The Dual Ladder Concept

The formal education and technical training of most scientists and engineers does not include much exposure to management-oriented courses. Although scientists and engineers are always practicing management in the conduct of their projects, the experience gained in the management of human resources is minimal when compared with that obtained in administrative jobs. This puts technically trained people at a disadvantage in terms of both education and experience if they must compete for promotions with people possessing more business expertise.

In order to provide promotional incentives and to eliminate the inequities involved in a comparison of a professional manager and a scientist, dual ladders have been adopted by many companies. A dual ladder offers promotional opportunities either within a scientific (or technical) hierarchy or within a management (or administrative) hierarchy. Scientists then may progress in the organization by following either route. The individual who is extremely competent technically and is very science-oriented would probably choose to be promoted up the scientific ladder. Another individual, who was not keeping up with the technical developments in the field but yet wanted to advance, could elect to follow the management promotional ladder. Generally, it would appear that people "peak out" more quickly in the scientific ladder because of a greater likelihood of skills becoming obsolete.

While the dual ladder concept provides an opportunity for scientists to advance in rank by displaying their technical competence, there are some disadvantages to the system. Any time there are two hierarchies within one organization, some coordination problems can be expected. In addition, there is the difficulty of maintaining an equitable power structure. Depending upon the nature of the firm and the contribution of those in the technical or scientific ladder, one of the hierarchies is likely to be the more powerful, have more status, and receive greater monetary rewards. When the organization represents positions as being on the same level but in operation one group is clearly in a more favorable situation, intergroup and interpersonal problems can develop.

The dual ladder approach has obviously not eliminated communication problems, but it has not necessarily magnified them. In some cases there has been some improvement in communications because the interchange has been limited to those who normally have the most contact on an interdepartmental basis. This simplifies the communications flow and enables the individuals at the top of both ladders to serve as buffers to the rest of the people below them.

THE ENVIRONMENT
OF KNOWLEDGE RESOURCES

For the most part the discussions of environment in earlier chapters (most notably Chapters 2, 3, and 5) are applicable in the management of the environment for knowledge resources. The discussion of the individual in the work environment in Chapter 2 is very relevant, as is the examination of the importance of job design in Chapter 3. Creating and maintaining an organizational climate as detailed in Chapter 5 is also most appropriately applied to knowlege resources. However, the work environment of scientists, technicians, and engineers is so significantly different from that of other professionals and managers that it should be treated separately.

The most favorable environment for scientists seems to be one that encourages a great amount of research, mental challenge, and mutual peer support. These are important factors for managers to remember when attempting to create a suitable organizational climate for scientists. Since this group of employees, probably more than any other group, has its own culture, management must be aware of ways to make the scientists feel as though they are in a "scientific environment." This special environment apparently starts early in life for most scientists. In Anne Roe's research of sixty-four eminent research scientists, she found that the background of the participants in the study was a significant factor in eventually determining their occupations. For example, 53 percent of the scientists had fathers who were professional men and none had parents who worked as unskilled laborers.[5] Other studies have had similar findings. It would thus appear that the environment and the culture of scientists is definitely somewhat different from that of the average working man in industry.

As scientists tend to identify more with their profession than with the organization for which they work, it would be a mistake to attempt to create a climate that is similar to that in a production unit or in a sales department. The climate required in order to increase the motivation of scientists is different from any other within industry. It means establishing a working environment that has fewer rules, restrictions, or directives.

It is difficult to enforce the same kind of work standards that are imposed upon the rest of the work force. The effective manager of scientists must realize that creative talent is not productive all the time. Usually the creative process will include periods of idleness that are just as necessary as the periods of stimulation. By the same token, there is a high risk factor as far as time is concerned. For example, a scientist may spend many days on a particular project with no concrete results to show for the effort. The successful manager of scientists must have a fairly high tolerance for ambiguity, as the scientific research process has a higher susceptibility to failure than does ordinary problem solving.[6] Quick answers and readily identifiable results are not likely to occur. As scientists have a very low regard for time and a very high regard for quality work, the time perspective of scientists is usually much longer than that of professional managers.

In addition, scientists may possess a different view of management than other members of the organization have. Because of their specialized training and the technical nature of their jobs, scientists may well view the management function as one that deals with the mundane. Good management may be thought of by such employees as having the physical facilities in the best possible condition, and inventorying and ordering supplies. It is doubtful that scientists will think of the manager's role in terms of increasing employee motivation and establishing the appropriate climate. This is to be expected, as motivated employees seldom are aware of specific management efforts toward encouraging a positive motivational disposition. In this regard a successful manager of scientists is much like a good referee of a ballgame. The good ones are unnoticed by the participants and the observers; the bad ones are readily apparent.

It is especially important that the climate be one that adjusts to the creative attitudes of scientists. An environment that is conducive to creativity should be a major objective in the management of scientists. The process of encouraging creativity is probably more effective through the use of indirect means. A direct approach, which may be appropriate for management to use in the encouragement of a greater sales effort, will simply not yield the desired results in a creative profession. The best management can do is control the environment to make creativity possible. Indeed, the organizational climate that encourages and rewards creativity will undoubtedly achieve the kind of output sought.

It is usually extremely difficult for management to exert much control over an individual's creative process. As researchers have discovered, "Cosmo(politans)-professionals demand and justify more autonomy than local technicians."[7] This is not only due to the nature of the people involved, but also is a function of the nature of the problems with which they are dealing. Of course, when management must devote its effort almost exclusively to the control of an environment, the results are likely to be less certain than when more direct controls over workers are utilized. While this is definitely an ever present problem, the risk of some loss of control is usually more than offset by the performance of scientists who feel they have considerable job freedom.

While creativity can often be attributed to one particular individual, most research and development attempts within industry are built upon the notion of a team effort. A research team must have full and open communication with one another at all times. Management must arrange conditions of work in such a way that there is nothing which impedes this interchange. While some researchers may never seem to be contributing to innovations, they may actually serve as catalysts. Many times creative people will develop ideas from conversations with one another. As various members of the research team develop particular roles, it is important that management be aware of these roles and encourage their development. In short, the environment within which scientists work must be equal to the creative potential of the people. Managers must remember that the unique talents of scientists require a fairly unique environment in which to work.

MOTIVATION OF KNOWLEDGE RESOURCES

Since knowledge workers have the same basic needs as any other employees, the motivational concepts discussed in Chapter 7 are equally applicable. However, the cosmopolitan orientation of most knowledge workers may be indicative of some slightly different or additional needs. The need to achieve professionally is usually quite high and causes the motivational disposition of knowledge workers to be oriented toward their professions. While the organizational rewards may or may not be directly correlated with what the knowledge workers see as professional achievement, it must be assumed that much of their satisfaction is obtained through the intrinsic qualities of work. Also, the possibility of peer recognition is probably valued more highly than the organizational rewards.

The cosmopolitan orientation and a high level of an achievement motive would imply that an individual is a self-starter. Even though this is not the case for all knowledge workers, it is indeed true for a good many engaged in creative research and scientific activities. Because of the nature of their educational and work backgrounds and because of the creative objectives that most scientists have, management must be aware of the necessity to provide a different type of leadership and motivation.

Almost without exception the leadership style that is best used by nonscientists in the management of scientists is one that sets some very broad parameters and allows as much freedom as possible. Some of the basic guidelines of acceptable organizational behavior must be established, communicated, and enforced. For the most part, these guidelines would be those designed to combat some of the more common manpower problems; rules on absenteeism, tardiness and safety would, of course, be enforced the same as within any work unit. But with regard to goal setting and the prerogative to make decisions which will affect their jobs, scientists should be allowed considerable freedom. Since an important element of creativity is the freedom to express oneself, autonomy in the conduct of research is valued quite highly. Research conducted by E. Frank Harrison and James Rosenzweig provides evidence that "role performance will be improved if the scientist is allowed and encouraged to participate actively in the goal-setting and decision-making process of the formal organization."[8] Harrison drew similar conclusions in a study of ninety-five scientists in three large research laboratories in which he found participation in setting objectives and making decisions was important to an improvement in perceived and actual role performance.[9] In this respect, management would be wise to relax some of the formality of the organization and allow more participation in both the planning phase and the evaluation of performance.

Among the motivational techniques that seem to be quite successful for scientists is the opportunity to work with others who are well known in the field. To be involved in a project with an individual who has received recognition from peers for a professional contribution represents a challenge and increases many of the inherent qualities of the job. When coupled with the freedom to select some of their own research projects, this can be a very powerful incentive to creative people.

In research conducted at the Marshall Space Flight Center, it was found that the motivators most important to scientists were:

- Interesting and challenging work
- Freedom to choose the approach for achieving goals
- The feeling of accomplishment
- Recognition[10]

Management continually seeks means of "turning scientists on" to the organization by making use of effective motivators and reward systems. If such means cannot be found, the formal organization will probably represent nothing more than a vehicle for satisfying the personal occupational needs of scientists.

Peter Drucker suggests still other ways to improve upon the productivity and satisfaction of all knowledge workers.

1. The key to productivity and achievement of the knowledge worker is to demand responsibility from him or her.
2. Knowledge workers must be able to appraise their contributions to the organization.
3. Knowledge workers should be allowed to do what they are being paid for.
4. Proper placement of knowledge workers is important to their productivity.[11]

Drucker's suggestions refer either directly or indirectly to intrinsic job factors. Because of their cosmopolitan orientation most knowledge resources will respond favorably to the intrinsic motivators of a job. This is not to say, however, that money is not important to knowledge resources. They must feel adequately reimbursed for their contributions. Failure to recognize the existence of the hygiene factors among cosmopolitans could lead to unnecessary turnover. Like anyone else, knowledge resources will want to avoid the dissatisfaction that could occur from inadequate hygiene factors.

MATRIX PROJECT MANAGEMENT

In many organizations a large number of knowledge workers may be assigned to perform duties for a particular project. For example, the project may be the result of a government grant wherein the work is to be completed in a specific time. Upon completion of the project, people will be reassigned to other projects or may go back to their functional departments. Organizations which are heavily involved with government contract work may make use of a matrix organization in order to accommodate simultaneous work on a number of projects.

Figure 14.1 is representative of what is known as a matrix management organization. The chart indicates that there is a sharing of authority. Line managers (shown as a vertical relationship) retain the functional authority over their department personnel. Project managers (shown as a horizontal relationship), however, are given the responsibility and the authority for scheduling the work in order to meet project work requirements. In order for a matrix organization to work, the project managers must have the full cooperation of the line managers to gain the necessary support in utilizing people within the line managers' departments.

Because the workers assigned to a particular project are caught between two supervisors, the potential for conflict is always present. In this regard the matrix approach to project management is somewhat similar to Frederick W. Taylor's functional foremanship, which suggested a different foreman for every different task an individual performed. This means that one of the so-called principles of management is violated—unity of command. If the project manager is given line authority, the determination as to who really has a decision-making prerogative, the project manager or the functional manager, is not always clear.

As shown in Figure 14.1, the project manager must cross functional lines, making the coordination of activities of all personnel involved in the project a major task. From the standpoint of studying the behavioral implications in the role of a project manager, there are several points to be considered:

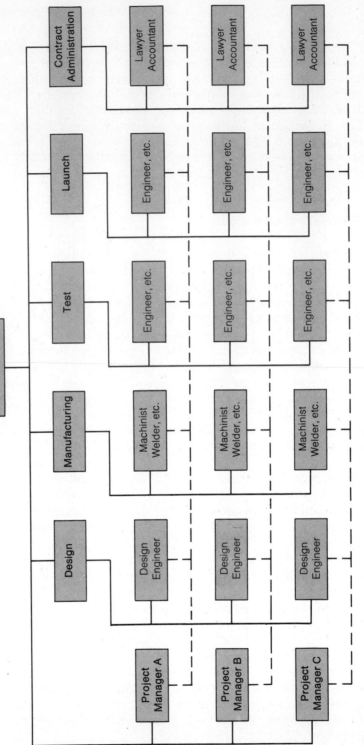

Figure 14.1 "Matrix" Project Management (Shared Authority)

Source: George A. Steiner and William G. Regan, Industrial Project Management (New York: The MacMillan Co., 1968), p. 10. Copyright © The MacMillan Co., 1968. Used with permission of MacMillan Publishing Co., Inc.

1. By nature of the matrix project organization, there is a built-in conflict situation between the project manager and several functional managers.
2. The project manager must successfully deal with people from different departments who possess diverse specialties.
3. Many times there is a mixture of line and staff people who are performing slightly different tasks than they normally perform.
4. Problems of loyalty often arise.

From an operational viewpoint, the problem of unity of command has done more to slow progress, reduce morale, and give employees an excuse for low productivity than any other problem associated with the matrix organization. The difficulties related to confusion over "who is my boss?" are not isolated at any one level. They occur at all levels of the organization. It does not really matter what level individuals are on from a behavioral perspective when they are caught between incompatible directives and expectations. Confusion and frustration are the probable results. When a conflict over the unity of command does occur, the severity of the problem seems to depend upon:

1. The abilities of the line and project managers
2. The life of the project
3. Team members' seniority in the functional organization
4. The amount and quality of communications that exist between the line manager, the project manager, and the team member
5. The professional challenge to the team member

Another problem frequently related to a matrix approach is the dilution of the talent of the line or functional organization. As the best professional talent is selected for work on projects, the capability of the functional department can be greatly reduced. Within some organizations people involved in a project may feel more loyalty to the project than to the functional department. Employee loyalty could be the opposite as well. Some individuals will feel an attachment to the department and will direct their efforts toward the accomplishment of project goals grudgingly. This will be more likely to occur in situations where the project is of rather short duration.

Much of the conflict over decision-making prerogatives can be avoided if the organization has established a clear set of "ground rules." When no compromise can be reached, it is generally understood that the superior having common authority over the project and functional managers will serve as an arbitrator. When a set of guidelines does exist, they may be quite similar to those proposed by David Cleland and William King:

Decision prerogatives of functional managers:
  "Who" will perform specific tasks
  "How" will they be accomplished
  "How well" they are accomplished
Decision prerogatives of project managers:
  "What" effort will be accomplished
  "When" it will be performed
  "How much" is budgeted
Areas of joint decisions:
  "Where" work will be accomplished
  "Who" will be the key senior man in the functional organization for that project[12]

Even in the presence of such guidelines there is likely to be need for some "give and take" on the part of both the functional managers and the project managers. Areas of joint decisions must be given careful attention by both parties, with an attitude of compromise prevailing.

An Example of Matrix Management.   Ball Brothers Research Corporation (BBRC) of Boulder, Colorado, uses matrix project management most successfully. Within BBRC the matrix structure is referred to as a "project overlay system." This system is designed to accomplish organizational and project goals by drawing people, equipment, and facilities from the functional (line) organization. Project managers are assigned full responsibility and authority for the achievement of project objectives. Top management determines total goal constraints of cost, delivery, and performance and must give the approval for the overall project plan. To overcome the problems of split loyalty, dilution of talent, and lack of unity of command, and to guarantee a continual dialogue between project and line managers, Ball Brothers Research Corporation has taken several important steps:

1. A strong functional organization with which people want to identify has been developed.

2. All project personnel are dependent upon the line organization for administrative and merit review.

3. People are trained and developed in a manner that encourages them to work as a part of a team.

4. Management has made an effort to continue to provide challenges for all functional (line) personnel as well as for those assigned to projects.

5. There is an emphasis upon the managerial and professional integration of goals.

While there are obviously many problems with the application of matrix project management, Ball Brothers Research Corporation has managed to overcome most of the difficulties. In fact, not only has their corporation made very effective use of this approach in making maximum utilization of their knowledge resources, but they have been able to turn the disadvantages of the system into problem-solving exercises for the development of people.

SUMMARY

As people spend more time today preparing for an occupation, their education and development experiences are causing these knowledge resources to feel a greater loyalty to their occupations than to the organizations that hire them. People who have greater occupational loyalty than organizational loyalty are known as cosmopolitans. Most knowledge resources who are being paid for applying their mental abilities seem to fall into this category. Employees who have more loyalty to organizations are known as locals.

Among the knowledge resources one particular group seems to be different in background, education, and the demands placed upon management; scientists appear to have several characteristics that make them unique. Some of these characteristics include the following: (1) a higher level of education, (2) a somewhat narrow view of management, (3) loyalty which is centered with the profession, and (4) a low degree of interest in progressing in the hierarchy.

The "management of scientists" is somewhat of a misnomer as the managerial effort should be directed more toward the management of the environment within which scientists work. Maintaining a high level of professionalism, encouraging creativity, and allowing scientists to be relatively independent are all elements of the managerial challenge of supervising scientists. Leadership must be fairly liberal in delegating authority to grant scientists more decision-making prerogatives.

Increasing the motivation of knowledge resources is not significantly different from increasing the motivation of other members of the organization. The same managerial knowledge and attitudes are needed; only the tools of implementation are different. Besides the inherent qualities of the work, some of the motivational techniques available to managers include dual promotional ladders, the opportunity to work with other scientists, freedom to select some of their own research projects, and provision of adequate research facilities and support.

Because much of the work done by knowledge resources—especially scientists—is of a very specialized nature, the organizational structure must be adjusted to accurately reflect the relationships of people working on projects. The matrix project management approach is an attempt to structure an organization so there may be a sharing of authority between line or functional managers and project managers. Although there are still many problems with matrix project management, it has provided a vehicle for many organizations to successfully accomplish organizational and project objectives.

In the final analysis, the successful management of knowledge resources requires managers to be aware of the special needs of creative people in the organizational environment. Through the integration of organizational goals and individual needs and the development of a team approach, management can make the best possible utilization of the knowledge resources.

NOTES

1. PETER DRUCKER, *People and Performance: The Best of Peter Drucker on Management* (New York: Harper's College Press, 1977), p. 271.

2. U.S. Department of Labor, Bureau of Labor Statistics, *Monthly Labor Review,* 98 (June 1975): p. 81.

3. See ALVIN W. GOULDNER, "Cosmopolitans and Locals: Toward an Analysis of Latent Social Roles," *Administrative Science Quarterly* 2 (December 1957): 444–80.

4. FREMONT A. SHULL, JR., ANDRE L. DELBECQ, and L. L. CUMMINGS, "Operating Task Group Structure Cell (4) Heuristic Strategy," *Organizational Decision Making* (New York: McGraw-Hill, 1970), p. 203.

5. ANNE ROE, "The Psychology of Scientists," in *The Management of Scientists,* ed. Karl Hill (Boston: Beacon Press, 1964), p. 50.

6. BERNARD WEISS, "How to Manage the Creative Person," *Management Review* Vol. 63, No. 12 (December 1974): 40.

7. SHULL, DELBECQ, and CUMMINGS, "Operating Task Group Structure Cell," p. 205.

8. E. FRANK HARRISON and JAMES E. ROSENZWEIG, "Professional Norms and Organizational Goals: An Illusory Dichotomy," *California Management Review* 14 (Spring 1972): 47.

9. E. FRANK HARRISON, "The Management of Scientists: Determinants of Perceived Role Performance," *Academy of Management Journal* 17 (June 1974): 241.

10. GEORGE C. BUCHER and JOHN E. REECE, "What Motivates Researchers in Times of Economic Uncertainty?" *Research Management* 15 (January 1972): 28–9.

11. PETER DRUCKER, *People and Performance: The Best of Peter Drucker on Management* (New York: Harper's College Press, 1977), pp. 272–73.

12. DAVID I. CLELAND and WILLIAM R. KING, *Management: A Systems Approach* (New York: McGraw-Hill, 1972), p. 345.

QUESTIONS FOR THOUGHT AND DISCUSSION

1. Why has the category of knowledge workers grown faster than any other group in the United States?

2. What are the major contributors to a cosmopolitan orientation? Does the growing number of people who are loyal to an occupation create any special problems for organizations? Explain.

3. Explain what management must do to create an environment that would be beneficial to the encouragement of creativity and motivation of scientists.

4. What kinds of managerial problems do matrix project management present? How can these problems be minimized?

KEY TERMS

The student should be able to discuss the significance of these terms to the study of human behavior in the work environment.

Knowledge resources
Occupational loyalty
Organizational loyalty
Cosmopolitan
Local

Dual ladder
Matrix project management
Project managers
Functional managers

CASE INCIDENT

Bernice Warren had been with the Carrolton Hospital and Nursing Home for only fourteen months. She was twenty-four years old and the youngest registered nurse in the nursing home. Now, for the first time, she wasn't sure she wanted to remain in nursing . . . at least not at Carrolton!

Bernice had grown up in Carrolton, an Arkansas community with a population of about eleven thousand. She liked the town, but thought she could "make more out of her life" if she moved to a bigger city. Once she had told her father, "I want to accomplish something in my lifetime. I'd like to be able to look back at what I've done someday and know that I've made someone or something better."

Bernice had graduated from Carrolton High School where she had a 'B' average in her classwork. She had attended the University of Arkansas for one year but then decided to go away to nursing school. Bernice had worked hard there and graduated close to the top of her class. At her graduation ceremonies one of her instructors complimented her, saying, "You're going to be a fine nurse. You not only learn fast, but you have a lot of good ideas. I'm sure you'll be a supervisor in a couple of years."

Bernice remained in the St. Louis area for two years. There, she worked with a newly created nursing home unit of a small hospital and had an opportunity to use much of her training. After two years with the hospital her name was placed before the board for promotion to a supervisory position. However, two days before the board was to make a decision, Bernice received some distressing news. Her father was ill and her mother had called to ask Bernice if she could come home and help out. She told her that she thought there was an opening in the Carrolton Hospital and Nursing Home. Bernice was disappointed that she would have to leave what appeared to be a fine opportunity. However, she knew that she was needed at home and immediately turned in her resignation.

Shortly after arriving in Carrolton, Bernice went to the hospital administrator's home. There, she explained what had taken place and asked the administrator if he had an opening in either the hospital or nursing home. Fortunately, such an opening was available and Bernice was given a job in the nursing home. Mr. Hanson, the administrator, knew Bernice well from her days in high school in Carrolton. In addition, Bernice had kept in touch with Mr. Hanson and Mrs. Clements, the head nurse, while in St. Louis by occasionally sending them articles about new concepts and equipment in geriatric care. During her job interviews, Bernice asked both Mr. Hanson and Mrs. Clements if they had received the articles, However, neither party said much about them.

After a few months Bernice began to get restless in her new position. She had continued to take a nurse's bulletin published in the St. Louis area and on occasion passed on the bulletin to other nurses if an article contained a new idea that she thought would benefit the individual or the home. From time to time she made suggestions to Mrs. Clements and Mr. Hanson concerning training and nursing techniques. However, few of her ideas were acknowledged and even fewer tried out.

Mrs. Clements at one point asked Bernice, "Why do you keep taking that paper? It must cost you something, and you know that we can't use those city ideas down here." After fourteen months with the Carrolton Hospital and Nursing Home, Bernice was confused. She had always honestly thought she wanted to be a nurse, but lately she wasn't so sure. That week she received a reprimand for failing to show up for her shift on time. She decided to approach Mrs. Clements about the matter and the following discussion ensued:

Bernice: I just wanted you to know that I am sorry about last week. But, I couldn't do much about it. I was looking over the information on the new telemedicine program we were considering, and my watch stopped. I'll be more careful the next time.

Mrs. Clements: You don't need to read about telemedicine or anything else, Bernice. Mr. Hanson and I will make that decision when the time comes.

Bernice: I just thought I could give you some ideas . . .

Mrs. Clements: You've got a lot of bright ideas—you always did. But I need nurses, not idea people. Wait until you are head nurse yourself. That's something I don't understand about you young people. You're too impatient. You all want to be supervising and changing things before you learn enough about the way things are around here. You know, I had to let a couple of nurses go two years ago for almost the same thing. Just take orders and do your job and everything will work out all right.

When Bernice left Mrs. Clements' office, she was lost in thought. She knew that her father and mother still needed help. But she wasn't sure she could remain with the Carrolton Hospital and Nursing Home much longer. "What's the future in it?" she thought.

Questions for Discussion

1. What factors have contributed to Bernice's present attitude?
2. Would you describe Bernice as a "local" or a "cosmopolitan"?
3. If you were Mr. Hanson, how would you advise Mrs. Clements about Bernice?
4. Can Bernice still become motivated at the Carrolton Hospital and Nursing Home?
5. How important is the organization to Bernice?

Case Contributor: Don White, Associate Professor of Management, University of Arkansas.

15

Women
and Minorities

LEARNING OBJECTIVES

Upon completion of this chapter, the student should be able to:

- Explain why a special chapter on women and minorities needs to be included in the study of human behavior in the work environment.
- Describe what is meant by the male managerial model and the problems it creates for women.
- Discuss the proposition that women need to work for the same reasons as men do.
- Describe the marked differences in salaries between men and women in similar jobs and trace the legal gains for women for improving their position.
- Explain why women in management have similar self-concepts and motivation-to-manage capabilities as their male cohorts.
- Recognize why culturally disadvantaged workers tend to place higher priorities on extrinsic factors (high salary, secure employment) than on intrinsic factors such as job challenge and growth.
- Discuss why black supervisors receive much higher ratings as supervisors when compared to their white peers.

Was Sigmund Freud accurate when he said "anatomy is destiny"? Many women who feel they have been discriminated against in industry would certainly agree that anatomy has determined their destiny. Others would expand upon Freud's statement to include color, religion, and ethnic backgrounds as determinants. Prejudice can be based upon any number of things, all more or less equally inane. While the discussions in this chapter are appropriate to all minorities in the work environment, the two major groups that have seemed to suffer the most from prejudice in the work force—women and blacks—will be emphasized.

While the ideas expressed earlier in this book on how to deal successfully with people in organizational life apply equally well to both sexes and to all races, we will see that women and blacks have had very different life experiences than white, middle-class males. These life experiences have had a strong impact on their frames of reference. A frame of reference influences individuals' perceptions and behavior and affects how they manage and are managed by others.

The concern of minorities was initially for more jobs on an organization's payroll. Later, their concern shifted toward landing more of the skilled jobs. Now, the concern of racial minorities, as well as of women, is for better representation on all levels of the organizational hierarchy. The need for this chapter arises from:

1. The lack of familiarity of business managers and policy makers with the work interests, priorities, motivations, and expectations of minority employees.

2. The opportunity costs incurred from not fully using the capabilities of women and minorities. Both groups are untapped reservoirs of supervisory and managerial talent.

3. The increasing amount of research on the influence of race and sex on such topics as hiring, promoting, paying, training, and supervising minorities.

4. The need to foster communication and increase managerial understanding of the aspirations, opportunities, and problems surrounding minority group members.

This chapter will discuss how low self-esteem, fear of success, fear of failure, and conflicting demands (mother versus worker) inhibit the upward occupational aspirations of women. A person displaying these characteristics will not engage in achievement-oriented behaviors consistent with the male managerial model in our culture. The successful managerial model in our culture, according to Douglas McGregor, is a masculine one:

The good manager is aggressive, competitive, firm and just. He is not feminine, he is not soft and yielding or dependent or intuitive in the womanly sense. The very expression of emotion is widely viewed as a feminine weakness that would interfere with effective business processes.[1]

Another description of the male managerial model which is incompatible with the stereotype female image is provided by Loring and Wells:

Men are supposed to be tough, concerned for the dollar, practical and objective enough to face the facts and act accordingly. Even if someone gets hurt in the process, a man is supposed to be strong enough to do what has to be done. Such strength, toughness, and total responsibility, even occasional, necessary violence are attributed to men as "natural." . . . He is expected to repress those aspects of himself which are associated with the feminine in our culture.[2]

Favorably or unfavorably, these two descriptions of the managerial model are widely accepted by practicing managers as valid and "right." The reader will learn later in the chapter that the motivation to manage of managerial women is as high or higher than that of males. The phrase "motivation to manage" refers to such activities as taking charge, being assertive, taking responsibility, and being competitive. There are certain actions women can take to confront stereotyped thinking in their climb up the organizational ladder. At the outset, it is especially important that everyone realize that the role of a woman and the role of an achiever are not incompatible.

WHY WOMEN WORK

According to a recent government economic report, "the labor force has grown by 1.5 million over the past year, with adult women accounting for 1.1 million of the increase."[3] The number of female workers has more than doubled since 1950 and has nearly tripled since 1940. Why are so many women now working?

Women work for the same reasons men work. They work for money and, once on a job, they want the same psychological benefits as men do. The Department of Labor reports that nearly half of the employed women are working because of "pressing economic need."[4] More than half of the 6.9 million women workers who were widowed, divorced, or separated from their husbands, particularly those who were raising children, were working just to survive. It may surprise many people to know that only 14 percent of divorced women are awarded alimony, of whom only about half collect it regularly.[5] Based on these hard facts, many divorced women must work or join the welfare rolls.

Of the women working in 1975, 23 percent were "never married" women who were working to support themselves, and 19 percent were "widowed, divorced, or separated" women employed to support themselves and their families. In addition, 29 percent of the working women had husbands earning less than ten thousand dollars a year and chose to work to bring their families into the middle income bracket.[6]

As noted in Table 15.1, 46 percent of all women with children under eighteen are working. This percentage jumps to 62 percent when husbands are not present in the household. An analysis of this data shows that it can be concluded that the vast majority of women work for economic motives in the same way that men do. The myth that women work just for "pocket money" or just to have something to do is without foundation.

One recent study examined the job factors desired by 101 women and 121 men.[7] Both were asked to rank the importance of four intrinsic and five extrinsic factors to their work lives. Regarding the intrinsic factors, the women reported that work pride was the most valued factor followed by opportunities for personal development, accomplishment, and self-esteem. The men ranked the intrinsic factors in the same order as the women.

Considering the extrinsic factors—defined, again, as those factors outside of the job being performed—a slight difference in ranking was reported. The male respondents ranked pay as the most important fol-

---

TABLE 15.1   Working Mothers and Their Children, March 1974

43 percent of all married women (husbands present) were working.

46 percent of all women with children under 18 were working.

65 percent of all working mothers have children between 6–17 years.

19 percent of all working mothers have children under 3 years.

62 percent of mothers without husbands were working.

6.8 million families, 12 percent of all families, were headed by women in 1974 (between 1970 and 1974, the number increased by over 1 million).

Source: To Form a More Perfect Union: Justice for American Women, *Report of the National Commission on the Observance of International Women's Year, no. 2 (Washington, D.C., 1976), p. 337.*

lowed by recognition from supervisors, fringe benefits, peer acceptance, and better working conditions. The women placed most importance on recognition from supervisors, followed by peer acceptance, high pay, fringe benefits, and better working conditions.[8] The idea that women differ significantly from their male counterparts in what they value from organizational life seems to be another myth that has no data supporting it.

TABLE 15.2   The Jobs Women Hold

OCCUPATION	PERCENTAGE OF WOMEN IN PARTICULAR OCCUPATIONS	
	1970	1985*
Ten Highest Paid		
Stock and bond sales agents	8.6	12.5
Managers and administrators	11.6	11.0
Bank officials and financial managers	17.4	23.5
Sales representatives, manufacturing	8.5	5.7
Real estate appraisers	4.1	8.7
Designers	23.5	30.3
Personnel and labor relations workers	31.2	28.7
Sales representatives, wholesale	6.4	9.9
Computer programmers	22.7	18.7
Mechanical engineering technicians	2.9	7.3
Ten Lowest Paid		
Practical nurses	96.3	97.8
Hairdressers and cosmetologists	90.4	92.4
Cooks, except private household	62.8	60.4
Health aides, except nursing	83.9	79.2
Nurses aides	84.6	88.9
Sewers and stitchers	93.8	93.5
Farm laborers	13.2	17.4
Dressmakers and seamstresses	95.7	94.2
School monitors	91.2	95.8
Childcare workers, except private household	93.2	88.4
All study occupations	35.9	40.5
All Occupations	37.7	39.0

*Projected

Sources: U.S. Department of Commerce, Bureau of the Census, Occupational Characteristics, 1970; *U.S. Department of Labor, Bureau of Labor Statistics,* Occupation-by-Industry Matrix Projections, 1974.

JOBS WOMEN HOLD

Despite the emergence of some women into high positions in large companies, the vast majority of women are still heavily concentrated in the lower paid, lesser skilled, service occupations which they have traditionally held. Table 15.2 shows the percentage of women in the ten highest paid and the ten lowest paid occupations. The imbalance in the 1970 figures is readily apparent. Given the current rate of progress being made, the figures will change in the future. By 1985 it is estimated that women will take a larger share of such jobs as stock agents, bank managers, real estate appraisers, and sales representatives.

The predominance of women in nine of the ten lowest paying occupations has been attributed to the similarity of these jobs to the activities typically performed by women in the home. Caring for children, nursing the sick and preparing meals are extensions of what women have traditionally done as homemakers. Typecasting not only hurts some actors and actresses, but it also affects women's efforts to secure good jobs.

THE EARNINGS GAP

It has been shown that the numbers of women in low paying occupations are disproportionately high. However, for those who have gotten past the low level jobs into the higher level jobs, there still exists a great disparity between what they make and what their male counterparts earn. Table 15.3 shows that the salaries of men in the "good jobs" exceeded women's by 15 to 49 percent. For example, in 1976 men in mathematics earned 50 percent more than did women in mathematics. Men in chemistry earned 48 percent more than did women. Men in the earth and marine sciences earned 43 percent more than did women in the same fields.[9]

In the relatively new fields of space and computer sciences, pay discrimination also exists. Even in industries where women are being accepted in entry level management positions, they are still having difficulties in receiving equal treatment in terms of salaries and promotions. This seems especially true in terms of the "executive suite" and most upper levels of middle management.

LANDMARK LEGAL GAINS

Once it had been established statistically that women were not receiving fair treatment in their work interests, the federal government started to take steps to improve the situation. Several of the more important legal gains are identified below.

TABLE 15.3   The Difference between Female and Male Pay on the Job

FIELD	MEDIAN SALARY Women	MEDIAN SALARY Men	PERCENT MEN'S SALARY EXCEEDED WOMEN'S
All fields	$11,600	$15,200	31.0
Chemistry	10,500	15,600	48.6
Earth and marine sciences	10,500	15,000	42.9
Atmospheric and space sciences	13,000	15,200	16.9
Physics	12,000	16,000	33.3
Mathematics	10,000	15,000	50.0
Computer sciences	13,200	16,900	28.0
Agricultural sciences	9,400	12,800	36.2
Biological sciences	11,000	15,500	40.9
Psychology	13,000	15,500	19.2
Statistics	14,000	17,100	22.1
Economics	13,400	16,500	23.1
Sociology	11,000	13,500	22.7
Anthropology	12,300	15,000	22.0
Political sciences	11,000	13,500	22.7
Linguistics	11,300	13,000	15.0

Source: U.S. Department of Labor, Employment Standards Administration, Women's Bureau, The Earnings Gap Between Women and Men *(1976), p. 9.*

- *July 1962:* President Kennedy ordered an end to sex bias in hiring and promoting federal employees.
- *June 1963: Equal Pay Act.* This act passed by Congress requires men and women to receive the same pay for the same work. Women now must be paid the same as men for equal work performed in the same location and under the same conditions.
- *July 1964: Civil Rights Act—Title VII.* This act passed by Congress prohibits discrimination because of race, color, religion, sex, or national origin, by a company, employment agency, labor organization, state and local government and educational institutions with fifteen or more people.
- *October 1967: Executive Order 11246* as amended by *Executive Order 11375.* This order prohibits discrimination because of race, color, religion, sex, or national origin by government contractors and subcontractors regardless of number of employees.
- *February 1970: Order Number 4.* This order by the President prohibits giving government contracts of $50,000 or more to contractors or subcontractors of fifty or more employees, until development of written

affirmative action programs. This means that a contractor must set goals and timetables to correct minority and female underutilization.

- *October 1974: Equal Credit Opportunity Act.* This act passed by Congress bans credit bias on the basis of sex or marital status.
- *November 1975:* The U.S. Supreme Court struck down a Utah law denying pregnant women jobless benefits during the last 17 weeks of pregnancy and the first six weeks after giving birth.

Although these laws and their provisions for women's rights have created a new awareness among managers, women in the 1970s have been experiencing what the civil rights leaders learned in the 1950s and 1960s: The government can create laws against inequitable and unfair treatment, but it is difficult to instill the spirit of integration. That is, the government's legislative effort stating that women cannot be kept out of good jobs does not mean they will get good jobs. That they are not landing good jobs is largely due to two reasons:

1. Corporate decision makers strongly believe in the validity of the male managerial model defined at the beginning of the chapter.
2. The myth suggesting that women do not really have to work or have a career is still very credible in the minds of many policy makers.

WOMEN IN MANAGEMENT

There are many people of both sexes who are not suitably trained or who lack the motivation for management positions. In fact, most people have not been trained in the management skills of conceptual and technical thinking and dealing with people. Some women who have had difficulties but who have nevertheless been successful were interviewed for their opinions of what it takes for a woman to make it in management. Their male co-workers were also questioned on the same topic. The ten characteristics identified as being important to women in management are:

- Competence
- Education
- Realism
- Aggressiveness
- Self-confidence
- Career-mindedness
- Femininity
- Strategy

- Support of an influential male
- Uniqueness[10]

According to the people interviewed, the aspiring woman must be especially competent and well-educated. If a woman is both of these things, she should not have to wait for that "lucky break" to get ahead. But even well-educated and competent women must face the fact that it may take an exceptional effort in order to receive a promotion. A hard situation mentioned by men who control promotions in one engineering firm is that "some women in management are working twice as hard as men, and getting half as much in the way of promotions and job responsibility."[11]

Aggressiveness and self-confidence are just as crucial for the aspiring woman as they are for the aspiring man. However, it appears that women must be able to disguise their aggressiveness as self-initiative. The image of women as being less aggressive than men is one that is still cherished by many men in the managerial hierarchy. Because of the kinds of feelings that exist in organizations and various "conditioning" experiences, self-confidence has been purported to be one of the more difficult attributes for women to develop. For this reason, many assertiveness training programs have cropped up across the country to train women to act more confidently and assertively. Successful women have found it to be essential for women to think highly of their own potential and avoid feelings of inferiority when competing with men.

Research results concerning central issues confronting women in management have recently been summarized by James Terborg. He found that many women described themselves and were described by men as being not suitable for managerial positions. In fact, many women were found to lack confidence in themselves or in other women as managers. Similarly, women who chose management as a profession, rather than one of the traditional work roles such as nursing, did not receive much support from vocational counselors or parents. It is not known, according to Terborg, if women who go into management have different self-concepts initially from those women who do not enter the managerial ranks. It is known that after several years in management women have interests, needs, and motives that are very similar to those of men in management.[12] It would, therefore, appear that the perceived managerial role is a much more significant determinant of women managers' behavior in the work environment than the perceived expectations of sex roles are.

There are still many stereotypes and prejudices to overcome. For example, one young man in explaining his decision to quit an otherwise good job said, "I just couldn't take it. My boss was a woman. Besides that, she was a former Army officer." His stay of two weeks was so short that it's doubtful his decision was based upon his supervisor's ability to lead or function as a manager.

Developing the Woman Manager

The more recent research studies seem to indicate very little sex bias or sex role stereotyping in the selection of people for entry level managerial positions. In fact, the person's major and scholastic standing play a more influential role in selection decisions than the candidate's sex or physical attractiveness.[13] Today, when some discriminating treatment occurs, it may be of a more subtle nature. For instance, it may be the lack of opportunity for women to attend management development programs. But it is possible, in fact very likely, that most of the perceived inequities are due to ignorance on the part of management. They may feel that they should do something special for the women, which may not be necessary, but are not sure what kinds of training would be best. Their problem is twofold:

1. Once a woman is hired and placed on an employment track leading to a managerial position, what activities can be offered that will increase the woman's capabilities for assuming a managerial role?
2. What kinds of programs can be offered to improve the effectiveness of an incumbent female manager?

The design of training and development programs must rest on some assumptions about women's needs and the requirements of the business. Assumptions which may apply to some female managers are identified below:

1. Women need to raise their self-esteem as managers of people.
2. Women need to learn new behaviors for dealing with interpersonal conflict.
3. Women need to develop leadership and team-building skills.
4. Women need help with career planning.[14]

The assumptions are largely based on the socialization process women experience in our culture. Our culture tends to instill in women the attributes of dependency, passivity, and conformity, while in men the characteristics of aggressiveness, competitiveness, and independence are ingrained. Two investigators have summarized the research on the socialization of women.[15] They concluded that:

girls in our society are socialized to be more oriented toward people, to be other-directed and dependent, whereas boys are raised to be more independent, aggressive and achievement-oriented. Girls develop a negative self-image when they accept society's more positive evaluation of males and masculine activities . . . to "work" is to demonstrate masculine traits, something most women are reluctant to do. Socialization to traditional feminine values results in lower occupational aspirations for women.[16]

Women's feelings of dependency, inferiority, and conformity are incompatible with the management role because subordinates do not want to follow a person with these qualities.

Many universities across the country offer training workshops where women develop managerial self-concepts and skills. The typical approach is to help each woman understand herself, better understand others, and better understand group functioning and group problem solving. At the outset of these workshops the woman is assured that the "role of a woman" and the "role of an achiever" are not incompatible. A woman can be both without internal conflict.

One major university has a short program which has received a good deal of attention.[17] After the three-day program many women have said that they had increased their self-awareness, self-confidence, and assertiveness. In the first part of the program, each woman learns about her own managerial behavior and practices the managerial skills of problem solving, decision making, and interpersonal communication. These skills are then developed through a variety of techniques which include case studies, role playing and immediate feedback activities. The second part focuses the women's attention on conflict-handling skills. Each woman has the opportunity to role play in a number of different conflict situations. The women are given help by the trainer in expressing and working with aggression and hostility. The last part of the program trains the women in career planning and in bridging the gap between what has been learned in the workshops and applying what was learned to their organizations. Two factors contribute to the success of this program:

1. The women are in residence, thereby isolated from other demands on their time.
2. Only women are allowed to attend. Mixed workshop sessions tend to inhibit the candid and forthright expression of women, particularly those learning new modes of behavior.

A helpful 1978 article titled "Training Women for Management: New Problems, New Solutions" summarized the situation and outlined some common problems to be overcome and several excellent women's programs offered by universities.[18] It concluded that:

Employment discrimination exists—women do not usually succeed in management despite their abilities. Although there are many ways to explain this phenomena, most can be readily summarized under the rubic of socialization: men and women are trained differently, expect differences in themselves and one another, and react as though the differences are real, whether they are or not.[19]

The authors added that appropriate training can offset these problems since the problems are learned rather than innate. Suggested training strategies included demythologizing management, providing role models, and presocializing female students to management, as well as sex-segregated workshops and classrooms.

How to Get to the Top

In a popular article about women in the executive suite, Margaret Hennig and Anne Jardin suggest that the reasons women are not in senior management positions are far more complex than simple bias among male executives or "fear of success" among women.[20] Men have been prepared for leadership roles early in life, learning how to work with others as early as their first Little League game. In early work experiences, men have learned the informal rules of business behavior. Most women have neither had the training that youthful team sports provide, nor have they been taught the informal codes of business conduct. They are brought up to be unsure of their futures, while men realize early in life that they will go to work and possibly lead others. Therefore, most women have not developed a long-term strategy concerning their careers. With the situation changing in terms of childhood experiences in team and individual sports and with parents who encourage their daughters to think in terms of their futures in business, women are becoming better prepared for a place in the executive suite. For the time being, Hennig and Jardin suggest that if women want to be in high places in corporations where the money and responsibility are, they should follow the eleven steps described below:

Step 1 Decide objectively whether you really want a career.

Step 2 Make a specific list of every job you have ever held, including how well you did at each, and the skills, knowledge and experience you gained.

Step 3 Make a five-year plan.

Step 4 Try to find ways to increase your experience in planning, problem solving and group leadership—all crucial skills for a successful career in management.

Step 5 Study the informal system of personal relationships that exists in your company.

Step 6 Try to establish an informal system of relationships with other women in the company.

Step 7 When dealing with male colleagues, don't try to engage in their male joking and camaraderie.

Step 8 Learn to control your emotions and the way you express them at work.

Step 9 Ask yourself why you are so vulnerable to criticism.

Step 10 Stop trying to separate the worlds of work and home.

Step 11 Stop waiting to be chosen, and start letting people at work know what you want.[21]

MINORITIES IN THE LABOR FORCE

Little systematic attention has been given to the influence of race and minority cultures on worker interests, concerns, and behavior. It is known that there appear to be differences in job attitudes among minority cultures and the white Anglo-Saxon culture. It is also known that many of the minorities, especially the blacks, have suffered from injustices in the work environment because of these cultural differences. In the past, commonly cited injustices include rejection from jobs, lack of promotional opportunities, and similar discrimination.[22] The "color of your skin" seems to many blacks to influence personnel practices. While the current situation is much better than it once was, there are still incidences of injustice, especially in terms of opportunities.

As Table 15.4 shows, there is a big difference in the unemployment rates between white and black people regardless of age or sex. While the unemployment rate for white men and women was between 3.4 and 5.3 percent, respectively, in 1978, the unemployment rate for black men and women was over twice as high—7.8 percent and 11.3 percent during the same year. Black teen-agers had a distressingly high unemployment rate of 37.1 percent in 1978. This means that between three and four of every ten black teen-agers who wanted to work could not find jobs. Although unemployment among white teen-agers is also quite high (11.6 percent), the white teen-agers have a much greater chance of finding work than do black teen-agers.

Table 15.5 shows that black men earn about three-fourths of what white men do. In 1976, the mean yearly earnings of black men was $7,180, while white men earned $11,604. The earnings picture is more equitable for black women if their earnings are compared to white women. White and black women earn about the same yearly salary. In 1976, for example, the mean yearly earnings for white women was $4,919, while black women earned $4,545.

TABLE 15.4   Unemployment Rates for Blacks and Whites (first six months of 1978)

Percentage of persons in the labor force who are unemployed

White Men	3.4
Black Men	7.8
Teen-age White	11.6
Teen-age Black	37.1
White Women	5.3
Black Women	11.3

Source: U.S. Department of Labor, Bureau of Labor Statistics, Monthly Labor Review, *101 (August 1978): 64–6.*

TABLE 15.5   Mean Earnings Year Round (persons with income, age 14 and over, 1976)

| White men | $11,604 | White women | $ 4,919 |
| Black men | $ 7,180 | Black women | $ 4,545 |

Source: U.S. Department of Labor, Bureau of Labor Statistics, Monthly Labor Review, *101 (August 1978): 64–6.*

TABLE 15.6   Occupations of Employed Men by Race (1977)

OCCUPATION	WHITE MEN	MINORITY MEN
Total employed—thousands	52,000 (mil)	5,179 (mil)
Professional and technical	16.0%	11.7%
Managers and administrators	11.4	4.4
Sales workers	7.0	2.5
Clerical workers	18.0	16.1
Blue-collar workers	32.6	37.6
Service workers	12.3	25.4
Farm workers	3.3	2.3

Source: U.S. Department of Labor, Bureau of Labor Statistics, Monthly Labor Review, *101 (August 1978): 64–6.*

As shown in Table 15.6, over one-third of employed black men are in blue-collar jobs and 25 percent are in low level service occupations. Only about 12 percent have professional and technical jobs, compared with 16 percent for employed white men. Only 4 percent are managers or administrators, while 11 percent of white men have such jobs. The preponderance of black women have very low level white and blue-collar jobs. The vast majority of black females are in either clerical, blue-collar, or low skill service occupations.

WHAT BLACKS WANT FROM THEIR JOBS

Do black workers differ in important ways from white workers in what they want from their jobs? Chapter 3 discussed that blue- and white-collar workers want about the same things from work. Both groups of employees want important and challenging work and good chances for promotion, as well as good pay. It is also known that women want about the same things from work as men do. Do blacks as a group also want to do meaningful and challenging work, or do they focus their attention more on money and job security?

This topic is more complex than it appears. Of course, all blacks cannot be placed into one category any more than we can put all whites in one category. Job priorities and job satisfaction among blacks will vary according to occupational level, expectations, and needs. Often, however, it has been found that culturally disadvantaged workers do tend to place a higher priority on extrinsic factors (high salary, secure employment) than on intrinsic factors such as job challenge and growth. In the minds of disadvantaged workers, good job performance does not lead to advancement or to increased job responsibility.

In 1975 data was collected on the job priorities of blacks and whites in two national opinion surveys.[23] Generally, the blacks studied were in lower level blue- or white-collar jobs. It was found, in sharp contrast to some previous research, that blacks are more likely than whites to prefer high incomes and less likely to prefer important, meaningful, and challenging work that gives feelings of accomplishment. The question posed to survey respondents is presented below:

Tell me which *one* thing on this list you would *most* prefer in a job?

(A) High income
(B) No danger of being fired
(C) Short working hours and lots of free time
(D) Chances for promotion
(E) Important work that gives a feeling of accomplishment[24]

Although there was a great difference between black and white workers on the importance of income and meaningful work, no significant differences were found on the other three job factors. Black and white workers preferred the other three factors (B, C, D) in about the same way. The researcher feels that the blacks' high concern for money and low concern for job content is influenced by their employment history. According to the author

the black worker's differentially higher preference for income and lower preference for interest and meaning in a job may, at least partially, be the result of what has been learned from a history of considerable insecurity in jobs in the less desirable occupational categories. Knowing that having a job is at best tenuous, the black worker may focus on the tangible, immediate security of income and be less mindful of the intrinsic satisfactions in his work, which are, in fact, comparatively few in the types of jobs blacks have traditionally held.[25]

One recent study of the quality of work life faced by blacks included 87 black and 131 white Certified Public Accountants.[26] Each was given a questionnaire that, in effect, asked "What do you want from your job?" The CPAs could express their feelings in terms of the following:

1. Security needs
2. Social needs

3. Esteem needs
4. Autonomy (independence) needs
5. Self-actualization needs
6. Compensation needs

Overall the black CPAs derived less satisfaction from their work than their white counterparts on all need areas except on the security needs. In other words, the white CPAs were significantly more satisfied with social needs, esteem needs, autonomy needs, self-actualization needs, and compensation needs. Some of the specific areas where the black CPAs desired more satisfaction are listed below:

- Opportunity to help people
- Opportunity for friendship
- Opportunity for self-esteem
- Opportunity for independent thought and action
- Opportunity for growth and development

The failure of black CPAs to have their social needs satisfied on the job may be related to the fact that there are very few black CPAs among the 100,000 Certified Public Accountants in the United States. The opportunity for developing social ties with other black CPAs is obviously very limited. There are important differences between work attitudes and preferences between black and white CPAs. Whether these findings can apply to other blacks in other occupations will have to await further research.

JOB SATISFACTION AND WORK VALUES
OF THE MINORITY WORKER

We commonly read in popular press reports that minority workers when compared to white workers are less satisfied with their work, have lower expectations toward personal growth, demonstrate lower needs for achievement, and do not see much need to plan for the future. However, many of these reports are poorly thought out and would not hold up to rigorous testing.

A recent study compared the level of job satisfaction and need fulfillment of both black and white male sailors occupying the same types of jobs.[27] Overall, job satisfaction of both groups was remarkably similar. Of fourteen areas of satisfaction, the groups differed significantly on only five, namely job involvement, work motivation, rules and regulations, pay, and opportunities to get a better job. Contrary to some popular earlier studies, the blacks were more satisfied in these five areas than were their white counterparts. The black and white employees had similar attitudes toward such factors as global satisfaction, security, ego factors, and self-actualization. In this study, there were no differences in satisfaction with the intrinsic job factors similar to those reported in the preceding section.

One possible explanation for these results is that the white individuals had stronger basic needs to fulfill than did the blacks. The white workers did have significantly stronger needs to fulfill in terms of social, autonomy, and self-actualization needs, doing a whole job, job challenge, and job variety. Since satisfaction is related to need fulfillment, an organization would have to offer more or give more to white workers than to the black individuals for the same satisfaction level to be felt. In the words of the authors:

Differences that were found were low to moderate in magnitude and tended to show black sailors as having more positive attitudes toward the Navy than were found for their white counterparts. Such differences appeared to reflect lower needs reported by black sailors rather than to differences in perceived work conditions. Satisfaction scores also appeared to reflect differences in comparison level, where the military offered a more attractive career option for the black (perhaps due to a perceived restriction of nonmilitary options).[28]

This study offered evidence that job satisfaction among black and white workers occupying the same type of jobs is about the same. In fact, when important differences were found, the black individuals were more, rather than less, satisfied. The study suggested that the relatively high level of satisfaction among blacks could be influenced by their need strengths and occupational expectations.

There are several other variables that influence the level of satisfaction among blacks other than need strength. Social class, age, family income, supervisory position, job autonomy, occupational prestige, sex, and educational level were studied as possible influences on satisfaction among black and white male workers in a national sample.[29] The workers occupied a variety of jobs in many industries and in many geographical locations. In answer to the question, "Is job satisfaction of black and white male workers influenced by the same things?", the study found that most of the factors were equally influential. Of those factors mentioned above, only sex and educational level did not have uniform influences on job satisfaction for both groups. All of the variables correlated with job satisfaction in a positive way; that is, as a variable increased, so did satisfaction. For example, as age increased, satisfaction increased; as occupational prestige increased, so did satisfaction; as work autonomy increased, satisfaction increased. The belief that black workers operate under a different value system from the whites clearly was not supported. Factors that influenced white job satisfaction also influenced satisfaction among blacks.

A person's values affect certain forms of activity and have been found to be related to managerial success. Values influence the way we look at things and the way we evaluate alternative forms of behavior. Values influence the way we look at other people and, therefore, affect our interpersonal relationships. Values strongly determine what we consider ethical and unethical. To answer the question "Do personal values of black managers differ in important ways from those of their white counterparts?", the values of sixty-four black and white managers were studied.[30] These individuals were asked to describe their values about some general topics, different groups of people, their own goals, and business goals. A person's earnings were used as a managerial index. The results showed that the values of both groups are quite similar and confirmed several earlier research efforts.[31] Overall, both groups were seen as pragmatic and moralistic. Black managers in the U.S. were found to be more like their white counterparts than like managers in Japan, India, or Australia.

BLACK VERSUS WHITE PERCEPTIONS OF FAIRNESS

The black worker plays two roles—one as an individual worker, the other as a black. This is especially apparent when one considers that the average black person in industry is much more concerned about injustices perpetrated against other blacks than are whites concerned about injustices to other whites. Companies with successful integration of black workers have dealt with black individuals on both levels. These companies have done something special in the way of "accentuating black group identity in the company rather than merely seeking to assimilate the individual black employee in the existing white-oriented organization."[32]

The way a person behaves in the work organization is strongly influenced by the person's perceptions of equitable treatment. Equitable perceptions will foster good behavior, while perceptions of inequitable treatment will foster unproductive behavior. In a recent study, black workers were asked to express their perceptions of the treatment they receive with the treatment they believe whites receive in such areas as hiring practices, compensation, promotion, and job satisfaction. Some perceptions of black workers are presented below:

1. Blacks believe it is easier to get a job if you are white.

2. Blacks do not believe the best qualified person gets hired. The color of your skin has some influence.

3. Blacks believe that the company's hiring and promoting practices are influenced by race.

4. Blacks believe that they have been treated "below average" with regards to their pay.

5. Blacks believe that supervisors treat white workers better than black workers.

6. Blacks believe that supervisors favor white employees over blacks.

7. Blacks believe that white workers have a better chance for promotion.[33]

These unfavorable perceptions held by black employees are damaging to both the individual workers and to the organization—both become less effective. Black individuals will be dehumanized and less willing to put forth an extra effort because there is no reason why black employees should be enthusiastic about doing something special beyond what is prescribed in the job description, if they do not believe favorable consequences will be earned. The company will be less effective because the unproductive beliefs of black workers will result in the underutilization of the firm's human resources.

It is possible that individual managers' use of organizational power for the satisfaction of personal goals and needs can contribute to this undersatisfaction. On some occasions these personal goals and ideas surrounding the use of power may be in conflict with organizational goals. One study was designed to measure how individual supervisors actually used their institutional power in the supervision of subordinates.[34] A checklist of twenty-seven items was used to evaluate power usage in similar situations involving white subordinates and black subordinates. All supervisors were white and there were no differences in the kinds of problems dealt with in terms of the black or white subordinates. Despite the same kinds of problems and the almost identical distribution of these problems among blacks and whites, supervisors were found to use more coercive power when dealing with the blacks. Thirty-two percent of the black subordinates compared with 14 percent of the white subordinates were fired, suspended, given written warnings, or recommended for disciplinary action.[35] In light of such data the perceptions of black workers being treated inequitably are not surprising. To remedy this situation, management or outside consultants must first talk with the workers to identify and study how perceptions of inequitable treatment originated, and secondly, meaningful programs with black participation must be designed to correct the unfair treatment.

LEADERSHIP AND MOTIVATION TO MANAGE
AMONG MINORITIES

In this section we will study the work interests, motives, and leadership styles of minorities in supervisory positions. In one study, it was found that black managers have a greater willingness to compete, take charge, exercise power, and assert themselves than their white counterparts.[36]

The phrase "motivation to manage" refers to a person's motives to influence others, to be strong, and to get things done.[37] We can measure the level of motivation to manage through a reliable survey questionnaire. An individual with a high motivation-to-manage score will usually develop and nurture a highly effective and efficient department with good productivity, teamwork, cohesiveness, and job satisfaction. An individual with a low motivation-to-manage score will probably fail to provide good leadership and will foster low group productivity, low teamwork, and general lack of good administrative direction. To John Miner there are six necessary requisites to a high motivation to manage:

1. Favorable attitude toward authority—Managers are expected to behave in ways that do not provoke negative reactions from their superiors; ideally, they elicit positive responses. Equally, a manager must be able to represent his group upward in the organization and to obtain support for his actions at higher levels.

2. Desire to compete—There is, at least insofar as peers are concerned, a strong competitive element built into managerial work; a manager must compete for the available rewards, both for himself and for his group. Certainly, without competitive behavior, rapid promotion is improbable.

3. Assertive motivation—There is a marked parallel between the requirements of the managerial role and the traditional assertive requirements of the masculine role as defined in our society. Although the behaviors expected of a father and those expected of a manager are by no means identical, there are many similarities: both are supposed to take charge, to make decisions, to take such disciplinary action as may be necessary, and to protect the other members of their groups.

4. Desire to exercise power—A manager must exercise power over his subordinates and direct their behavior in a manner consistent with organizational (and presumably his own) objectives. He must tell others what to do when this becomes necessary and enforce his words through positive and negative sanctions.

5. Desire for a distinctive position—The managerial job tends to require a person to behave differently from the ways his subordinates behave

toward each other. He must be willing to take high visibility; he must be willing to do things that invite attention, discussion, and perhaps criticism from those reporting to him; and he must accept a position of considerable importance in relation to the motives and emotions of others.

6. A sense of responsibility—The managerial job requires getting the work out and staying on top of routine demands. The things that have to be done must actually be done; constructing budget estimates, serving on committees, talking on the telephone, filling out employee-rating forms, making salary recommendations, and so on.[38]

In the study mentioned above, the questionnaire was given to seventy-five white males, thirty-six white females, and twenty-three minority male managers from a major automobile manufacturing company.[39] The results showed that the minority managers scored significantly higher than did their male and female white counterparts. (Additionally, there was no significant difference between the male and female white managers on motivation to manage.) One argument explaining the high scores for the minority managers can be referred to as the "stockpile" effect. According to Miner:

It is possible that prior discrimination had operated over the years to stockpile minority managerial talent at the first level of supervision, rather than spreading it evenly through all levels of management as deserved promotions occurred. Under this hypothesis, minorities with high motivation-to-manage scores would be blocked from further promotions and held at the first level, whereas their white counterparts would move up and therefore would not appear in the same numbers at the bottom of the managerial hierarchy.[40]

He suggests that aspiring blacks are an untapped reservoir of managerial talent, and that the findings of this study are significant because:

[It] provides the first evidence supporting the hypothesis that minorities who move into management have unusually strong motivation to manage. At least in terms of motivational requirements, the data indicate that the upgrading of minorities into positions of increased managerial responsibility presents a feasible solution to the twin problems of compliance with equal opportunity legislation and managerial talent shortages.[41]

This study focused on the self-reported motives of black and white supervisors and found that the blacks had a superior motivation-to-manage profile. But the study did not consider subordinates' reactions to their leaders' actual behaviors. How are black supervisors viewed by black followers? By white followers? Likewise, how are white supervisors viewed by black followers? What are the influences of a racially mixed department toward black and white supervisors? These questions were studied among 16 black and 17 white male supervisors in three midwestern industrial plants.[42] These supervisors had a total of 123 subordinates of whom 72 were black, 36 white, and 16 Chicano. The investigator asked the subordinates to rate their supervisor across these leadership dimensions:

- Managerial Support—behavior toward subordinates which lets them know that they are worthwhile persons doing useful work.
- Goal Emphasis—behavior which stimulates a contagious enthusiasm for doing a good job.
- Work Facilitation—behavior which removes roadblocks to doing a good job.
- Interaction Facilitation—behavior which encourages subordinates to develop close, cooperative working relationships with one another.[43]

The results presented some very positive data about black supervisors. First, black supervisors were seen by white, black and Chicano subordinates as more effective leaders on all four leadership dimensions than were the white supervisors. Secondly, subordinates did not bias their assessment of their leaders in favor of a supervisor of the same race. That is, a white subordinate did not "fudge" in favor of white supervisors and black followers did not "fudge" for black supervisors.

Three interpretations were offered for the superior rating of black supervisors:

1. The black supervisors are simply better qualified.
2. People in a racially mixed department have special perceptions of good and bad supervision.
3. Supervisors behave differently toward subordinates of different races.

More support is offered for the first interpretation than for the others with "neither the second or third being in direct conflict with the first." The most logical explanation seems to be that "black supervisors may be better supervisors than their white peers due to superior qualifications required by blacks for promotion—a result of systematic discrimination in promotion policies."[44]

THE BLACK MBA

The master of business administration degree (MBA) is believed to be a ticket to high organizational places. Blacks have been entering MBA programs across the country in increasing numbers to improve their chances of promotion within the typically white managerial hierarchy.[45]

Has the MBA helped the earning power and promotability of the black manager? Unfortunately, the answer is "Not a great deal." According to two experts on the subject:

"Relative to their white counterparts, black MBAs are not doing well in the corporate business world. . . . Black MBAs from predominantly black schools receive starting salaries several thousand dollars below those of white, as well as below those of black MBAs from mixed schools."[46]

The investigators studied the earnings and salary progression (over twenty-six months) as well as the vertical movement of 161 black MBAs from mixed schools, 20 black MBAs from black schools, and 680 white MBAs from predominantly white schools. These facts were uncovered:

1. Taken as a group, black MBAs received starting salaries averaging $14,037, slightly higher than their white cohorts.
2. The average starting salary of black MBAs from predominantly black schools was $11,800, substantially lower than that of black and white MBAs from mixed schools.
3. The starting salary picture is even worse for black female MBAs from black schools. Their starting salary was $9,700.
4. The salary progression of blacks is much slower than of whites. During the 26 month period, the typical white MBA salary increased 54 percent while the black's increased 23 percent. In dollars and cents, the average yearly increase for the whites was $2,100 compared to $1,508 for blacks.
5. Of the 26 black MBAs from predominantly black schools 69 percent were still occupying entry level positions four to five years following their graduation. Of the 680 white MBAs out of college from four to five years, only 27 percent were still occupying entry level positions.
6. On a ten point job satisfaction question, 0 (very dissatisfied) to 9 (very satisfied), black female MBAs average score was 5.8 while the black male average score was 6.5. Taken as a group, black MBAs are moderately dissatisfied with their jobs.[47]

This information clearly shows that there is a need to make employment opportunities equal. The researchers advise us to look for the "whys" behind the discrimination:

Future research should explore the "why" behind the present findings, perhaps through longitudinal studies, in order to determine and trace what happens to black

MBAs on the job . . . we need to know more about the specific discrimination events.[48]

BARRIERS TO EMPLOYMENT
AMONG THE DISADVANTAGED

Disadvantaged people, regardless of race, are those who have great diffi-culty getting and holding jobs. Some of this difficulty is rooted in poor work attitudes, underdeveloped skills, legal problems, or in outright dis-crimination. Some companies have created successful "outreach" pro-grams to find and recruit people who have had consistent difficulties in landing jobs that last and that pay the bills. Typically, these companies scrap their traditional recruiting and selection procedures, which are geared to the nondisadvantaged workers. The new recruitment proce-dures literally involve going "to the streets" to find the disadvantaged. Such places as bars, youth centers, and community centers are searched to secure disadvantaged people.

One successful program developed to help disadvantaged workers uses a checklist to identify specific worker problems.[49] The creators of the program work with local governments to find jobs for people on welfare rolls. They question the people on welfare about the barriers they experi-ence in finding work. The barriers range from interpersonal conflicts, and financial and legal problems, to drug abuse. Once the barriers are iden-tified, a program is undertaken to remove the barriers, allowing the person to leave the ranks of the unemployed. For example, one person was not able to find work simply because he did not own his own hand tools. This person received financial help in terms of a loan to purchase tools and since receiving the loan has been fully employed. Another person was unable to find work because of transportation problems. The counselors were able to arrange adequate transportation. This type of program, ac-cording to its originators, can easily be supported by a local government, since the government benefits by the reduced costs of welfare payments.

SUMMARY

Contrary to the thinking associated with traditional sex roles, the role of a woman and the role of an achiever are not incompatible. A woman in a managerial position has needs, interests, and motivations which are very similar to her male counterpart. Unfortunately, women's efforts to gain entry into managerial positions have been blocked by some myths, par-ticularly that of the successful male managerial model. Douglas McGregor defined the successful model in our culture as a masculine one. He said "the good manager is aggressive, competitive, firm, and just. He is not feminine, he is not soft and yielding or dependent or intuitive in the womanly sense. . . ."[50] This kind of stereotype image of a manager and some correctable skill deficiencies are prohibiting the large scale integration of women into industry.

Women work for the same reasons men work. They work for money and once on a job they want the same psychological benefits as men do. Women feel that work pride is the most important psychological outcome from work, followed by personal development, accomplishment, and high self-esteem. Men rank these factors in the same order as women.

Fifty-five percent of employed women are in the two broad occupational categories of clerical workers and service workers. Very few are in administrative and managerial jobs paying $25,000 or more. The predominance of women in the lowest paying occupations is attributed to the similarity of these jobs to the activities performed by women in the home. Typically the housewife will play roles as a nurse, waitress, secretary, and maid. These kinds of service-oriented jobs are usually low paying jobs that account for a sizable proportion of the jobs held by women.

Once a woman has made it into a good but low level managerial position, there are several guidelines she can follow to accelerate her progress. One suggestion is to increase her competence in planning, problem solving, and leadership skills. Such skills can be learned in formal courses offered by colleges of business and through various seminar and workshop programs. Some other areas identified for training include increasing self-esteem as a manager of people, learning new behaviors for dealing with interpersonal conflict, and improving team-building and career-planning skills.

These needs for training were largely created by women's socialization in our culture. Men and women have been trained differently, expect differences in themselves and one another, and react as though the differences are real, whether they are or not. Some training strategies include demythologizing management, providing role models, and presocializing female students to management, as well as offering sex-segregated workshops and classrooms.

Job priorities and job satisfaction among black workers is just as complicated to understand as among white workers. We cannot place all blacks in one category any more than we can put all whites into one category. Job priorities and satisfaction will vary according to occupational level, expectations, and needs. Very generally, however, culturally disadvantaged workers do tend to place a higher priority on extrinsic factors (high salary, secure employment) than on intrinsic factors such as job challenge and personal development. This preference in job outcomes is influenced by the considerable insecurity felt by blacks from being in jobs in the less desirable occupational categories and by the inequitable treatment they often receive from supervisors. Also influencing blacks' attitudes toward jobs is the fact that the unemployment rate for black men and women is about twice as high as that for white men and women.

Black managers and white managers have very similar values. Both are very pragmatic and moralistic. When the motivation-to-manage capabilities of black and white supervisors were compared, it was found that black supervisors had higher scores on all areas of the test—being competitive, exercising power, taking responsibility, seeking distinctive positions, and asserting themselves. In one study of first-line supervisors in a Detroit automobile plant, black supervisors were rated higher than white supervisors by both black and white subordinates. The better qualifications of the black supervisors were thought to be the reason for the high ratings.

Neither male nor female black MBAs have fared very well in business hierarchies in terms of salary and promotions. The salary progress of blacks averages about $1,500 yearly while that of whites is about $2,100. Blacks earning their MBA from schools where students are predominantly white earn much more money and are promoted more often than are blacks from black business schools. Black female MBAs from black schools are particularly discriminated against in terms of equal opportunity and employment treatment.

NOTES

1. Douglas McGregor, *The Professional Manager* (New York: McGraw-Hill, 1967), p. 23.

2. R. Loring and T. Wells, *Breakthrough: Women in Management* (New York: Van Nostrand Reinhold, 1972), p. 92.

3. *To Form a More Perfect Union: Justice for American Women*, Report of the National Commission on the Observation of International Women's Year, no. 2 (Washington, D.C.: 1976), p. 57.

4. U.S. Department of Labor, Employment Standards Administration, Women's Bureau, *The Myth and the Reality* (May, 1974).

5. Leonard A. Lecht, "Women at Work," *The Conference Board Record* (Washington, D.C.: U.S. Department of Education, September, 1976).

6. U.S. Bureau of the Census, *Current Population Reports*, no. 114, p. 60.

7. G. G. Alphander and Jean Gutman, "Content and Techniques of Managerial Development Programs for Women," *Personnel Journal*, February 1976, pp. 76–9.

8. Ibid.

9. U.S. Department of Labor, Employment Standards Administration, Women's Bureau, *The Earnings Gap Between Women and Men* (1976), p. 9.

10. MARION M. WOODS, "What It Takes for a Woman to Make It in Management," *Personnel Journal*, January 1975, pp. 38–66.

11. Ibid., p. 39.

12. JAMES R. TERBORG, "Women in Management: A Research Review," *Journal of Applied Psychology* 62, No. 6 (1977): 647–64.

13. For a discussion of recent research on the influence of sex in the selection process, see PATRICIA ANN RENWICK and HENRY TOSI, "The Effects of Sex, Marital Status, and Educational Background on Selection Decisions," *Academy of Management Journal* 21, No. 1 (1978): 93–103.

14. STEPHEN HEINER, D. MCGLAUGHLIN, C. LEGEROS, and J. FREEMAN, "Developing the Woman Manager," *Personnel Journal*, May 1975, p. 283.

15. JOHN DELAMATER and LINDA FIDELL, "On the Status of Women," *American Behavior Scientist* 15 (1971): 163–71.

16. Ibid., p. 165.

17. HEINER, MCGLAUGHLIN, LEGEROS, and FREEMAN, "Developing the Woman Manager."

18. LAURIE LAKEWOOD, MARION WOODS, and SHEILA INDERLIED, "Training Women for Management: New Problems, New Solutions," *Academy of Management Review* 3 (July 1978): 584–601.

19. Ibid., p. 591.

20. MARGARET HENNIG and ANNE JARDIN, "Women in the Old Boys Network," *Psychology Today*, January 1977, p. 78.

21. Ibid.

22. JOHN SLOCUM, JR. and R. STRAWSER, "Racial Differences in Job Attitudes," *Journal of Applied Psychology* 56, No. 1 (1972): 28–32.

23. CHARLES WEAVER, "Black-White Differences in Attitudes Toward Job Characteristics," *Journal of Applied Psychology* 60, No. 4 (1975): 438–41.

24. Ibid., p. 439.

25. Ibid., p. 441.

26. SLOCUM and STRAWSER, "Racial Differences in Job Attitudes."

27. ALLAN JONES, JOHN BRUNI, and S. B. SELLS, "Black-White Differences in Work Environment Perceptions and Job Satisfaction and Its Correlates," *Personnel Psychology* 30 (1977): 5–16.

28. Ibid., p. 15.

29. CHARLES WEAVER, "Black-White Correlates of Job Satisfaction," *Journal of Applied Psychology* 63, No. 2 (1978): 255–8.

30. JOHN WATSON and JOHN WILLIAMS, "Relations Between Manager Values and Manager Success of Black and White Managers," *Journal of Applied Psychology* 62, No. 2 (1977): 203–7.

31. As reported in J. G. WATSON and SAM BARONE, "The Self-Concept, Personal Values, and Motivational Orientations of Black and White Managers," *Academy of Management Journal* 19, No. 1 (1976): 36–48.

32. MICHAEL JEDEL and DUANE KUJAWI, "Racial Dichotomies in Employment Perceptions: An Empirical Study of Workers in Selected Atlanta-Based Firms," *Academy of Management Journal* 19, No. 2 (June 1976): 284–91.

33. Ibid., p. 289.

34. See DAVID KIPNIS, ARNOLD SILVERMAN, and CHARLES COPELAND, "Effects of Emotional Arousal on the Use of Supervised Coercion with Black and Union Employees," *Journal of Applied Psychology* 57, No. 1 (1973): 38–43.

35. Ibid., p. 41.

36. JOHN B. MINER, "Motivational Potential for Upgrading Among Minority and Female Managers," *Journal of Applied Psychology* 62, No. 6 (1977): 691–7.

37. JOHN B. MINER, "The Real Crunch in Managerial Manpower," *Harvard Business Review* 51, No. 6 (1973): 146–58.

38. Ibid., p. 149.

39. MINER, "Motivational Potential."

40. Ibid., p. 695.

41. Ibid., pp. 696–7.

42. WARRINGTON S. PARKER, JR., "Black-White Differences in Leader Behavior Related to Subordinates' Reactions," *Journal of Applied Psychology* 61, No. 2 (1976): 140–7.

43. Ibid., p. 146.

44. Ibid.

45. HAROLD A. BROWN and DAVID L. FORD, JR., "An Exploratory Analysis of Discrimination in the Employment of Black MBA Graduates," *Journal of Applied Psychology* 62, No. 1 (1977): 50–6.

46. Ibid., p. 54.

47. Ibid.

48. Ibid., p. 55.

49. C. D. MILLER and GENE OETTING, "Barriers to Employment and the Disadvantaged," *Personnel and Guidance Journal*, October 1977, pp. 43–51.

50. McGREGOR, *The Professional Manager*, p. 23.

QUESTIONS FOR THOUGHT AND DISCUSSION

1. Think of three people who in your opinion are effective managers. These people may be friends, parents, other relatives, or just people you happen to know. Do these people reflect the types of attributes in the male managerial model described in the beginning of the chapter? Why do women have a difficult time behaving in that fashion?

2. Ask three women what they want to get from the work experience. Give them choices among three intrinsic factors and three extrinsic factors. Have them rate each on a ten point scale with 1 being most important and 10 being

the least important. For example, use job challenge, recognition, and personal growth as intrinsic factors and pay, social interaction, and good supervision as the extrinsic factors. Are their answers about equally divided between extrinsic and intrinsic concerns? After this, ask three men what they want from their work experience. Compare the results. Generally, do women want the same things from work as do men?

3. Comment on this quotation from this chapter, "Many women described themselves and are described by men as not being suitable for managerial positions. In fact, many women were found not to have much confidence in themselves or in other women as managers."

4. It was reported in this chapter that black supervisors are more effective than white supervisors. Why?

5. How do black MBAs fare in the work arena in terms of salary and frequency of promotion compared to white MBAs?

KEY TERMS

The student should be able to discuss the significance of these terms to the study of human behavior in the work environment.

Male managerial model
Motivation to manage
Equal Pay Act
Civil Rights Act
Equal Credit Opportunity Act

The spirit of integration
Socialization
Values
Disadvantaged
Discrimination

CASE INCIDENT

Format:

Men in the class are to interview women in the class (then reverse the roles) using the questions listed below. They are based on ideas presented in the chapter in another form. These questions are helpful to many people in the task of developing a future plan. The interviewers are requested to write down the replies, and, to the best of their ability, assess the clarity and completeness of the answers.

1. Why do you want a career? How will your career affect your spouse and children?

2. Name three of the jobs you have held in the last five years. Briefly tell me the skills you learned in each. Will these skills aid you in reaching your ultimate goal?

3. Since management positions involve skills in planning, problem solving, and group leadership, tell me how you plan to acquire skills in these areas.

4. What job do you want in five years? Detail to me the types of training or experience you will need to get that job.

5. Since "who you know" sometimes can influence your chances of landing a promotion, tell me how you are going to get to know the right people.

6. What talents have you developed for keeping your on-the-job relationships with people of the opposite sex task-oriented rather than social-oriented?

7. Name at least three situations that get you upset in a work environment. What can you do to control your emotions regarding these problems?

8. Do you feel small and vulnerable when criticized? Since all people receive criticism from time to time, what can you do to not feel badly when criticized?

9. Which people at work have been informed of your interests for either a different job or a higher one? Or, if you're not employed in a relevant job at present, which individuals will you inform when you do begin a career position?

16

Unions and Labor Relations

LEARNING OBJECTIVES

Upon completion of this chapter the student should be able to:

- Discuss the role of unionism in the United States.
- Explain the growth patterns of unionism.
- Define the nature of the collective bargaining relationship.
- Identify the sources of bargaining power for both labor and management.
- Describe in general terms the bargaining strategies of the parties to collective bargaining.
- Discuss why management has not always practiced good human relations in dealing with unions.
- Explain how the union-management relationship can be improved through better human relations practices.

A large, midwestern corporation with a sizable fleet of trucks found that many of the drivers were becoming more and more interested in what a union could do for them. Suddenly, the firm seemed to become more concerned about the drivers and listened to some of their complaints. It appeared as though somehow management gained compassion overnight for the drivers of the large semitrailers and granted a request that the drivers had been making for years. Air conditioners were put into the cabs to relieve the drivers from the oppressive heat and humidity of the midwestern summers. But the company did not have enough money to put the units in all the cabs. Coincidentally those drivers who were known to be antiunion got the air conditioners. Those who were believed to be prounion did not get the cooling units. But strangely enough, within a few weeks when the threat of unionism had passed, management found enough money to put air conditioners in the rest of the cabs.

This incident showed management not to be too knowledgeable or ethical regarding human relations practices. Indeed, they also displayed their lack of knowledge of labor law as they put themselves in a rather poor position legally. Why was the company so afraid of the union? Why did they ignore labor's requests until threatened with the presence of a union?

In this instance, the answer to the second question would probably provide an answer to the first. Poor management teams generally have more to fear from unions than good ones. In fact, it can be argued that a good management team would probably not provide the employees any real reason to unionize. But even if a union was present, a good management team would seek to work with it and create a cooperative work environment.

The purpose of this chapter is to provide a broad overview of the role of unions, to discuss the nature of the union-management relationship, and to look at how the presence of a union influences the behavior of union members and management alike. Since this book is primarily concerned with human behavior, the laws and the judicial and quasi-judicial decisions will be treated as parameters within which the interaction of the union and management must take place. Therefore, the legal intricacies of labor-management relations should be considered beyond the scope of this book.

THE ROLE OF UNIONISM

The role of unions has changed only in minor ways since their beginning. Unionism is still concerned with the protection and representation of the membership in matters concerning the conditions of employment. The role of protector is less important today than in times past when workers needed some means to end abusive treatment from management. Working conditions, wages, and benefits are much better in the modern industrial environment than they were early in this century, thanks in part to the role of the unions as protectors of the working people.

People who possessed skills and abilities that were widespread throughout the population were the first to recognize the need for some type of protection. Managers who believed themselves to be in a buyer's market when it came to labor usually were inclined to treat workers as any other resource. People, of course, grew tired of being looked upon as being "a dime a dozen" resources that could be replaced at a moment's notice. Unions understandably had a strong appeal to such workers and slogans such as "In union there is strength" caused memberships to grow rapidly during the thirties and forties.

That growth has since dissipated. Union membership now constitutes approximately one-fifth of the total work force. While total union membership has increased in absolute terms, it has declined as a percentage of the labor force. As can be seen in Table 16.1 this percentage decline is especially true when considering employees in nonagricultural establishments.

Today the union role is more that of an agent or representative than a protector. The union represents the membership in negotiations with management in an attempt to constantly improve upon the conditions of employment. Through payment of the union's initiation fees and dues, members gain the benefit of having someone serve as spokesman for them in the effort to get more wages, fringe benefits, and better working conditions. By having a united membership that is willing to back the union officials in the negotiations, the union members are able to enforce their demands by striking. While the economic strike is the primary weapon of the unions, their ability to bring together large numbers of people for boycotts or political action should also be recognized as a major source of power. The use of power by both labor and management has come to be an accepted part of the collective bargaining relationship.

TABLE 16.1   U.S. Union Membership, 1960–76*

Year	Total membership (thousands)	TOTAL LABOR FORCE		EMPLOYEES IN NONAGRI-CULTURAL ESTABLISHMENTS	
		Number (thousands)	Percent union members	Number (thousands)	Percent union members
1960	17,049	72,142	23.6	54,234	31.4
1961	16,303	73,031	22.3	54,042	30.2
1962	16,586	73,442	22.6	55,596	29.8
1963	16,524	74,571	22.2	56,702	29.1
1964	16,841	75,830	22.0	58,331	28.9
1965	17,299	77,178	22.4	60,815	28.4
1966	17,940	78,893	22.7	63,955	28.1
1967	18,367	80,793	22.7	65,857	27.9
1968	18,916	82,272	23.0	67,951	27.8
1969	19,036	84,240	22.6	70,442	27.0
1970	19,381	85,903	22.6	70,920	27.3
1971	19,211	86,929	22.1	71,222	27.0
1972	19,435	88,991	21.8	73,714	26.4
1973	19,851	91,040	21.8	76,896	25.8
1974	20,199	93,240	21.7	78,413	25.8
1975	19,473	94,793	20.5	77,051	26.3
1976	19,432	96,917	20.1	79,443	24.5

*Membership includes total reported membership excluding Canada. Also included are members of directly affiliated local unions. Members of single-firm unions are excluded.

Source: U.S. Department of Labor, Bureau of Labor Statistics, News,USDL: 77–771, p. 5.

THE COLLECTIVE BARGAINING RELATIONSHIP

The term "collective bargaining" is often thought to be descriptive of the negotiation process between labor and management when the terms of the labor agreement are determined. Collective bargaining does include negotiations, but it also includes aspects of conflict resolution and the day-to-day administration of the contract.[1] The collective bargaining relationship can therefore be viewed as encompassing all formal interactions between the union and the company.[2] It is essentially the process of negotiating, living by, and maintaining the labor-management contract.

The Third Party

Any given bargaining structure in industry also includes at least one other party. Legislative, judicial, and quasi-judicial roles are filled by the federal government in order to insure industrial peace. Although the role of the government is meant to be that of an unbiased referee, there are always accusations that one party is favored over the other. But just the presence of a third party that has the power to intervene serves as a catalyst to labor and management to solve their problems themselves. In most circumstances the parties to collective bargaining would like to be able to reach agreement without depending upon an outsider to determine what the nature of the labor-management relationship will be.

On occasion, when disputes cannot be settled or negotiations reach an impasse, the third party may be required. Most contracts, for example, include arbitration as the final step in the grievance procedure. If an employee cannot settle a grievance with his or her supervisor, the procedure provides for a meeting of union officials (union steward, then the union committee) with the department head and the personnel manager successively. If after going through the various steps of the grievance procedure a settlement has not been reached, an agreed upon arbitrator is brought in to hear the case and make a binding decision.

The federal government is usually referred to as one party, but all branches of the government are involved with the collective bargaining relationship. The legislative branch, of course, passes laws that regulate the labor-management interchange. The judicial branch hears cases and the executive branch becomes involved through executive orders and statutory provisions for intervening in labor disputes that threaten the welfare of the nation. Thus, the efforts to maintain industrial peace are quite complex and go far beyond the "two" parties to collective bargaining.

Bargaining Power

Bargaining power can be interpreted as "a party's ability to impose its demands upon its bargaining counterpart or to resist successfully the attempts of an imposing party to enforce its demands."[3] This means that in most bargaining relationships power is measured in relative terms as it is in part determined by the opposition. The ability of management to continue to operate an oil refinery in the midst of a strike is power to resist union efforts to enforce demands. Power for management may be derived from technological capabilities that allow for a rapid build-up of inventory or the ability to continue operations without labor.

Union bargaining power may stem from a large and cohesive membership. In fact, when it comes to a strike, it may go beyond just the striking union. Other unions may refuse to cross the picket lines of the strikers, multiplying the impact of the strike. As mentioned earlier, boycotts may be started by a particular union and gain support from many segments of the population, union and nonunion alike. A boycott of Coors Beer, for instance, was supported by college students and others who were sympathetic to the strikers' cause.

Strike funds and the general financial well-being of a union can also be a source of power. It takes a lot of money to support a strike and to provide strikers with a modicum of income to support their families. While it is usually hoped that a strike will be short, as this is one measure of success, there will be times when a strike fund becomes very important to the membership.

Regardless of the source of power, it will be applied by either party to enforce demands and/or resist the demands of the other party. When to use power, how much power to use, and what kind of power to use are tactical decisions that are an important part of overall bargaining strategy.

Bargaining Strategy

Union's bargaining strategy over the years has come to be characterized by one word—"more." Labor unions traditionally have been involved with seeking more members, more union security, and more control over jobs.[4] As would be expected, the major concern of unions is the welfare of the membership and the survival of unionism. To these ends unions continue to push management in order to continue to make gains. The union strategy then can be said to be primarily offensive in nature.

Management, on the other hand, usually must operate from a defensive position in an attempt to protect those management rights thought to be inalienable. By granting too many concessions at the bargaining table it is possible that management could seriously affect the firm's ability to compete. In order to maintain operations and profits at an acceptable level, management will seek to limit those areas in which unions can become involved. So while unions are primarily interested in the gains to be made by the members and the union itself, management is most concerned with the avoidance of granting and yielding too much to labor. Management's strategy could be said to be one of containment.

CHANGES IN UNIONISM

Increases in white-collar employees, the greater participation rate of women, and the gains being made by minorities have brought about some changes in unionism. In addition, technology is doing away with many jobs that have been traditional strongholds of unionism. With some of the manufacturing jobs disappearing, union organizing attempts have had to turn to other segments of the work force.

Membership Numbers and Makeup

From 1974 to 1976 total union membership declined by 767,000 or by about 4 percent. Much of this decline occurred in manufacturing and construction where employment fell off by nearly 1.4 million workers.[5] A relative decline (union members to total work force) in unionism was recognized over a decade ago. It was the feeling of many that there were simply no more meaningful battlegrounds left in which to engage management. Alfred Kuhn expressed unions' problems as a "mission accomplished with no new mission in sight."[6] At about the same time, Leonard Sayles and George Strauss concluded from a study of local unions that the labor movement was no longer a movement.[7] Ironically, it seems that the success of unions in accomplishing their goals has been contributing to a weakened labor movement.

The rewards of unionism are much less obvious to members than once was the case—oppressive work conditions are gone, there is more job security, there are laws forbidding discrimination, grievance procedures have been established for nonunion employees, and there is little difference between union and nonunion wages. Even though the unions played an important role in the attainment of such benefits, today's younger members want to see a positive contribution now.

Union leadership has had to undergo some changes as organizational efforts are being directed more toward women, white-collar workers and public employees. The public sector is the fastest growing area of union membership. As shown in Table 16.2, unionization of federal employees has remained rather stable with the growth taking place in state and local governments. In fact, the public sector is growing so fast that the most successful recruiters of new members over the past decade have been the state, county, and municipal employee unions and teachers' unions.[8]

Union membership among white-collar workers continues its long-term growth. As can be seen in Table 16.3, white-collar membership in unions has increased from 15.7 percent of all members in 1968 to 18.4 percent in 1976. It should also be noted that after many years of growth women union membership declined from 1974 to 1976.

TABLE 16.2   Union Membership by Employment Sector, 1968–76*

	PRIVATE SECTOR			GOVERNMENT		
Year	Total	Manu-facturing	Nonmanu-facturing	Total	Federal	State & Local
1968	20,210	9,218	8,837	2,155	1,351	804
1970	20,689	9,173	9,198	2,318	1,370	947
1972	20,838	8,920	9,458	2,460	1,355	1,105
1974	21,585	9,144	9,520	2,920	1,391	1,529
1976	21,006	8,463	9,533	3,009	1,300	1,710

* Includes membership outside the United States, except members of locals directly affiliated with the AFL-CIO. Because of rounding, sums of individual items may not equal totals.

Source: U.S. Department of Labor, Bureau of Labor Statistics, News, *USDL: 77–771, p. 6.*

TABLE 16.3   White-Collar and Women Union Membership, 1968–76

YEAR	NUMBER (THOUSANDS)	PERCENT OF TOTAL UNION MEMBERSHIP
White-collar members		
1968	3,176	15.7
1970	3,353	16.2
1972	3,434	16.5
1974	3,762	17.4
1976	3,857	18.4
Women		
1968	3,940	19.5
1970	4,282	20.7
1972	4,524	21.7
1974	4,600	21.3
1976	4,201	20.0

Source: U.S. Department of Labor, Bureau of Labor Statistics, News,USDL: 77–771, p. 4.

Besides the changes that have occurred, in terms of numbers of members, of equal significance is the change in the characteristics of the union members themselves. Unions are becoming increasingly aware of the presence of a new generation of labor that quite obviously does not share the same viewpoint as its elders.

Behavioral Causes of the Changes

Today's typical union member has never experienced a severe depression and was not present to witness the organizational drives of the thirties and forties. Thus, today's typical member has an entirely different image of the union and its activities than do some of the older members of the work force. While it may be an overstatement to say that union members today have a total lack of interest, there is surely a lack of enthusiasm for the labor movement. Although most union members are well aware of and in agreement with the economic objectives of the union, few are willing to become actively involved in the internal workings of the union.

The underlying causes of this apathy are many. Sayles and Strauss made use of "projective tests" to find why such an ambivalent attitude existed among union members. Their findings included:

- Shame in accepting help
- Sensitivity to community antipathy
- Reluctance to attack the company
- Fear of management reprisal[9]

Just as managers must take part of the blame when apathy exists among their subordinates, so must the union officers share the responsibility for the lack of interest and enthusiasm among the rank and file. The lack of interface between union leaders and the membership is causing the union to lose contact with the people. Again the analogy of the relationship between a manager and the subordinates can be applied. When the manager becomes too concerned with the nonhuman elements of the job, the human factor is ignored and the attitudes, behaviors, and the productivity of the workers fall off dramatically. In other words, to a large extent unions have fallen victim in their internal relationships to the very kinds of managerial practices they were formed to resist.

For example, new union members are literally informed of the union and "recruited" by a company's personnel officer. Seldom do union officials have anything to do with bringing new employees into the union fold. Even once employees have joined the union, they still have little, if any, contact with the union and/or its officers. This lack of communication definitely has an impact upon the behavior of union members. It is unfortunate for the unions when these situations exist. The behavior by the members and the officers tends to be negative and creates an environment of hostility and conflict. When there is internal disagreement among union officials and the membership, it only serves to enhance the rather negative image of unions that exists.

HUMAN RELATIONS VERSUS UNION RELATIONS

Many management teams and much of the general public have a negative image of unions. This image may exist in people's minds although they really know very little about unionism. Unions are often viewed as an opponent to management with little to contribute other than strikes and conflict encouraged by leaders with reputations more similar to criminals than to businessmen.

When the backgrounds of most management personnel are considered, it is not hard to understand the existence of a negative perception of unions. Most management and professional personnel within an organization usually come from middle class backgrounds that tend to be non-union. Parental discussions were probably overheard that blamed unions for inflation as well as other social and economic ills. As students, their education was usually business-oriented with little attention given unions other than how they must be dealt with. It is little wonder that many managers separate union or labor relations from human relations.

Unfortunately, too often management forgets good human relations practices when dealing with unions. Of course, it is not clear which party is to blame for the nature of the relationship, as unions have also displayed a fair amount of aggressive behavior.

A study which compared supervisors' methods of handling problems found that foremen were much more likely to use coercive power in a unionized situation than when dealing with nonunion employees.[10] Threats and reprimands were used over twice as much (38 percent versus 16 percent) by supervisors of union employees. Similarly administrative punishments were much more frequent (19 percent versus 7 percent) in the unionized work environment. However, the presence of a union seemed to protect people from being fired as nonunion subordinates were fired more often (8 percent versus 3 percent).[11]

CONFLICT IN THE WORK ENVIRONMENT

Some of the human behaviors that are always present in the work environment stem from conflict. The conflicts between unions and management seem to be ongoing because the conflicts that occur are highly publicized and are described in terms that make the parties to collective bargaining sound more like combatants. In fact, living the contract is a series of compromises. On one occasion one party may come out better than the other, but usually both parties will make some gains and suffer some setbacks.

Conflicts within the work environment are of two types:

1. Institutional
2. Interpersonal

The interpersonal conflicts are usually the result of personality differences, value differences and/or faulty communications. Institutional kinds of conflicts are those which include differences that result because of the structural relationship. The labor-management conflicts and interdepartmental conflicts are thus classified as institutional rather than interpersonal. This is not to say that institutional kinds of conflict cannot degenerate into interpersonal conflicts. They can and often do.

The conflict that occurs between labor and management is not all bad. In fact, there are many positive aspects of their adversary roles. Today there is a trend among behavioralists to stimulate conflict with the idea that it can be managed. Some of the processes of managing conflict will be examined following a discussion of the sources of conflict.

Nature of Union-Management Conflict

Perhaps the greatest contributor to labor-management conflict is the different set of goals held by each party. As mentioned earlier in the chapter, unions have been concerned with getting more for their membership. To make these gains something has to be received from management. Management, of course, is seeking to protect what they have. Thus, labor and management necessarily have diametrically opposed viewpoints.

These different objectives come into conflict in several areas. One issue that seems always to be a source of conflict is the controversy surrounding management prerogatives or management rights. This is basically a question of what is bargainable and what is an inalienable right of management in terms of making decisions. While some unions have made inroads into what were once thought to be management prerogatives (such as the hiring decision), other unions have chosen to direct their attention toward gains in the area of wages and benefits.

Inadequacies of communication seem to exaggerate the differences in goals of the two parties. Most organizations that are unionized have a formal grievance procedure. Management should monitor this grievance machinery frequently to guarantee a free flow of communications without disruptions such as overloads or underutilization. The failure to communicate can cause otherwise minor problems to become major.

As with interpersonal conflict, a conflict cycle applies to the union-management relationship. Louis Pondy has described the stages of conflict as follows:

1. Latent conflict—At this stage the basic conditions for potential conflict exist but have not yet been recognized.

2. Perceived conflict—The cause of the conflict is recognized by one or both of the participants.

3. Felt conflict—Tension is beginning to build between the participants, although no real struggle has yet begun.

4. Manifest conflict—The struggle is under way, and the behavior of the participants makes the existence of the conflict apparent to others who are not directly involved.

5. Conflict aftermath—The conflict has been ended by resolution or suppression. This establishes new conditions that will lead either to more effective cooperation or to a new conflict that may be more severe than the first.[12]

These stages of conflict serve as a rough guide to the evolution of a conflict. Not all conflicts will go through all stages but the general framework does help in the understanding of conflict situations. It is hoped that with a better understanding can come better management of conflict.

The Management of Conflict

It is ironic that many of the collective bargaining models have been used in managing interpersonal and intergroup conflicts. While these models do an excellent job of describing the process of compromise, they do not always deal with solving the problems. Consequently, there is no recipe approach that can be given to improve the union-management relationship. There are a number of things that can be tried, but like any other situation involving two or more people or two or more formal or informal groups, the success of a relationship is dependent upon the interchange between the parties involved. A certain action is not guaranteed to bring about a particular response. In most cases, though, a reciprocal response can be expected. Management should be the initiator and make the positive moves necessary to gain the cooperation of the union. The following represent some of the actions management can take. Some are really more involved with changes of attitude than with specific procedures. The important thing is that these suggestions are representative of the kinds of things management can do that will allow unions to respond positively.

Problem-Solving Approaches.   There are several different techniques that rely upon the basic problem-solving model. Most of these techniques try to arrive at the real source of the conflict. Nominal group techniques as described in Chapter 13 are among the problem-solving approaches that can open the lines of communication between labor and management. Problems are defined, alternatives suggested, and solutions arrived at through some form of compromise. When there is a great difference in goals and values of the two parties, the compromise can be difficult to arrive at.

Training the Foremen.   To employees the immediate supervisor is the company. Foremen should be trained in dealing with unions and handling human relations problems. The foremen can do more than any other group of managers to create a positive company image as they have more direct interaction with union members.[13] Keeping foremen well-trained and informed can be extremely critical to the improvement of union-management relations.

Open Communications.   Management should try to promote better communications with the union in terms of both quality and quantity. This means an ongoing dialogue should be sought. Communications become negative when they are confined to conflict and negotiation situations. Management may view contract administration and grievance procedure as being negative kinds of interchange. Most good managers feel that they could solve the minor issues with employees if it were not for the formal systems such as the grievance process. If management would invite union opinion and keep the union and employees informed, perhaps some of the negative aspects of the formal relationship could be minimized. This does not mean, however, that management must give up any decision-making prerogatives.

Attitude and Climate Surveys.   The administration of climate surveys and the data feedback can have a positive effect on conflict in an organization. Allowing people to express their opinions and then discussing the results has a positive effect on attitudes. Like other techniques it does not deal directly with controlling conflict, but rather breaks down barriers and opens up the possibility of an ongoing dialogue. This survey feedback method will be discussed in more detail in the following chapter on organization development.

Creating a More Productive Climate.   As suggested in Chapter 5 management has the responsibility for creating the organizational climate. Many variables (including communications) are part of this effort, but the first step should be one of adopting a more positive attitude toward working with the union. A company that has unionized employees must face the fact that there is another formal organization working within the corporate structure. Some corporations may actually have several different unions to work with. In such circumstances, management cannot afford to treat the unions and the membership as the enemy. By working with and seeking the cooperation of the union, management can create a productive work environment.

This is not to say that the problems can be easily solved. Perhaps the best thing management can do is to realistically recognize what the presence of the union means. Unilateral decisions concerning employees and their conditions of employment cannot be made. Nor should management become involved in a contest with the union to win employees' loyalties.

Recognition of Dual Allegiance.   Loyalty or allegiance refers to a sense of belonging and may be viewed as the degree to which individuals are psychologically inclined to accept the organization as their own.[14] This goes beyond just formal membership by suggesting that a person identifies with a certain organization. Informal groups and personal relationships within that formal organization may determine to a large degree the allegiance to the formal group.

Allegiance to the company is usually thought to be in conflict with allegiance to the union.[15] Unfortunately this "either-or" philosophy contributes to the existence of interpersonal conflict (role conflict) and institutional conflict.

Stereotyping workers as loyal to the union or loyal to the company can only compound problems. Such stereotyping is not only damaging to union-management relations, it is also an incorrect assumption on someone's part that there is a necessity to choose up sides.

Each individual will differ in degrees of loyalty, but both management and unions should realize that split allegiances are possible. Both parties should realize that dual allegiance, not unilateral company or union allegiance, is the stabilizing and constructive factor in industrial relations.[16] In light of the fact that unions represent employees but the company hires and pays them, some split of loyalties should be expected. If the unions and management would willingly deal with the situation as it is and not constantly compete to win the workers over to one side or the other, industrial relations would be improved. In fact, in many instances it is the employee who feels no loyalty to the union or to management who may be the troublemaker. Employees who are loyal to the union will probably also feel some allegiance to the organization. Recognition of dual allegiance is simply a process of recognizing individuals' feelings and not forcing them to make a decision for or against unions or management. In other words, it is good human relations practices applied to the labor-management relationship.

SUMMARY

Although the traditional role of unions has not changed appreciably, the membership has. Jobs long considered union strongholds in manufacturing and construction have been disappearing. The economy and technology have contributed to a shift in the labor market. Consequently labor union members have decreased as a percentage of the work force during the sixties and seventies. White-collar workers and public employees constitute the segments of the work force that are now the fastest growing in terms of union membership.

The collective bargaining relationship is becoming more and more a three-party relationship instead of two. Legislation, executive orders, administrative agencies, and the courts make the government an important part of labor-management relations. Even though the various branches of the government are concerned with maintaining industrial peace, it is obvious that the role of government is not always that of an unbiased referee.

Generally speaking, unions and management would prefer to solve their problems without the need of intervention from a third party. In order to live together in a work environment that is productive and relatively free from labor problems, management must take the initiative. Management must recognize the presence of unions and employee loyalties to them and apply good human relations practices in working with the unions. By working in a cooperative fashion, it is possible for the union and management to benefit from an organizational climate that allows more open communications. The existence of an ongoing dialogue between labor and management would be a major step toward more constructive industrial relations.

NOTES

1. See CARL M. STEVENS, *Strategy and Collective Bargaining Negotiations* (New York: McGraw Hill, 1963), pp. 1–2.

2. Also see EDWIN F. BEAL and EDWARD D. WICKERSHAM, *The Practice of Collective Bargaining* (Homewood, Ill.: Richard D. Irwin, Inc., 1967), p. 1.

3. G. JAMES FRANCIS, "The Influence of Technological Change on Collective Bargaining," *Business Perspectives* 8 (Spring 1972): 30.

4. Ibid.

5. U.S. Department of Labor, Bureau of Labor Statistics, *News*, USDL: 77-771, p. 4.

6. ALFRED KUHN, *Labor: Institutions and Economics* (New York: Harcourt, Brace and World, Inc., 1967), p. 38.

7. LEONARD R. SAYLES and GEORGE STRAUSS, *The Local Union* (New York: Harcourt, Brace and World, Inc., 1967), pp. 158–9.

8. *News*, USDL: 77-771, p. 6.

9. SAYLES and STRAUSS, *The Local Union*, p. 133.

10. DAVID KIPNIS, ARNOLD SILVERMAN and CHARLES COPELAND, "Effects of Emotional Arousal on the Use of Supervised Coercion with Black and Union Employees," *Journal of Applied Psychology* 57, No. 1 (1973): 41.

11. Ibid.

12. LOUIS R. PONDY, "Organizational Conflict: Concepts and Models," *Administrative Science Quarterly* 12 (September 1967): 300–5 and LESLIE W. RUE and LLOYD L. BYARS, *Management: Theory and Application* (Homewood, Ill.: Richard D. Irwin, Inc., 1977), p. 250.

13. MICHAEL J. SHERSHIN and W. RANDY BOXX, "Building Positive Union-Management Relations," *Personnel Journal* 54 (June 1975): 327.

14. KUNIO ODAKA, *Toward Industrial Democracy* (Cambridge, Mass.: Harvard University Press, 1975), p. 89.

15. Ibid., p. 91.

16. Ibid., p. 123.

QUESTIONS FOR THOUGHT AND DISCUSSION

1. Compare the role of unionism in the first half of this century with the role you believe they will have to play throughout the second half of the century.

2. Do you believe it is true that labor and management prefer not to allow a third party to make decisions regarding the labor-management relationship? Explain.

3. What are the sources of management bargaining power?

4. Comment on the following statement: "The labor movement is no longer a movement."

5. How can management initiate steps to improve the labor-management relationship?

6. Is it possible for loyal union members to also be loyal to the organization for which they work?

KEY TERMS

The student should be able to discuss the significance of these terms to the study of human behavior in the work environment.

Role of unionism   Boycott
Collective bargaining relationship   Bargaining strategy
Grievance procedure   Institutional conflict
Arbitration   Conflict cycle
Bargaining power   Dual allegiance

CASE INCIDENT

Hal Donofria is the president of a medium-sized, full-line advertising and public relations organization in the mid-Atlantic region. The company, Donotria Enterprises, employs 280 people of whom 120 are union members. These people occupy such jobs as drivers, copy writers, artists, production helpers, draftsmen, and other service maintenance personnel. Hal is a responsible, conscientious, participative top level manager. Although he manages in the best way he can, several employee problem areas have surfaced, especially among the union employees.

Hal noticed that in 1978 the number of complaints from union members increased 18 percent; the number of grievances filed increased 15 percent; the number of suggestions was down 26 percent; absenteeism increased 11 percent; and turnover increased 14 percent over the preceding year. He knows that the ultimate responsibility rests with himself. He believes in supportive, democratic practices and tries hard to implement humanistic techniques in his day-to-day management practices.

His twelve subordinate managers are largely technical experts in the advertising field. About 70 percent of their time is spent on individual projects, leaving 30 percent to be devoted to actual supervision. Several have business educations as well as several years of management experience. During a February 1979 meeting with these managers, Hal expressed a concern about the unfavorable trends in some behaviors shown by the union members. The managers attributed the trends to vaguely defined societal changes, economic conditions, a lowering of the work ethic, and to a greatly increased work load for the entire company in 1978. When asked if the troubles among the union personnel could be attributed to their supervisory behavior toward union members, the managers agreed among themselves that they were not to blame. They added that they were doing "things like they always do things."

To gain some additional information about the situation, Hal and his managers thought it would be a good idea to hire a consultant to survey the attitudes of union members to try to identify areas of discontent. After reaching an agreement with the company's union representative, they selected a management professor from a local university to conduct the survey. The consultant, Hal, two subordinate managers, and the union leader met and developed a survey questionnaire, part of which is shown below with the union members' answers.

| | 1 | 2 | 3 | 4 | 5 | 6 | 7 | 8 | 9 | 10 |

0   5   10

Do supervisors act friendly? **(7.3)**

0   5   10

Do supervisors pay attention to workers? **(7.6)**

0   5   10

Do supervisors listen to workers' problems? **(7.6)**

0   5   10

Do supervisors encourage best effort? **(7.3)**

0   5   10

Do supervisors maintain high standards? **(6.6)**

0   5   10

Do supervisors set good examples? **(9.3)**

0   5   10

Do supervisors help workers improve job output? **(6.3)**

0   5   10

Do supervisors help employees schedule work? **(7.6)**

0   5   10

Do supervisors offer new ideas for solving job-related problems? **(7.3)**

0   5   10

Do supervisors encourage team work? **(7.3)**

0   5   10

Do supervisors encourage the exchange of ideas? **(8.0)**

0   5   10

Do supervisors inspire trust and confidence? **(6.6)**

0   5   10

Do supervisors receive trust and confidence? **(7.0)**

0   5   10

Do supervisors schedule enough meetings with the workers? **(7.2)**

0   5   10

Are supervisors human relations oriented? **(3.0)**

0   5   10

Are supervisors sufficiently informed in management principles? **(4.4)**

0   5   10

Do supervisors have well placed priorities? **(3.4)**

0   5   10

Are supervisors skilled in administration? **(6.8)**

0   5   10

Are supervisors skilled in the practice of human relations? **(4.4)**

0   5   10

Do supervisors need more freedom? **(4.4)**

0   5   10

Do supervisors show enough concern for the employees? **(4.4)**

Union Members' Responses to Survey

Other questions and responses included:

- Why do people work hard in this organization?
  Just to keep their jobs and avoid being chewed out—33%.
  To keep their jobs and to make money—0%.
  To keep their jobs, make money and to seek promotions—0%.
  To keep their jobs, make money, seek promotions and for the satisfaction of a job well done—33%.
  To keep their jobs, make money, seek promotions, do a satisfying job, and because other people in their work group expect it of them—33%.

- How are differences and disagreements between units or departments handled in this organization?
  Disagreements are almost always avoided, denied, or suppressed—16%.
  Disagreements are often avoided, denied, or suppressed—16%.
  Sometimes disagreements are accepted and worked through; sometimes they are avoided and suppressed—33%.
  Disagreements are usually accepted as necessary and desirable and worked through—16%.
  Disagreements are almost always accepted as necessary and desirable and are worked through—16%.

- Which of the following best describes the manner in which problems between units or departments are generally resolved?
  Little is done about these problems, they continue to exist—66%.
  Little is done about these problems, they work themselves out with time—16%.
  The problems are appealed to a higher level in the organization but often are still not resolved—0%.
  The problems are appealed to a higher level in the organization and are usually resolved there—16%.
  The problems are worked out at the level where they appear through mutual effort and understanding—0%.

- How are objectives set in this organization?
  Objectives are announced with no opportunity to raise questions or give comments—33%.
  Objectives are announced and explained, and no opportunity is given to ask questions—16%.
  Objectives are drawn up, but are discussed with subordinates

and sometimes modified before being issued—50%.

Specific alternative objectives are drawn up by supervisors, and subordinates are asked to discuss them and indicate the one they think is best—0%.

Problems are presented to those persons who are involved, and the objectives felt to be best are then set by the subordinates and the supervisor jointly, by group participation and discussion—0%.

Questions for Discussion

1. Why can the managers score high in "being friendly" while scoring low in "human relations"?

2. List four problem areas you believe should receive attention.

3. Drawing from the section of this chapter titled "Human Relations versus Union Relations" as well as from the four leadership chapters, suggest corrective remedies.

PART SEVEN

HUMAN BEHAVIOR AND ORGANIZATION DEVELOPMENT

One of the few elements of the work environment that is recognized as being constant is change. Often change is viewed as a disrupting influence on the organization that has the potential to negatively affect human behavior. Consequently, people tend to resist changes in the work environment that will have some impact upon them personally. This is especially true when the results of some change are not easily predicted or there has not been a full disclosure by management of the exact nature of the change.

Organization development has become an accepted tool for the management of change. It represents an attempt to apply behavioral techniques to identify organizational needs and bring about positive changes. Change in all facets of the organization is brought about through participation of organizational members and with the assistance of an outside change agent or interventionist. Because OD makes extensive use of behavioral science to increase organization effectiveness, it represents a composite of knowledge of human behavior in the work environment.

Chapter 18 provides an overview of what has been presented in the preceding seventeen chapters. It discusses the advantages and disadvantages of a behavioral approach to management and shows how money may actually be saved and earned through more concern for the human resources. As a capstone chapter it provides a summary for putting the behavioral approach into a managerial perspective.

17

Organization Development and the Management of Change

LEARNING OBJECTIVES

Upon completion of this chapter, the student should be able to:

- Define organization development.
- Discuss how effective changes in organizational processes can lead to greater efficiency and output.
- Trace the steps in implementing an organization development effort.
- Explain the role of a change agent in the organization development process.
- Identify and explain several organization development change treatments.
- Distinguish how survey feedback differs from other diagnostic techniques.
- Differentiate between job expectation techniques and sensitivity training.
- Describe the various change treatment categories.

Any announcement of changes within the work environment seems to be received with some resistance. Regardless of the magnitude or importance of the changes, there will be people who feel threatened by any alteration in the work environment. Perhaps people are fearful of the unknown consequences or perhaps they are comfortable with the way things are and just do not want to see them changed. But an even more obvious explanation of the usual resistance to change could stem from the manner in which the change is made.

When a change is "announced," people will, at the very least, react with some token resistance or mistrust of the new ways of doing things. It is also quite possible that the people affected most will become defensive, uncooperative, and resentful of management's unilateral action. In other words, frequently the resistance is not so much a reaction to the change itself as it is to the methods by which the change was implemented. Just as with other types of decisions, if people have the opportunity to participate in a decision regarding change, they will be much more committed to it. This vested-interest approach is probably one of the most successful in bringing about an effective change. However, there are many different kinds of changes that take place and that need to occur in the work environment. Some may be quite complex and require a great deal of control over the processes that are necessary to bring about the changes. These needs for a more organized and systematic treatment have been met by a technique known as organization development. Organization development (OD) is being used quite effectively as a tool for the management of change. It includes several processes that are designed to assist in the planning, implementing, and controlling aspects of the change process. Typically, OD efforts include an emphasis on leadership styles, organizational communications, decision-making practices, management of conflict, goal setting, and team building. This chapter will serve as an introduction to OD by providing definitions and by examining the various OD processes and their applications.

ORGANIZATIONAL CHANGE

Nearly all organizations undergo changes. Some will be in a constant state of change while others will feel the impact of change only periodically. But given the nature of our society and the premium the business world places on innovation and technology, the rates of change for all organizations will probably continue at a rapid pace.

These rapid changes present society with myriad problems that must be solved before we can more fully appreciate and utilize the potential of our technology. The fact that the physical sciences have advanced more rapidly than the behavioral sciences in no small degree contributes to the human problems that seem to accompany innovation and technological change. It is estimated that within the past three decades we have witnessed more technological progress than has been accomplished in the rest of the entire history of the world. Therefore, it may be speculated that because we are progressing at a faster rate than ever before, we may be paying a higher price for our advancement. Social costs of rapid change can be observed in all segments of society.

To keep pace with these changes, organizations must seek to further behavioral knowledge and continue to improve upon techniques for increasing job satisfaction and performance. This means overcoming the resistance to change that seems always to occur regardless of how well conceived the change process is. For this reason it is important not only to decide if a change is needed but also who should be involved in the change and how these people should be involved.

Most human behavior in organizations is strongly influenced by sets of certain factors or conditions in the work environment. Some of these include:

- Goals
- Organizational principles
- Resources
- The design of jobs
- Leadership
- Communications
- Development of a favorable climate

Many of the "people problems" that occur within an organization are the result of poor human relations and management practices applied in one or more of these factors. Problems in any of these factors may be an indication of a need for change.

Effective management of change and change treatments can minimize those problems that are jeopardizing organizational effectiveness. In Figure 17.1 some of the possible areas where change treatments may be applied are shown with the expected consequences of a positive change. All of the areas for change can be improved through a participative approach by management. Even an improvement in the appropriate kinds and levels of resources is related to human relations in that problems such as blame orientations, complaints, excuses, and low job performances can be corrected. But equally important as the changes is the method by which changes are made. Involvement of people in managing changes that will affect them is necessary to insure their cooperation. Just as with organizational climate, there is a reciprocal effect in the management of change that greatly influences the success of any change.

EFFECTIVE CHANGES HERE . . .	LEAD TO THESE CONSEQUENCES
Goals	
Organizational goals (long- and short-run) Department goals Project goals (short-term activities)	Employees know what is expected of them; encourages goal-oriented behavior and the compatibility of organizational and individual goals.
Organization Principles	
Clear lines of authority Unity of command Clear supervisory responsibilities Authority is equal to responsibility Effective use of delegation Effective specialization of abilities	Employees can do their work without interferences, barriers to performance, or conflicts; there is a minimization of conditions that can lead to role conflict and role ambiguity.
Resources	
Tools and machines Procedures for utilizing all resources Appropriate budget Human resources	Employees have resources to do what is expected of them.
Job Design	
Proper amount of: Task significance (makes a job important) Task identity (makes a job whole/complete) Variety (makes a job nonroutine) Job feedback (insures knowledge of performance) Autonomy (makes a job independent)	Employees can feel important and competent through doing meaningful work.
Human Relations Practices	

Leadership
  Concern for people
  Concern for production
  Concern for worker participation
	Employees can work in an atmosphere of support, encouragement, and trust where they participate in decision making.

Communication Flow	Employees are well informed and feel as though they are an important part of the organization.

Peer Leadership
  Concern for people
  Concern for production
  Concern for teamwork
	Employees work with people who strive to contribute to a climate that is productive, cooperative, and supportive.

Figure 17.1   Some Major Areas for Change in Organizations

In most situations the more vested interest people have in a change or development, the greater the chance the change will be effective. When management applies good human relations practices, employees will reciprocate with appropriate on-the-job performance. However, the need for good human relations skills transcends the effective management of change. It can be related to the central reason for existence for most organizations—the bottom line. By utilizing human relations skills, better service and productivity can be achieved in the long-run by both profit and nonprofit organizations. In the final analysis, the effective management of people and the work environment is directly related to good human relations practices.

Organization development achieves this integration of knowledge of the management of people and the work environment. The emphasis placed upon the application of behavioral techniques in OD processes suggests the importance of good human relations to a successful OD effort. It is no secret that OD consists of a compilation of managerial practices that were being put to use well before the term "organization development" was coined. However, the study of OD as a unified technique helps us to see how the various theories and practices of management can fit together.

DEFINITIONS OF ORGANIZATION DEVELOPMENT

Like other popularized managerial tools and techniques, the definitions applied to organization development are about as numerous and diverse as the users. This is not necessarily bad. There is usually a common thread running throughout the definitions that links all of them to generally accepted OD processes. When there are several slightly different definitions of a particular concept, it suggests that the tool is being used and that it has the flexibility to meet the unique needs of each organization.

The definitions that follow are very compatible in most respects, with only minor variations. They can be considered representative of the existing attempts to apply an all encompassing meaning to the term organization development.

Warren Bennis offers the following definition:

Organization development is a response to change, a complex educational strategy intended to change the beliefs, attitudes, values, and structure of organizations so that they can better adapt to new technologies, markets, and challenges and the dizzying rate of change itself.[1]

Wendell French and Cecil Bell apply different terminology when they refer to OD as

... the emerging applied behavioral science discipline that seeks to improve organizations through planned systematic, long-range efforts focused on the organization's culture and its human and social processes. The goals of organizational development are to make the organization more effective, more viable, and better able to achieve both the goals of the organization as an entity and the goals of the individuals within the organization.[2]

While the end objectives in his definition are the same, Raymond Miles defines OD in terms of identifying and removing barriers to good performance.

In theory OD is a coordinated effort by organization members (usually with the aid of outside consultants) to uncover and remove attitudinal, behavioral, procedural, policy, and structural barriers to effective performance across the entire socio-technical system, gaining in dynamics so that future adaptations are enhanced.[3]

All definitions are concerned with the management of change and the improvement of performance over the long-run. Organizational processes and the social system of the work environment are usually emphasized as critical to the successful intervention. In general terms, then, OD can be said to be long-term planned interventions to improve upon organization performance through the application of behavioral knowledge to the organizational processes and the organizational climate.

INDIVIDUAL WORK VALUES AND ORGANIZATION DEVELOPMENT

The major thrust of organization development is the involvement of employees in nearly all stages of planning and implementing change. This involvement does present some human behavior problems that management has sometimes been unaware of or chosen to ignore. Only fairly recently has it been recognized that workers may have a number of different work values. These work values are more than likely to be different from those of management, but many managers mistakenly believe that everyone in the work environment has the same aspirations, motivational drives, and attitudes as themselves. There are, unfortunately, many people who are primarily concerned with putting in their time and collecting their pay. The existence of such attitudes should serve notice on managers that it is most difficult to project their own work values onto their employees.

Charles Hughes and Vincent Flowers have done a considerable amount of research and consulting in the area of worker value systems.[4] The framework they have developed is based upon Clare Graves's "Levels of Existence."[5] They believe their framework is helpful to managers in gaining understanding of themselves as well as others and can thus minimize many interpersonal problems. When considering the value systems presented below in Table 17.1, the student of human behavior in the work environment should see once more the importance of a behavioral approach and the possible application of contingency management to human relations practices and an OD effort.

One of the contributions of the framework of worker value systems is the comparison of managers' and subordinates' values. Hughes and Flowers suggest the most compatible match-ups regarding employee values and the management style used by a manager. For instance, employees who are sociocentric will be most responsive to and satisfied with a supervisor who uses group participation and emphasizes the human relations aspects of individual performance.[6]

Understanding the value systems of subordinates is important in the everyday management of people. It is even more critical when an organization is trying to bring about changes that will improve performance. Once a manager has more knowledge about subordinates, it will be easier to apply a management style that will be conducive to creating a work climate that is receptive to change and innovation. The next section will trace the steps in implementing an OD attempt.

STEPS IN ORGANIZATION DEVELOPMENT

Organization development can be implemented in a number of different ways; however, there are usually some steps that are always taken in the process of bringing about change. Figure 17.2 demonstrates the sequential steps that would be common to a typical OD effort. The figure is meant to show the order in which events usually take place. Change treatments (OD processes) will be discussed in some detail later in the chapter.

The first step in bringing about any change is the recognition that a change is necessary. A manager may identify specific performance problems, barriers to performance, or areas of possible improvement. In many cases management will initially be dealing with a symptom of the problem and may not know the real causes of a performance deficiency. At this point, a change agent (interventionist) may be brought into the firm to speak with several of the firm's key managers and supervisors as well as with a segment of the rank-and-file workers. Following this, the interventionist may begin to formulate some ideas of what the problem is. More interviews and perhaps a formal questionnaire survey may be administered in order to gather as much information as is needed. This information is broadly summarized into "areas to be worked on" and is given to the heads of the firm's departments as well as to the top level managers.

TABLE 17.1 Worker Value Systems

SYSTEM	VALUES
System 1—Reactive	Values are absent. It characterizes infants and individuals with serious brain deterioration, and therefore is not likely to be applicable to employees.
System 2—Tribalistic	At this stage the individuals derive their values from others such as a father or boss. These people value highly routine work, friendly autocratic supervision, and a compatible work group.
System 3—Egocentric	This describes rugged individuals who are usually tough and aggressive. They are likely to take any job so long as they get the money they want. They need and respect a boss who is tough and controls employees closely.
System 4—Conformist	Employees at this level exhibit the rather traditional traits of loyalty, hard work and attentiveness to duty. They prefer to work in a place where structure, policy, and procedure are clearly defined, and where supervision is consistent. Security and fairness are important to this type of individual.
System 5—Manipulative	Materialism, activity, goals, achievement, and advancement are valued by the employees at this level. They like work that allows "wheeling and dealing" and a boss who understands company politics.
System 6—Sociocentric	People count more than situations for employees with sociocentric values. Harmony in the work group, friendly supervision, and equality for mankind are important to them.
System 7—Existential	Individuals at this level like work that allows freedom and creativity, and jobs with open structure. Money and advancement are less important than challenge and an opportunity to learn and grow.

Source: Modified and adapted from: Charles L. Hughes and Vincent Flowers, "Toward Existentialism in Management," The Conference Board Record 12 (September 1975): 61.

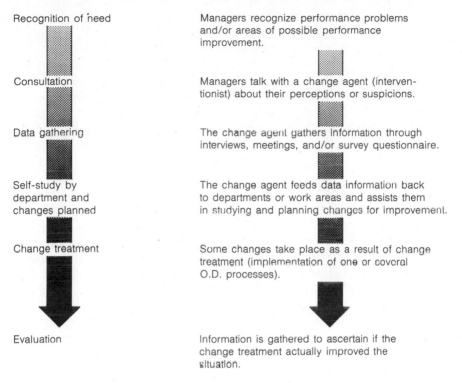

Figure 17.2   Model of Organization Development

During a self-study workshop the top management group studies itself to determine how the group accomplishes work. The "how" refers to the processes such as decision-making, planning and goal-setting methods; and communication manner and style. From this self-study, the group, in collaboration with the interventionist, will be able to develop programs to upgrade areas of performance needing improvement. This type of self-study workshop will also occur concurrently within each of the departments (target departments) to be exposed to the OD effort.

In some instances the OD effort will involve only the feedback of the data gathered. But when another change treatment is to be used, it is at this point, after data feedback, that other OD methods would be applied. This may involve team building, communications training, leadership training, or any number of the OD processes, some of which will be explained in the next section.

After the change treatment has been implemented, it is necessary to determine if the change was successful. Some controversy surrounds the time period that must elapse before studying the effects of a change. The nature of the change will in part govern the amount of time needed by workers to perceive and adjust to a change. For example, a change in the compensation system will be "picked up on" rather quickly when compared to a change in top management's leadership style. A change in leadership style at the top of the hierarchy will probably take time to filter down through the firm. There are no guidelines for determining when a remeasurement should be conducted. However, management should try to ascertain when the total effects of a change reach a plateau and remain stable. When this plateau stage is reached, a remeasurement would be appropriate.

ROLE OF THE CHANGE AGENT

Individuals, usually from outside the organization, who assist in organization development are referred to as interventionists or change agents rather than as management consultants because of the nature of their roles. Change agents work with the people of an organization and actually assist them in a manner which allows the employees to solve their own problems. Change agents never just give a report to top management and leave, but rather work hand in hand with the people in the work units that are undergoing change. This method of improving organizations purposely places a great deal of responsibility in the hands of the firm's employees. Basically, the role of the employees in organization development involves describing the way work is presently done and the problems encountered in the way people and work are organized. The employees then, with the help of the change agent, plan how work should be done in an ideal sense and develop programs to move the firm from ''what is presently happening" to what "should be happening."

Although it is not imperative, the change agent is normally from outside the organization. Companies that have in-house consultants may be able to use such people if it is felt they can be effective change agents. An outsider in the role of a change agent offers several advantages to an organization:

1. No preconceived notions as to the nature of the root cause of existing problems
2. An objective appraisal of organizational climate and conditions of employment
3. No vested interests in any one department, division, or work unit
4. No stigma of being associated with a particular department that has not been too effective in the past

5. Not part of the political or social systems that exist within the organization

Generally speaking, because of the above reasons an outsider will be a more effective change agent than someone internal to the organization. Since the role of a change agent is one of a facilitator rather than a problem solver, the nature of the expertise required is somewhat different from that of a management consultant. The change agent should, therefore, be someone who can offer effective ways to work on problems, not answers to problems.[7]

ORGANIZATION DEVELOPMENT CHANGE TREATMENTS

Change treatments are actually the forms of intervention or the organization development processes. In practice the OD umbrella has come to include nearly every behavioral-based management tool. There has been a proliferation of new names applied to old techniques, some new techniques, and even some undisguised proven techniques that are now seen as OD processes. We will examine some of the OD change treatments that have been used. There are many others that are somewhat different, but each change treatment is designed to bring about a change that will result in improved organization performance.

Basically, change treatments will fall into general categories derived from the target of change or that part of the organization that is treated. Although it can be argued that ultimately the target is always the same— the human element—the means to bring about performance changes can be quite different. Some change treatments deal directly with the development of individuals, while others treat a part of the work environment directly which in turn has an indirect impact upon personal performance. The following breakdown of change treatments into categories (Table 17.2) describes the kinds of OD processes that are likely to be applied within each. It should be noted that there is a strong interrelationship and interdependence between these categories. This, of course, means that some overlap is possible and categorization of some processes would be difficult. However, the categories should be approached as means to identify parts of the organization that may be treated and the possible areas of development within each category. A very precise classification is neither possible nor necessary.

Wendell French and Cecil Bell have identified six major kinds of treatments that include some specific processes:

TABLE 17.2   General Categories of Change Treatments

CHANGE TREATMENT CATEGORIES	POSSIBLE AREAS OF EMPHASIS
Personal Development	Interpersonal skills, beliefs, attitudes, communication skills, conflict resolution, leadership styles, decision making, individual goal setting
Group Development	Team building, intergroup processes, coordination of activities, conflict resolution, group problem solving, group goal setting
Task Development	Formulation of task objectives, analysis of work-task situation, job design
Structural Development	Organizational hierarchy, formal structure, formal interdepartmental relationship, relationship of jobs, formal communication networks
Data Utilization	Gathering data, analysis of data, feedback of data, data discussion

FRENCH AND BELL'S SIX MAJOR WAYS TO CHANGE ORGANIZATIONS

Diagnostic Activities: fact-finding activities designed to study the "way things are." Available methods of fact-finding include interviews, survey questionnaires, and meetings with departments or work area personnel.

Team-building Activities: activities designed to improve the teamwork, cooperation, and coordination among members of a single department. Topics studied include evaluating the way things are done, the needed skills to accomplish tasks, the resource allocations needed to get work done, and the nature and quality of personal relationships between department members. Sensitivity or T-Group training, the Job Expectation Technique (Jet), and Survey Feedback are three of the more popular methods of strengthening a department.

Intergroup Activities: activities designed to improve the relationship between departments. Cooperation, coordination, and teamwork are the important focuses of attention. The Intergroup Team-building Technique is one of the better ways to improve the overall effectiveness of two or more departments which need to interact.

Survey Feedback Activities: related to and similar to the diagnostic activities mentioned above. These activities center around actively working with data produced by a survey and designing improvement activities based on the survey information. In brief, a department or work group studies information about itself and takes corrective action.

Organizational Principles Activities: are generally concerned with insuring that a company operates on the proper management and organizational principles outlined in most basic management textbooks. This change area deals with a number of topics such as lines of authority, the authority and responsibility, relationship, delegation, and work specialization.

Education and Training Activities: activities designed to improve skills, abilities, and knowledge of individuals. This area may involve helping people improve technical skills required for effective job performance or may be directed toward improving interpersonal skills. Other focuses of attention include leadership issues, responsibilities and functions of group members, training in problem-solving, goal setting and planning. The techniques used in this area cover a wide range and may include educational training in college and universities, educational workshops at the work site, specific job training on the job, and T-Group training.[8]

Their attempt to categorize change treatments is based upon the nature of the activities. Some categories are quite broad (organization principles and education and training) while those based on the use of data and group activities are somewhat more specific. These latter, more specific change treatments, as well as some other OD processes used to bring about change, will be discussed separately.

Diagnostic Activities

Diagnostic activities refer to programs undertaken to study the "way things are." Normally, these things include the following factors:

- Leadership
- Group processes
- Organizational climate
- Job satisfaction
- Communication
- Decision making
- Motivation

The interventionist collects information on these factors through interviews, departmental meetings, and pencil-and-paper surveys. Diagnostic activities help identify problems and show where improvement is needed. This is generally the first step in the OD effort as it serves as an analysis of need and provides base-point data. One of the weaknesses of many OD efforts is that they do not have this base-point data so they have no effective way of measuring OD's contribution.

Survey Feedback

Survey feedback in its data-gathering stage is very similar to the diagnostic activities but this treatment is distinguished by the feedback of the data to the employees. The data are discussed, evaluated, and used to assist the group in planning, decision making, and problem solving.

When a change agent is brought into an organization, there is usually a perceived problem or a need to control rapid changes. The change agent will typically spend some time in observing operations and talking with people in order to get a feel for the organization and the perceived problems. Once some tentative problem areas have been identified a questionnaire will be developed. This phase of survey feedback can be considered as being the same as diagnostic activities. Usually a survey will cover several topics and will include questions such as the following:

- GOALS
  Does the company have clear and reasonable goals?
  Does your department have clear and reasonable goals?
  Do you have clear and reasonable goals?

- MANAGERIAL LEADERSHIP
  Are managers supportive and friendly?
  Do managers encourage best effort?
  Do managers offer new ideas?

- GROUP PROCESSES
  Do members of a department plan together?
  Do members of a department share information?
  Do members of a department have confidence and trust in each other?

- PEER LEADERSHIP
  Are your co-workers friendly?
  Do your co-workers listen to your problems?
  Do your co-workers help you maintain high standards?

- SATISFACTION
  Are you happy with your job?
  Are you happy with your pay?
  Are you happy with your promotion opportunities?
  Are you happy with your supervisor?

- ORGANIZATIONAL CLIMATE
  Is your company interested in your welfare?
  Does your company try to improve working conditions?
  Does your department have an influence on the company, overall?

- STRESS
  Do you feel certain about how much authority you have?
  Do you know what is expected of you?
  Do you have two or more supervisors?

Most of the questions relate back to the key human dimensions discussed in Chapter 1. To review briefly, Chapter 1 emphasized that most disruptive worker activities like absenteeism, quitting, poor morale, and motivation are affected by a handful of factors or conditions which include managerial and peer leadership, group processes, organizational climate, and job satisfaction. The information gathered during the observation stage will greatly help the change agent tailor the questions on the survey to the company's needs.

Once the survey questionnaire has been designed and perhaps pretested, it will be administered to the employees of the organization. The interventionist needs to emphasize the anonymity of the respondents in order to receive forthright and candid information. The employees must be assured that the survey is not a "witch hunt" where the top managers would be informed of people giving unfavorable responses to the survey questions. An entire development effort can fail if people do not have confidence and trust in the change agent. It may be desirable to have the president of the firm send a letter to each of the employees participating in the survey stating the purpose of the project and that survey responses will not be identified with any one individual. A second letter from the president should accompany the survey questionnaire as a cover letter. This letter should again emphasize the importance of honest answers as well as guaranteeing the anonymity of a person's responses.

Once the survey questionnaires have been completed, they must be scored and tabulated by departments or work areas. Figure 17.3 shows one effective way to present survey feedback results. High scores (to the right of 5) are favorable, low scores (to the left of 5) are unfavorable. By profiling a department's responses in this manner, department workers can easily see where improvement is needed. These are real scores of one department in a medium-sized firm. The people in the department apparently feel that work is not as sensibly organized as it should be, workers are not sufficiently informed about company activities, decision making is not being pushed down the line far enough to satisfy needs for participation, and employees do not feel valuable. In most cases the change agent will compare the profile of one department with the profile of the entire organization in such areas as leadership, group processes, satisfaction, and goal clarity, and then work with each department to upgrade any areas needing improvement.

For this method to be of most value to the firm, the following steps should be followed when using survey feedback:

1. Top managers are involved in the planning and use of the survey.
2. Information is collected from all workers and employees.
3. Survey results are fed back to the top people first and then down through the organization.
4. A manager conducts a meeting with members of the department where (a) the survey results are discussed, (b) members are asked to

	1	2	3	4	5	6	7	8	9	10

0   5   10
Do supervisors act friendly? (8.5)

0   5   10
Do supervisors pay attention to workers? (8.8)

0   5   10
Do supervisors listen to workers' problems? (8.7)

0   5   10
Do supervisors encourage best effort? (8.9)

0   5   10
Do supervisors maintain high standards? (8.3)

0   5   10
Do supervisors set good examples? (9.0)

0   5   10
Do supervisors help workers improve job output? (7.4)

0   5   10
Do supervisors help employees schedule work? (7.6)

0   5   10
Do supervisors offer new ideas for solving job-related problems? (8.1)

0   5   10
Do supervisors encourage team work? (8.3)

0   5   10
Do supervisors encourage the exchange of ideas? (7.2)

0   5   10
Do supervisors inspire trust and confidence? (7.4)

0   5   10
Do supervisors receive trust and confidence? (7.5)

0   5   10
Do supervisors schedule enough meetings with the workers? (7.0)

0   5   10
Are supervisors human relations oriented? (3.3)

0   5   10
Are supervisors sufficiently informed in management principles? (4.1)

0   5   10
Do supervisors have well placed priorities? (4.5)

0   5   10
Are supervisors skilled in administration? (5.4)

0   5   10
Are supervisors skilled in the practice of human relations? (3.7)

0   5   10
Do supervisors need more freedom? (4.7)

0   5   10
Do supervisors show enough concern for the employees? (4.4)

Figure 17.3 A survey feedback instrument

(Source: Adapted and modified from ISR "Survey of Organizations." Center for Research on Utilization of Scientific Knowledge, Institute for Social Research, University of Michigan, Ann Arbor, Michigan.)

help interpret the information, and (c) plans are made for outlining programs to improve the department's profile.

5. The change agent discusses how to conduct a feedback meeting with each manager and provides information that will clarify the meaning of special terms or activities.[9]

Step 4 is particularly crucial for success. Once the survey information has been collected and scored, workers must study the reasons for their low survey profiles. The profiles show the "results" or consequences or some mode of operating or practice in their department, but do not point to the causes or reasons for a low profile. The reasons for low profiles need to be brought out by the department members in their discussions of the survey results.

Team-building Activities

Team-building activities are programs designed to upgrade teamwork, cooperation, and coordination among members of a work unit. Usually the topics of communication, decision-making, job responsibility, and leadership are central concerns of team building. These four areas can be improved through T-group training, the job expectation technique, and survey feedback.

Intergroup activities are forms of team building that are designed to improve the working relationships between two work units such as departments. When the perceptions of people in one department of the people in another department are causing poor working relationships, an intergroup team-building program is usually necessary. Generally, this type of program allows people in the two departments to share their perceptions and feelings about each other and allows each department to respond to the other's perceptions. Most interdepartmental problems are caused by the failure of one department to understand the nature of the work and problems faced by the other.

T-Groups or Sensitivity Groups.   T-groups or sensitivity groups resemble small informal groups of people talking to each other about whatever is bothering them. Bothersome topics may include such factors as a person's job, supervision, the organization, or the other people in the group.

The "t" in t-groups stands for training. Participants are trained in several different skills that are intended to improve their human interaction, communication, and job skills. Typical goals of t-groups include the following:

1. Increased understanding, insight, and self-awareness about one's own behavior and its impact on others

2. Increased understanding and sensitivity about the behavior of others
3. Better understanding and awareness of group and intergroup processes
4. Increased diagnostic skills in interpersonal and intergroup situations
5. Increased ability to transfer learning into action
6. Improvement in a person's ability to analyze his or her own interpersonal behavior[10]

The idea that "the better a person perceives reality the better a person can function" appears to be at the heart of the six goals. Reality refers to knowledge about oneself and one's relations with other people. Because of the extent to which organizational life involves interpersonal and group interaction, many organizations have turned to t-groups to help solve human problems in such areas as perception, communication, and cooperation.

There are basically three types of sensitivity or t-group designs. In the "family" type all members are from the same work group, department, or division and probably know one another fairly well. In the "cousin" group, members are from the same organization but do not know one another very well. Finally, there is the "stranger" type where members are from different organizations. Sometimes knowing other people in the sensitivity group can be a problem. The presence of other people from the same company may prevent a person from being forthright and candid in exchanging perceptions and understandings. This is particularly true when a person's immediate supervisor is present. Who would volunteer a series of damaging observations about a supervisor with the supervisor present? For this reason, leaders of sensitivity or t-group programs usually separate supervisors from their subordinates.

The stages of a sensitivity group are usually similar to the following:

1. At the start there is an intended lack of formal leadership, power, and status. There is no agenda, stated goals or purpose. This admittedly uncomfortable condition will create a vacuum which members will fill with examples of traditional behavior. That is, each member will act in his or her customary manner at least for a while.

2. During this stage, the trainer evaluates how he/she feels in the group in a nonevaluative manner. The trainer becomes open and empathetic. This behavior will include others in the group to describe their feelings about what they feel is occurring.

3. In this stage, following a period of give-and-take between members, interpersonal relationships develop. Each member is exploring with new personal and interpersonal behavior.

4. The last phase tries to help the members explore how to use their new understandings of interpersonal and group behavior when they return to their organization.[11]

In short, sensitivity groups are characterized by the absence of formal authority, agenda, explicit goals, and instruction from others. Learning through sensitivity training is thus accomplished by exploring or experimenting with different personal modes of behavior. This new type of social interaction allows people to test different ways of reacting to other individuals.

A recent review of one hundred studies does not give high marks to sensitivity training, but neither does it receive low marks. The review concluded that sensitivity training:

1. Often leads to increased self-awareness.
2. Induces members to feel that their behavior is more controlled by themselves than by others, such as their supervisors.
3. Did not have any consistent effect on changing a person's prejudices toward others. Some participants were more prejudiced, others less prejudiced; in others there was no change.
4. Temporarily increased a member's tendency toward assuming a leadership role (or at least a participative role).
5. Temporarily improved communication skill.
6. Temporarily changed the perceptions of a member's peers and superiors toward that member.[12]

Another review of the overall effects of sensitivity training concluded that:

Laboratory education (t-groups or sensitivity training) has not been shown to bring about any marked change in one's standing on objective measures of attitude, values, outlooks, interpersonal perception, self-awareness, or interpersonal sensitivity. In spite of these essentially negative results on objective measures, individuals who have been trained by laboratory education methods are more likely to be seen as changing their job behavior than are individuals in similar settings who have not been trained.[13]

This review suggests that there may be some on-the-job changes as a result of some form of laboratory training. This, of course, is where changes are most sought but where solid evidence supporting t-groups is most lacking. Sensitivity training appears to have more of an effect on employee attitudes than on actual work behavior.

Perhaps some of the failures of t-groups can be blamed on administrative procedures. Top level managers have been known to direct sensitivity training to the middle and lower level managers before they, themselves, experience the learning outcomes offered by sensitivity training. Emulation is probably the most common way managers are developed. Lower level managers tend to perpetuate the style of their own managers. This style may include such processes as method and style of communicating, manner toward subordinates, expressed attitudes and dispositions toward others, and leanings toward worker participation in organizational decision making. A conflict may arise when people in sensitivity training learn that open communication and worker participation upgrades the quality of work life and then fail to be offered such opportunities by their immediate supervisors. To be most effective, sensitivity programs must be experienced by top managers before such programs are offered to subordinate managers and other workers.

Job Expectation Techniques.   Job expectation techniques (JET) are aimed at classifying job responsibilities between two or more people. Because of the interdependence of most jobs today JET can be most helpful in:

1. Establishing job understanding between people who have never worked together in the same department
2. Establishing job understanding among workers in an already established department where some job ambiguity or conflict is either reported or observed
3. Establishing job understanding between present workers and a newly acquired member[14]

In each of the above situations there is an obvious need for getting a person's job responsibilities "out in the open." Most of us have been in situations where our effectiveness was dampened by others not understanding our responsibilities. For example, the coordination required by members of a football team in carrying out an offensive play illustrates the need for everyone to be clearly aware of others' job duties in order for each person to do his or her own duties. The same level of coordination is necessary within most organizations.

JET can be used to clarify job understanding between a leader and subordinate but is most often used to clarify job responsibilities among people in a single department. Each person has the opportunity to discuss and outline his or her job in front of the other people in the department. When used in this way, the following steps are followed:

1. The individual whose job is being discussed lists, on a flip chart, his or her perceived job duties and responsibilities. Throughout the process, all other members of the management group are encouraged to

add their comments and to agree or disagree with the perceptions as expressed by the individual whose job is being discussed. In other words, the entire group contributes to the job definition.

2. When the members of the group have reached consensus on a particular job definition, the incumbent is responsible for writing a description of the activities which are now felt to constitute the job. Later, a copy is distributed to each participant to make certain that the group has developed a full understanding and agreement of each individual's role.

3. This procedure continues until the job expectation analysis has been completed for each member of the group. Generally, it is wise to start with lower level jobs and end with the job of the group's overall supervisor.[15]

During a year's time, a person's job will probably change a little or need to be changed and these changes communicated to co-workers. Thus, it would be useful if these JET activities were repeated annually to insure that workers in a department understand their job responsibilities and authority as well as those of other people in the department. After the initial session, subsequent sessions will be less time consuming and more productive relative to the time spent.

Other OD Change Treatments

Once a diagnosis has revealed the areas of needed improvements, the interventionist and members of management may agree to do any of a number of different things to correct the weaknesses. In this way OD has come to include just about whatever techniques practitioners feel are appropriate in improving organizational effectiveness. Training may be given employees in the following:

- Contingency management
- MBO
- Leadership
- Communications
- Problem solving
- Motivation
- Management of conflict
- Interpersonal skills
- Behavior modification
- Technical skills
- Management principles

Job design and job enrichment may also be included as part of an OD effort. In other words, almost anything that has the potential to improve performance while achieving organizational and individual goals can be included as a viable technique of organization development.

SUMMARY

In order to bring about effective change, managers must be aware of their subordinates' value systems. Charles Hughes and Vincent Flowers have designed a framework for categorizing individuals' values. The framework is helpful in assisting individuals to better understand themselves as well as others. Being able to identify the values of subordinates enables supervisors to adopt a leadership style that is the most effective with certain types of people.

When compatibility exists between employee values and leadership style, management is in a much better position to implement changes that will influence performance. Typically changes may occur in one of the following areas: goals, organizational principles, resources, job design, or human relations practices.

Organization development seeks to improve organizational effectiveness through planned, systematic, and long-range efforts that are focused upon the firm's human and social processes. Some of these organizational processes that are typically dealt with include goal setting, leadership, teamwork, problem solving, and communications. Because organization development is an overall effort to improve organizational effectiveness, OD goals are attained over relatively long periods of time.

Organization development emphasizes a participative rather than a unilateral approach to change. Important roles in the planning and development efforts are played by the organization's members rather than by management. Employees have a part in gathering data, in studying how they are presently accomplishing work, and in detailing how they should accomplish work. In essence, organization development offers members of the organization the opportunity to create their own work environment.

While many different techniques may be used in bringing about planned change, there is a recognized procedure for developing organizations. After the need for an OD approach has been recognized, an interventionist is selected. The interventionist plays the role of a facilitator and works closely with management in designing the complete OD effort. Observation and diagnostic activities serve to assess and provide base-point data for measuring change. Data is then fed back to members of the organization who use it to plan changes for improving performance. Change treatments and training are then implemented in an attempt to correct diagnosed deficiencies, to improve certain operations, and to manage growth and change. Following the implementation of the change treatments and training there should be an attempt to measure the success of the changes. This evaluation should be repeated over a period of time in order to ascertain where more attention is still needed and where satisfactory progress is being made.

Organization development should be viewed as being an action-oriented method for influencing organizational effectiveness. In practice it has come to include many different training and development techniques. The emphasis is on the application of behavioral knowledge to organizational processes and the work environment. As such OD has provided industry and the public sector with a tool that has the capability of improving organizational processes while achieving organizational and individual goals.

NOTES

1. Warren G. Bennis, *Organizational Development: Its Nature, Origins, and Prospects* (Reading, Mass.: Addison-Wesley Publishing Co., 1969), p. 2.

2. Wendell French and Cecil H. Bell, Jr., *Organizational Development* (Englewood Cliffs, N.J.: Prentice-Hall, Inc., 1973), p. 3.

3. Raymond E. Miles, *Theories of Management: Implications for Organizational Behavior and Development* (New York: McGraw-Hill, 1975), p. 191.

4. Charles L. Hughes and Vincent Flowers, "Toward Existentialism in Management," *The Conference Board Record* 12 (September 1975): 61.

5. Clare Graves, "Levels of Existence: An Open System of Values," *Journal of Humanistic Psychology* (Fall 1970): vol. 10, No. 2, pp. 131–5.

6. For a more complete discussion of the matching of management style to worker values, see Charles L. Hughes, "If It's Right for You, It's Wrong for Employees," *The Personnel Administrator*, June 1975, pp. 14–19, and Thomas M. Rohan, "Should a Worker's Personality Affect Your Managing?" *Industry Week*, 5 May 1975, pp. 28–38.

7. Wendell L. French, Cecil H. Bell, Jr., and Robert A. Zawacki, *Organization Development: Theory, Practice, and Research* (Dallas, Texas: Business Publications, Inc., 1978), p. 10.

8. Wendell L. French and Cecil H. Bell, Jr., *Organization Development: Behavioral Science Interventions for Organization Improvement* (Englewood Cliffs, N.J.: Prentice-Hall, Inc., 1973), pp. 102–3.

9. French and Bell, *Organizational Development*, p. 130.

10. John Campbell and Marvin Dunnette, "Effectiveness of T-Group Experience in Managerial Training and Development," *Psychological Bulletin* 70 (August 1968): 73–103.

11. ANDRE DELBERG, "Sensitivity Training," *Training and Development Journal* 24 (January 1970): 32–5.

12. P. B. SMITH, "Controlled Studies of the Outcome of Sensitivity Training," *Psychological Bulletin* 82 (May 1975): 597–622.

13. MARVIN D. DUNNETTE and JOHN CAMPBELL, "Laboratory Education: Impact on People and Organizations," *Industrial Relations* 7 (January 1968): 23.

14. EDGAR HUSE, *Organizational Development and Change* (St. Paul, Minn.: West Publishing Co., 1975), p. 181.

15. Ibid., p. 182.

QUESTIONS FOR THOUGHT AND DISCUSSION

1. How does organization development differ from personal development and personal training programs?

2. Why do people resist change?

3. Why is an external change agent more likely to be successful in bringing about change than an internal change agent?

4. How does job design (Chapter 3) fit into an OD attempt?

5. Compare Table 17.2 with the six change treatments identified by French and Bell. How are the two lists compatible? How do they differ?

KEY TERMS

The student should be able to discuss the significance of these terms to the study of human behavior in the work environment.

Organization development
Worker value systems
Change agent (interventionist)
Change treatment
Change treatment categories

Diagnostic activities
Survey feedback
Team building
T-groups
JET

CASE INCIDENT

The need for organization development can be indicated through collecting information on a company's climate or personality. The following survey feedback instrument shows actual information for two departments in a small company. High scores are favorable, low scores are unfavorable. Departments 1 and 2 are doing about the same type of work and are in the same city.

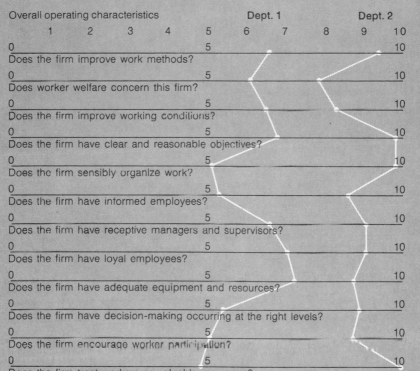

Overall operating characteristics					Dept. 1			Dept. 2	
1	2	3	4	5	6	7	8	9	10

0 ————————————————— 5 ————————————————— 10
Does the firm improve work methods?

0 ————————————————— 5 ————————————————— 10
Does worker welfare concern this firm?

0 ————————————————— 5 ————————————————— 10
Does the firm improve working conditions?

0 ————————————————— 5 ————————————————— 10
Does the firm have clear and reasonable objectives?

0 ————————————————— 5 ————————————————— 10
Does the firm sensibly organize work?

0 ————————————————— 5 ————————————————— 10
Does the firm have informed employees?

0 ————————————————— 5 ————————————————— 10
Does the firm have receptive managers and supervisors?

0 ————————————————— 5 ————————————————— 10
Does the firm have loyal employees?

0 ————————————————— 5 ————————————————— 10
Does the firm have adequate equipment and resources?

0 ————————————————— 5 ————————————————— 10
Does the firm have decision-making occurring at the right levels?

0 ————————————————— 5 ————————————————— 10
Does the firm encourage worker participation?

0 ————————————————— 5 ————————————————— 10
Does the firm treat workers as valuable resources?

Two Very Different Climates or Cultures. Exhibit shows that the people in Department 2 perceive much more emphasis on good work methods and conditions, worker welfare, clear objectives, worker participation, and treating people as valuable resources.

(Source: The instrument is adapted and modified from ISR "Survey of Organizations," Center for Research on Utilization of Scientific Knowledge, Institute for Social Research, University of Michigan, Ann Arbor, Michigan.)

The people in Department 2 obviously have a better attitude toward the organization than do the individuals in Department 1. Two vastly different organizational cultures or climates are shown. People in Department 2 perceive the firm as being highly supportive, concerned about worker welfare, and democratic; whereas the members of Department 1 perceive the company as being nonsupportive, unconcerned about worker welfare, and autocratic. The employees in Department 2 see the company as emphasizing good work methods, work conditions, worker welfare, clear objectives, worker participation, and treating people as valuable human resources.

Questions for Discussion

1. How can people working in the same company see the firm in such different ways?

2. How should this information be used?

3. What people should see this information?

4. How would you improve the profile of Department 1?

5. What OD change treatments might help Department 1 become more like Department 2?

18

Putting the Behavioral Approach into a Managerial Perspective

LEARNING OBJECTIVES

Upon completion of this chapter the student should be able to:

- Discuss reasons why a behavioral approach to management is a cost effective way to manage.
- Identify costs associated with poor human relations practices.
- Recognize the possible drawbacks of a behavioral approach to management.
- Discuss some of the characteristics of organizations that encourage a behavioral approach to management.
- Explain what the behavioral approach to management is and how it contributes to organizational effectiveness.

The discussion of the change treatments, values, and philosophies of organization development demonstrates new behavioral techniques are still being found and applied. However, for the most part organization development is a compilation of behavioral techniques that have been found useful for a number of years. Thus, not only are new behavioral approaches to management being discovered, but many proven techniques are being applied as part of a new systemwide effort to bring about greater organizational effectiveness. The fact that organization development with its emphasis on the behavioral and cultural aspects of the organization has been so successful illustrates the recognition of top level managers of the possible benefits of better human relations practices.

WHY A BEHAVIORAL APPROACH TO MANAGEMENT?

As was pointed out earlier in the book, a behavioral approach pays off not only in humanistic terms but also in dollars and cents. Research since the early 1960s has shown that absenteeism, turnover, tardiness, and complaints are closely related to how the employees feel toward their jobs and toward the organization. Although these consequences of poor work attitudes appear to be obvious, there have been only a few studies that have actually measured the dollar costs associated with different levels of satisfaction and motivation.

One of these research efforts was conducted by Philip Mirvis and Edward Lawler in which they studied 160 bank tellers working in twenty branches of a midwestern bank.[1] They set out to determine how much work dissatisfaction, low job involvement, and low motivation were costing the bank and how much money the bank could save through improving satisfaction and motivation levels. The research measured work satisfaction, job involvement, and work motivation. In addition, the levels of absenteeism, turnover, and shortages (mistakes) were examined.

As shown in Table 18.1 an absent employee cost the bank $66.45 a day while the costs related to a worker quitting amounted to $2,522.03. Job dissatisfaction was determined to be very costly to this bank since dissatisfaction was found to lead to absenteeism and turnover.

The study also asked if the happy employee was an efficient worker. In short, the answer was no. High work satisfaction was not found to cut down significantly on the number of teller mistakes. Although it was found that job dissatisfaction strongly influenced decisions to be absent and to quit, job dissatisfaction did not affect productivity levels. In other words, the more a teller likes the work, the less chance there is of that teller either being absent or quitting, but he or she will not necessarily be a better worker on the job.

How much money could the bank save by improving worker job satisfaction, involvement, and work motivation? Could a dollar amount

TABLE 18.1   The Costs of Absenteeism and Turnover

VARIABLE COST (IN DOLLARS)

Absenteeism

Absent employee	
Salary	23.04
Benefits	6.40
Replacement employee:	
Training and staff time	2.13
Unabsorbed burden	15.71
Lost profit contribution	19.17
Total variable cost	23.04
Total cost	66.45

Turnover

Replacement acquisition	
Direct hiring costs	293.95
Other hiring costs	185.55
Replacement training	
Preassignment	758.84
Learning curve	212.98
Unabsorbed burden	682.44
Lost profit contribution	388.27
Total variable cost	293.95
Total cost	2,522.03

Source: Philip Mirvis and Edward Lawler, III, "Measuring the Financial Impact of Employee Attitudes," Journal of Applied Psychology 62, No. 1 (1977). p. 4. Copyright 1977 by the American Psychological Association. Reprinted by permission.

be put on it? Years ago this could not be done because the state of the art in management had not advanced far enough. Today, there are techniques of attaching dollar savings to improvements in the human organization. Table 18.2 shows how much money the bank could save by improving worker satisfaction, worker involvement, and worker motivation. At the time of the study the level of work satisfaction was costing the bank $5.44 a month per teller in absenteeism costs, $17.04 a month per teller in turnover costs, and $25.27 a month per teller in costs due to mistakes. Likewise it was found that the level of teller work motivation was costing the bank $5.44 a month per teller in absenteeism costs, $17.04 a month per teller in turnover costs, and $25.27 a month per teller in shortage costs. It should be noted that an increase in satisfaction, involvement and motivation could lead to a substantial savings for each employee. For 160 bank tellers, the direct savings for one year would be $17,664. Overall, the potential total cost savings would amount to $125,160 per year if more concern for the human element would be demonstrated.[2]

In another study involving a manufacturing firm employing 800 workers, it was estimated that poor human relations cost the firm over two million dollars in a single year.[3] The breakdown of these costs is

TABLE 18.2   Dollars Saved through Improving Satisfaction, Involvement, and Motivation

		COST (IN DOLLARS)			
Attitude	*Change*	*Absenteeism*	*Turnover*	*Shortage*	*Total*
Intrinsic satisfaction	Increase	2.40	10.17	25.98	38.55
	As is	5.44	17.04	25.27	47.75
	Decrease	8.48	23.93	24.55	56.96
Job involvement	Increase	5.74	7.08	23.62	36.44
	As is	5.44	17.04	25.27	47.75
	Decrease	5.14	27.01	26.91	59.06
Intrinsic motivation	Increase	4.45	11.55	24.41	40.41
	As is	5.44	17.04	25.27	47.75
	Decrease	6.43	22.54	26.13	55.10

*Source: Philip Mirvis and Edward Lawler, III, "Measuring the Financial Impact of Employee Attitudes,"
Journal of Applied Psychology 62, No. 1 (1977): 6. Copyright 1977 by the American Psychological
Association. Reprinted by permission.*

shown in Table 18.3. The costs of absenteeism, tardiness, turnover, grievances, and poor work performance were definitely cutting into profits.
For example, employees being late to work cost the company $56,920 in
one year. Absenteeism cost the firm over $500,000 in a single year. When
one worker stayed home rather than going to work, the company lost
$62.49 per day. Poor worker attitudes and low worker motivation were
also costly in dollar and cents terms.

Poor quality of work, an increase in mistakes, and accidents are often
the results of poor attitudes and motivation. Behavioral experts no longer
must argue on the traditional humanistic or quality-of-life basis for upgrading the human organization. An organization is simply losing money
by failing to do what it can to improve the calibre of human relations
experienced by workers. When there is a good quality of work life, there
are low levels of absenteeism, tardiness, turnover, and complaints, and a
high will to work.

POSSIBLE DRAWBACKS
OF THE BEHAVIORAL APPROACH

The ideas studied in this book would suggest that giving employees more
responsible, interesting, and challenging work will benefit all workers. A
common mistake of managers who believe themselves to be behavioralists
is the assumption that everyone wants to achieve and wants to progress
within the organizational hierarchy. This is not true. There are indeed

TABLE 18.3   Costs of Poor Human Relations

Behaviors and Performance	PERIOD 1 1972–1973		PERIOD 2 1973–1974		PERIOD 3 1974–1975	
	Estimated cost per incident ($)	Estimated total cost ($)	Estimated cost per incident ($)	Estimated total cost ($)	Estimated cost per incident ($)	Estimated total cost ($)
Absenteeism						
Absences	55.36	$ 286,360	53.15	$ 510,453	62.49	$ 431,494
Leave Days	—	—	55.04	687,229	61.64	821,795
Tardiness	4.86	56,920	—	—	—	—
Turnover						
Voluntary	120.59	18,089	131.68	33,973	150.69	18,083
Involuntary	120.59	14,230	131.68	21,859	150.69	18,686
Grievances	32.48	1,851	34.44	1,378	56.10	2,300
Quality below standard	19,517	663,589	19,517	573,800	19,5-7	409,857
Production below standard	22,236	266,838	22,236	335,764	22,236	255,714
Total costs		$ 1,307,877		$ 2,164,456		$ 1,957,929

Source: Adapted from Barry Macy and Philip Mirvis, "A Methodology for Assessment of Quality of Work Life and Organizational Effectiveness in Behavioral-Economic Terms," Administrative Science Quarterly 21 (June 1976): 219.

some people who will be satisfied to remain in an intrinsically nonrewarding job and receive the extrinsic rewards.

In addition, it should be remembered that a participative or behavioral approach is not always the most productive technique for all situations. There are some instances, as explained in Chapters 11 and 12, when a more directive or autocratic approach is desirable. In the short-run an autocratic leadership style may indeed be more beneficial. Thus, time, potential costs, the need for more consistent decisions, the nature of the task being performed, and the people supervised are among the important determinants of leadership style.

There is also the possibility that a participative style of management is in conflict with an individual's philosophies and personality. In such a case this person may come across as being a phony and will be less effective than if he or she adopted a leadership style more in line with his or her personality.

An organization's climate may not be conducive to a behavioral approach. If top management is typically autocratic or paternalistic, it will be very difficult for someone at a lower level in the organization to be participative. The short time spans allowed for decision making as well as other demands placed upon the individual from above will simply not allow a manager the luxury of being participative.

However, many of these possible drawbacks, as well as others that could exist, can be overcome if the support of top management can be obtained. By the same token, while all workers do not want added responsibility and job challenge, the number of workers whose job satisfaction and motivation can be improved through upgrading work is larger than managers would suspect. It is important to remember that many employees have not had the opportunity to experience meaningful work; therefore, managers do not know how many workers would behave on such jobs.

CHARACTERISTICS OF ORGANIZATIONS THAT ENCOURAGE A BEHAVIORAL APPROACH TO MANAGEMENT

Organizations are goal-seeking social units made up of leaders and followers working within a system of jobs, departments, rules, regulations, and procedures in some form of hierarchy. The potential for conflicts between the parts of an organization and each member is real and immense. When these parties understand human behavior at work, there is a greater chance that they will accommodate and conform to each other's goal-seeking behavior.

Effective organizations set goals not only for financial and marketing targets but also for such human concerns as:

- Satisfaction
- Employee training and development
- Climate
- Morale
- Absenteeism
- Grievances
- Turnover

When concern is shown toward the quality of work life experienced by employees, an organization is described by its employees as open, honest, supportive, encouraging, and participative. People working in organizations which do not pay attention to the needs and interests of workers will describe their work experience using terms such as exploitive, discouraging, or blame-oriented.

Future research will continue to be directed toward the topic of the quality of work life. Some broad questions that are presently providing direction for ongoing research include:

1. What is wanted and valued by different occupational groups?
2. Is the quality of life decreasing or increasing across American industry?
3. What sociological factors or environmental factors are influencing the quality of work life?
4. What are the dollar costs of poor or inadequate attention to employees?

While a more behavioral approach to management will not solve all problems in a work environment, it is the key to nearly all people-oriented problems. When looking at the improvements that have occurred to date in managerial techniques and organizational efficiency, it is easy to see the value of the behavioral approach. A brief overview and summation of the topics discussed throughout this book will serve as a most appropriate reminder of why the behavioral approach can be an effective way to manage.

HUMAN BEHAVIOR AND THE WORK ITSELF

One of the great dilemmas of organizational life concerns the relationship between the needs of people and the needs of the organization. Most of the time both management and employees must compromise their respective ideas of the perfect situation for mutual benefit. Although there is no denying that the employees make more adjustments than the organization, there is still a special sort of "socialization" process where people are learning about the organization and the organization is learning about its members. It involves the process whereby individuals try to conform to the organization and accommodate to other people. People are asked to give up some of their idiosyncrasies and special demands while the organization tries to adjust some of its rules, regulations, and policies to fit what is wanted by the majority of its work force. Regardless of how hard both try to work and accommodate to each other, conflicts will occur.

People enter the work place with certain expectations about organizations, about bosses, and about the jobs they will hold. The more the firm can match what it offers with the expectancies of employees, the better off both will be. A mismatch occurs when the needs of workers are not compatible with the demands of the work situation. In this unfavorable situation, workers will become dissatisfied and will lower their commitment to the job, to the supervisor, and to the organization. The organization will feel the pinch in dollar costs linked to higher tardiness, absenteeism, grievances, and turnover rates since these unproductive behaviors stem from people avoiding unpleasurable situations.

Conflicts in organizations may be in the form of value conflicts, personality conflicts, and role conflicts. One type of conflict is called job ambiguity. Ambiguity is felt when an employee does not understand what work is to be done, how the work is to be done, and what authority can be assumed in getting the work done. When, for some reason, a person's values or understanding of the work assignment are in disagreement with what he or she has been told to do, a role conflict exists. Role conflict thus refers to problems a worker has in doing the work once the work to be done has been explained. In these conflict situations, one party in the employment relationship has failed to accommodate to the other.

Job design is a critical factor in attaining mutual compliance and accommodation. To most people the job itself is the most important factor in the work environment, and therefore special care needs to be taken when changing the nature of the job. Some people prefer and expect simple and routine jobs; whereas others want more complex and challenging tasks. Giving an achievement-oriented person a challenging and complex job will lead to very favorable consequences. Unfavorable consequences can be expected if this same job is given to a person low in achievement need. Broadly speaking, past experiences influence what a person values and expects in terms of need fulfillment.

Once a person has entered an organization and assumed a work role complete with a supervisor, co-workers, pay, promotional opportunities, and other situational factors, a feeling of satisfaction or dissatisfaction will develop. When a job fulfills a person's important values, the person will be satisfied. On the other hand, when a job does not fulfill an individual's values, the person will be dissatisfied. While the relationship between satisfaction and performance is circular rather than direct on the individual level of analysis, the collective level of satisfaction among all employees strongly affects the success of a company. This is to be expected since the consequences of worker dissatisfaction—for example, absenteeism and quitting—are so costly to organizations.

Future research is needed to further evaluate the importance of proper organizational socialization and to test existing job redesign theories. A large number of managerial workshops can be expected to occur to help practicing managers determine when job redesign is needed as well as how to develop a practical method for altering jobs.

HUMAN BEHAVIOR AND THE CLIMATE OF THE WORK ENVIRONMENT

Part 2 of the book discusses the idea that many undesirable employee behaviors are influenced by an inadequate socialization process and by poor job design. The purpose of Part 3 is to examine two other strong influences on human behavior at work: organizational climate and job stress. A climate refers to an organization's personality or atmosphere. The personalities of organizations differ in the same way that the personalities of people vary. A good climate is one that helps the organization meet its objectives while allowing individuals to satisfy their goals and needs.

While a good climate may be thought of as a collective sign of general organizational health, the level of job stress can be viewed as a sign of health for a single individual. A certain level of stress may be good for people. It keeps them alert, aware, and psychologically and physiologically comfortable. However, most often stress in the work environment is unproductive. Job stress may be caused by many things. Some powerful influences include job ambiguity, job conflict, work overload or underload, insecurity, and employee nonparticipation in decision making. Apathy, hostility, wasted time, sabotage, and aggression are some observable examples of the ways people react to stress. The level of job stress among employees can be measured and changed using the same methodology that is usually suggested for measuring and changing organizational climate and job satisfaction.

UNDERSTANDING MOTIVATED BEHAVIOR

The three chapters in Part 4 deal with the broad topic of motivation, i.e., "the will to work." The chapters are related and build upon each other. The first chapter on motivation presents a discussion of several human needs and comments on rewards that are typically useful in fulfilling employee needs. The reinforcement chapter goes into greater detail in explaining that the timing or the giving of rewards must be scheduled appropriately to induce people to work harder. Not only must a manager give a worker the right reward but, in addition, the reward must be given at the right time for motivated behavior to result. An individual must be convinced that a certain reward—for example, supervisory praise—is linked to a certain behavior for that person to be motivated to repeat the rewarded behavior. The chapter on pay ties the previous two chapters together by showing that money can fulfill most needs directly or indirectly and that money can be made contingent upon performance in an authentic behavior modification sense.

Several principles underlying human motivations have been identified. First, the worker must be ready to be motivated. This implies that the work must be properly organized so that people are not preoccupied with unproductive concerns. It is nearly impossible for a person to be motivated if he or she is concerned with being fired, working under a terrible supervisor, being unjustly passed over for a promotion, or being inadequately paid. The mind of an employee must be fairly free of these types of concerns. Secondly, influencing the motivation of people is easier when people believe that they are using important skills and abilities. People do not get turned-on using unimportant skills. Thirdly, to maintain motivated behavior a manager must give the worker an important reward at the right time. Finally, a worker must know that the productive workers are receiving better and more rewards than are the unproductive workers. This observation will insure employees that the organization is putting forth a genuine effort to observe and reward good performance.

Organizations want people to be motivated to do several things. People should be motivated to arrive at work on time, to do high quality work, to do a high quantity of work, and to work safely, creatively, and compatibly with supervisors and co-workers. The principles outlined in the text can be useful in increasing the likelihood of each of these types of actions. It is all a matter of giving the right person the right reward at the right time. Future research should focus on: (1) identifying what type of rewards are best for different types of people, and (2) identifying what type of rewards are best for reinforcing each of the several behaviors desired by organizations.

LEADERSHIP AND HUMAN BEHAVIOR IN THE WORK ENVIRONMENT

Part 5 focuses on leadership and communication since these processes are so inextricably linked. Leaders do much of what they are required to do through communications. The first chapter in this part emphasizes the dynamics of the communication process and offers suggestions for clearer communication between the leader and follower. The chapter on leadership styles defines what leadership actually means and discusses the different styles of leadership people may adopt. The next chapter, on participative management, presents ideas on how leaders can create real employee participation where people can feel a sense of ownership of their work lives. The chapter on effective group performance focuses on how leaders stimulate teamwork and effective group problem solving.

Leaders get things done through communications. Each manager is, in essence, an information center and thus a critical link in the upward, downward, and lateral flow of communications. Chapter 13 explains communication process, barriers to communication, and ways to improve the accuracy of communication. Communication is accomplished when a meaning is somehow transferred from one person to another. The total communication process involves message formulation, sending the message, receiving the message, interpreting the message, feedback, and interpretation of the feedback. The best way to improve individual communication is to be aware of and work with the various barriers that interfere with the transfer and understanding of a message. One of the main barriers is that people inadvertently interpret communications in terms of their own self-interests. While the communication process is quite complex, the ways of overcoming barriers to effective communications are really quite simple. These rules and guidelines should be followed and other ways of improving upon communication styles should be developed by a manager as effective communication can be the key to successful management.

Leadership refers to an action orientation by a person designed to bring about group commitment to and accomplishment of group goals. Good and appropriate leadership styles will vary with the situation. Since there are many different situations, there is no best leadership style for all situations. A supervisor emphasizing getting the work done and deemphasizing consideration or human relations may be good in some circumstances and completely ineffective in others. Moreover, a style emphasizing both dimensions—the task and people concerns—will usually work better than a leadership style that is either task- or people-oriented. The appropriate style of leadership is dictated by characteristics in the leader, the followers, and the work situation.

The amount of realistic and useful employee participation in decision making will vary from situation to situation in much the same manner as do leadership styles. There is no best level or amount of participation that will be appropriate across different situations. The involvement of subordinates in decision making accomplishes several things. First, it allows superiors to spend more time on important opportunities and problems than would be otherwise possible. Second, participation will develop subordinates for high level positions. Third, since decision making is pushed down to the point of impact, the quality of the decision made will be increased. And fourth, people tend to commit themselves strongly to decisions they make themselves.

The factors that influence the amount of participation to be sought include: the time aspect, the managerial system, the capability of subordinates, and the personality of the leader. When time for a decision is short, participation is unlikely since involving many people will be time consuming. The managerial styles of the very top managers have a tremendous impact upon the amount of participation throughout an organization. That is, when there is a large amount of participation at the very highest level in an enterprise, there will typically be a large amount of participation in the lower levels. The last constraint on the amount of participation is the real or imagined ability of subordinates. When superiors have trust and confidence the abilities of subordinates, participation is fostered. When there is a lack of trust and confidence, participation is unlikely. Authentic participation is welcomed while pseudoparticipation is viewed by subordinates as patronizing, insulting, and a waste of time.

A good deal of time in organizational life is spent in committee meetings of one sort or another. Since most are problem-solving groups, Chapter 13 focuses on the leadership of these groups. The central issue concerning leaders of problem-solving groups is how to structure the communication process so that each person can contribute in a free and uninhibited fashion. The contributions of people in group settings are influenced by the presence of a superior, by the presence of others, and by the person's confidence in his or her own ideas. People generally fear the unknown and often become tight-lipped in fear situations. Groups or team problem-solving sessions are replete with fear-arousing factors. The superior, being an authority figure, is likely to be a source of fear. The possible reactions of co-workers may not be very predictable and thus will arouse fear. A person will generally not volunteer ideas in a group situation when there are many fear factors. People do not want to make themselves look stupid or uninformed. The role of a group leader is to limit and minimize the number and magnitude of these inhibiting factors so that each participant can contribute in a systematic way. The Delphi and nominal group techniques are noninteracting approaches to problem solving that allow everyone to contribute without the fears or problems that occur in most interacting groups.

SPECIAL GROUPS AND THEIR INFLUENCE ON BEHAVIOR IN THE WORK ENVIRONMENT

The purpose of studying the work behavior of knowledge resources, women, minorities, and unions is to determine if their work interests and attitudes are appreciably different from those of other organizational members. The two main reasons for studying these groups in a textbook on employee behavior are that managers are generally not familiar with the work interests and motivations of members of these groups and that there are human and dollar costs related to this lack of understanding.

The chapter on knowledge resources examined the different backgrounds and experiences of various kinds of knowledge workers. Employees included in this category are professionals, scientists, technicians with advanced academic training, engineers, managers, and administrators. Their numbers are on the increase in private, public and nonprofit organizations. Engineers, scientists, and other technically trained people are in positions quite atypical in terms of the organizational environment and must be given special attention regarding the management of their efforts and the management of their environment. They are different from most employees in regard to the following characteristics: They have more education; they have a narrow view of management; their loyalty is aimed toward their profession rather than toward the organization; they generally have a low interest in advancing into managerial positions.

The "management of knowledge workers" is somewhat of a misnomer as the managerial effort should be directed more toward the management of their environment. Maintaining a high level of professionalism, encouraging creativity, and allowing scientists to be relatively independent are all elements of the managerial challenge of supervising scientists. Leadership must be fairly liberal in delegating authority to grant scientists more decision-making prerogatives. Increasing the motivation of scientists is not significantly different from increasing the motivation of other members of the organization, but a different perspective is needed. Besides the inherent motivational qualities of their work, some other motivational techniques available to managers of knowledge resources include dual promotional ladders, the opportunity to work with other scientists, freedom to select some of their own research projects, and provision of adequate research facilities and support.

Chapter 15 explains that the psychological makeup of women in management is remarkably similar to that of their male counterparts. Women work for the same reasons men work. They work for money and once on the job they want the same psychological benefits as men do. Overall, women feel that work pride is the most important psychological outcome from work, followed by personal development and high self-esteem. Unfortunately, women's efforts to gain entry into managerial positions have been blocked by some myths, particularly that of the successful "managerial model." This model is a masculine one in our culture and has proven a difficult one to change.

While women have been put at a disadvantage because of the masculine model of a manager, some black supervisors seem to have benefited from it. They received better ratings as supervisors than did their white counterparts in several studies. The reason for the better ratings is that they were simply better qualified. Blacks are finding entry into business organizations easier now than in the past, but black supervisors with managerial potential are not being fairly integrated into managerial hierarchies. Some experts believe this lack of integration is causing a stockpile effect whereby black supervisors are being stockpiled in the lower levels of the organizations. Unfavorable and unfair stereotypes have hurt the promotability of blacks as well as women.

The chapter on labor unions provides a broad overview of the role of unions, discusses the nature of the union-management relationship, and looks at some of the human behavior problems stemming from that relationship. The chapter begins by stating that poor management teams generally have more to fear from unions than do good ones. In fact, it can be argued that a good management team probably would not provide the employees any real reason to unionize. But when a union is present, a good management team will seek to work with it and create a cooperative work environment.

The latter part of the chapter addresses some behavioral concerns surrounding labor unions. Management tends to forget the behavioral approach when dealing with unions and union members. Foremen are much more likely to use coercive power, threats and reprimands, and other administrative punishments toward union members than toward nonunion employees. Some ways to improve the human relations between unions and management include training the foremen in interpersonal skills, improving the quality of open communications with the union, creating a more productive climate, and encouraging people to have dual loyalty (loyalty to the union and loyalty to management).

HUMAN BEHAVIOR AND ORGANIZATION DEVELOPMENT

As mentioned earlier, people have important goals such as high self-esteem, belonging, and purposefulness that can be readily fulfilled in a healthy organization. Unfortunately, employees from all different kinds of organizations report that their human capabilities are not being fully tapped and they feel underutilized and moderately dissatisfied with organizational life. The more that employees report these feelings, the more ineffectively their organizations will function. Organization development (OD) offers an approach to bringing about a positive change in organizational efficiency. This emerging, behavioral science discipline refers to a planned, organizationwide effort to increase organizational effectiveness through changing the methods or processes by which work is done.

The activities referred to by the phrase "methods or processes" include any technical, human, and social process by which an organization accomplishes its work. Topics such as leadership, teamwork, climate, culture, job design, MBO, participation, communication, and decision making are among the areas of concern to the organization development expert. The main outcome of developmental efforts is an improved organizational climate. An emphasis is therefore placed upon the organization and employee norms and values concerning what work should be done and how it should be done. Generally, OD places great importance on the role of collaboration among all employees. Since an organization is essentially a group of teams, OD emphasizes teamwork, group problem solving, and self-diagnosis.

OD operates on the "bottom-up" rather than the "top-down" approach to change. This approach means that an important role in development is played by the members of the organization rather than having the change implemented only by top management or a consultant. Organization members study how they are presently accomplishing work and detail how they should accomplish work in an ideal sense. A planned system of changes among the organization's technical, human, and social processes is scheduled with the help of an outside resource person. In the top-down approach, an outside management consultant studies how work is accomplished and makes recommendations to the top management group. More often than not, these recommendations are imposed on the lower level workers. OD offers all employees the opportunity to help create their own work environment as a means of heightening their feeling of ownership and commitment.

In this regard OD represents an accumulation of behavioral techniques that are being consolidated in a systemwide attempt to develop the entire organization. Since OD is primarily concerned with applying what has been identified as good human relations practices, it is, for the present, the ultimate model for a behavioral approach to the management of people and the work environment.

NOTES

1. PHILIP MIRVIS and EDWARD LAWLER, III, "Measuring the Financial Impact of Employee Attitudes," *Journal of Applied Psychology* 62, No. 1 (1977): 1–8.

2. Ibid., p. 6.

3. BARRY MACY and PHILIP MIRVIS, "A Methodology for Assessment of Quality of Work Life and Organizational Efficiency in Behavior-Economic Terms," *Administrative Science Quarterly* 21 (June 1976): 212–26.

QUESTIONS FOR THOUGHT AND DISCUSSION

1. What are the costs associated with poor human relations management?

2. Why is the happy employee not necessarily the efficient employee?

3. How does the quality of work life contribute to the productivity of employees?

4. What are the possible drawbacks of a behavioral approach to management? How can they be overcome?

5. What, in your opinion, is the most important factor in making a behavioral approach to management successful? Support your answer.

Name Index

417

Subject Index